Acclaim for Ann Hulbert's

Off the Charts

"What can we learn, in a society dedicated to high-achieving children, from children who seem 'naturally' off the charts in their achievements? . . . [Hulbert] does the good work, throughout, of resisting morals or too neat generalizations."
—Adam Gopnik, *The New Yorker*

"In this beautifully written, thoroughly reported look at young 'geniuses,' Hulbert poses fascinating questions about the roles of both genetics and pushy parents."　　—*Booklist* (starred review)

"Captures the complicated lives of child prodigies without descending into voyeurism or caricature. [Hulbert] has tried to 'listen hard for the prodigies' side of the story,' to her great credit."
—*The New York Times Book Review*

"The richness of the book, and the pleasure of it, is in the human stories. . . . Hulbert has chosen her wunderkinds carefully, recognizing them not only for their individual brilliance but also as pint-size portraits of their eras."　　—*Minneapolis Star Tribune*

"Fascinating if at times disturbing. . . . Hulbert makes clear, in this nuanced and meticulous book, that when it comes to the prodigy's gift, the peril is indivisible from the glory."　　—*Newsday*

"Sophisticated, well-researched, and thought-provoking. . . . [Hulbert] shows the prodigies' own perspective of their experience, revealing the pressure that accompanies being labeled exceptional at an early age."　　—*The National Book Review*

Ann Hulbert

Off the Charts

Ann Hulbert is the author of *Raising America: Experts, Parents, and a Century of Advice About Children* and *The Interior Castle: The Art and Life of Jean Stafford*. Her articles and reviews have appeared in many publications, including *The New York Times Book Review*, *The New York Review of Books*, and *The Atlantic*, where she is the literary editor. She is a graduate of Harvard University and spent a year at Cambridge University. She lives with her husband in Washington, D.C.

ALSO BY ANN HULBERT

*Raising America: Experts, Parents,
and a Century of Advice About Children*

*The Interior Castle: The Art and Life
of Jean Stafford*

Off the Charts

Off the Charts

The Hidden Lives and Lessons
of American Child Prodigies

ANN HULBERT

VINTAGE BOOKS
A Division of Penguin Random House LLC
New York

FIRST VINTAGE BOOKS EDITION, JANUARY 2019

The Library of Congress has cataloged the Knopf edition as follows:
Names: Hulbert, Ann, author.
Title: Off the charts : the hidden lives and lessons of
American child prodigies / Ann Hulbert.
Description: First edition. | New York : Alfred A. Knopf, 2018. |
Includes bibliographical references and index.
Identifiers: LCCN 2017003438
Subjects: LCSH: Gifted children—United States.
Classification: LCC HQ773.5 .H85 2018
DDC 371.950973—dc23
LC record available at https://lccn.loc.gov/2017003438

Vintage Books Trade Paperback ISBN: 978-1-101-97132-1
eBook ISBN: 978-1-101-94730-2

Book design by Betty Lew

www.vintagebooks.com

Printed in the United States of America
10 9 8 7 6 5 4 3 2 1

7. 2019

In memory of my mother

Contents

Prologue

"When is a boy not a boy?" In the summer of 2005, a six-year-old named Marc Yu was eager to stump me as we stood in a hallway of the Colburn School of Music in Los Angeles before his cello and piano lessons began. An adorable little guy in a red Pacific Oaks Children's Center T-shirt and matching red socks, he was deep into his repertoire of riddles, awarding a point for every punch line I came up with. "When he turns into a store," I answered, after briefly debating whether to play dumb.

Marc practically danced into his classroom, ignoring the requests of his cello teacher and his mother, Chloe Hui, that he please settle down. An hour later, after I heard him play Vivaldi's Concerto in G Minor for two cellos on a quarter-size instrument several inches bigger than he was, another answer occurred to me: "When he's a prodigy." During his next lesson, I watched Marc's tiny hands racing through Bach's Concerto in F Minor for the piano. His bony shoulders moved with the music and the effort of producing remarkable clarity and phrasing, and I felt the full force of the riddle. As he slipped down from his booster seat on the piano bench, begging his teacher to let him tackle at least a part of Rachmaninoff's Second Piano Concerto, I couldn't help wondering what he might actually turn into.

Several months later, I watched as Marc became a poster boy for a mission to "stop wasting our brightest young minds" in an era of global competition. He was awarded a $10,000 fellowship for his "prodigious work" by the Davidson Institute for Talent Development, founded six years earlier to support and proselytize on behalf of "profoundly gifted" children. Sixteen mostly teenage superstars joined him, honored for their portfolios of intellectual and artistic feats, which they submitted along with testimonies about their labors and tributes to mentors. The fellows, hailed as a precious but imperiled national resource, got a taste of advocacy as well. As part of the celebratory festivities in Washington, D.C., the prize-winners paid visits to Capitol Hill to speak about their hard-won accomplishments.

For Marc, the classic child prodigy in a group of bigger and gawkier students, the credential brought crossover stardom, too. On a tour of the talk shows—Ellen DeGeneres, Oprah, *The Tonight Show*—he told jokes and got off funny one-liners. Then he removed the red gloves that kept his hands warm and played a sample from a repertoire that ranged from Mozart to Gwyneth Walker. ("She is still composing," Marc deadpanned, "unlike most of the composers I like, who are decomposing.") When a more earnest morning show interviewer asked him if he thought he was gifted, he looked flustered. "I don't know." He shrugged, mumbling a guess about a possible "gift from God." What Marc wanted to talk about was his hard work, not a topic typically associated with child wonders, who are supposed to soar without sweating. In his many media appearances, he spoke out whenever he could as an ambassador for a resurgence of American excellence, ready with advice. Marc, who had lately lost three teeth, had come up with a lisping sound bite: "You should play Game Boy less, and you should practice more."

The democratic zeal of the message, and of its six-year-old messenger, was inspiring. Marc wasn't smug. He seized every chance to salute his immigrant mother and her tireless guidance. Marc didn't scold. He delivered the counsel with sincere fervor and irrepressible energy. Here was a boy who sometimes stole to the piano at night, Chloe reported, drawn by a favorite passage he'd toiled over during the day. As Marc swayed on the bench, playing with unusual feeling, his eyes closed and face uplifted, his transport inspired a neck-prickling awe not just at the music pouring forth but at the mysteries of human potential. How often do we underestimate children's untapped powers and phenomenal capacity to learn? "The possibilities are extraordinary for a child with a child's imagination and a child's heart," marveled a conductor stunned by Marc's adult-level mastery. With momentum like his, what might maturity bring?

At the same time, the spectacle of Marc couldn't help but stir more mundanely discomfiting sensations, a variation on the what-is-American-youth-coming-to worry that every generation of parents, along with pundits and policy makers, succumbs to. Warnings about a rising China, and about widening achievement gaps in the United States, were hard to ignore. "Tiger parenting" had yet to enter the lexicon: Amy Chua's shocker of a book, *Battle Hymn of the Tiger Mother*, about goading two daughters to virtuoso extremes, lay half a decade ahead. But the fraught ethos of early superachievement was already familiar enough, as hard to like as it was to shake.

You didn't have to be a parent with two overscheduled high school kids, though I was, to feel off-balance. In an ever more competitive world, what is the promise—and the price—of honing youthful potential ever earlier and more avidly? What happens to those imaginations and hearts? The not-so-democratic consequences of America's meritocratic mystique were obvious: stressed-out, helicopter-parented, test-prepped, accelerated children bent on exceptional performance from cradle to elite college—and left-out children, lacking adult guidance and challenging goals, derailed by obstacles. I sighed at the proto-prodigy expectations: Was this a likely route to social equality, or resilient autonomy, or bold creativity? I signed up my privileged, omni-enriched kids for SAT prep anyway.

This is a book about prodigies like Marc, who aren't merely amazingly good at something before they lose all their baby teeth or hit puberty. I've chosen young marvels in modern America who have also tapped into a very public concern about precocious achievement, which baby boomers and their successors are far from the first to feel. To display adult mastery as a child—or, in several cases in this book, as a teenager—is usually to draw notice. But different talents seem to attract heightened interest in different decades, inviting scrutiny as auguries for the rest of us. Over the past century, the zeitgeist has swept some prodigies to special attention as emblems of social progress or as victims of worrisome pressures— or often both at once. Who they are, and what particular skills they display and how, touches a nerve. Marc, a captivating miniversion of the virtuoso piano celebrity Lang Lang and, with his mother, an outspoken proponent of perspiration over inspiration, was a standout made to order for a China-focused, college-frantic moment preoccupied with "grit," the latest lab-tested talent development secret on the lips of psychologists, educators, and parents.

At anxious junctures, in other words, you could say we single out the child wonders we deserve—which doesn't mean those remarkable children get treated the way *they* deserve. Or, for that matter, the way parents and mentors, and other meddlers and an avid media, claim they are treated. This book began with curiosity to get to the bottom of stories about some American superchildren who seized the spotlight—and to tell those stories as unsentimentally, and unsensationally, as possible. My previous book, *Raising America*, was a cultural history of twentieth-century child-rearing theories peddled by a succession of experts, each promising—with great confidence and shaky evidence—that scientifically informed nurture would liberate untold human potential. Phenomenally accomplished children offered a chance to explore practice, rather than theory, at those eagerly anticipated new frontiers of performance.

My choices, from math prodigies at the start of the twentieth century on up to Marc, are glaring exceptions to prevailing rules—boys and girls whose exploits have seemed to offer timely discoveries about talent development. They aren't representative or exemplary in the sense of typical, and that is the point: ours is an era, as a popular adviser of parents has put it, when Lake

Wobegon–style insistence on above-average children is "yesterday's news," overtaken by an anxious credo that "given half a chance, all of our children would be extraordinary." If versions of today's message in fact go back further than we think, let's take a closer look at prodigies who have been heralded as emissaries of that drive to excel early—the living, breathing, superbly high-performing proof of what is possible, and how, and with what results. Let's revisit the public debates over their rare achievements and unusual regimens, and probe for the private realities behind the headlines. Not least, let's listen hard for the prodigies' side of the story. After all, how they understand their experience is what matters most, certainly for them as their lives unfold. And the rest of us—caught up in an ever less playful, increasingly purposeful ethos of childhood—could really use their advice.

I wasn't fully prepared for how elusive the goal of getting at the child's-eye view would be—though I set out to tackle it precisely because ignoring or misjudging kids' perspectives is so easy to do, despite the best of intentions. Parental empathy runs deep but not straight. Though childhood was a country we all once inhabited, our early selves become foreigners: blurry forebears who pull at our sleeves, whispering mixed messages about the people we've become, and about how our children might redeem us. Parenting experts are hardly immune from the urge to project grown-up agendas either. Even the strictest advisers I wrote about in *Raising America* prided themselves on child-focused enlightenment. They touted empirical data about immature beings whose needs, their studies showed, were very different from ours. Yet again and again, the experts' own hopes, fears, and memories—along with wider cultural anxieties—shaped their views more than rigorous science did.

To say that eager champions of prodigies are prone to be even more buffeted by their dreams and frustrated desires is not to deliver news: the stage mother stereotype thrives. And unlike Dr. Spock and his expert ilk, whose advice is more often invoked than studiously obeyed, on-the-ground mentors and parents of young wonders exert real clout. Prodigies are children, after all, small people who rely on all kinds of help from those who loom over them. Exceptionally talented and driven though they may be—their feats are astonishing—they aren't in the driver's seat. Adults may revere them, and families revolve around them, but prodigies remain dependents, subject to circumstances they didn't choose and usually have limited power to change. They get many chances to show off but may have to wait until they're grown up, and looking back, to fully and truly tell their elders off.

Yet as I've pursued their stories, I haven't simply discovered tales of voiceless victims and myopic, narcissistic oppressors—or of triumphant young talents and model mentors either. Except, not surprisingly, in the press. In just about every case, media accounts have been short on veracity, long on lurid voyeurism, and very aware that suspenseful dramas sell. Is this or that early bloomer a weirdo headed for burnout, true to popular lore? Or is the wunderkind bound for creative glory, as modern experts have hoped to prove? And what behind-the-scenes forces other than his or her genius explain precocious mastery? Such loaded questions are the underside of off-the-charts expectations. They're writ large in prodigy media coverage, and they lurk between the lines for lesser superkids groomed to excel, too: the same intense anticipation that can help spur children onward sets them up to disappoint as well, saddling them with goals that can daunt and doubts that corrode. Adults also pay a price for the high-stakes prospects. As they anxiously eye the future, they're prone to forget that childhood happens only once and goes by very fast.

Every one of the stories gathered here has sad or shocking moments; a few are tragic. But my goal isn't to pile on the stark cautionary fare. Nor am I aiming to crack some "talent code," though the children in these pages do share remarkable curiosity and stubbornness—and that latter quality, predictably, distinguishes many mentors and parents as well. Instead, I've taken my cue from Norbert Wiener, the turn-of-the-twentieth-century child prodigy who opens the book and who, as a grown-up, warned against the allure of told-you-so lessons or seven-steps-to-stardom advice. In his memoir *Ex-Prodigy* (1953), the founder of cybernetics laments that the only young marvels "the public ever hears of are those who 'point a moral or adorn a tale,'" when untidy life arcs can reveal much more:

> There is a tragedy in the failure of a promising lad which makes his fate interesting reading; and the charm of the success story is known to all of us. Per contra, the account of a moderate success following a sensationally promising childhood is an anticlimax and not worth general attention.

I can imagine Wiener pausing to tug on his white goatee and push up his heavy-rimmed glasses before proceeding to type, "I consider this attitude of extremes toward the infant prodigy false and unjustified. In addition to being unjustified, it is in fact unjust."

It also misses, he might have noted, what is most fascinating about the unfolding of exceptional childhoods. From Norbert Wiener at one end to Marc Yu at the other, I probe legends—Bobby Fischer, Shirley Temple—along with now-forgotten girl writers, pioneering computer geeks, an autistic jazz pianist and composer, and more. Psychologists obsessed with giftedness—Lewis Terman, Julian Stanley—make appearances, too. In every case, confident predictions and programmatic methods morph into wishful projections and unanticipated challenges.

Look closely at personalities, families, and actual trajectories, with detours and snags included; step back to scan the historical scene, since talents, however unbidden, thrive in particular times and places. The revelation is that off-the-charts achievers aren't good grist for moralistic fables after all, whether about ill-fated freaks or about superstars for a meritocratic century. That is the real virtue of stories at once strange and familiar. They expose very recognizable confusions behind a zeal for early prowess that by now has gone mainstream—fueling hopes of success, and no end of stress. Not least, prodigies offer reminders writ large that children, in the end, flout our best and worst intentions.

I was expecting to encounter an oppressively elitist tone among champions of exceptional childhoods but was surprised to discover instead an upstart rebelliousness, in young and old alike. Norbert Wiener's father, proudly touting his twelve-year-old college matriculant as a model, hoped to jolt genteel Americans into following suit in their families, but he wasn't betting on it. Like so many of the excited promoters of prodigies in later chapters, Leo Wiener was an outsider (a Jewish immigrant from Russia) who held forth as a liberator of children. A version of his message gathered momentum over the century: freed from the unscientific prejudices of their complacent and conformist elders, boys and girls could surge forward amazingly quickly, given the right guidance. What's more, the remarkable young achievers would do it easily and eagerly, without getting spoiled or stigmatized or snooty.

Of course, the promise has never been as simple as that sounds. Who calls the shots, and how, can be murky. That was true back when grown-ups like Leo presumed they were boss and children, however exceptional, did their bidding. It was true generations before that in the Old World as well. "Next to God comes Papa," wrote twelve-year-old Wolfgang Mozart, the patron saint of modern prodigies, a century and a half earlier. Papa's sway was indeed vast, but he also knew he owed his son a dose of obeisance: Leopold hailed Wolfgang as a "miracle, which God has allowed to see the light in Salzburg"—and counted on him to keep the family afloat. The current term is *codependency:* prodigies capitalizing, as best they can, on the resources of elders who are vicariously invested in their glory. And by the post–World War II era, as old rules of deference to maturity eroded, enterprising young standouts made the most of their new authority. Later chapters in this book attest to that. As adults became more solicitous and systematic in their enabling, prodigies became more defiant handfuls, proudly intent on doing things their way. Bobby Fischer didn't just imitate the masters; he knew how to intimidate. So did Bill Gates. Lang Lang lashed out.

Introducing her portraits of eminent Victorian marriages in *Parallel Lives,* Phyllis Rose astutely wrote that at the core of every alliance between spouses is a pair of narratives about power relations. Trouble arises when those views cease to mesh, when "the understanding about the balance of power breaks down, when the weaker member feels exploited or the stronger feels unrewarded for his or her strength." The same holds for child prodigies and their mentors—with a vengeance. After all, no matter how richly collaborative a bond children forge with grown-up guides, some version of divorce is inevitable. It's what modern experts would call developmentally appropriate. That doesn't mean the process is smooth. In the case of prodigies, the usual age-based scripts get rewritten from the start, as they speed ahead of their peers to the applause—and unease—of adults keen to facilitate the phenomenal progress of their talents. Upheaval is guaranteed: however carefully monitored or mentored an extraordinary childhood may be, power relations get recast in the turmoil of adolescence. And all along the way, twists and turns in family circumstances may propel, or derail, a prodigy's course. So may social pressures or opportunities that nobody saw coming.

Just about all the unusual children assembled here implicitly or explicitly convey a version of the same message to the eager promoters of an American meritocracy over the century: back off. That is not what proponents of whisking the best and the brightest onward, starting the younger the better, have ever really wanted to hear as they champion youthful genius as a crucial national resource. But if you listen closely to these prodigy stories, which play out in successive decades in a country increasingly committed to fine-tuning and fast-tracking talent development, the message gets louder and clearer.

It's not that these children are desperate to chill out, or slow down, or quit striving, or even cease astounding their elders. What they want, and need, is the chance to obsess on their own idiosyncratic terms—to sweat and swerve, lose their balance, get their bearings, battle loneliness, discover resilience. How else does anyone shape a self, never mind a phenomenal skill? Extraordinary achievement, though adults have rarely cared to admit it, takes a toll. It demands an intensity that rarely makes kids conventionally popular or socially comfortable. But if they get to claim that struggle for mastery as theirs, in all its unwieldiness, they just might sustain the energy and curiosity that ideally fuel such a quest. That is no guarantee of mature creative genius, but it is a good bet for future happiness.

Like us, our predecessors over the course of a century have been thrilled by the thought that rapidly growing young bodies and flexible brains are primed to navigate change and meet new challenges in ways that adults can't. Like us, our predecessors have also been unnerved by upstart impulses and lopsided young lives, not to mention uncertain futures. The urge to domesticate prodigious children—to anoint them not as misfits but as marvels whose streamlined paths promise to realize our hopes and ambitions—has proved understandably hard for modern American strivers to resist. Phenomenally talented boys and girls have been swept along, though not as effortlessly as their mentors have wanted to suggest—and not as obediently either. Decade after decade, prodigies in the spotlight have stirred up debates, weathered ordeals, and delivered surprises, as the stories in this book reveal. Their experiences betray secrets about their struggles—with their gifts and with their guides—from which they learn a lot, sometimes too late. It's time to resurrect their stories and see what they might tell us.

PART I

NATURE

vs.

NURTURE

CHAPTER 1

The Wonder Boys of Harvard

· 1 ·

"The first thing my April Fool's boy wanted from the great outside world was the moon," wrote a young mother named Sarah Sidis, recalling her firstborn's arrival in the family on the cusp of the twentieth century.

> We stood at the window of the apartment together in the evening, with Billy in Boris' arms, and admired the moon over Central Park. Billy chuckled and reached for it. The next night when he found that the moon was not in the same place, he seemed disturbed. Trips to the window became a nightly ritual, and he was always pleased when he could see the "moo-n."
>
> This led to Billy's mastering higher mathematics and planetary revolutions by the time he was eleven, and if that seems to be a ridiculous statement I can only say, "Well, it did."

The moon-gazing scene is a classic parental experience, a memory likely to stick, even if it goes unrecorded in a baby book. A brilliant sphere or sliver hangs in the sky. The baby arm reaches out, pointing, and the round eyes are even brighter than usual as they look first at the moon, then into your eyes, then back at the light out there in the darkness. "Moon," you say, a word almost as mesmer-izing, in English, as the sight. The tiny lips purse, and out comes a sound that no cow could imitate. "Yes, moon," you say again, and the future seems full of promise for a young soul excited by a new word and fascinated by the view. This baby, who doesn't want to turn away, will surely go far in life—and in the cool moonglow, you feel thrilled and perhaps also a little terrified at what may be in store for both of you.

Sarah Sidis told her unusual version of the story years after the birth on April 1, 1898, of one of the first, and for a time most famous, child prodigies of the modern era. Billy's full name was William James Sidis, after the renowned Harvard psychologist who was her husband's mentor and the boy's godfather. At eleven, enrolled at Harvard, Billy made headlines when he delivered a lecture on the fourth dimension to the university's Mathematical Club, "with the aid of a crayon which he wielded with his little hand," wrote *The New York Times.*

By then Sarah and her husband, Boris, had made it their mis-sion to jolt turn-of-the-century Americans with a thrilling, and terrifying, message: learning, if it was begun soon enough, could yield phenomenal results very early and rapidly. Russian Jews, they had fled the pogroms in Ukraine for the garment sweatshops on the United States' East Coast in the mid-1880s. Within ten years they had worked their way to the top of American higher educa-tion. Sarah, by 1898 a rare woman with an M.D. (from Boston University School of Medicine), considered her husband "the most brilliant man in the world." After tutoring Sarah, Boris had racked up a B.A., an M.A., and a Ph.D. in psychology at Harvard within four years. But inborn talent had nothing to do with their feats, or their son's, they insisted. Billy was not miraculous, and Boris's bril-liance was more honed than inherited. (Reared in a polyglot world by a bookish merchant, he had been multilingual and a voracious young reader, who boldly began educating peasants as a teenager—for which he was imprisoned by the tsar.) The long-standing fear that precocity was the prelude to early degeneracy was groundless. An as-yet-unimagined potential lay in every child, and it was time parents started cultivating it, Boris urged. The country, more than ever, needed "the individuality, the originality, the latent powers of talent and genius" too often wasted.

Their zeal will sound familiar, echoed by current apostles of the "10,000 hour rule" of "deliberate practice," begun the younger the better. The impatience with low expectations remains a refrain. So does the warning that if we heedlessly neglect childhood opportunities to excel, we're jeopardizing a valuable national resource. The opposite concern, conveyed by William James in a letter, is alive and well, too. "I congratulate you on W.J.S.—what you tell of him is wonderful," he wrote of his four-year-old godson in 1902. But he was clearly alarmed. "Exercise his motor activities exclusively for many years now! His intellect will take care of itself," he told Boris. Did James realize that the rest of his letter—he cited a Harvard colleague's prodigious son as a cautionary example—risked egging the Sidises on? That problem is familiar as well. James noted that the university's first professor of Slavic languages, Leo Wiener— another remarkable émigré from tsarist Russia (he had taken the Bialystok high school entrance exams at ten and knew that many languages by his teens)—was several steps further along with his phenomenal son, Norbert. "Now at the age of seven," James reported, the boy "has done all the common school work, and of course can't get into the high school, so that his father is perplexed what to do with him, since they make difficulties about admitting him to the manual training schools in Cambridge."

Seven years later, when both boys converged on Harvard—there was no stopping the mission—their fathers, with Boris in the lead, had the eye and ear of the public as they sounded a democratic call to Americans to get busy enriching their children's fast-growing minds. An influx of underage standouts at the nation's most prestigious university put them all in the spotlight. In the fall of 1909, Norbert, almost fifteen, arrived as a graduate student in zoology after getting his B.A. in math at Tufts in three years. Billy, now known as William, was admitted at eleven as a "special student." They were joined by two children of the Reverend Adolf Berle, an ambitious Congregationalist minister in Boston—Adolf Jr., fourteen, and his sister, Lina, fifteen, at Radcliffe—and a scion of a blue-blooded Boston family, Cedric Houghton, also fifteen. (The following fall, a fourteen-year-old musician named Roger Sessions enrolled.)

The two superprecocious sons of the immigrant professor and doctor, outspoken men with bushy mustaches and accents, inspired the most interest—and the most suspense. The world was in ferment, and Harvard along with it. The basic contours of the flux haven't changed. A new century of global migration and international tensions was under way. The pace of scientific progress had picked up. The fledgling field of psychology was taking off—Freud visited the United States in 1909—and Einstein's revolutionary papers of 1905 had stirred baffled interest. The arrival of these brilliant boys, with their unusual pedigrees, fit the mission of Harvard's outgoing president, Charles W. Eliot, a liberal Boston Brahmin and staunch believer in equality of opportunity. He aimed to open university doors to "men with much money, little money, or no money, provided that they all have brains." And not just brains, Eliot warned complacent WASPs, who mistook "an indifferent good-for-nothing, luxurious person, idling through the precious years of college life" for an ideal gentleman or scholar. Eliot had in mind an elite with "the capacity to prove by hard work that they have also the necessary perseverance and endurance."

Boris and Leo, more radically egalitarian than Eliot, promised that anyone's children could soar like their sons—and do so without undue strain, if parents were prompt enough and pursued the right methods. The prospect stirred great interest, but also wariness, on campus and beyond. A. Lawrence Lowell, Eliot's far stuffier Brahmin successor, was said to worry that the "new immigrants" from Eastern and Southern Europe just didn't mix well with the "Anglo-Saxon race," whose ascendancy he assumed. "What will become of the wonder child?" asked a *New York Times* article announcing William's arrival at Harvard. The attention was tinted with suspicion: "Will he go the way commonly supposed to be that of most boy prodigies," the *Times* went on, "or will he make a name for himself?" Boris had just given a speech at the Harvard summer school about liberating youthful genius. Norbert's father was ready with the assurance that his son "was not forced. He is even lazy." For one boy, an embattled and lonely quest for privacy lay ahead. For the other, a formative role in the information age awaited. More emblematic fates for two pioneering modern prodigies would be hard to find—which doesn't mean that one path is a model and the other neatly conveys a cautionary moral. Both, as the boys understood sooner and better than their fathers did, were minefields.

· 2 ·

"I tried at one time to unite the five of us into a sort of prodigy club, but the attempt was ridiculous for we did not possess a sufficient element of coherence to make a joint social life desirable," Norbert Wiener wrote years later in his memoir *Ex-Prodigy*. The effort was a valiant, and rather poignant, gesture by a teenager well versed in the struggle to fit in while standing out.

> In all of our cases, our social relations were better taken care of elsewhere than by a close social contact with those of our own kind. We were not cut from the same piece of cloth, and in general there was nothing except an early development of intelligence that characterized us as a group. And this was no more a basis for social unity than the wearing of glasses or the possession of false teeth.

When they arrived on campus in Cambridge, he and William certainly bore no physical resemblance. Round-faced Norbert was a stocky adolescent verging on plump—though he went to the gym every day, an article noted. Short and clumsy and severely myopic, he wore thick wire-rim glasses. There was no disguising that he was a "greasy grind," the collegiate term for scholarly types. But having already graduated to long pants, at least he wasn't obviously underage. In a photograph that circulated in the avid newspaper coverage that fall, Norbert looked like an unpriggish goody-goody. He conveyed confidence, a bow tie setting off a sober yet open expression. William, in bangs and short pants, was still very much a child. He sometimes even wore the neckerchief that was part of a grade-schooler's uniform. What was most striking about the photograph of him that kept cropping up wasn't the odd farmer-boy hat on his head, accentuating his stick-out ears. It was the sullen set to his mouth and his aggrieved gaze.

Their backgrounds blurred, though, in the welcoming press accounts that greeted the unusual new students. That fit right in with their fathers' overarching purpose. Boris and Leo presented their sons and themselves as readily imitable examples, cut from a common cloth. As one headline in a long feature about "Harvard's Four Child Students" put it, "Parents Declare Others Might Do Likewise." Their boys had started out no different from other "bright" children. Their new methods were neither customized nor complicated—nor coercive. But they could work wonders. They opened "up to the human race vistas of possibilities and achievement unreached in any epoch of the history of the world." So announced the Boston journalist and popularizer of psychology H. Addington Bruce, who claimed prime magazine space at a time when compulsory schooling laws were spreading, along with "child study" groups and new interest in early development. As Boris and Leo's self-appointed quasi-publicist, Bruce created a de facto prodigy-fathers club.

It was a club whose maverick members were far too busy with their own work to hold any meetings, and whose educational mission definitely needed Bruce's rhetorical polish. With his recent 1909 Harvard summer school address, "Philistine and Genius," Boris had invited dismissal as a Cassandra. He issued dire warnings of catastrophic violence ahead for a benighted world that schooled its children in fear and obedient conformity, suppressing "the genius of the young." As for Leo, his son later noted that he "could be overwhelming through the very impact of his personality, and he was constitutionally incapable of allowing for his own forcefulness." That was a polite way of saying he could be a bully.

Yet with Bruce's genteel help, Boris and Leo drew notice as the opposite of Old World scolds as their boys arrived at Harvard.

There was no hint of the duress that Isaac Babel (Norbert Wiener's exact contemporary) later evoked in his famous short story "The Awakening." Among Jewish families back in Odessa, a prodigy industry churned out little violin virtuosi—"with thin necks like the stalks of flowers, and a paroxysmic flush upon their cheeks"—to satisfy their parents' dreams of cultural distinction if not fortune. The young marvels in Cambridge were not to be mistaken for New World freaks either. They bore no resemblance to lopsided "lightning calculators" like Zerah Colburn, a Vermont farm boy born in 1804 whose father had toured him through Europe: big-headed wonders able to "perform vast sums in arithmetic, as some children have done," as Boris put it. "Mere 'reckoning machines,'" Bruce called such specimens, noting their otherwise often limited horizons. These émigré fathers promised that to cultivate well-rounded early genius was to reap, later on, a "liberal-minded citizen, devoted soul and body to the interests of social welfare."

Boris and Leo boasted an enlightened modern advance beyond even the most illustrious Anglo-Saxon precedent. John Stuart Mill, the outstanding prodigy of a century earlier, had surged ahead on his father's chilly regimen, only to suffer a depressive crisis as he reached maturity. His American counterparts got the same basic, and humbling, paternal message the young Mill did—that their only real distinction was having a father, as James Mills indicated, "willing to give the necessary trouble and time" to teach them. But they had the advantage of a curriculum weighted toward science, believed more suited to "children's needs of the concrete," one doctor noted, than the Millian diet of classics, heavy on abstractions.

Norbert and Billy also thrived on cutting-edge pedagogical insights that promised to banish old-fashioned fears of debilitating precocity produced by "forcing." Children's "minds are built with use," Boris taught, their brains undergoing rapid growth beginning in infancy. Seizing the window between two and three was crucial, and teaching must also appeal to their feelings. Boris's signature contribution was "the psychology of suggestion." Fascinated by hypnosis, he advocated the well-timed use of unconscious, emotionally charged associations and urged subtle priming to stimulate a child's interest; the mind, he advised, was especially receptive before sleep.

Boris also promoted the theory of "reserve energy." He claimed co-credit with William James for discovering this idea of "second wind," which Leo swore by, too. Hitherto unknown levels of energy were accessible to those with real focus, the psychologists had decided. For adults, the emphasis was on endurance, working through initial fatigue to draw on otherwise unused sources of mental strength. The application to children, who were naturally given to scattered interests, was breezier. The point was to inspire effortless, deep absorption, which fueled the kind of learning that late-starters never tapped into. Once bad habits set in and vulnerable young minds were clouded by superstitious nonsense and fears—the crass staples of American child-rearing—the moment had been missed.

Lessons, harnessing imaginations that might otherwise wander, needn't be long or onerous. The ideal result, far from a frail-necked specialist, was an accomplished generalist who thrived on a varied curriculum. Though Boris made no mention of group activities, he picked up on the refrain of the contemporary kindergarten movement: purposeful play. "That is the key to the whole situation," he liked to emphasize. "Get the child so interested in study that study will truly be play." Leo stressed the anticram theme and the importance of following a child's inclinations. His son Norbert didn't "learn by [rote], as a parrot might, but by reasoning." Leo took a swipe at a school system that rewarded not "the child who thinks best but the one who remembers most"—and that shut its doors for months each year. Summer breaks were "one of the absurdities of American life," the Reverend Berle agreed, when children "absolutely forget that they [have] brains . . . which must be kept active in developing habits of observation, attention and self-control."

Boris and Leo didn't have brain scans to back up theories very similar to notions that now carry the imprimatur of the lab—about early brain plasticity, the benefits of exploratory play, the creative experience of "flow," the problem of extended school vacations. Instead they lucked into extraordinarily curious and focused boys who supplied evidence that went to their fathers' heads. Boris and Leo could generalize grandly as William and Norbert arrived at Harvard because they could point to amazing results in sons who were not narrow prodigies at all—although they were hardly average children either. The boys' pre-Harvard feats, often jumbled by an initially awed press eager for anecdotes, merged into an updated version of John Stuart Mill's trajectory. Which boy had accomplished what by when wasn't the point: they were an amalgam of the wonder child hidden in every child.

The milestones began with mastery of the alphabet before two and full literacy by three or four. Norbert drew letters in the sand with a nursemaid; Billy had ABC blocks dangling in his crib and his parents played letter games with him. Avid reading ensued, mostly of nonfiction. The boys then speedily amassed languages (Latin, Greek, German, French, and Russian for both, and some Hebrew, Turkish, and Armenian for Billy). Their intense scientific interests (anatomy and astronomy for Billy, chemistry and naturalist zeal for Norbert) inspired unusual strides before school age as well.

At which point—keeping up with Mill, who wrote a history of Rome at six—the wonder boys became eager knowledge producers as well as consumers. Between six and eight, Billy was especially busy. He invented his own language, Vendergood, and wrote a forty-page explication of it, in a style that veered from whimsical to pompous. He designed a grammar for teaching three languages at once and, according to his list of authorial accomplishments, also produced an astronomy textbook. Surely spurred on by Boris's prolific psychological output, Billy turned a passion for calendars into a primer, too. At eleven, while *his* father was toiling away on a translation of the total Tolstoy oeuvre, Norbert wrote a paper on "The Theory of General Ignorance." Carefully copied over in ink in a brown notebook, it represented his own step-by-step philosophizing, not a presentation of others' views. Leo, understandably impressed by his son's lucid argument for "the impossibility of man's being certain of anything," rewarded him with a special trip to Maine.

· 3 ·

Yet of course neither the men nor the boys—nor their families—were cut from the same cloth at all. That much was certain, a grown-up Norbert noted in his memoir. Their intellectual feats lumped them together as fascinating new Harvard outliers. But as Norbert appreciated in retrospect, and seems to have intuited even as a boy, what really mattered was how their social relations were, as he put it, "taken care of." Or, more accurately, not taken care of. By the time they arrived on campus, the boys' experiences had been strikingly different—each distinct from the other's, and neither in line with the effortless harmony that Leo and Boris liked to advertise for their avid tutees. Look behind the scenes, and the recalcitrant details leap out, especially in—who would have guessed?—Norbert's and Billy's less-than-smooth mastery of math. For two singular children, both supersmart but otherwise a study in contrasts, temperaments and family dynamics counted far more than paternal theories or pedagogical tactics ever could. Which didn't mean that their fathers (and, for Billy, his mother) were marginal. They were crucial, but in ways neither Boris nor Leo began to fathom.

Life in the Wiener household was a whirlwind, despite the best efforts of Leo's wife, the very proper former Bertha Kahn of Missouri, reared in assimilationist gentility by her businessman father and southern belle mother. Norbert, contrary to his father's claims, was anything but lazy. An insatiable learner who pored over books early, Nubbins—Norbert's family nickname—had the freedom, and the inclination, to be as vigorous as he was intellectually curious. He had a model: Leo, a tireless scholar and farmer and mushroom hunter. (Leo had set out from Germany at nineteen on a quest to create a vegetarian utopia in Belize, and when that voyage was aborted, he embarked on a long and circuitous American journey as a jack-of-all-trades—pausing in Kansas City to get semi-domesticated by the woman he courted—before his lucky landing at Harvard.)

As a small boy in Cambridge, Norbert eagerly sought out friends. Chunky and full of physical energy, he threw himself into neighborhood games, despite his bad eyesight and coordination—and more fearfulness than he cared to admit. From a young age he especially loved the outdoor "tramps" his father encouraged, and the "element of *élan,* of triumph, of glorious and effective effort, of drinking deep of life and the emotions thereof" that romantic Leo brought to them. Indoors, the Wieners' "house of learning" overflowed with visitors, conversation, books, and emotional outbursts. A sister Constance, four years younger, was a baby to quarrel with before she became his beloved companion. Another sister and a brother followed. With a husband whose "shaggy unconformity" and temper she vainly tried to tame, Bertha Wiener had her hands full. That her zealous firstborn was a nub off the old block taxed her further.

By the time Norbert was seven, his father decided it was time for third grade at the local Peabody School in Cambridge. There the stellar reader was bumped up to fourth grade, only to run into math difficulties with a mean teacher. Norbert didn't know his multiplication tables and didn't take to rote learning, though he was speeding ahead in math reasoning through avid problem solving with his father. Leo, math-minded himself, pulled him out of school to offer "a greater challenge and stimulus to my imagination," as Norbert put it in his memoir. There was plenty of that during two more years of home-based learning, much of it outsourced in wonderful ways—a lovely Radcliffe tutor for Latin and German,

NORBERT WIENER

a chemistry student who helped set up a lab, and endless time in the Agassiz Museum at Harvard, not to mention roaming with friends.

But math studies were another story. His father, whom he praised in his memoir as "a poet at heart, amid the frigid and repressed figures of an uninspiring and decadent Boston," was also a fierce taskmaster. Norbert's later bright-eyed photograph didn't betray the behind-closed-doors reality that had come before. In public, Leo prided himself on setting store by "the blessedness of blundering." Making children "work out problems" gave them the chance to fumble, and to "acquire that sense of mastery, that joy of triumph, which is of itself an incentive to further effort." So Leo explained his approach to his biggest journalist fan (whom Norbert later anointed H. "Addlehead" Bruce). In his memoir, Norbert put it rather differently: "No casual interest could satisfy my father's demand for precise and ready knowledge." Norbert's description of algebra lessons with Leo reveal a habit of thundering.

> He would begin the discussion in an easy, conversational tone. This lasted exactly until I made the first mathematical mistake. Then the gentle and loving father was replaced by the avenger of the blood. The first warning he gave me of my unconscious delinquency was a very sharp and aspirated "What!" and if I did not follow this by coming to heel at once, he would admonish me, "Now do this again!" By this time I was weeping and terrified. Almost inevitably I persisted in sin, or what was worse, corrected an admissible statement into a blunder. Then the last shreds of my father's temper were torn, and he addressed me in a phraseology which seemed to me even more violent than it was because I was not aware that it was a free translation from the German.

Leo let loose with *brute, ass, fool, donkey*. The lessons being blessedly short, sturdy Norbert weathered the tirades. But they "often ended in a family scene. Father was raging, I was weeping, and my mother did her best to defend me"—only to watch Leo later belittle Nubbins in company. Another hurdle his father wasn't about to publicize, because it suggested just what he denied—a boy under strain—left a more constructive mark: at eight, eye trouble for Norbert necessitated a half-year ban on reading or writing—doctor's orders. Leo's orders were to learn by ear. Those months spent working out algebra and geometry problems in his head introduced Norbert to a powerful ally: a highly unrote memory. In the bargain, he staked out a private inner sanctum and discovered his own unusual skill. "I relearned the world," Norbert later told an MIT colleague. "My mind completely opened up. I could see things I never saw before."

And then came another "unorthodox experiment," as Norbert put it in his memoir. His father, now consumed by the herculean challenge of translating twenty-four volumes of Tolstoy in twenty-four months, decided to send his son to high school. The choice hardly seemed auspicious for a nine-year-old, especially a boy newly stranded by the family's move to the rural Massachusetts town of Harvard. (Leo was in full Tolstoy mode, eager to farm.) But at nearby Ayer High, Norbert lucked into an ideal mentor. More accurately, Miss Laura Leavitt—a classics teacher whom Wiener later described as the "brains and conscience" of the school—was a maternal protector. She eased Norbert into kid-brother status among the students (even letting him sit on her lap at the intimidating start, before he learned "schoolroom behavior"). She made sure he connected with middle schoolers who shared the building. And her nephew became his best friend, just the company Norbert needed after homework recitations with a multitasking Leo, his eyes glued to Tolstoy—his ears alert as ever to any blunders.

Three years later, in the fall of 1906, Norbert graduated from Ayer High, fortified by "a sense of roots and security" (though recently buffeted, he also recalled in his memoir, by a severe case of "calf love"). Now almost twelve, he was a matriculant at Tufts College, in Medford, where the Wieners had moved for that purpose. The idea was to spare him the full glare of the spotlight that would have been his fate on the Harvard campus, which didn't mean his college debut went unnoticed. He got an upbeat send-off for a

prodigy. A Sunday magazine feature in the *New York World* pronounced Norbert "The Most Remarkable Boy in the World," her-
alding his wholesomeness as much as his phenomenal progress. If
his speech was a bit "prim and quaint"—"philosophy is a fairyland
to me," he told the reporter—his spirit was judged anything but.
Norbert set off daily for campus with his dog at his heels, and he
was a hit with the college guys. His eyes, "big and black and blazing [with] . . . something almost uncanny in their gaze," conveyed
the opposite of fragile precocity.

Billy's home world was a calm idyll by comparison with the
Wiener maelstrom. Officially at least, no family friction intruded
on his mathematical awakening, or on anything, for that matter. "The most important thing we agreed on was that we should
always agree," Sarah wrote of the pact she and Boris had made
about applying the Sidis approach to their son back at the moon-
gazing start. Sarah Mandelbaum herself had missed out on the
early learning that was purportedly so crucial. She had spent her
childhood tending to siblings, but when she arrived in the United
States at thirteen, unschooled, she was undeterred. So was her
tutor, seven years her elder, who helped her ace her high school
exams by eighteen and married her. By the time their baby was
due six years later, her medical degree was behind her. Her focus
was now the speedy progress of Boris (for whom clinical work
with insane patients at New York's recently established Pathologi-
cal Institute was a prelude to his pursuit of yet another Harvard
degree, an M.D.)—and of Billy.

Sarah, who later wrote it all up, said she ignored the latest
American counsel against too much cuddling and swore by her
husband's principles, applying no fearsome discipline. Not that
she was a laid-back mother. She appealed, she emphasized, only to
Billy's desire to please—her, for starters. As Boris had discovered
in his role as her tutor-suitor, gratifying Sarah could be arduous but
brought lots of plaudits for brilliance. She also imbued Billy with
her own Boris-worship, eager to spur him on to efforts to awe his
father, whom she described as besotted with his son. And "like all
normal little fellows," Billy loved being "the center of attention,"

she claimed, which spurred him to feats of learning. Or did she love making him the center of attention? It was telling that Sarah proudly recounted how a wealthy neighbor in New York used to summon Billy to her apartment to show off for her guests.

At home, Billy at five months was joining his parents for meals, observing and listening to everything, learning to use a spoon by trial and error. Sarah described herself as omnipresent, joining Billy on the floor as she banished all baby talk and made learning a game, from alphabet blocks onward. Ever at hand (the Sidises' second child, Helena, wasn't born until a decade later), Sarah was ready to answer or help him research any question. Her account, though, suggested that the partnership was rather one-sided. Billy got swept up in whatever subject was introduced or captured his interest, and early on he let his mother know he could look things up on his own. At around three, he found her old Latin trot, for example. Sarah reported her surprise when one day he excitedly revealed his mastery to his stunned father and some visitors. Boris supplied Billy with calendars to familiarize him with days and numbers. By five, the hyperfocused little boy had figured out by himself how to calculate the day on which any date fell.

But Billy wasn't simply a convivial bundle of curiosity; nor were his parents the models of progressive insight and flexibility they imagined. Outside the home cocoon, at the Adirondack resort where the Sidises spent summers among academic company during their New York years, the family style made an especially dramatic contrast to the free-range spirit of the philosopher John Dewey's brood. Sarah watched bemused as the educational reformer's children ran wild, confirmed in her own vigilance. Not that her son was clamoring to join in the unstructured peer chaos. (Sports held no interest for Billy, Sarah said, because Boris mocked them: so much for William James's advice about motor activities.) At breakfast, served between eight and nine, Billy threw a fit when food arrived at seven-forty-five, according to the account of another guest who took notes and published them later. He inventoried every guest by his or her room number, and pets by their kennel numbers. Ask him to display his expertise, on that subject or any other, and he

WILLIAM J. SIDIS

was stubbornly unresponsive; betray some bit of ignorance in his presence, and he was encyclopedic.

When the family moved back to the Boston area so Boris could go to medical school, among Billy's favorite pastimes was drilling his father on his anatomy studies. "Aha, you forgot the fifth cranial nerve," his mother would hear him sing out. He also headed off, now six, to a Brookline primary school. There he was an impatient handful for teachers, according to a later press account, covering his ears when he was bored, irrepressible when he was interested. At recess Billy was a loner, avoiding all games and "expounding the nebular hypothesis" to less-than-attentive schoolmates. And he balked at math, even as he zoomed through seven grades in the half year he lasted in school.

At least that was Boris's story, though Billy's fascination with calendars and numbers suggests a different struggle at work: a boy absorbed by a rule-bound realm and eager not to be disturbed, and a father determined to prove that his methods could produce more than mere narrow calculating prowess. In any case, Billy's math resistance gave his father a chance to make targeted use of his pet concept—the psychology of suggestion. Boris began the subtle strategy as homeschooling resumed. After sessions with dominoes and other math games, and staged conversations between Sarah and Boris about the many delights and uses of math, Billy at eight was busy inventing a new logarithmic table. No Leo-style eruptions were entailed—but no soul-bonding excursions transpired either. Mother-son trips to the hilltop behind the house to stargaze in the evenings were not Billy's idea of fun. "He soon told me," Sarah noted, "he could see better and think more clearly when he was alone."

Before long Billy was back in school—a real gamble, as his parents surely could have anticipated. In retrospect, some have reached for an Asperger's diagnosis, but no label is, or was, required to appreciate that a loner so woefully lacking in practice with peers was in for trouble. Boris and Sarah may well have cited Norbert's path as an example when they approached Brookline High about letting Billy, now eight, attend for several hours a day in the fall of 1906: the Wieners had just arrived in Medford, and their high school grad was making headlines at Tufts. But personable young Norbert, who had won over teachers and teenagers in out-of-the-way Ayer High, was not a helpful precedent at all.

A physics teacher at Brookline High showed special interest, but neither nurture nor, it seems, nature had predisposed Billy to endearing behavior. (Even his awed cousins found him odd and unapproachable—and their aunt Sarah domineering and heartless—recalled one of them, the critic and quiz show host Clifton Fadiman.) Billy interrupted the principal's Bible-reading to declare his atheist opposition. He gave academic help to classmates, who nicknamed him "professor." Let's hope some meant it fondly. The same fall of 1906 that Norbert got the "remarkable boy" press treatment at Tufts, Billy's high school foray elicited notably less favorable gawking in an article headlined "A Phenomenon in Kilts." Its author had unobtrusively observed the scene as teenagers thundered past the small interloper on the stairs between classes. After making his way to an empty physics lab to finish assembling a clock, Billy began "skipping and dancing about the many-windowed room like a child in his nursery." The reporter, unsettled rather than charmed, seized on Billy's gaze as confirmation of dire prodigy lore: "There is something weird and 'intense' in his gray eye, and the way he looks out under his eyebrows."

· 4 ·

Might everything have turned out differently—for both boys, but especially Billy—had the Sidises taken their cue from the Wieners' post-high-school decision to shield Norbert from the Har-

vard limelight? It's tempting to wonder. Instead, the Sidises aimed
to pick up the pace. When Billy was only nine (he had soon left
Brookline High and then sped through calculus and read Einstein
on his own), they were already pressing for admission to Harvard.
The thought of engaging high-powered tutors (Boris's former line
of work, after all) apparently never occurred to them. Possibly their
motives were ones that latter-day meritocrats would recognize: to
give their son an edge in the superchild spectacle, and his father's
reputation a boost. Doubtless Sarah was impatient to see Billy—
who so revered and resembled Boris, she constantly said—become
another brilliant outlier welcomed into the most prestigious ivory
tower. ("Our undisciplinables," William James once announced at a
Harvard commencement dinner, "are our proudest product.") How
Billy viewed the plan, particularly after his misfit experiences in the
Brookline schools, nobody evidently felt the need to ask. What the
inevitable campus hoopla would be like, the Sidises either didn't
consider or didn't care—though in theory, of course, Billy wasn't
supposed to become self-conscious about his specialness. Their
nephew Clifton Fadiman later brutally diagnosed Boris and Sarah
as lacking in "*wisdom,* even any common sense. They were, except
intellectually, fools."

Social obtuseness seemed to be Billy's style, too, which was a
blessing of sorts, at least at the outset, when Harvard, overcoming
its qualms about his lack of maturity, admitted him at eleven. The
boy who had happily skipped around the Brookline High lab displayed a frisky imperviousness in Cambridge, too. "I was certainly
no model of the social graces," Norbert wrote of his sightings of
William, "but it was clear to me that no other child of his age
would have gone down Brattle Street wildly swinging a pigskin
bag, without either order or cleanliness. He was an infant with a
full share of the infractuosities of a grown-up Dr. Johnson." William gave no sign of being fazed that he didn't fit into a world of
polished young gentlemen. Nor had awed adulation (and a rash
of newspaper coverage) gone to his head, a big Sunday magazine
profile in the fall was pleased to report. William was "utterly without self-conceit, but still with a broad grin for the humor of the

situation: 'It's very strange,' he remarked in his high, clear voice, 'but you know, I was born on April Fool's Day!'" A mind busy with vector analysis—he was enrolled in only one class the first term, advanced math—could tune out the fuss and the awkwardness.

But of course the purpose of William's being at Harvard wasn't to remain off in his own orbit. And in fact, Sarah had seen to it that he had been hearing about his unusual feats for years. Whether or not William much liked it, she had made performing and pontificating a habit. Mixed in with his cluelessness was what could be taken for arrogance—and certainly was in his parents' case. Their message, after all, not so subtly implied that those who didn't match the Sidises' pedagogical success (which was everybody) were mere slackers. Under the circumstances, the idea that Billy would deliver a lecture to the Mathematical Club in January 1910—an event arranged by a Harvard math professor whose father, a retired faculty member, was a family friend of the Sidises—was as loaded as it was alluring. Not least, another round in an ever more intense spotlight was guaranteed. Now the stakes had been raised, inviting stark questions no child should have to face and the public can rarely resist: Was he keeping up the pace, on the way to becoming a creative genius? Or was he a victim of parental ambition, headed for failure?

The substance of William's talk was impressively incomprehensible: that was the gist of accounts by reporters inclined to suggest that what was over their heads was beyond the rest of the audience, too. One informed listener was Norbert, who found the discussion original in the sense that William had consulted no sources in formulating a notably full account of the fourth dimension—a real achievement for anyone, never mind an eleven-year-old. It was William's style that entertained the press. He had his professorial act down—introductory patter, gestures, arcane vocabulary, diagrams, even a closing glance at his watch. Not least, he was impatiently supercilious with the assembled professorial elite. Rapidly recapping a point for one questioner, William inquired, "Is that any plainer now?"

The retired Harvard professor whose son had arranged the talk was on the alert for trouble, socially attuned as his old friend Boris clearly was not. At Harvard, if anywhere, "such a mind should find its home," the professor wrote of William in a letter to the *Harvard Graduates' Magazine*, worried that the boy was becoming a mere freakish spectacle. The university, he urged, should "do its best for the preservation and protection of that new type." William was a potential guiding light, not merely another phenomenal calculator. The Mathematical Club got a chance to make the comparison with another performer, a month after William's talk, when "Marvelous Griffith," a farmer, displayed his prowess in the same Sever Hall. Young Sidis probed concepts, but Griffith's "system depended too much on his own inherent genius for mathematics to be of any general service in their instruction system," a faculty member concluded.

But by then, William had stirred a press backlash that revived an old-style type of prodigy—an exploited specimen, enfeebled by ill-advised precocity. On January 27, 1910, a front-page article in *The New York Times* reported that young William had been "weakened recently by overstudy" and had been felled by a cold after his lecture. A longer account inside the paper diagnosed a "breakdown" and blamed Boris. To say that Dr. Sidis's "new and better system of education" had backfired, the *Times* duly noted, might be premature. But he had unquestionably failed to shield his sensitive son from "the morbid excitements and excessive attention to which he probably has been subjected" due to his feats, and which could be fatal. The article was a particularly unsavory instance of just such voyeurism, an irony that went unnoticed. It was also based on false rumors.

Yet the story—in spirit, though not fact—was accurate. William, under stress, had been stranded. In addition to being fools, Clifton Fadiman judged in retrospect, his aunt and uncle, "though not cruel, had no truly paternal or maternal feeling: they could educate a child but not rear him, which is a different thing." For William, happy when he could focus on his own interests, the Boris-emulation ceaselessly promoted by his mother seems to have been what passed for emotional intimacy in the household. Warmly insightful empathy, at any rate, wasn't a family strong suit. William had in fact caught a cold after his talk. Though he apparently didn't suffer a collapse of any sort, he did stay home for some time. But solicitous stocktaking wasn't on the agenda.

Boris was in the throes of opening a sanatorium for "nervous patients" up the coast in Portsmouth, New Hampshire, on an estate bequeathed to him by a wealthy benefactress. If the innuendoes had been truer—and the young genius had gotten at least a dose of concerned expert attention—perhaps William would have benefited. Boris's announced specialty, curing "persons who are hobby ridden," was at least pertinent. William, who hadn't let classwork eclipse his various independent projects (he devised, for example, an elaborate constitution for a utopia he called Hesperia), had developed an obsession with trolley transfers. But Boris had new patients to worry about, and in any case, parental protective gestures, such as they were, tended to irk William. Sarah had made a point of taking the streetcar with him to and from Cambridge during the fall—never mind that he'd learned all about Boston's growing public transportation system and yearned for a solitary commute between Harvard clamor and home. Now Sarah, with young Helena to tend to, was about to take on the management of the sanatorium as well. Like Boris, she had her hands full.

William was on his own as he entered adolescence, and more of an outsider than ever on campus. Under suspicion now of being mentally unbalanced, he was prey to continued press hounding. An article noted that when he found his math class tedious, William indulged in distracting antics like twirling his hat despite requests that he stop. His lack of social awareness, no longer a shield, left him painfully exposed. With the family's New Hampshire move, the plan was for him to try Harvard dorm life. But he was at sea with fellow students, the dupe of pranks that mostly turned on his awkward ignorance about girls. Bullying soon drove him to a rooming house on Brattle Street. There, approaching thirteen and not exactly practical, William had to cope alone all week—

though at least he was spared a mother whose aggressive nagging had intensified under the stress of her added burdens at the Sidis Psychopathic Institute.

Meanwhile, Boris, evidently feeling beleaguered too, erupted as a public scold, precisely the kind of parent no prodigy needs. In June 1911, Boris's "Philistine and Genius" lecture appeared in updated form as a short book in which he pulled no punches. Extolling his remarkable son (though not by name), he excoriated a "drift into national degeneracy" and warned that war was imminent. Sidis was "bent on repelling, offending, and estranging," remarked one reviewer. It was the screed of a man who had concluded that his message about America's backward approach to education wasn't getting across after all. "Poor old college owls, academic barnyard-fowls and worn-out sickly school-bats" was just one litany of derision. Boris never paused to consider who would pay the price for his venom. Decades later Sarah recognized that her husband had "pulled down upon his stout head, and upon Billy who was so very young—the anger that comes from hurt pride. Educators, psychologists, editorial writers and newspaper readers were furious with him. And their fury was a factor in Billy's life upon which we had not counted."

What she didn't say, or see, was that Boris had also bequeathed plenty of his own fury directly to his son, which wasn't part of the Sidis theory. That William was already feeling fiercely embattled became clear when, his college career at an end, the press cornered him once again. He graduated cum laude at sixteen in June 1914, with a wide array of courses (and a batch of Cs in junior year) under his belt. The *Boston Herald* was ready with salutes to his record-breaking prowess. He was "mentally . . . regarded by wise men as the most remarkable youth in the world" and was on his way to becoming "the youngest college professor in the world," with an appointment to teach math at Rice Institute. As for William's own thoughts about the path ahead, or about his Harvard ordeals, he at first seemed wisely determined to keep them to himself. He offered this brusque—or perhaps anxious—brush-off to the hovering reporters he hated: "I want to live the perfect life.

The only way to live the perfect life is to live it in seclusion. I have always hated crowds."

But William wasn't going to get away so easily. What were his one-of-a-kind plans for his personal, never mind intellectual, future? Such an inquiry promised ideal grist for the press. It was also the stuff of adolescent crisis for William, who got sucked in by an insinuating reporter. He needed to talk, and the *Boston Herald* was ready to listen. The picture that accompanied the two-page spread showed a filled-out young man in a suit, complete with a small daisy tie-pin, looking very mature for his age. It was William's graduation photo, in which he offered a reserved smile and a warm gaze. Two sidebars excerpted temperate statements of Boris's core educational tenets. But the headline brimmed with mockery: "HARVARD'S BOY PRODIGY VOWS NEVER TO MARRY Sidis Pledges Celibacy Beneath Sturdy Oak, Has 154 Rules Which Govern His Life, 'Women Do Not Appeal to Me,' He Says; He Is 16."

William even let the reporter into his Brattle Street rooms. The interview began in the vein of a therapy session in which a patient describes dire pain while deep in denial of just that. With odd pride, William laid out his obsessive-compulsive rituals for steering clear of women, though he also seemed half-aware of how peculiarly self-entrapping they might appear. "Many of my rules are checks rather than hard and fast laws," he explained. "They act as safety valves." It sounded like advice from Boris-the-hobby-expert on keeping compulsions within bounds. But rules for tempering rigidly rule-based thinking are easier to cite than to apply, especially for a teenager faced with a huge transition.

Readers didn't need to know the family drama to detect an alienated son, though William was working hard to keep his fury under wraps. He was caught up in his own version of the struggle for balance and meaning that had sent a twenty-year-old John Stuart Mill into a depression. Where Mill, fearing he was merely a "manufactured man," recognized a desperate need to reconnect with his feelings, a younger William grasped at equilibrium by denying them: "I had made up my mind that sentiment would make too much of an upset in my life," he told the *Herald* reporter.

It wasn't just romance and sex but anger that he needed to keep at bay—anger that ran in the family. "I have a quick temper; ergo, I will not mingle a great deal with the fellows around me, then I shall not have occasion to lose my temper."

But the anger he barely suppressed seemed to be aimed above all at his parents. Without directly addressing his own past, he indicted the family as a prison for the young. William declared himself "not at all a believer in home life" or in "forcing children in the early stages of their education." In one puzzling and poignant swipe, he all but abolished childhood: "No one should be dependent upon the good-will of others for support when too young to support himself." He announced that he was "in a way . . . a Socialist," perhaps not such a surprising allegiance for a prodigy who was feeling sabotaged by filial dependence, Harvard snobbery, and media prurience—and loneliness. His goal, he announced as he informed his interviewer that his earlier interest in the fourth dimension had entirely faded, was to "seek happiness in my own way."

· 5 ·

When Norbert arrived at Harvard at fourteen, he quickly figured out that William wasn't going to be a companion. But the unkempt boy swinging his pigskin bag seems to have inspired a fraught sense of fellowship in Norbert, who began his graduate studies in zoology already battling feelings of deep inadequacy, ostracism, and, worst of all, ill-fatedness. He did more than worry about William, who as the youngest oddity on campus was a magnet for the unwelcome glare that Norbert knew he was lucky to be mostly spared. (He knew better how to elude it, too, sometimes even fleeing down Cambridge alleyways to avoid reporters.) William was also a figure with whom he could readily identify—and wished he couldn't. Norbert came to Harvard newly, and intensely, haunted by predictions of failure for a "freak of nature," or nurture, of the sort the two of them were.

He had spent the summer of 1909 in acute crisis after three

years at Tufts. He had thrived there on the academic challenges, but four decades later in his memoir he described feeling off-balance, and not just in the lab, where he was hopelessly clumsy. Majoring in math while eagerly exploring biology and philosophy, he was "nearly completely a man for purposes of study." Heading home each day to siblings and neighborhood buddies, he was "wholly a child for purposes of companionship." Wherever he was, hormones left him feeling guilty and confused. And his father consistently kept him in his place. Leo, unlike the Sidises, zealously practiced what he preached about the dangers of singling a boy out for his brilliance—yet failed to consider the risks of eroding youthful confidence. His "Donkey!" explosions were bad. Perhaps worse was his refrain, in company and in the press, that Norbert was not just average but lazy. Leo surely didn't believe it, especially once he had initiated his two bright daughters and younger son into his regimen, only to discover that they failed to make anything like Norbert's progress—and were thoroughly intimidated. Still, Leo didn't let up, even in his son's presence.

As the end of Norbert's time at Tufts approached, he was an exhausted teenager with "severely lacerated self-esteem" who found himself preoccupied with death—calculating how many years he and everyone he knew might have left, and what he might accomplish. Self-doubt swamped him when he didn't make Phi Beta Kappa and learned that the reason was "doubt as to whether the future of an infant prodigy would justify the honor." Such a view stunned him. Votes of no confidence now seemed to be closing in. As the "prodigy comes to realize that the elders of the community are suspicious of him," Norbert wrote later, "he begins to fear reflections of this suspicion in the attitude of his contemporaries." He slipped into a real depression over the summer, with a lingering low fever and no sense of his future.

By the time Norbert started at Harvard, he was armed with social awareness that he saw poor William could have used—but it brought a burden, too: acute self-consciousness about his status as a misfit in a setting where, as he put it in his memoir, "a gentlemanly indifference, a studious coldness, an intellectual imperturbability

joined with the graces of society [to make] the ideal Harvard man."
In a maladroit hurry in the lab (he shifted from zoology to biology),
Norbert was always breaking glass and messing up procedures, to
his embarrassment. He later remembered his chagrin when some
classmates bought him a watch: he'd had no idea he was bothering
them by constantly asking for the time. Norbert went ahead and
threw himself, as he always had, into more than his studies. He
dared to join in pick-up basketball games in the gym basement
but quickly realized his glasses couldn't take the rough games even
if he could. A commuter, he mingled happily in the library of the
Harvard Union between classes. That was where the intellectual,
unclubbable sort hung out—generating murmurs of disapproval as
anti-Semitism became more overt under President Lowell. Norbert's mother had primly disparaged Jews throughout his childhood, and somehow the topic of the family's own heritage never
arose in the household. Now she urged him to spend less time in
the Union. Norbert, who allied himself with his father in boldly
pursuing truth and overcoming bigotry, was distressed.

Leo meanwhile had decided he wasn't particularly pleased with
his son's prospects in biology, so in the fall of 1910 he dispatched
Norbert to Cornell on a scholarship to study philosophy, for which
he had shown talent as a preteen at Tufts. Compared to William,
whose parents sought out exposure and skimped on support, Norbert had a fiercely protective guide in coping with what now goes
by the term *multipotentiality*—high abilities pointing in a confusing array of directions. Still, Leo's bossy approach to the blundering was hard on Norbert, who welcomed some distance from the
man who was hero and taskmaster in one. Nearly sixteen, he stumbled into what turned out to be a "black year of my life." He faced
a daunting endeavor his father did *not* direct: a struggle to claim
an identity and the feelings of agency that go with it—just what
prodigious children appear to have early but soon enough discover
they need urgently. William was at a similar crossroads as he, also
sixteen, left Harvard four years later.

The day his father dropped him off at his boardinghouse at

Cornell, Norbert glimpsed just how disorienting his quest for perspective on himself was going to be. The two of them paid a visit to an old friend of Leo's, a professor of ethics, who had agreed to keep an eye on Norbert during the year. In the course of conversation, the rumor that Maimonides was an ancestor of the Wieners somehow cropped up. Norbert promptly went off to investigate this unfamiliar philosopher who seemed to be a relative, only to be shocked to discover that the great Aristotelian had headed the Jewish community of Egypt. The implication hit him: his family was Jewish. Norbert gazed in the mirror at features he could now recognize as Semitic. He looked at his beloved sister's photograph and saw she wasn't just a pretty girl, but a pretty Jewish girl.

And suddenly his parents were exposed not just as social pariahs—if he was to credit the genteelly anti-Semitic Bertha Wiener's views—but as, in essence, liars. Norbert found it next to impossible to forgive his mother's prejudice; he went on to explore her forebears and realized that her maiden name, Kahn, was in fact Cohen. He struggled to excuse his assimilationist father, who had always conveyed respect for Jews; Norbert decided he must have wanted to spare his children the "consciousness of belonging to an undervalued group." Norbert never mentioned what must have been the other revelation: he and William were now joined as double outliers.

He was miserable, he wrote in his memoir. A "confused mass of feelings of resentment, despair, and rejection" overwhelmed him. Just coping day to day felt like more than he could manage. For the first time, Norbert didn't have his mother to hound him about cleanliness and his father to enforce disciplined study. He floundered in his one math course, and his philosophy papers were so crabbed that he was asked if German was his first language. In his letters home, Norbert staged no confrontation, betrayed no collapse. He kept saying things were "OK" and duly reported on his finances, which he had never handled on his own before. "My only want is some boy companion, but boys are scarce hereabouts," he wrote his mother, and in a postscript asked his favorite sister, Constance, for news of "W.J.S." (William) and the Berle children, and his non-Harvard friends.

But Norbert also began staking out new ground with his father as he wrote home. Leo, conscious of his status as a brilliant but marginal figure in his Slavic field, had often hashed out philological points in his son's company. Now Norbert, struggling with his deepening sense of himself as an outlier, seemed to be pushing his father to be a bolder model. If he could see him not as an oppressive Pygmalion but as part of a tradition of unconventional thinkers that reached back to Maimonides, perhaps he could banish his own fearful expectations: Norbert didn't put it this way, yet finding sustenance in social solidarity—not just looking for it within—had always been his instinct. Deeply confused, he never contemplated embracing the Jewish faith, but here was a broader context for his own prodigyhood. As he later noted of the Sidises, the emphasis on honing rabbinic learnedness in every generation was still fresh in Jewish émigrés. Perhaps Maimonides, a Jew steeped in Muslim tradition who left his mark on Western philosophy, offered a cosmopolitan ideal: a bold and resilient outsider receptive to new ideas from exotic sources.

Amid his Cornell woes, Norbert kept up with his father's linguistic studies. He raised questions ("What is the Egyptian word for goose?") and weighed in on Leo's theories, one of which had lately been challenged by a scholar. "Give it to him!" Norbert urged, eager for "a good philological fight." Here was a son/student trying to turn the tables. It was "devastating," Norbert wrote later, to learn that Leo had spread the notion "that my failures were my own but my successes were my father's." Still, he wanted Leo to be an undaunted success himself. His mother was always urging her bristly menfolk to fit in—which, given what he now knew, perhaps made Norbert bridle more at her conformism. He seemed to be pushing for a combative, productive example as he foundered. Norbert wasn't failing by any means, but a professor had informed him that his work wasn't what had been expected—hardly the verdict a boy worried about fading promise needed. Nor was the news, as the term ended, that his fellowship wouldn't be renewed. "How is your work?" he wrote his father in May, underscoring four times the demand that followed. "I want more concrete news!!!!!!!!"

For Jews, the way ahead was all uphill, which could serve as a kind of relief: it was an alternative to the downward flameout augured for a prodigy. An avid hiker like his father, Norbert knew the terrain. In fact, for Norbert, the steeper the path the better, to judge by drawings he sent as postscripts to his sister Constance in his letters from Ithaca. His pen and ink efforts showed the two of them heading nearly vertically up Mount Washington's Boott Spur trail, and *not* falling off. Norbert's fears and depression had fueled a sense of himself as "nervous" in temperament. But he also set great store by the stamina that had allowed him to weather Leo's treatment.

The sense of "filial servitude" lingered as Norbert finished his Ph.D. at Harvard in June 1913, writing a dissertation on Alfred North Whitehead and Bertrand Russell's *Principia Mathematica*. But now eighteen, he was on the brink of a much broader apprenticeship, with plenty of detours in it. As Norbert doubtless appreciated, his father was in no position to demand that he keep up the dizzying pace of superachievement. Indeed, Leo now emphasized to the press that there was no hurry. His son—"he is so young, only eighteen"—had "plenty of time. . . . He has not begun to specialize yet" and would probably be heading abroad.

Leo himself, having set sail for America in 1882 at nineteen, was over thirty by the time he settled into his life and work. He had never regretted his picaresque journey from New Orleans to Kansas City, picking up odd jobs and curious acquaintances—and yet more languages (including Gaelic!). "Just Missed Becoming a Great Merchant," read the headline of a profile of Wiener Sr. in *The Boston Daily Globe* in 1914, which went on to note, "Passion for Languages Finally Fitted Him Into His Life Work." Fortuitous swerves plus zealous focus: for anybody heading into young adulthood, not merely a former prodigy, counting on both is to be recommended—but not, Norbert and William discovered, as anything like a surefire formula for success.

As Norbert and William navigated their way amid wartime uneasiness, what made the difference was temperament, social circumstances, and luck, as much as paternal guidance or neglect—not that the factors could be readily disentangled, and not that their fathers ceased to be important. For William, a resolve to sabotage Boris's enterprise unfolded not just tragically but ironically. In his effort to escape the public attention and expectations thrust upon him, he turned his back on achieving recognized greatness—only to end up very much his father's son, feeling isolated and besieged. Further exposure to academia didn't go well. As a seventeen-year-old math teacher at Rice, William was yet again mercilessly teased by undergraduates older than he was. Enrolled after that at Harvard Law School, he dropped out in his third year, not the collector of credentials his father had been. If his growing interest in radical politics encouraged any new bonding with Boris (the erstwhile tutor of Russian serfs), a bitter break with his parents was in store after William got arrested at a Boston May Day Socialist march in 1919 that dissolved into mayhem.

By now twenty-one, he was sentenced to eighteen months in prison on charges of rioting and assaulting a police officer, though he had done neither. In William's later version of events, his actual fate was worse. Before he could appeal the initial sentence, he was "kidnapped" by his parents and forcibly kept in the New Hampshire sanatorium for a year, after which they whisked him to California—eager to keep him not just out of court and prison but also out of touch with fellow Socialists in Boston. (Among them was an unrequited romantic interest: Martha Foley, who had marched alongside him and who went on to found *Story* magazine—a friend he courted ardently but without success.) Upon finally escaping to New York and low-level accounting work, he was spooked, in flight from his parents' "protection," press attention, his reputation (he promptly quit if officemates learned who he was), the legal charges. In 1923, when Boris died at fifty-six of a cerebral hemorrhage, William didn't go to the funeral. But he did write to a

Harvard Law School faculty member, eager to discover whether his case had been dropped. William got good news, though he was shielded from learning the grounds for the dismissal of charges: Sarah had testified that her son was "mentally abnormal." Already determined to avoid his mother at all costs, William hardly needed to find that out in order to hate her, as he often said he did.

William's sister, Helena, kept in fond touch—grateful for her big brother's tutorial efforts as she grew up (their parents having decided she was too fragile for more than haphazard schooling) and gratified that he counted on her common sense. Not that her advice to try more challenging jobs made a dent. "I just want to work an adding machine, so I won't have to use my mind on it," he told her. "I want to use my mind for other things." William, though mostly phobic about math, was as eclectic as ever in seeking happiness in his own intense and now anonymous way.

Writing under pseudonyms, he pursued a wide array of topics: the collection of streetcar transfers, the contributions various Indian tribes had made to American colonists' notions of democracy, collisions on highways, trivia about his beloved city of Boston (for a magazine called *What's New in Town*), and more. He put his name on his most ambitious endeavor, *The Animate and the Inanimate,* which was published (perhaps at his own expense) in 1925 to no notice. It set forth his ideas about the possible reversibility of the second law of thermodynamics, and was later judged by some—among them, Buckminster Fuller—to have anticipated versions of the big bang theory and black holes.

Be careful what you wish for seemed to be William's belated message for Boris, who had never cared about conventional success or money and had fiercely championed the antiphilistine generalist. Not unlike his aggrieved father, William finally did erupt publicly, devastated by a reprise of the exposure that had begun with Boris and Sarah. In 1937, he was dragged back into the limelight in a cruelly patronizing *New Yorker* profile in the magazine's "Where Are They Now?" series. It was written by James Thurber (under a pseudonym) and bore the title "April Fool!" Worse than a portrait of a burned-out recluse, the piece mercilessly mocked William's still very busy mind. He broke his vow of seclusion to sue for invasion of privacy and malicious libel. The judge dismissed the case, which has become a classic in privacy law, and William, who worked on the briefs, lost the appeal. Once a public figure, always a public figure, the judge ruled, even as he lamented the ruthless intrusion. Once Boris Sidis's son, always Boris Sidis's son: that thought follows not far behind. William persisted with his various causes, especially active in defense of pacifism and of limited government, alienating allies again and again with his bullheadedness. In 1944, at forty-six, he died of a cerebral hemorrhage.

Norbert, who vented his outrage at the *New Yorker* article in his memoir, risked sounding harsh in his assessment of William (by then dead): a "defeated—and honorably defeated—combatant in the battle for existence." As for himself, Norbert's verdict was stringent, too—that he was a near casualty, still struggling. In contrast to William, already at odds with his ill-attuned parents as he graduated from Harvard, Norbert left Cambridge with the opposite problem: a revered father who still couldn't resist butting in, even if he was no longer bossing in the old way.

For Norbert, unable to overtly rebel against his hero, traveling a path beyond Leo's ken proved crucial. Norbert surged onward academically, though not exactly smoothly. He won a prestigious Harvard postgraduate traveling fellowship and headed off to study at Trinity College, Cambridge, with Bertrand Russell, who had been assured (by Leo) that a sturdy specimen was on his way: "physically strong (weighing 170 lbs.), perfectly balanced morally and mentally, and shows no traits generally associated with early precocity. I mention all this to you that you may not assume that you are to deal with an exceptional or freakish boy, but with a normal student whose energies have not been misdirected."

But Leo, of course, couldn't guarantee good chemistry between them. Russell proved to be a ruthless mentor, and a homesick Norbert sent an unvarnished account to his father. Russell complained that Norbert's views were a "horrible fog," his exposition of them worse, and accused him of "too much confidence and cocksureness." Norbert had heard a lot worse in his day, and though wounded, he was hardly undone. Russell, he complained in turn, was "an iceberg. His mind impresses me as a keen, cold, narrow logical machine, that cuts the universe into neat little packets, that measure, as it were, just three inches each way." His own mind, Norbert was discovering, was fertile—and more versatile in math than he had known. When things didn't click the way they did in the brilliant G. H. Hardy's math class at Cambridge, bearing down brought results. He was able to show dubious professors (and himself) that he could keep up with the rest of the class and feel gratified by his progress.

Norbert, not his father, was now maturely trying to decide where his real interests lay—in philosophy or math, perhaps applied math—and he was finding his place in a world of donnish collegiality and intense discussions. At the same time, he could sound like the college-age youth—or the still-precarious postprodigy—that he was. He harped on his work habits in his letters home, now assuring his parents that he had his nose to the grindstone, then assuring them that he wasn't overtaxing himself. He was searching for the discipline he had depended on his father to provide, and complying as best he could with Leo's counsel: "Do not work too hard, but do not become lazy at the same time." ("I have occasionally taken a glass of beer, as no other cheap liquid refreshment is available," Norbert informed his parents, itemizing the amount and costs. "If you object to my doing as I have done, I shall not take any more.")

If Norbert was "loafing," as he admitted he was as the summer of 1914 arrived, he was pretty sure he wasn't "idling." The young man who had known depression recognized the importance of rest. He needed to fend off the feeling that his studies were "a dead drag" and to restore his "enthusiasm over my work." It was very gratifying to have his father proudly salute several of his published projects as "fine, especially fine, since I do not understand a word in them." Still, Norbert felt more under Leo's thumb than he wanted to be when he returned to the United States in 1915 to figure out what he might do next. Now twenty-one, he began jumping among jobs (some lined up by Leo), happier the farther away he was from home. "It may seem a step down to follow years of pre-cocity and early academic degrees by the somewhat routine tasks of a shopworker, a hackwriter, a computer, and a journalist," Norbert noted in his memoir, but real-world immersion held glamour. His stint in 1918 at the U.S. Army's Aberdeen Proving Ground—he was summoned thanks to his mathematical talents, not paternal contacts—was especially rewarding. Mood swings continued. Yet busy doing invaluable work on antiaircraft targeting with fellow mathematicians, he found the camaraderie and independence he yearned for.

And soon, in a now-flourishing postwar academic market for the brainiacs needed in a science-guided era, Norbert found his niche. At MIT, down the road from increasingly anti-Semitic Harvard, social graces and pedigrees didn't count for much, and wartime technical experience like his did. He got hired. The latest mathematical tools were much in demand as electronic communication technology took off in the 1920s. By then he was seeing the woman he finally married in 1926 and with whom he had two daughters. Norbert was also deep into the prescient endeavor of fathoming the endlessly elusive process at the heart of the computer age: the flow of information.

Cybernetics, "or control and communication in the animal and the machine," as Norbert summed up his new pursuit, has been hailed as the catalyst of the first genuinely *American* scientific revolution. A notably hybrid undertaking, it was at once theoretical and practical, concerned with both mind and matter. Cybernetics laid crucial groundwork for modern automation and is back in the spotlight with recent cross-disciplinary developments in robotics, prosthetics, synthetic biology, and more. It "sired, inspired, or contributed to dozens of new technical and scientific fields," Wiener's biographers write, "from artificial intelligence and cognitive science to environmental science and modern economic theory." That a pioneering modern prodigy had sired it seems particularly fitting. Norbert's work helped usher in the computer, which one of his many successors, Seymour Papert, heralded as "the children's machine" and the key to a newly youth-driven "age of learning."

Norbert, who died in 1964, surely would have been excited. But in a memoir haunted by the depression he suffered on and off throughout his life, he aimed to remind readers of the human challenges of growing up. Every child, however extraordinary his mastery of a skill may be, "struggles in a half-understood world" of adults as he strives for autonomy. William Sidis probably wasn't far from his mind, nor was his own imposing father, when Norbert distilled a low-tech secret of success. Based on his experience, he concluded that the key wasn't expert early tutelage, grateful though he said he was for the "rigorous discipline and training" he received (if "perhaps in rather excessive portions"). What counted most for a boy like him, he wrote in an article that he hoped might help others, was more modest: the hard-won "chance to develop a reasonably thick skin against the pressures which will certainly be made on him and a confidence that somewhere in the world he has his own function which he may reasonably hope to fulfill."

CHAPTER 2

"A Very Free Child"

· 1 ·

Out in the foggy and untamed San Francisco Bay area, a golden-haired boy was born in 1897, a year before Billy Sidis and three after Norbert Wiener, to two bohemian-anarchist writers committed to giving him the fullest freedom to flower. Or to eat gravel, as happened one morning while Harry and Clarissa Dixon Cowell were busy inside their tiny Menlo Park cottage in the hills behind the brand-new Stanford University campus. Henry, roughly two, was happily playing outside. A young university student who had become friendly with the family was waiting nearby for the milkman to give her a lift to class. Turning to hug the strikingly beautiful boy, "I noticed his eyes were staring, his face was purple, he was gagging," she recounted. She seized Henry, held him upside down, and forced his teeth apart. "His cheeks were packed with gravel," and she struggled to clear his airway. Finally she heard a strangled cough. After soothing the sobbing child, she brought Henry in to his parents. Their response on hearing what had just happened was to ask, "You did not use violence?"

It is a rare parent who doesn't have at least one early close call seared in memory—that day when, say, your Lego fan decided to see how different colored bricks tasted. What if you hadn't been in the next room (you were not hovering) and heard him choke? Years later, that thought can still make your heart pound. In Clarissa and

Harry Cowell's case, principle took precedence over panic. As the Stanford student commented with some awe, "There was never a deviation, never any momentary temptation on the part of Clara or Harry to bear down on the child . . . in any way." One day not long after that morning, Henry decided to go walking on his own. He got far enough along the road that Clarissa, who was in her late forties, had trouble catching up, but she still didn't dream of chiding him. Instead she asked him why he had taken off. "He says, 'Choo-choo say, Run away, run away, run away,' imitating with his voice the monotone of carwheels running over railendings." Clarissa noted this in her diary, along with entries about—among many other things—all the humming he did in his high chair. Henry picked up whatever childhood songs his not particularly musical parents sang. Harry, who had emigrated from Ireland after what he liked to portray as a restless youth, favored Irish airs. Clarissa's staple was Ozark mountain songs she learned growing up in a fundamentalist family in Iowa. And before Henry could really talk, his mother noticed, he was improvising his own melodies.

"I find much in Henry which I am unable to account for on generally-accepted scientific principles. He seems to be part-angel and wise with inexplicable wisdom," Clarissa wrote some fifteen years later. Sick with cancer in 1914, she was gathering her diary entries as potential "material for a biography" of her now teenage son. Henry had recently been hailed as "an artist of unusual talent" in a newspaper review of a piano recital in which he played his own compositions. The headlines echoed the East Coast tributes to the Harvard boys of several years earlier: "Lad Shows Signs of Real Genius," announced the *San Francisco Chronicle* in March 1914. "Youthful Wonder Has Charm of Genius," reported *The Daily Palo Alto Times*.

But the story of the boy who became one of America's preeminent modern composers could hardly have been more different. Almost everything about Henry's trajectory would have driven the father-experts in Cambridge crazy. True to her hands-off philosophy, Clarissa steered clear of structured academics as she and her son charted an itinerant route across the country during his childhood. A fast track held no allure. And Henry acquired a mentor in a Stanford psychologist whose core conviction was precisely the view that Boris Sidis and Leo Wiener scoffed at. In a century surging with immigrants and new educational opportunities, Lewis Terman emphasized that youthful intelligence was distributed unevenly. It needed to be assessed and ranked, and then trained accordingly. A former brainy boy from an Indiana farming family with deep rural American roots, he was determined to prove that geniuses of all kinds were born, not bent, that way.

For both Henry and Terman, the connection turned out to be formative. Terman was poised to revise the French psychologist Alfred Binet's test of children's mental abilities for wide American use. He needed evidence for his view that general intelligence was inherited, readily measurable in childhood, and stable throughout life. Not least, he was eager to prove that it was sure to be impressively high in talented individuals of all different stripes. Binet had focused on the bottom, intent on identifying children who might benefit from remedial help. Terman embraced the opposite goal, to single out those he considered natural superachievers. Here he agreed with the Bostonians: in a philistine country in a newly fast-paced era, it was high time that intellectual promise ceased to be associated with young misfits. The image of brainiacs as "especially prone to be puny, over-specialized in their abilities and interests, emotionally unstable, socially unadaptable, psychotic, and morally undependable" was in dire need of debunking. Where Boris and Leo focused on an enlightened citizenry, reared to resist the "mob spirit," Lewis envisaged a leadership elite.

For his starter sample, Terman had a son, Fred, who revealed an unusual mind well before starting school, which his father was in no hurry to have him do. At nine, when Fred first entered a regular classroom, he had already done lots of independent wandering and inventive tinkering; ham radio had become a specialty. (On a near par with the Sidises in sexist handling of a firstborn's little sister, Terman didn't pay much heed to his daughter, Helen, whom he considered "average.") But America's IQ-test crusader needed a pool of subjects to study. He was fascinated to learn from a colleague that "a very free child" with highly unusual musical gifts lived in the area. In Henry, Terman found an ideal outlier. In Terman, Henry found a kindly professor who offered attention and resources. He ended up being Terman's most unforgettable subject.

It was a curious partnership. Terman embodied the standardizing ethos the nonconformist Cowells prided themselves on shunning. Henry confounded many of Terman's claims, exposing the narrowness of his testing tools. But each had something to learn from the other, about the limits of tidy measures of innate intelligence and about the limits of fervent faith in freedom for raw talent. Together they could have knocked some humility into Boris and Leo, so obsessed with adult-style mastery and so heedless of children's own distinctive powers of discovery. And as William and Norbert might have especially appreciated, Henry cast new light on youthful eccentricity.

· 2 ·

Plump-cheeked Henry, whose blue eyes are dazzlingly clear even in black-and-white photographs, was all the more prodigious for not being a prodigy in anything like a conventional sense. His mother recorded that he spoke three words at twenty months. That was two months older than Billy and Norbert were when they mastered the alphabet. Henry made swift progress after that, and at three—when the Boston boys were already reading—Clarissa noted that he recognized twenty-five words at sight. She half-apologized for that retrograde trick: "Both his father and I disapprove of beginning formal education when a child is very young; but when a baby points to a letter or a word and fairly demands to be told the name of it, what's to be done?" By then, Henry had also moved on to humming original tunes in his high chair, but Clarissa didn't pretend to be a knowledgeable judge of his improvisational talents. He wasn't surrounded by music at home.

What stands out in Clarissa's jottings on Henry's earliest years is not any remarkable achievement of his, much less any rigor in her experiments in child-driven nurture. Instead, the account conveys his angelic spirit and her highly unusual blend of fervor and flexibility. She pronounced that, as an older mother who had borne a first child at nineteen back in Iowa, she now had "strong convictions on many subjects bearing on child-life and the relation of the child to its parents and to society." She invoked the "three great forces for happiness: love, wisdom, freedom." But she also freely, and wisely, confessed that her "notions about methods of securing freedom for my child were exceedingly hazy."

She mocked herself for one of her efforts: to determine Henry's favorite color, she presented him with an array, and "his eyes rested on pink." Henceforth, she wrote, "I think I overdid the lavishing of his favorite color upon him." Given lots of choices, big and small, Henry evidently didn't fret the way children often do when overwhelmed by options. Clarissa wasn't fazed either, even when the "castoff finery of ladies" turned out to be his fashion preference. Saying "he wished to be a girl and wear dresses because they were prettier than boys' clothes," Henry did just that until he was eight or so. Meanwhile, Clarissa and Harry (fifteen years her junior) were coping with more consequential domestic issues. They needed to put food on the table. When it was Harry's week in their egalitarian domestic arrangement, meals tended to consist of crackers.

Even when, at the age of four, Henry first displayed unmistakable signs of a musical gift, Clarissa and Harry's response took a laid-back form. The family was now living in a tiny San Francisco apartment on the edge of Chinatown, and Henry's singing inspired a friend to give him a mandolin harp ("like a zither with a keyboard," he later described it) for his birthday. Soon he "played familiar airs and made original variations on them." His parents were thrilled, and especially pleased to feel they had no proprietary role in this talent. That fit right in with their emphasis on "the development of initiative, intelligent choice, self-government, in the child." Another admiring neighbor gave Henry a quarter-size violin, and Clarissa then bought him the even smaller one he needed. In her diary she marked the day of his first lesson—

November 16, 1902. It was hardly the beginning of steady or spectacular tutelage, however.

Before long, Henry was studying with the British violinist and composer Henry Holmes, a former prodigy himself, then in his seventies. (Holmes's daughter, who got Henry off to a good start on the instrument, had to stop when she injured her hand.) Holmes took an old-school approach, dictating the repertoire (eighteenth-century music) and demanding deference and commitment, not the best match for a freedom-loving five-year-old. Assigned lots of Louis Spohr exercises, Henry learned them and improvised eagerly on his own. It quickly became clear he had absolute pitch, and Clarissa gushed that

HENRY COWELL

"not a single unpleasant sound ever issued from his tiny instrument." But she also noticed that her usually cheerful son seemed irritable, his shoulder twitching after just a few minutes of practice.

The symptoms (of chorea, it later turned out, a nervous system disorder sometimes triggered by a strep infection or rheumatic fever) meant he had to ease up. She made a point of not reminding him about his lessons and ruled out any invitations for Henry to perform for friends. Harry showed no such compunction. Yearning after "the long deferred literary life," he seems to have quietly nursed the notion that a performing child might be an entrée into the creative limelight. He liked having Henry in circulation and dragged him around late at night to visit one of the couple's heroes, Jack London, and others—to Clarissa's distress. But she also didn't want to interfere in the father-son bonding, since she and Harry had recently separated.

All in all, Henry had very intermittent lessons over the course of about two years—surely not under pressure from Clarissa, who wasn't about to make him quit either. Henry called the shots, even when he didn't quite mean to. One day, now eight and struggling to correct a mistake while Holmes kept finding fault, Henry retorted: "I cannot play because you put me out." That was the end of regular lessons with Holmes. (Clarissa, who was present, felt Henry was simply explaining, not impertinently whining.) Henry seemed disinclined to work further on his own—though he had made good progress with what amounted to scant instruction, playing easy movements in Mozart and Haydn. "Henry showed no strong impulse toward working without a teacher," Clarissa noted. "I made no step to get another . . . because I feared that his nerves would be shattered if he continued work."

But he was avidly listening to Asian music in nearby Chinatown. And what she didn't know was that Henry had decided to be a composer and had devised his own invisible regimen. He wrote later that "all the children I played with went in from four to five in the afternoon, exactly, to practice the piano, and of course, everybody was out again at 5:01 to play. I didn't want to be left out of such activity." So he went in, too. "I sat down at the desk and practiced listening to sounds in my mind. I did this very methodically," Henry recalled, eager to emphasize his own inner discipline. ". . . Although I lived among people who were very romantic about composition, I myself supplied a method, and this method was to cultivate my mind to hear sounds which became more and more complicated as time went on."

Clarissa, now a single mother, moved back to Menlo Park from San Francisco. She later inveighed against the public school habit of "crushing all children into a shapeless, pulpous mass and then pouring them into molds, like hot tallow" (a rare echo of Boris Sidis). But she sensibly decided that Henry needed "at least enough of it so that he could bear understandingly such parts of it as he could not love but could not evade." She was being practical on her own behalf, too: Clarissa needed him steadily supervised and occupied so that she could write and earn some money. Henry arrived at the local elementary school with his long hair and was severely beaten by some bigger boys—Portuguese and some blend of Spanish, Mexican, and Indian, she noted, and evidently threatened by "the young god so manifestly different from them." Henry recovered and went back, only to get another drubbing. He didn't return.

In her biographical notes, under the heading "Groping Among Educational Methods (I do the groping. The child leads.)," Clarissa did her best to portray the muddling that ensued as an approach made to order for Henry. He was a child who "loved successively, ardently, one subject at a time," she wrote. "While the love lasted he mastered difficulties with readiness and insight that seemed little short of magical." Like William and Norbert, he wasn't obsessively given to one form of accomplishment, in music or elsewhere, yet he plainly could summon the sort of single-minded focus that often makes effort seem less effortful.

"Reserve energy," Boris called it, promising that all children, given suitably playful instruction, could draw on it. Clarissa took a different view. She believed there were children "who feel no special voluntary interest in anything, and need to be prodded and pricked and roused to look about them and see what sort of world they live in." But not Henry. All he needed was to be spared distractions. She was lyrical on the subject. "The child must be delighted with his work," she wrote.

> He must study the thing he wants to know while he wants to know it. . . .
>
> It is not the way of wisdom to hold Geometry before the face of a dreamer while he is at his dreams. First let him wake to the presence, if not the beauty, of angles in the world.
>
> One study at a time, and that the one utterly beloved— for the time.
>
> That became my cult.

Her standards for mastery were not exactly punctilious. She judged Henry to have "learned" the violin in under four months. In three weeks of brief daily work, she boasted, her eight-year-old

plowed through a "language lessons" textbook designed to con-
sume hundreds of hours of classroom study. Not at all perturbed
that his "careless habits" continued—his spelling and punctuation
were hopeless several years later—Clarissa lauded her wonderful
conversationalist.

In what time she could spare for Henry's studies at home—she
acknowledged it wasn't much—Clarissa read widely to him, and
they discussed all kinds of things. The San Francisco earthquake of
1906, which closed Stanford and left Menlo Park a disaster area,
introduced a new level of improvisatory adventure to his curriculum. He spent an "impassioned" six weeks absorbed in geology
after it happened. And then Clarissa, seeing no good alternative
to flight, took Henry's education on the road. They headed east to
Clarissa's sister in Kansas, then to her first son and other relatives
in Des Moines. Their cross-country journey sparked an interest in
geography and a bout of eager stamp collecting. In Iowa, she made
another stab at formal schooling for Henry. Finding the right class
for him was a challenge—way ahead of the third graders in reading
and arithmetic, he was a mess in writing—but after four months, it
was sickness that sabotaged him. Tonsil and adenoid trouble were
followed by measles, and finally he quit. Henry returned briefly
for fourth grade, only to be pulled out upon being diagnosed with
Saint Vitus' dance (as chorea was then known). Clarissa concluded
that school was most effective in spreading germs.

In the Des Moines public library, Henry quickly outgrew the
children's section. Suspecting him of skimming, Clarissa tested
him and found he could give eloquent summaries of the books he
claimed to have read. An outing to *Il Trovatore* inspired him to
learn the stories of twenty other operas. Loaned a piano, Henry
began playing and sent his father a song he had written and set
to music. Harry didn't think much of the melody but admired the
clever words. Clarissa, still dreaming of a literary career for herself,
decided they would head for New York, where she somehow soon
finagled grand Greenwich Village lodgings in exchange for care-
taking while the place was being renovated. Henry's bleaker memory was of huddling in bed, cold and hungry, some of the time.

In a letter to Harry, Clarissa clung to her hopes of "getting fitted into my own place, if life holds one for me, and I still believe it does." And she gave an upbeat account of their son, now eleven. "Henry likes New York, of course. He belongs where life is stirring and full, though he is capable of filling it himself with small resources." The absence of peers went unmentioned, but Henry was indeed good at keeping himself eclectically occupied, and she was grateful. While Clarissa finished writing a curious novel about a young girl and her best friend, which was published to next to no notice, Henry had his own creative projects. He reported to his father that he was composing music for a Longfellow poem and reading Greek poets—and still playing with his blocks, enjoying them "like a baby."

In his mother's descriptions, which mixed Rousseauism and realism, Henry was curiously ageless and unspoiled.

> He loves a land of art galleries and libraries, and big grand opera advertisements—even if he can't go in and pay for a seat. He is absorbed in his stamp collection and really does learn a surprising lot of geography and history, and the political status of all nations from this source. I am growing rather tired of the subject. I suppose it is a sort of measles that he has to go through.

Henry's own report at twelve confirms the impression. "I have had enough of New York," he wrote to Harry in the spring of 1909, but he wasn't complaining. "I have learned much by coming here. I know what it feels like to live in the largest literary centre of the U.S. I have the history of the ancient world on the tip of my tongue. The city libraries are a help but now I wish to go back." Harry, though still floundering himself, wrote to his ex-wife to say he found Henry inspiring. But, alluding to Thomas Carlyle's definition of genius, Harry also couldn't help feeling his son was a little slapdash: "I wish that he had had an infinite capacity for taking pains with his music commensurate with his genius. But alas!"

Clarissa and Henry arrived back in Menlo Park in the fall of

1910, after another pause to work on her sister's farm in Kansas, where Henry took pains instead with flowers. They had become his passion. "Sweet peas, phlox, petunia, portulaca, eschscholtzia and scarlet flax are all blooming," he wrote his father of his garden, but "I am not as much interested in any of these things as I am how to get to California." There they found their old cabin overrun by nature in their absence. With neighborly help, they reclaimed it. Henry also found time for a new collecting obsession, not stamps or flowers but—if only William Sidis had known—pre-earthquake San Francisco streetcar transfers!

Clarissa's meager freelance income had dried up, and the two of them were scrounging, so Henry at thirteen turned his mind to making the family living. He did janitorial work at the local elementary school. He also launched a fern- and flower-gathering enterprise, showing a new persistence as he headed into the hills and then sold what he picked to Stanford faculty members. "The plant business was never worse because most wild things have died down and people won't buy what isn't there!" he reported to Harry in the summer, having urged his father to be his salesman in San Francisco. "Am making some rustic hanging baskets."At the same time, Henry stumbled onto an incongruous pair of mentors, one scientific and the other artistic. Lewis Terman, recently hired as an assistant professor in Stanford's new education department, wasn't alone in being smitten with Henry. So was Ellen Veblen, the estranged wife of the economist Thorstein Veblen. Unlike Henry's free-spirited and impractical parents, they were poised to help him find and pursue his true focus.

· 3 ·

At roughly the stage that William and Norbert were coping with overweening fathers and a merciless spotlight focused on their every misstep after their precocious starts, Henry experienced the opposite. After years in isolated obscurity, he suddenly had admirers, and they were especially taken with his untutored idiosyncrasies. For the bohemian Ellen Veblen, childless and wealthy after a divorce from her womanizing husband, Henry was the ideal surrogate son-cum-protégé. Clarissa was in turn infatuated with Veblen, welcoming her practical and inspirational contributions. Soon after Henry told his mother that he couldn't live without a piano, Veblen paid to replace the decrepit one that had been all he and his mother could afford. "Hour by hour she listened carefully, patiently to new compositions," Clarissa wrote, "pointing out weakness and strength with rare taste and fine appreciation." As important, Veblen introduced the boy to an array of mystically inclined artists—writers, photographers, painters, playwrights—who had gathered in and around Carmel on the Monterey Peninsula. As one of the company later put it, "She is a big soul with queer Karma on."

For Lewis Terman, Henry offered a rare case of what he took to be potential all but untainted by formal tutelage—an ideal specimen for a hereditarian obsessed with inborn gifts. The thirty-four-year-old psychologist met him, fittingly enough, in the fields near the Termans' garden and was struck by his departure from anything resembling a norm. Terman lingered with fascination over his anomalies:

> As a boy of a dozen years, Henry's appearance was odd and interesting in the extreme. His speech was quaint, and rather drawled and stilted; his face was childish, but he looked at you with eyes that seemed utterly void of self-consciousness; his clothes were often ragged and always ill-fitting; his hair hid his ears and straggled down to his shoulders; his face and shoulders twitched occasionally with choreic spasms.

It was a portrait of a creature who wasn't quite feral but wasn't an ordinary terrestrial either—much less a celestial Mozart. "Everybody considered Henry as queer, not to say freakish," Terman summed up. "If employed to weed a lawn he was likely to forget what he was doing while trying to compose and whistle a tune. His janitor work was hardly more successful."

Enchanted by Henry's primitive waywardness, Terman seemed unconcerned that he was hardly a poster boy for the physically vigorous, socially well-adjusted, intellectually well-rounded profile of genius he had in mind. Nor did he dwell on any possible tension between the unschooled, budding artist and an IQ enterprise that enshrined "schoolhouse gifts," the verbal and mathematical skills the test assesses. Terman was entranced. What was one to make of a boy like this? What would a boy like this make of himself, and how?

In 1911, when Henry was fourteen and a half, Terman was extremely pleased to add him to the early round of children he was examining as he worked on a tentative first revision of Binet's test. He couldn't have found a better antidote to the precocity on display at Harvard, or a better example of natural originality. Henry's notable success on parts of the test clinched Terman's belief that his measures truly did tap into powers of intelligence independent of schooling. He was evidently so excited that a boy without anything close to a regular education performed so well that he sometimes couldn't resist inflating the results. Clarissa, leery though she was of pouring children into molds, was thrilled to have the glowing imprimatur of a high score on a standardized appraisal. Henry was "the brightest child to whom he had ever given the tests," she exulted, taking it as confirmation of her hands-off approach. Even Henry boasted to his father about how well he stacked up. In fact, Terman assessed his IQ at 131, not close to the highest in his survey—but also, as he acknowledged some years later, not a very relevant or revealing measure for a boy like this one: "Although the IQ is satisfactory, it is matched by scores of others among our records; but there is only one Henry."

Terman probed well beyond the test items for insight into a specimen whom he considered in a class of his own, with scientific *and* artistic gifts developed in quirkily impressive ways. He jotted down notes on Henry's descriptions of improvising music in his head. He explored the boy's own sense of himself and his vocation ("only two things considered—1) A hybridizer of flowers—florist 2) Music composer"). He even coaxed a messily written obituary-style biographical entry out of Henry, who took a mocking tone as he complied with the exercise in imaginative projection:

Henry Cowell was a very Ordinary man, who cultivated flowers extensively and successfully, and whom some records say, made feeble attempts to compose music, which was rotten, but I, personally, do not believe this. the only thing for which he might be at all noted was the reproducing of a new and slightly better kind of garden beet but as this is all I can find about this person I will come to an end.

Basking in the newfound attentions of adults more expert than his adored mother, Henry quickly outgrew his humility. By 1913, now sixteen, he had acquired a sense of himself as a not very ordinary youth. A year earlier he had stirred interest at the Pacific Musical Society's anniversary celebration in San Francisco when, all unplanned, he got to play a piece of his for the large audience. His intermittent efforts at composing music had given way to fervor—first on his own piano in their cabin, soon in Ellen Veblen's cabin in the Carmel colony, where he mingled with artistic adults and their families. Within the year, he had produced some sixty pieces, skimpy on structure and development but full of restless motion and striking melodies. One night as he babysat, he produced a gorgeous setting for a poem, "St. Agnes Morning," in which the future playwright Maxwell Anderson, then a young M.A. student in English at Stanford, evoked sleepless turmoil during the calm between dawn and sunrise. Teenage Henry found inspiration in the contrast.

He was in his element. As Clarissa noted, Henry was highly receptive without being unduly impressionable. "Always he has worked mostly alone," she observed, "browsing for information, when he felt need of it, wherever a door opened." Henry's youthful isolation hadn't made him a social recluse. Instead, it had given him the habit of independence and nonconformity—and infrequent bathing, "the dirtiest little shrimp you ever ran into," a teacher later said. (Henry was barely over five feet tall.) It was a recipe for fitting right in with the Monterey Bay scene. A lack of formal musical training wasn't a liability in an ethos that emphasized attunement with nature and exploratory energy over rigor. Naturally ingratiating, Henry dedicated his little pieces to area artists, and then to resident children. At the same time, he impressed the open-minded spirits of the Carmel realm with an experimental boldness that he got a chance to display in recitals.

In the summer of 1913, Henry's most ambitious piece so far, "Adventures in Harmony," featured the first use of his signature "tone clusters"—adjacent notes played with the forearm, or fist. It was, literally, a striking performance. He was asked to speedily produce music for a vatic play called *Creation Dawn* by one of Carmel's creative stars, Takeshi Kanno, whose meditative quest had brought him from Japan to commune with the sea on the American West Coast. Henry employed his new technique to evoke the "hungry ocean in the human soul," as he scrawled on the score. Performed later that summer in the Forest Theater, an outdoor amphitheater, the result reportedly won Henry acclaim that echoed through the woods. A music critic offered an assessment that verged on the oxymoronic: "a total presentation of chaos which is excellent in conception."

Beyond the woods, Henry's conceptual clarity, or lack of it, came under greater scrutiny as he approached college age and gave more concerts. In Stanford's well-tended precincts and in the San Francisco area, he was acquiring a broader circle of admirers drawn in by Terman's interest and mounting press attention. Samuel Seward, a Stanford English professor, had already stepped in to work with him on his writing. Known for his devotion to his students, Seward tailored his lessons in craft to the unusually expressive mind he discovered in Henry. He also sounded out music teachers and contacts, aware that guidance for Henry was tricky. What was the next step? For precociously trained William and Norbert, after their post-Harvard doses of more academia, that inevitable question about the maturing prodigy had a daunting answer: a dose of independent real life. For Henry by 1914, the opposite course seemed reassuringly obvious. The untutored marvel would benefit, Terman was sure and reviewers agreed, from "the steadying hand of instruction."

The adjective was key—steadying. Strictness was not the goal in handling this "turbulent" genius, except in the blunt view of the *San Francisco Examiner's* critic, writing about his San Francisco debut in March 1914. Impressed by Henry's talent, he was impatient with compositions that he judged "very lawless; they do not show much melodic originality. They are dithyrhambic impressionizing without so much as a hint of counterpoint." He prescribed "a thorough schooling . . . several years drill in a conservatory": that was just the antidote Henry needed, surrounded as he had been by "idolizing womenfolk who mistake anarchistic rhapsodizing for inspiration." Clarissa, who had recently had a mastectomy, missed his concert at the San Francisco Musical Club but bridled at the verdict. Rules were "useful to modest talent," she felt, but "they hamper genius, which learns them in order to break them with larger wisdom."

Other critics split the difference, calling for not harsh "but reasonable discipline" and confident no influence could squelch Henry. "Whether anybody can teach this lad how to compose, I very much doubt," one reviewer judged. "All that can be done for him is to instruct him in the value of rules which he now breaks with the charming simplicity of a Wagner-in-the-making." Reared on resistance to "received wisdom," Henry himself was primed, thanks to Seward's attentive efforts, for some more formal pedagogy.

Terman had been prodding his test subject, too. His mission went beyond quantifying exceptional youthful potential. In Henry, he found an ideal occasion to pursue his quest to prove that early genius, far from burning out, would be borne out in an illustrious future, given the right educational guidance. He served as a conduit to other Stanford faculty, and with Henry's 1914 success, interested supporters established an education fund that enabled Henry to go to Berkeley. It was among the first of many interventions for his gifted testing subjects that Terman continued to provide down the decades—blithely stacking the deck in favor of his optimistic predictions for his "Termites," as they came to be called. For Henry, the three and a half years as a special student were certainly well timed.

Musical iconoclasm in the decade after the tumultuous debut of Stravinsky's *Rite of Spring* in Paris opened up unusual room for an untrained talent like Henry's to flower. The faculty wasn't about to frown on a young composer who had already "gone . . . far along his own lines," as one teacher described Henry. He was exposed to traditional theory and also had a chance to explore new approaches. In Charles Louis Seeger, Jr., whose "dissonant counterpoint" foreshadowed twelve-tone writing, Henry found a teacher congenially ambivalent about the idea of academic musical training. Henry hardly mingled with students, especially not girls (several of whom complained about his grungy appearance—and actually got him to take a bath). Among other things, his mother's bizarrely adamant view that sexual relations were wicked scared Henry off. What time he had for a social life, he mostly devoted to a theosophical community led by John Varian, whose Temple of the People was based farther south, in Halcyon, but had an active Palo Alto branch. The eccentric Irish poet and father substitute was a man given to such pronouncements as "There is a new race birthing here in the West. We are the germic embryonic seed of future majesties of growth."

But mostly Henry was tending to his music and above all to his by now ailing mother. Since surgery in 1913, Clarissa's condition had been anything but steady. He kept in solicitous touch even when he was away, caught up in the new associations that she encouraged. "You know how well and Dearly I love you, though it embarrises me to speak of it," Henry wrote at sixteen from Carmel. "Oh, but he was a splendid comrade!" Clarissa was writing in her diary at roughly the same time, reflecting on their itinerant years together and feeling proud that her teenager was making a name for himself. "More like a man than a child, he was my friend and close, sympathetic companion through dark days or bright. Never a word of complaint passed his lips." He was a loyal caretaker during the Berkeley years, too, commuting to campus from Menlo Park as she got sicker. At a Palo Alto concert in early 1916 to showcase the results of his college experience to his assembled patrons, the audience wanted to hear Henry's setting of one of her poems again as an encore. By mid-May, his mother was dead.

Urged on by patrons eager for him to acquire the East Coast

imprimatur of rigor, Henry at nineteen set off in the fall for the Institute of Musical Art (later Juilliard) in New York. But he hated the place, with its rich students and "rotten" teachers. "Everyone here composes along the old lines, or merely stupid new ones, using discords without reason," he wrote to a California friend. Henry yearned for the unconventional company out west. After Clarissa died, he had officially joined the Temple of the People, not swallowing any doctrine, he assured Ellen Veblen, but plainly in need of a larger sense of purpose and a place for himself. John Varian looked to him as the creator of a "music soul" for the group's often murky, mythic ethos. It was with Varian's son Russell—left back four times in school and now a budding engineer fascinated by sound—that Henry eagerly shared new notions of rhythmic counterpoint, not with the institute "cads."

But New York did supply a catalyst outside the classroom. Henry went to a recital by a composer named Leo Ornstein, several years his senior, who was hailed as a "futurist" pianist and "the Keyboard Terror." Ornstein's specialty, dissonant clusters much like Henry's own, was making audiences furious and him famous. Henry described getting worked up to quite a fevered pitch himself about the music. When this "genius," as Henry rated him, agreed to meet and praised Henry's work as the most promising that Ornstein had encountered, Henry was ecstatic. At a dinner with Terman not long after, he conveyed his sense of formative developments under way. Terman made sure to record this turning point for his files, but he wasn't merely being methodical. His notes reveal his own excitement about Henry's account of creative contagion. Ornstein's verdict was that Henry's music was "crude but that the material was there. That H. must learn what to leave out," Terman jotted down in breathless style. "That altho H. was working in the dark, he needed only to find himself."

· 4 ·

When Henry set off for New York in 1916, Terman was tooling up for a project that embodied the ambitions and the confusions—

and the elusive predictions—that have marked gifted research
and education ever since. That year Terman published the Stanford revision of Alfred Binet's scale for measuring intelligence. He
promptly put it to use in identifying the most select group he had
yet examined: some sixty children in the Bay Area with IQs of 140
or higher, a cut-off that would have ruled out Henry. (It eliminated
the future Nobel Prize–winner William Shockley: singled out for
assessment by his elementary school teachers, he went on to score
only 129 and then 125, to his and his mother's disappointment.)

Five years later Terman, like Henry, had bigger plans in mind.
The war had given them both a taste of broader influence, Henry
as a bandleader in the army, and Terman as a developer of group
intelligence tests for military recruitment. Terman emerged a pros-
elytizer of widespread mental testing. His goal was to shake up
perceptions, though in a spirit very different from anticonven-
tional Henry's. While Henry was riling audiences in Europe and
at home with his chord clusters and his "string piano"—plucking
and banging the instrument's innards—Terman set out to show
that extraordinarily bright children were anything but weird, much
less doomed. He aimed to supply data where mere anecdote had
prevailed, and to help reorganize education.

Boris Sidis and Leo Wiener urged parents to get busy tutoring their toddlers; Terman soon became a spokesman for school
tracking. Armed with generous funding, he embarked in 1921
on an even larger roundup of gifted California schoolchildren to
participate in what he titled his *Genetic Studies of Genius*. He was
launching the first youthful-talent search, and one of the earliest
longitudinal studies. He was aware that no one knew when or how,
or which, precocious signs of brilliance might ultimately lead to
mature distinction, though he shared Wiener and Sidis's bias in
favor of early blooming. And as he had done with Henry, Terman
eagerly assumed the role of participant-observer, not mere tester.
He was poised to record the trajectories of his subjects—which
in itself, many Termites later said, gave them a confident sense of
specialness—and to offer assistance as they progressed.

The result was not exactly rigorous science. Terman's helpful interventions inevitably undermined the purity of his predictions. He also ran into selection bias, a problem nearly unavoidable in gifted research. Given his methods, it was not a great surprise when the Termites proved on the whole to be exemplary schoolchildren, not eccentrics at all. Terman's testing tool was designed to measure general intelligence. It had been devised in and for an academic setting, focusing on verbal and logical and memory skills, which meant scores at the high end that correlated closely with classroom success. His fieldwork further ensured a sample low on idiosyncratic characters. Terman and his assistants couldn't possibly examine the more than a quarter of a million students in third grade through high school in the California school districts he was using. So he enlisted teachers to help make the first cut. They supplied him with the students they considered the best, a group unlikely to include twitchy, unevenly developed kids—or, obviously, homeschooled anomalies.

Testing this cohort—as well as other batches of bright children he had rounded up earlier—Terman emerged with a sample of roughly fifteen hundred students with IQs above the 135-to-140 range, or about the top 0.6 percent. His methods selected for a conscientious breed of parents as well: lengthy questionnaires about their children were part of the drill. A score from "most rare" to "high average" for their progeny was also part of the reward. Along with that often came decades of counsel from Terman, who remained in touch with an amazingly large percentage of his subjects for years to come. Their loyalty was crucial to his longitudinal project. It was also encouraged by the process. Though Terman's team hoped to keep the study's participants as unselfconscious as possible, the selective nature of the enterprise was hard to keep secret. The members of this prodigy club, and their parents, were not the sort to drift off the radar screen of a man who had singled them out for greatness.

The data reviewed in the first volume of findings in 1925 did more than demolish "the widespread opinion that typically the intellectually precocious child is weak, undersized, or nervously unstable." Terman's inventories—of physical and personality traits, books read, intellectual and recreational interests, family background—revealed children more muscular, responsible, and mature, never mind much more successful at school (where 85 percent of them had skipped grades), than a nongifted group used for a rough comparison. On the East Coast, the psychologist Leta S. Hollingworth of Teachers College came up with similar findings about the gifted children she studied in two public schools. For the truly rare children with IQs of 170 or higher, the record was somewhat more mixed on the question of social adjustment. Hollingworth focused on difficulties engaging in play at school. But home life in her samples' comparatively well-off—and small—families seemed enviable. "Fortunately," Hollingworth agreed with Terman, "the majority of gifted children fall by heredity into the hands of superior parents, who are themselves of fine character and worthy to 'set example.'" Terman went a step further. His winnowed elite disproportionately featured white, native-born, male, middle-class specimens. This clinched for him the hierarchy of racial stocks and genders. By now an outspoken eugenicist, he dismissed the role of environmental forces.

Except for his reading habits, sickly young Henry, a peculiar loner as a child, hadn't conformed to the hearty image Terman was now broadcasting. And though his northern European heritage fit the prejudices, his parents' economic and occupational status did not. Nor was a boy who had bumped along without schooling, but with constant if unorthodox learning, much of an advertisement for Terman's message at the close of the first volume of his study. "The great problems of genius" require urgent educational attention, he announced, by which he had in mind homogeneous grouping in school from the start. Terman's own data suggested that his sample was also doing quite nicely without more systematic enabling. He was up against a conundrum faced by advocates of support for gifted youths down the decades: If they're such paragons, how much special help do they really need?

Perhaps Terman's sample was performing all too competently. In a follow-up volume of the study in 1930, the Terman team betrayed a hint of defensiveness that reappeared in the twenty-five- and thirty-five-year follow-ups. Anticipating later critics, he and his associates now entered a caveat about the g-word and cautioned against disproportionate expectations of the cohort. "The title is not meant to imply that the thousand or more subjects who have entered into the investigations described are all potential geniuses in the more common meaning of that term. A few of the group may ultimately achieve that degree of distinction, but not more than a few." Still, he stuck by his title, even as he acknowledged the possibility of "utter failure" in his flock.

The urge to predict drives research on childhood giftedness, yet precocity can be misleading. Early feats of learning needn't be an augury of future disaster, as Terman joined the Cambridge fathers in proclaiming. But precocity, especially as measured on a scale like Terman's, doesn't turn out to be a very reliable precursor of outstanding mature performance either—particularly of a mold-breaking variety. Terman did his best to keep at bay that disappointing realization, which crept up on him. While he was waiting for his Termites to grow up, he encouraged a colleague, Catharine Cox, in a peculiar effort to link great achievements to early supersmartness. She set out to compute, retrospectively, the youthful IQs of three hundred adult eminences from the past by a curious method. She delved into their biographies for examples of childhood accomplishments—Voltaire writing verses "from his cradle," Coleridge reading a Bible chapter at three, Balzac flubbing exams but making "remarks or answers of singular penetration and meditative wisdom" when very young—and then aligned them with mental-test standards.

The available evidence of youthful capacities varied wildly, and the calculations were at best wobbly, but that did not trouble Terman and his team. The numbers Cox came up with were mostly high. (Eight-year-old Goethe's literary work, for example, was judged of "adult superiority," and his IQ was estimated to be 200, which was "probably too low.") She took some care to stress the importance of qualities other than intelligence, especially "persistence of motive and effort, confidence in their abilities, and great strength or force of character," which biographical stories could capture more vividly than any numerical score. Cox presciently warned that "the tests . . . cannot measure spontaneity of intellectual activity; perhaps, too, they do not sufficiently differentiate between high ability and unique ability, between the able individual and the extraordinary genius." But in her conclusion, she italicized to match the Termanite line. *The extraordinary genius who achieves the highest eminence is also the gifted individual whom intelligence tests may discover in childhood.* Cox's big caveat—"the converse of this proposition is yet to be proved"—did not receive any emphasis.

Proof that high-testing children routinely go on to become extraordinary geniuses was not so easy to come by. Might good IQ-test-takers (not least those hovered over by academic psychologists) turn out to tend toward conformity? Might creative types prove to be lousy test-takers? The Stanford research, and the studies it inspired, did not address such unwelcome possibilities head-on, but various findings hinted at them. Hollingworth's case studies, focusing on a small cohort of children with IQs above 180, raised some questions. The high scorers excelled at winning prizes and honors for academic and intellectual work as they matured. But she wasn't sure what to conclude about creativity and originality, plainly disappointed that her sample didn't display more of either—perhaps partly due, she speculated, to their nurture: "so harnessed to the organized pursuit of degrees," in one child's case, and subjected to an "education . . . so scrupulously supervised and so sedulously recorded that he had little time for original projects" in another.

When Terman reflected on Henry, even he had to acknowledge similar reservations about test-based solicitous advancement of unusual youths. In his 1930 volume, he saluted Henry's "rapid rise to international fame, despite the handicap of the most crushing poverty, and despite the utter lack of formal schooling"—and, he might have added, despite the lack of a superhigh IQ. Terman then paused. "It is interesting, however, that Henry himself is thankful for these 'handicaps' and believes that he owes to them whatever originality he possesses. It is his opinion that an orthodox musical training would have hindered rather than fostered his creative ability." Ever so tentatively, Terman all but concurred: "We are inclined to suspect that there is ground for this opinion." To be sure, Terman wasn't about to second-guess the goal of test-driven meritocratic streamlining as he devised and revised yet more assessments of achievement and ability to help sort the rapid influx of schoolchildren. He firmly believed that school efficiency—and social stability and national greatness—was at stake. Still, he couldn't shake his interest in creative outliers.

The appeal of the IQ measurement lay in its broad relevance, and the "globally gifted" child with school smarts was the figure he and his team fixed on. Yet with Henry's example to inspire him, Terman also paid attention to "special abilities" when they were spotted in the high-IQ mix—only to be flummoxed. Nonacademic talents weren't what the Stanford-Binet tested for, and they proved volatile, hard for systematizing researchers to handle. Fewer than half of the children who had shown distinctive abilities stuck with those interests, though musicians were more likely to. (Even in music, the field best known for spawning prodigies, the yield of distinguished mature artists is low. Out of an unusually big batch of seventy young musical marvels in the San Francisco area in the 1920s and '30s—all too young to be tapped by Terman—six went on to notable adult careers: Leon Fleisher, Ruth Slenczynska, and Hephzibah Menuhin on the piano, and Isaac Stern, Ruggiero Ricci, and Yehudi Menuhin on the violin.)

A female colleague of Terman's focused on a batch of precocious literary girls, whose works she set out to compare with the juvenilia of eminent writers of the past, in hopes of gauging the predictive value of early creative output. But quality and development tended to be highly uneven. That was obvious, for example, in a sampling of the one hundred poems produced between ages six and eight by the prolific Betty Ford (a pseudonym), an engaging girl with an IQ of 188 who was said to skip and dance as she dictated her poetry, if she wasn't feverishly typing it out by herself, often appending morals to her verses. Nor did the juvenilia of great poets provide a steady standard. A panel of judges composed of Stanford seniors rated poems by the young Longfellow and Shelley below those of Betty and various Stanford students when they perused them without knowing the authors. Terman joined his associate in concluding, "One would hardly be justified in attempting to devise methods for predicting adult literary accomplishment. Too many factors other than natural ability go to determine the amount and merit of achievement." Spontaneous Betty certainly did not betray high poetic ambitions, according to an anecdote her mother liked to relate: "'Mother,' she said one day, 'I am not proud because I can write verses; they just come themselves. But if I could only learn to control my temper, then I would be proud.'"

· 5 ·

In 1936, half a decade after Terman's first follow-up volume, Henry's own trajectory suddenly seemed in doubt. The musician who had emerged as an ultramodern pioneer, championing Charles Ives and other unorthodox composers, was arrested in his Menlo Park cabin on charges of oral sex with a seventeen-year-old. The issue was the act, not the age; fellatio was illegal, but by law the youth was a consenting adult. Instead of hiring a lawyer, Henry promptly confessed, then appealed for leniency with a tale of tangled bisexuality. Terman loyally lent his voice to Henry's cause, eager as ever to smooth a protégé's path to normalcy. But Terman's expertise—he had lately shifted his focus from mental traits to sexual tendencies—was of no immediate avail. At the age of thirty-nine, Henry went to San Quentin and a year later received a maximum sentence of fifteen years.

Henry was hardly thankful for the "handicap" of prison, but he proved as undaunted as ever in the face of deprivation. He was assigned to help the prison's bandmaster in the education division and for the next four years was a whirlwind of musical productivity. He wrote music. He wrote about music. He taught music to prisoners. He taught himself to play new instruments. In 1940 Cowell's model record and the lobbying of friends (and getting labeled as a likely candidate for "heterosexual adjustment") won him parole. The following year he married the ethnomusicologist

Sidney Robertson, a woman whom he had first met years earlier in Menlo Park. Henry continued to compose, and helped out the wartime effort of "cultural defense" by encouraging musical exchanges with Latin America. He secured a pardon and went to work in the music division of the Office of War Information, becoming the senior music editor. Henry, a solitary child who had thrived on eclectic company during a highly unusual adolescence, never ceased to be a catalytic anomaly—not a joiner, but an outsider who could galvanize groups.

When Terman's twenty-five-year follow-up volume appeared in 1947, its most interesting finding was one largely borne out by Henry, although his story wasn't included in it. The Termites, contrary to early high hopes, had not yet proved to be across-the-board successes, never mind geniuses. There had, of course, been a depression and a war, but the Terman team didn't put much stock in larger social influences. Instead the researchers undertook a comparison between the most and least successful of the Termites, aiming to identify the source of their different fortunes. It definitely wasn't IQ. Extra points did not account for more accomplishment. What made the clearest difference was, not surprisingly, family background. The children of better-educated, more successful parents clustered in the top group of those with the best jobs, the most extensive schooling, and the highest incomes. Yet the researchers also singled out several individual qualities shared by those who had thrived: perseverance, self-confidence, and the well-adjusted sense of purpose they referred to as "integration toward goals."

It was quite a bourgeois triumvirate, but a boy buffeted by a bohemian upbringing—and a man who had weathered further blows—had become an embodiment of them. Henry, who was more than a decade further along in life than the average Termite, had demonstrated remarkable assurance from very early on. The focus his mother had remarked on had served him well, despite all kinds of distractions. So had the discipline that romantic Clarissa tended to play down but that Henry emphasized in his own way. A theme might present "itself to me in a flash," he later said. "But it must be given material form, and I may work long hours

to get the scheme down in a form which adequately represents it."
And Henry's ordeals seemed to have smoothed the rough edges of
a nonconforming eccentric. In his composing work, he migrated
from the radical fringe of new music to embrace a more inclusively
panethnic vision of global music after his rehabilitation. He began
representing American music at conferences around the world.
"I was bristlingly modernistic when I was quite young," was how
Henry himself put it, "but I have become much simpler since."
Some avant-garde colleagues like Charles Seeger took a harsher
view. Henry, once daring, was playing it safe. But his wide-ranging
influence—as a pioneer who transcended boundaries in his explorations of sound, of performance technique, of non-Western musical traditions, and of homegrown talents—is now clearer than ever,
even if his music is rarely performed.

Henry's success was a bold fulfillment of dreams that the rest
of Terman's endeavor had not delivered on. In 1956, now seventy-
nine, Terman was at work with an associate on the thirty-five-year
update of "the gifted group at mid-life" while he nursed a bad back
and struggled to recover from a stroke. In the latest survey of "my
1,400 gifted 'children,'" as Terman fondly referred to them, the
glow of early hopes for exceptional eminence had faded. As his
colleague finalized the text for what turned out to be a posthumous
volume, she worked hard to play down any disappointment. At
the average age of forty-four, the male Termites as a group were
highly educated for the time, professionally accomplished, and
well adjusted. The female Termites' less-than-illustrious fortunes
elicited this strained assessment: "There are many intangible kinds
of accomplishment and success open to the housewife, and it is
debatable whether the fact that a majority of gifted women prefer
housewifery to more intellectual pursuits represents a net waste of
brainpower."

Terman's own son, Fred, a ham radio obsessive decades earlier,
had just been named Stanford's provost in 1955. He had proved a
true standout among the Termites—and was about to outdo his
father in the genius-incubating sweepstakes. In the decades since
doing graduate work at MIT (some of it under Norbert Wie-

ner), Fred had made Stanford an engineering hub and shown the foresight to encourage two students named William Hewlett and David Packard to found a Palo Alto company. Fred also lured William Shockley back to Stanford, and his father's genius-study reject hit the jackpot. In November 1956, shortly before Terman suffered a second stroke that left him mostly unconscious for the last month of his life, Shockley shared the Nobel Prize in physics for his role in inventing the transistor. Who knows, maybe that early rejection from the genius study served as a goad for a figure who went on to alienate many a colleague. Terman didn't live to discover that Shockley's eugenicist extremism—not so different from Terman's own—made him a pariah during his final decades.

The last chapter of the midlife volume, published in 1959, concluded wistfully that "the group has produced no great musical composer and no great creative artist," with an asterisk noting that "a man of rare creative genius was not included." Henry, who went unnamed, had been spotted ten years too late, and his IQ "was not definitely established in childhood," so he didn't officially count. But the summer before his death in December 1956, Terman had gotten back in touch with Henry to let him know that he considered him the true star. "Two weeks ago today I happened to have my radio tuned on KNBC at 7:30 and heard the announcer say that Henry Cowell's 4th Symphony was next on the program," he wrote him in late July. "I was deeply moved by it and after it was over, kept thinking of the days so long ago when I lived near you and of the solid reputation you have built up since then. Hardly anything has given me more satisfaction. Of course I am no critic of music, but I enjoyed all four parts of your symphony and most of all, the third part."

That "satisfaction" was Terman's implicit way of taking some credit, which he surely was due—although not thanks to his test or his theories. Henry was indebted to Terman's personal interest and his luckily timed interventions in a life that might otherwise have been as marginal as Harry and Clarissa Cowell's careers were. And Henry knew it. He seems to have emerged well aware of how much he owed to his circumstances, the freedom and the "handicaps" of his youth as well as the helping hands just when he needed them. He promptly responded with a letter that has not surfaced but was evidently full of gratitude. He also slipped in some publicity material about himself, leaving the boasting to others. Terman wrote right back, by hand.

What he sent Cowell (who died nine years later) was the sort of humble tribute the Harvard boys never got from their fathers. He conveyed his awe at Henry's efforts to shape a path he could call his own. Terman, who dropped all professional reserve, couldn't resist liberally invoking the signature word of his career, *genius*. But he drew real inspiration from Henry's astonishing resilience in the face of setbacks, something no intelligence test could ever measure:

> I don't know when I have received a letter that gave me as much joy as yours of 8/4. I have read it over and over and have read all of the pamphlet at least twice. I am moved beyond words to know that you are regarded by many musical critics as among the foremost composers in America, and by some as one of the most creative musical geniuses in the world. I am not surprised that you had and have the necessary genius, but only that you brought it to flower despite the paucity of formal education in the early years and despite the tragic experience that would have wrecked the career of all but the bravest soul. I recall "that day" . . . when you told me you would do your best to "pick up the pieces." And how you have succeeded! You have built the pieces into a structure that may be as grand as anything you could have wrought if the tragedy had not occurred. Perhaps it only made you try the harder.

PART II

DAUGHTERS

and

DREAMS

CHAPTER 3

"A Renaissance of Creative Genius in Girlhood"

· 1 ·

Nathalia Crane didn't just type when she sat down at her typewriter in the book-strewn Brooklyn apartment where she lived with her father, Clarence, a war veteran in his fifties, and her much younger mother, Nelda, who had married him straight out of high school. She beat time with her foot and sometimes took a hand off the keys to slap out a rhythm. Her usual good cheer disappeared, her father said of the frail, big-eyed child who at nine had begun to compose her poems this way. "When she is writing she becomes a different girl," he told a reporter after her first book of startlingly accomplished poetry, *The Janitor's Boy,* came out in 1924, the year she turned eleven. "She frowns and is concentrated and will not permit any one to interrupt her."

Barbara Newhall Follett demanded freedom from intrusion, too. In January 1923 her family had moved temporarily from rural Connecticut to a New Haven apartment when her father, Wilson, having taught English at a number of elite New England colleges, became an editor at Yale University Press. The typed sign she posted on her bedroom door was mostly meant for her mother. Helen Thomas Follett, coauthor with her husband of various literary essays for *The Atlantic Monthly,* was a former high school teacher.

> Nobody may come into this room if the door is shut tight (if
> it is shut not quite latched it is all right) without knocking.
> The person in the room if he agrees that one shall come in
> will say "come in," or something like that and if he does not
> agree to it he will say "Not yet, please," or something like
> that. . . .

The sign went on: "Reason. If the door is shut tight and a person
is in the room the shut door means that the person in the room
wishes to be left alone." Barbara, who wore braids, was typing away
on a very long story about a child who becomes a fairy. She hoped
to finish in time for her ninth birthday. Her aim was to surprise
her mother with it, a reverse present-giving tradition Barbara had
invented. The notion that the story would end up as a published
novel had not yet occurred to her, or to her father.

Most young bookworms—off in a corner, eyes glued to the
page—don't churn out pages themselves. But the small child who
does is bound to pique curiosity. (Check out what she's clicking
away at on the computer, and who knows whether you'll be greeted,
right then, as an annoyance or a captive audience.) Both girls' parents assumed they were blissfully unaware of it, but Nathalia and
Barbara—who never met each other—belonged to what one critic
called a "renaissance of creative genius in girlhood" as the 1920s
arrived.

Many adults sat down at *their* typewriters to muse about this
"epidemic," the term that often surfaced in the press. All across
war-weary Europe, the poet and anthologist Louis Untermeyer
noted as the decade began, prodigious child artists—working with
paints or in clay, or with words on the page—were suddenly winning praise. He was especially excited to see that "America has
rushed into the fast-filling breach" with young writers, mostly
female. He was also pleased to note that scientists were perplexed
by the phenomenon. (Betty Ford's output certainly baffled Terman.) No "army of professional educators, statisticians, eugenists
[*sic*], psychologists," bent on early testing and accelerated training, could presume to chart this fresh form of genius. Child writ-

ers, then as now, came trailing clouds of imaginative spontaneity their elders could only envy. Untermeyer joined a chorus of calls to draw sustenance from these creators and their wonder-tinged creations. Communing with them was a cure for what ailed a disenchanted age.

The Harvard boys, more traditional math-minded prodigies, had inspired no such romantic fervor. Off the beaten track, a musical original among the mystical-souled in Carmel, Henry Cowell had been a precursor of sorts. But with the creative girl "craze" (another word that cropped up), the fascination with innocent insight went mainstream. The literary boomlet, which wasn't as spontaneous as it seemed, had an obvious external catalyst. It was an unwittingly satiric British novella written by an obscure nine-year-old girl and published in 1919 to extraordinary acclaim. Daisy Ashford's *The Young Visiters, or Mr. Salteena's Plan* got a boost from a preface by J. M. Barrie, whose stage version of *Peter Pan* had been drawing crowds of all ages since the turn of the century, the Harry Potter of its moment.

An American publisher signed up *The Young Visiters*, and the book and an exported stage version took off. Daisy, who was decidedly not "parshial" to proper spelling, brought naïveté to a sharp-eyed tale of social climbing and amorous pursuit. Sales surged further amid a controversy over whether Barrie was actually the author. He wasn't. But he was the star in a newly thriving children's literature market, and his imprimatur made him the godfather of a subgenre ready to take off, child authorship. Amid Jazz Age jitters about flappers and radical cultural ferment, girlishly wise voices promised a wholesome frisson. Modernist flux opened doors for immature experimenters in literary form (as Henry had found in music). Add in, too, a spectacular success like Daisy—plus the popularity of the front-strike typewriter, which even little fingers could operate. The ingredients were at hand for a vogue in precocious self-expression. Prodigies thrive on receptive culture, whatever impetus nature or concerted nurture may supply. "All the mother's darlings in the country," a newspaper reported in the arch tone the phenomenon tended to elicit, "began writing books."

The inner catalysts that drove the young authors—writers named Hilda Conkling and Opal Whiteley opened the decade, ahead of Nathalia and Barbara—were much more of a mystery. That was an essential part of the romantic delight their work inspired. Untermeyer saw the child artist "drawing its substance directly from the unconscious . . . tapping that vast source of intuitive wisdom" no longer available to the adult, "lost among his own machines." All children, in fact, were "embryonic" artists, their creative energy suppressed by a civilization intent on "efficient industry." His friend the Imagist poet Amy Lowell joined in celebrating the unmediated vision of youth, a revelation to more occluded elders. "How beautiful! How natural! How true!": that gut response to girl outpourings, she felt, signaled that "one has stumbled upon that flash of personality which we call genius."

But the inner mystery also stirred up debate and doubt. There was a reason for the rumor that Daisy Ashford was really Barrie in disguise. She spelled like a child, yet how did a mere child acquire the familiarity with adult themes—most notably, sex and snobbery—that she displayed? These girls weren't prodigies in the usual sense of eliciting awe primarily with their mature technical mastery, though Nathalia did that, too—and what vocabularies they had! Their gift lay in their immaturity. Yet that state was all too perishable. The flip side of imaginative purity, as a bookish tween may remind you if you've forgotten, is impressionability, which can be as unsettling as it is enchanting. Look at what's there on the computer screen: she's a sponge not for math facts, you may discover, but for grown-up manners and morals—which she absorbs, in her own way, more avidly than you realized.

The young writers were readers, not just fantasizers. They were also the daughters of parents who were book lovers themselves, with romantic ideas about children—and about communing with them, often over books. The same sentiments thrived among the creative girls' literary admirers, writers like Untermeyer, Lowell, and Barrie. And the audience primed to appreciate their work was a generation reared on *Peter Pan,* whose biggest fans went on waving handkerchiefs and chanting their belief in fairies during performances. What if the child-writing wasn't quite so spontaneously natural after all? What if adult-pleasing, imitative urges crept in? Were the creations then so beautiful and free—or true? Lock your library, pack your poetic daughter "off to Tahiti," avoid college: so Untermeyer (who never graduated from high school himself) was known to preach semifacetiously even as he mentored the imaginative girls who so intrigued him. "The subconscious," he warned, "is going to have a hard time of it if it remains too close to poets, professors, and publishers."

And yet if the fleeting child visions and voices were to be shared, the attention of poets, professors, publishers—and parents—was surely required. The girls presented a new prodigy puzzle. The pressing question wasn't whether to train young brains in a hurry or let heredity be the guide. The focus, likely to sound familiar, was on parent-child bonding—how much of it, and what kind, might help or hinder that youthful creative potential. Nathalia's frown and Barbara's sign suggested that it was not as easy to get the answer right as their mentors hoped. So did public debates over what to make of such unnervingly articulate young females.

· 2 ·

Straightening up the family's Flatbush apartment one day in late 1922, Nathalia's mother threw some stray typed pages into the trash she sent down the dumbwaiter—only to be met by wails from Nathalia, then nine, in search of her "songs." The household did not come to a stop. Nelda Crane told her daughter, with an apology and a little impatience, to put away stuff she wanted to save. She had been aware that Nathalia was spending lots of time tap-tapping behind her bedroom door. Whatever she was up to seemed to make her feel better, so Nelda hadn't paid much attention. This was her husband's terrain, though his style of doting wasn't finely attuned either.

Nathalia's father had taught her to type before she entered first grade at seven, not long after he had returned from the Western front, where he had been wounded and gassed; that was the last in a long string of combat adventures that had begun with his enlist-ment in the Spanish-American War a decade or so out of high school. Along with the typing lessons, Nathalia got endless stories. Clarence Crane was an avid raconteur, and though his wife prob-ably didn't need to encourage father-worship in their only child, who would blame her if she did? Nelda, still in her twenties, was no doubt thrilled to cede her place as his rapt listener. In an ornate monotone, often by candlelight, Clarence regaled his daughter with tales of battle and aired an autodidact's old-fashioned opin-ions on poetry and a generally dim view of the modern world, along with a fervent belief in the superiority of women. He also read poems aloud, rarely venturing past Kipling. And he answered the constant questions of an unusual child drawn to unusual books. Nathalia wasn't an avid reader in general (and initially not much of a student), but she adored her two-volume *Standard Dictionary* of 1895. Her next favorite was Johnson's *Universal Cyclopedia* of that same year, missing two of its eight volumes, those covering *F* through *Mos.*

When Nathalia brought two new poems to her father a few days after her mother's faux pas, he was very impressed, as he told

it, but wanted a more expert view. He suggested she send them to an editor at the *Brook-lyn Daily Times* whom he knew vaguely from his short stints at various copy desks before reen-listing when the United States entered the First World War. There was a flurry of atten-tion at the *Times,* and Nelda started sending out more of Nathalia's work, some of which was apparently published with-out further fuss. So a year later, when Edmund Leamy, the poetry editor of the *New York*

NATHALIA CRANE

Sun, accepted a poem that Nathalia was said to have sent on her own, he had never heard of her. He assumed the author was an adult. After all, in his experience, no "child would ever submit any work from his or her pen without adding the words 'Aged __ years.'" And "The History of Honey," rhythmical and ingeniously rhymed, bore no obvious literary mark of immaturity. Nor was there girlish handwriting to supply a clue. When Leamy invited this new contributor named Nathalia Crane to drop by to confer about another poem and have lunch, he mistook her mother for the poet. Flustered to learn that "Miss" Crane was the "little, long-legged, bright-eyed child," he forgot about the promised meal, as Nathalia noted years later.

To dip into the start of Nathalia's twenty-four-line iambic meditation on an old book about ancient Chinese reverence for honey is to see why Leamy was disoriented:

> *"The History of Honey"—by an aged mandarin,*
> *And I bought it for the pictures of the burnished bees therein.*
>
> *For the dainty revelations, masquerading up and down,*
> *For the odor of the sandalwood that talked of Chinatown.*
>
> *According to the mandarin, the Oriental bees*
> *Were the first to hoard their honey in the mountain cavities.*

Several couplets on, she swerves from history into a weird little flight of spirituality:

> *Imprisoned in this honey, aging as the aeons wane,*
> *Are the souls of all the flowers, waiting to be born again:*
>
> *Every lotus, every poppy, every tulip, every rose.*
> *And those who sip the honey slip beyond all human woes,*
>
> *Dream again of youth's digressions, index misty ways of joy,*
> *Turn unto the pagan pastimes of Confucius—as a boy.*

And she closes with a faintly titillating return to her mandarin:

> *But the mandarin, he made no map, contented in old age*
> *To draw the clinging love scenes of the bees on every page.*
>
> *There he found an inspiration antedating all the Mings,*
> *And he got the ancient essence of the very sweetest things.*

If anything, such a "rhythmical, lilting production," as Leamy described it, suggested an old-school writer—perhaps a grizzled poet with a collection of rare books and a habit of couching sexual themes in birds-and-bees style imagery. It didn't sound like the work of a cutting-edge young modernist, experimenting with new forms and frankness. It was utterly different from the juvenile poetry then enjoying a vogue, Hilda Conkling's bucolic free verse, which her mother, the poet Grace Conkling, wrote down as she uttered it.

An editor of the *Brooklyn Daily Times* had been as astonished as Leamy was that a young girl had produced the poems he had received. One of them, "The Janitor's Boy," was chosen as the title piece in Nathalia's first book, which came out in 1924. It was the work she was asked to recite for the rest of her life. The childlike poem—with a jaunty echo of "The Owl and the Pussycat" in its ballad stanzas and theme—had an undercurrent that didn't seem entirely innocent:

> *Oh I'm in love with the janitor's boy,*
> *And the janitor's boy loves me;*
> *He's going to hunt for a desert isle*
> *In our geography.*
>
> *A desert isle with spicy trees*
> *Somewhere near Sheepshead Bay;*
> *A right nice place, just fit for two,*
> *Where we can live alway.*

Oh I'm in love with the janitor's boy,
     He's busy as he can be;
And down in the cellar he's making a raft
     Out of an old settee.

He'll carry me off, I know that he will,
     For his hair is exceedingly red;
And the only thing that occurs to me
     Is to dutifully shiver in bed.

The day that we sail, I shall leave this brief note,
     For my parents I hate to annoy:
"I have flown away to an isle in the bay
     With the janitor's red-haired boy."

Nathalia was dealing in fantasy, but it wasn't the usual juvenile kind, with talking animals or fairy rings. Her themes were sex and class. And her assured way with rhyme and meter was astonishing, but disconcerting, too. Her predecessors so far, including Daisy Ashford, the terrible speller, had been quaintly unpolished when it came to form. Prowess like Nathalia's didn't just burble up from the unconscious—or could it?

The Janitor's Boy strayed from innocent female terrain, too, though much more tamely than Edna St. Vincent Millay had four years earlier, titillating readers in the dawning Jazz Age with "My candle burns at both ends," and more. It was no surprise that Nathalia's book provoked a gut response very different from Amy Lowell's beautiful-natural-and-true test of genius: *How unusual! How unnatural!* was the tenor of the reception. No one was yet saying, *How implausible!* But Nathalia had critics on edge. One reviewer emphasized the "lack of childishness" in *The Janitor's Boy.* "Strictly speaking, there is not a purely child-poem in the book." Others were relieved to find intermittent silliness, as in another bee-related effort, which ended "I sat down on a bumble bee, / But I arose again; / And now I know the tenseness of / Humiliating pain." But they, too, were taken aback by perceptions of a sort that didn't seem associated with a child's directness of vision or immediacy of emotion. "The work was alternately juvenile and mature, frivolous and profound, absurd and mystical," Louis Untermeyer, one of the earliest champions of Nathalia's genius, wrote later; "it was a mixture but not a fusion."

Barrie's preface to Ashford's novella had set a precedent of sending children's work into the world with an expert chaperone. Nathalia's debut had three, all awkwardly promoting her while doing their best to protect her. In his foreword, the poet and soon-to-be *Saturday Review* editor William Rose Benét's assessment was in tune with Untermeyer's view, though more stringent. He dismissed much of her work as proving "nothing except that she is a little girl with a lively fancy." But he saw glimpses of "the thing we call poetry" in her instinct for metaphor and memorable phrasing. Above all, he was struck by the depth of Nathalia's thought in several poems. Her repertoire extended beyond Ming culture and erotic shivers to aesthetic ruminations. Benét singled out these couplets from "The Blind Girl":

> *In the darkness who would answer for the color of a rose,*
> *Or the vestments of the May moth and the pilgrimage it goes?*
> . . .
> *In the darkness who would cavil at the question of a line,*
> *Since the darkness holds all loveliness beyond the mere design.*

"These lines and the meditation from which they spring were the spontaneous phrasing and the natural meditation of—a child of ten," he marveled. ". . . Strange insight for a comparative infant!"

Benét thought it unlikely that "she can possibly realize the philosophical implications of her best poems," but that didn't detract from their power. He wasn't about to predict her future, which was also the message of Nathalia's two other chaperones—Leamy of the *New York Sun*, who wrote an afterword, and a reporter who met her early on and contributed a testimonial. She was a little girl who played with her dolls and with the janitor's boy, and who wrote when and what it pleased her to write. How refreshing in a jaded time. She should be left alone to continue to do just that, wherever it led. It was clear they were crossing their fingers.

A year and a half later, in September 1925, shortly after Nathalia's twelfth birthday, her second book of poems, *Lava Lane*, came out. This time the work stood alone, accompanied only by an advertisement that announced she had been invited to be an honorary member of the British Society of Authors, Playwrights, and Composers, presided over by Thomas Hardy. It was a distinction, her publisher claimed, shared by no other American poet since Walt Whitman. The news made headlines. So did reports that Nathalia's father might be absconding with sizable royalties. Corrections to both soon appeared. Sales of the two books hadn't earned anyone a fortune. And Nathalia wasn't being specially celebrated. It turned out that Clarence Crane had merely paid the standard dues to join a group that otherwise had no admission criteria. "Looking shyly out at the world," the *Brooklyn Daily Eagle* noted of Nathalia, "there was a wistful and haunting quality to the child's face that went directly to the heart."

Nathalia's publisher, Thomas Seltzer, removed the honor from ads, but by November he had a better—and accurate—claim to generate publicity: this fascinating young talent had become the post–Daisy Ashford "Literary Storm Center." Open the new book to the title poem, and the vocabulary was already staggering: *cicatrix, peris, ferneries, parasangs, fane*. The biblical and historical allusions piled up quickly: Bel and Balthazar, Theban pylons, lines like "I am an ancient lady / Cross-legged upon a dais / Reading of Cleopatra, / Lesbia, Phryne and Thais." Could an eleven-year-old—whose teachers said she wasn't remarkable, and whose parents, one article noted, hadn't gone beyond high school—really have written these poems? The same article quoted Nathalia's own publisher saying, "I am as much mystified as anybody. Nathalia Crane is either a miracle or she is the most colossal hoax in history." Or perhaps there was a third alternative. "Sometimes I wonder if Nathalia Crane is not a medium." Seltzer emphasized that he refrained from grilling this fragile girl on the sources of her more gnomic creations, for fear of making her "self-conscious." That, all agreed, was fatal to innocence.

The notion of Nathalia as a medium gathered momentum. Childish insight, channeled through solicitously attentive elders, had great allure. *Peter Pan* was proof of that. "A poet is continually trying to recapture the vision which a child has instinctively," Untermeyer said in his romantic vein. "A child sees the world fresh. The rest of us are dull; we have lost that first freshness." Tapping back into it purified adults. And what about the other way around—mature insight channeled through a singing girl? Untermeyer, Nathalia's staunch defender and by now an acquaintance, endorsed the basic idea: like all children, she had inherited "the wisdom . . . of the race" and had the rare gift of expressing it for elders who had lost their spiritual bearings. Others were more perplexed about "how a child could absorb so much of grown-up life."

Nathalia, gawkier now than the slight girl whose quaint habit of curtsying had often been mentioned, was still reassuringly childlike in her inability to shed any light on her powers. Words "just come" to her was her standard line to reporters, whom she mostly avoided. Prodded about how such "big words" made their way into her poems, she curtly responded, "They always fit." But two women from the *Brooklyn Daily Eagle* strode into the Cranes' small Brooklyn Heights apartment (they had moved from Flatbush) for a fuller interrogation. What did the author of that line about roses in darkness possibly know about the physics of prisms? Nathalia at first clammed up, then countered by asking why she couldn't have taken a rose into a dark room. The visitors raised other points, and before leaving, they posed the question perhaps foremost on their minds: "Nathalia, tell us what you know about Sex." Nathalia was silent for a long time, then got up and went over to the poet Jean Starr Untermeyer, who was there with her husband, and cried quietly on her shoulder.

Nathalia's inquisitors were not the only ones who had decided that Nathalia couldn't account for her creations because she was merely a conduit, not for unconscious insight, but for a conniving grown-up. The honorary president of the Poetry Society of America, the ancient poet Edwin Markham, suggested that "Nathalia Crane" was, as *Time* put it, "born upon the back of a menu card." She was an invention cooked up by Untermeyer, Benét, perhaps the frothy novelist Faith Baldwin, and Edna St. Vincent Millay over coffee in Manhattan. They denied it. Eager to fan the commotion, the *Brooklyn Daily Eagle* opened its pages to other views.

Among the most elaborate was a psychoanalytic reading by the opinionated poet and writer Clement Wood, who had weighed in earlier. He diagnosed Nathalia's father as a Svengali figure. According to his theory, Clarence Crane's own failure as a young poet (a book he had written at about thirty went nowhere) had inspired a sort of Oedipal rejuvenation through his daughter. Wood had the frustrated father all but dictating to Nathalia poems that unconsciously confessed to his crime of usurped creativity. A panel of experts—literary and psychological—was proposed to assess Nathalia and pronounce on the plausibility of her feats. Upon reflection, Clarence decided to spare his daughter the ordeal, which raised further doubts. All the agitation, not least Wood's, itself cried out for a diagnosis: Which aroused more fascinated alarm, the spectacle of parasitic men or of precocious girls? In an era of feminist ferment, when flappers had their elders on edge, the Crane story tapped into both at once—never mind that Nathalia gave every sign of being a surprisingly old-fashioned daddy's girl.

Clarence's semi-séances with his daughter were evidently something they both loved, but those who knew the odd man dismissed the idea that he was telling her what to write. It's impossible to know how much of an editor he was, or needed to be. Nathalia was an enthralled audience, and she had an uncanny ear. Such a child may well need no prodding to produce lots of semiderivative work. Young Mozart began by churning out plenty of that (and Leopold, while portraying his son as divinely inspired, surely tinkered as he transcribed the boy's earliest creations). In the realm of imaginative literature, Barrie evoked adult-child collaboration as, ultimately, a merging of visions. "The following is our way with a story," an autobiographical narrator in one of his books explains, describing his coauthorship with a young boy. "First I tell it to him, and then he tells it to me, the understanding being that it is quite a different story; and then I retell it with his additions, and so we go on until no one could say whether it is more his story or mine."

In fact, that kind of intense reciprocity doesn't seem to have been the rule in Nathalia's Brooklyn Heights apartment, tiny and overheated though it was. ("The windows were never opened and the phonograph was never off," Untermeyer remembered.) There was more chaos than claustrophobic, child-centered hovering. Clarence was not the "new father" type, advised by interwar experts to take conscientious note of his child's healthy social and personal adjustment. By the standards of the time, he was an old parent, and "prematurely aged by lingering traces of gas." He clearly lacked a psychologizing bent as he held forth, stoked by cigarettes and coffee. "The Cranes were at their best when things were most feverish," Untermeyer wrote—the music loud, the phone ringing, Clarence declaiming about the nobility of war and the delusions of progress, Nelda yelling from the kitchen, "the parrot Sinbad screaming vituperatively." Nathalia was soaking it all up, including the sense that you could run with any outlandish, outdated idea that might strike you.

But she also had her own pastime, literally in the middle of it all: her favorite dictionary, which along with several others was out on the floor. A reporter once got Nathalia talking, and she revealed a little about the world she found there. "I read them for hours," she said:

> They have so many fine words I never heard before; words that make me want to know them and love them. Yes, I love words, sweet words and noble words, too, because each word has a soul. How do I know that? Why, I just feel it. They come to me and I get to know them, like precious friends.

She was like a stamp collector, a jigsaw puzzle adept, only with words. Those were Untermeyer's analogies, and a more stereotypically girlish hobby might shed light, too. Words were partly a kind of dollhouse play, impelling her to make up stories, set in different eras, which entailed rearranging the furniture to go with particular rhythms. New words inspired new tales and new settings, incorporating things her father spouted, which she then explored in her encyclopedia, packed with yet more unfamiliar words. The possibilities must have seemed endless, and at nine she got immersed. Clarence was around, and Nathalia was doubtless pleased that he was entranced. But he also knew better than to interrupt her when she was beating out her lines.

The press storm died down without a consensus on girl genius but with Nathalia on a new private school path. During the turmoil of the fall, the principal of the Brooklyn Heights Seminary awarded her a recently endowed scholarship to the progressive institution. Her new benefactors judged it an ideal setting for "this gifted girl" because it was "in type the smaller modern school that devotes itself to the full development of the individual student." The educational landscape had evolved since Nathalia's prodigy predecessors had coped with bumpy improvisations—early intensity for the Boston boys, catch-up tutelage for Henry Cowell, in-and-out-of-school irregularity for them all. Carefully paced progress, under enlightened auspices, was a new ideal, at least for the lucky few who could afford it. Such an alternative seemed especially timely for a girl whose creative powers had been deemed a little outré.

Untermeyer had worried about the encroachments of poets, publishers, and professors as child writers matured. But earlier incursions by the press hadn't occurred to him, nor had invitations from solicitous private schools, where the whole point was for the young to be "moulded by well-meaning teachers." That was just the domesticating of untamed talent he prided himself on warning against. On the brink of adolescence, Nathalia certainly did receive a big dose of attention, and she was becoming a more self-conscious, ambitious writer. Then again, of course she was. She was getting older, and her dealings with Untermeyer (who didn't think to add anthologists to his list of influences to beware of) revealed a writer who was trying with surprising self-assurance to hold her own with her elders.

When he included some of her poems in his 1925 revision of

his *Modern American Poetry*, tinkering with the last line of one of them without telling her, Nathalia responded like a pro. First she flattered him and his wife, whose own "wonderful" poems also made it into the collection. Then she praised his presumptuous editing, doing her best to claim ownership. She sounded, at twelve, like a fellow seasoned critic. "But Oh, you are so cunning in verse making," she wrote. "You know very well what it was—you knocked out two foolish words in the last line of The Blind Girl and put in the winged things and made it right. . . . The 'better things' sounded like a prayer meeting," she said, with a wry dig at her own sentimentality. "Sir Louis," as she sometimes addressed him, had made the hackneyed into something haunting:

> *In the darkness who would answer, in the darkness who would care,*
> *If the odor of the roses and the winged things were there.*

After *Lava Lane*, it was the quantity more than the quality of Nathalia's work that now seemed prodigious, as reviewers pointed out. If she noticed the critics, though, she wasn't intimidated. Nathalia seemed unstoppable, rather like her father. Still evidently quite a homebody, she wasn't letting the public fuss deter her from pursuing her interests. In 1926 Nathalia produced another book of poems, *The Singing Crow*, and also published a first novel. *The Sunken Garden*, she confessed, didn't "just come" to her. She struggled to yoke her fondness for historical exotica to a conventional theme. Her protagonist, a young British duchess who is shipwrecked, falls in love with a gorgeous boy on the island, once home to castaways during the Children's Crusade. Already in her prologue, it was obvious that her love of words wasn't going to rescue her plot:

> Through the wizardry of a storm a yacht with a girl near the wheel is wrecked upon a barbarous strand, and a sun-gilded wilding, a forest youth, is torn from a shore covert and driven, amid weltering forest debris, into the frenzied breakers.

A year later, at fourteen, Nathalia won first prize—and $500—for a Kiplingesque poem commemorating Lindbergh's flight, beating established poets like Babette Deutsch. By 1930, the year she turned seventeen, she had written six books (including a second novel, about a child with wings), and was ready to ask forty-five-year-old Untermeyer a favor. She had just written an epic called *Pocahontas*. Would he blurb it, and write something about her, at the behest of her publisher—and do it quickly? Though nonplussed by her "phantasmagoria," he did her bidding, briefly reviving the authorship storm. In Nathalia's strange poem, he figured as Clovis Vanderspire, leader of a band of eight other faintly disguised poets who join the reincarnated Indian princess to beat back a Communist invasion. Another wave of reviewers smelled a hoax—not because of the work's maturity.

Nathalia lucked into a new benefactor, this time anonymous, who wisely decided to encourage a lower profile. Another scholarship, to attend Barnard College as a general studies student, came Nathalia's way—under one condition: that she publish no further work until she graduated. She eagerly accepted, later emphasizing her lucky trajectory. After a prolific adolescence, in which she had avoided directing undue "attention . . . toward the college entrance exam" (and, she primly added, "commercial amusements"), Nathalia welcomed college—and time abroad in Spain—as good for her writing. She quietly kept up her creative work, pleased to be more self-critical.

Nathalia retained her ageless aura in the press accounts that greeted her return to print in 1936 with a collection called *Swear by the Night*. She was still living in her parents' apartment, where her ailing father was more eccentric than ever. "Nathalia at 22 is grown up, wears long skirts and thinks about a wave in her hair," reported the *Brooklyn Daily Eagle*, "but the same mystic quality that made folks wonder when she was 10, has not changed much. . . . The child has matured but there was something mature about her as a child." Nathalia's poetry, too, had a curiously static and anachronistic quality, the critics agreed, even Untermeyer, whom she enlisted to write an introduction, after being out of touch.

It was a peculiar transaction on both of their parts. Was Nathalia expressing her dependence, or semiexploiting a former mentor? If she had hoped for a fond foreword, she got a bluntly mixed tribute that must have startled her but probably stirred interest in her book. Untermeyer staked out a new distance, while retaining his status as adjudicator of youthful genius. Nathalia, once the center of a critical storm, continued to be creatively buffeted, "by turns unusually graceful and surprisingly awkward," in his view. Her language veered between the instinctively musical and the overliterary, her insights between "clairvoyant illumination" and naïve pedantry. The subtext—that the best in Nathalia's curiously unblended work came unbidden—emerged in the most quotable line of all: "It may be an erratic genius that dictates this poetry, perhaps an only half-conscious genius, but genius in any case it is." Nathalia had puzzled Untermeyer from the start, he wrote, and she still did.

His praise was double-edged, yet he acknowledged Nathalia's quirky consistency, and he didn't presume to predict where her avid writing might take her—or perhaps more to the point, where she might take it. (Juvenilia, Lewis Terman's associate agreed, wasn't much of a guide to literary futures.) In any case, Nathalia's father seems to have bequeathed an imperviousness to conventional creative expectations early on. Steeped in his battle lore, she had set off on word-strewn, rhythmic journeys, often to uncanny places far from typical girlish haunts. Meanwhile, her educational patron, as discreet as Clarence was verbose, had been the ideal enabler. She (or was the benefactor a he?) helped secure Nathalia some adolescent privacy and gave her the chance to broaden her horizons. As varieties of noninvasive support go, a former prodigy could hardly ask for better.

Yet finding a mature poetic path is not easy, and Nathalia never did. Culture, perhaps even more than nature and nurture, can be fickle. The same literary ferment that helped create an audience for an offbeat girl poet may well have been just what a loyal, rhyme-entranced daughter of a literary throwback couldn't thrive on. Nathalia published two more books before she was thirty. The reviews of one, a coauthored collection of humorous alphabet verses, were not kind. It's possible that the other—a long poem, set partly in hell, about the death of poetry—reflected some bitterness. And yet Nathalia was as undaunted as her father. To keep poetry alive, she continued to write commemorative poems and publicly read them, with "The Janitor's Boy" an often requested encore. Her first husband, with whom she had no children, died in 1968. Four years later she married a philosophy professor at San Diego State, where she taught in the English department for many years. After Nathalia Crane's death at eighty-five, a former student recalled her "frequently and rapturously" invoking the phrase "reverence for life."

· 3 ·

Barbara Newhall Follett, born half a year after Nathalia, in March 1914, inspired a double dose of word-besotted parenting from the very start. Shortly after her birth, her mother, Helen, began making entries in a baby diary, addressing Babbie directly as she noted down observations and conveyed endearments. "Remember you're mine all through the day-times; remember your little mother when you are being fondled by your dream-mother-bird," she wrote one summer evening after putting Barbara down. A maternal acolyte of J. M. Barrie, Helen was channeling his myth of the original bird-stage of child life. She had the Darling children's escape to Neverland in mind, too. "Come back to me in the morning my Precious!" she urged. Helen promised she would make it worth Barbara's while. "Just sunshine, joy, laughter, the brown-bird twittering, and love, much love—these things are yours. And they shall be yours, my Precious, just so long as we can help to keep them yours." They would read together, she rhapsodized several months later when a friend sent Barbara a storybook about birds.

Barbara's father, Wilson, didn't hang back. When he took a turn in the diary that first summer, he added his share of enchanted, anxiously possessive mulling. Even as Barbara's gurgling filled him with wonder, he worried about all that was eluding him. "Only—one does not know the language! One cannot know it; one can find no key to the obscure code of your choosing," he wrote. "And so this whole period of your unfolding (a period that you yourself are going to forget while you are still only on the verge of understanding it in our crass and arbitrary terms) baffles and must baffle us. . . . O! how we want to understand!" Like Helen, he looked at a sleeping baby girl lost in her "own drunken-world of fairies and moonshine" and hoped that with parents so eager to commune, she would stay to keep them company in a drabber world.

The entries tapered off as Barbara grew into voluble toddlerhood in Providence, Rhode Island, where the family settled in the fall of 1914, when Wilson left Dartmouth for a new teaching job at Brown. Their modest house was as tweedily cultured and child-centered as the Cranes' apartment was chaotic and Clarence-centered. After a hiatus—"war, I suppose, has made us all restless," Helen reflected—she noted that Barbara, at three and a half, was "now using the Corona typewriter intelligently," typing various words over and over, including "bluebird." Two months later Barbara had "caught on to the reading game with (to us) astounding rapidity and never ceasing eagerness." Their romantic idyll of childhood worship had very quickly turned writerly.

As both Folletts told the story, Barbara had taken the initiative. Shortly before she turned three, she stood mesmerized beside one and then the other of them as they typed, which they were often doing. Each claimed credit for seizing the teachable moment and putting aside work to introduce her to the typewriter's marvelous powers. Barbara cranked the platen, pressed the keys, zipped the carriage, was entranced by the bell. Progress was swift because she kept coming back for more, eager to produce her own marked-up paper. Helen started with dictation, first letter by letter and soon word by word as Barbara slowly typed. She especially loved punctuation marks.

Her parents grew enthralled, too, as it occurred to them that this "piece of machinery—the indispensable tool of business and commerce," as Helen later wrote, could also serve a very different purpose: as a child's early means of expression, liberating her from handwriting, unwieldy work when fine motor skills are still immature. By four, Barbara was spelling and typing out her own thank-you notes—Helen's suggestion—as well as reading. She was so pleased with her first typewritten letter that she slept with it for several days before letting it be mailed.

Barbara's parents were so pleased that Helen felt inspired to pursue homeschooling, having stumbled on an "educational scheme . . . as practically sound as it was romantically adventurous." A constantly typing Barbara would hone her expressive skills, at the same time revealing the unknown resources in the child soul that adults yearned to discover. Wilson, in an article in *Harper's* in 1919, felt emboldened to share their ideas about "Schooling Without the School" with other disenchanted postwar parents eager to rescue the creative powers of childhood from the standardizing pressures of school and modern civilization in general. Wilson made very clear theirs was not a call "to let your son or daughter run wild, form associations by accident, and be taught mainly by experience and necessity." It was a summons "to pour yourself into your child" and develop a child's urge to pour herself into words as part of both work and play. That such an enlightened course might prove a mistake was, he granted in a rhetorical gesture, a possibility:

> Fostering a child's natural sense of order and beauty may be, for all we can say, a sorry preparation for life in a world of prevalent dullness and ugliness; giving such guidance as we have given may lead only to a more painful disillusionment in a scheme of things in which every one is ultimately left to flounder undirected.

But he and Helen, who served as the hands-on project manager (he assumed the hero-in-the-wings role), didn't really doubt their careful choreography.

A childish urge for disorderly camaraderie had no place on their agenda. What kept their kindergartner from wanting to run off to school upon hearing the morning bell ring in Cheshire, the town outside New Haven where they now lived, Helen wrote, was the proud pleasure of sitting down promptly at her beloved typewriter. The home lessons that ensued were "no shilly-shally affair, subject to unwarranted moods and interruptions." Helen made out a schedule for every morning, and Barbara followed it. Meanwhile, her mother tended to her own affairs and housework, on call but not constantly at hand. The Folletts officially disapproved of undue intrusion, though a subtle invasiveness lay at the heart of their endeavor. As Helen described it, the typewriter was the adult's accomplice and a peer substitute rolled into one. It constantly nudged Barbara to copious description and self-revelation, not just at her lessons. The machine also wanted news of her solo wanderings, a homeschooled child's luxury:

> All the doors and windows of this five-year-old's world were wide open. The typewriter had helped to open them, and it would now help to keep them open. As soon as it imprisoned in words one fact from her world, one scrap of imaginative beauty, one echo of laughter or of a dream, it asked for more and still more. Where she went, what she did, what she saw—the typewriter enticed her, by urging its own simple magic upon her, to tell in her own words.

The imagery—every fleeting, private experience "imprisoned in words" for a parent's perusal—was curiously oppressive, especially given that Barbara's creative liberation was the goal. Helen, an educated woman who had been her husband's collaborator, didn't hesitate to emphasize that the process was also designed not "to be a bore to *me;* I was quite as much concerned over that as I was over what might or might not happen to her." She was a cutting-edge mother, as attuned to her own fulfillment as to her daughter's and confident in complete synchrony between the two. Compared to Clarence Crane, happy to natter on and be adored, Helen had very particular ideas. She was not about to "limit my relationship with the child to that of nurse, social secretary, cook, or general adviser.

I wanted something more permanent and lasting than any of these things; I wanted a friend and intellectual companion."

Barbara wrote constantly. She responded daily to her mother's prompt: "Let's say something in words about . . ." That was how Helen posed the expressive challenges, which elicited work that was perhaps not always quite as fresh as she claimed when she touted her methods. On one occasion, Helen proposed clocks as the topic, picking up on "the consuming passion of Barbara's existence" at the time. They got down to work, side by side that day. Helen wrote about numbers and clock mechanisms while Barbara typed out lively tales about Mrs. Clock. Helen was quite thrilled to have her own prosaic adult style upstaged: "As for me, wasn't she showing me how much writing could be enriched through the injection of personality?"

Yet as Helen noted in passing, Barbara wasn't drawing directly on her own imagination. She was recycling clock stories told to her by one of her special friends, Holdo Teodor Oberg, an elderly Swedish antique restorer whom the Folletts had met while Wilson was teaching at Brown. He was the most fondly attentive of a whole coterie of grown-up correspondents who had become central to Barbara's curriculum. She kept up with them by mail, her letters a way to work on expressive and literary, not just typing, skills. She wrote more than thank-you notes. She evoked her days and relayed her thoughts—"her world," in a way, except that Barbara's peer-pressure-free life was not exactly an idyll of pure childish independence. Barbara was well aware that a maternal eye would look over what she produced, which often got retyped several times until it was right. "Mention the exquisiteness of the bundle" was Helen's directive on one bread-and-butter effort.

But Barbara was also just writing. She produced "masses of stuff, about everything under the sun, just for the pleasure and relief it gave me," she later remembered, describing her "hours of good practice in descriptive writing," though she wasn't mostly thinking of her pastime that way then. What emerged from those hours was not glimpses into alien child-soul terrain, but evidence of ample reading in the best of children's literature: Walter de la Mare,

W. H. Hudson, Kipling's *Just So Stories,* fairy tales. At six, Barbara wrote a magical fantasy about Mrs. Spinning-Wheel (a present from Mr. Oberg) and Mr. Horse (a rocking horse given by her parents). It was remarkable more for its ambition and execution—four chapters, over four thousand words, brisk pacing, lots of dialogue, great sentence structure, all carefully typed—than for its conception, which involved a quest for a fairy's magic wand to work various transformations.

Barbara later described her "little battered typewriter" as "a constant companion, and the most important thing in my life. When I was happy or sad, ecstatic or anxious, I . . . poured out my heart to it." She was also excited to begin violin lessons, but it was writing that gave her a proud sense of connection to her father, the man she adored, who was always toiling on manuscripts himself. He worked on revisions with her, teaching her proper copyediting and proofreading style. Her delight in the lessons confirmed his sense that children shouldn't be treated like broad-brush primitives; they love the fine points of writing. When his students were reading Dickens with him, so did Barbara. The two of them sang together.

But their outdoor life together—in "my native element," she called it, echoing her parents' view of childhood—formed their deepest bond. She was Wilson's "comrade of trail and river," as he was hers. He was the presiding spirit of Lake Sunapee summers in New Hampshire that she began looking forward to as early as February. At eight, Barbara made her breathless anticipation a theme of her letters to the dean of the Auburn Theological Seminary, another of her adult correspondents, and one who joined her in worship of "Nature's wonders":

> I want as long as possible in that green, fairylike, woodsy, animal-filled, watery, luxuriant, butterfly-painted, moth-dotted, dragonfly-blotched, bird-filled, salamandrous, mossy, ferny, sunshiny, moonshiny, long-dayful, short-nightful land, oh that fishy, froggy, tadpoly, shelly, lizard-filled lake—oh, no end of lovely things to say about that place, and I am mad to get there.

In New Hampshire she got lost in pretend fairy games with several children: summer's bounty included human company. She loved "dressing up in a green dress which I took the sleeves off of, putting berries or sprigs of pine in my hair, and dancing in the beautiful pine grove." But hikes into the mountains with her father were the highlight. Barbara began to devote herself to nature writing, which she did in lovingly exhaustive detail—in keeping with Wilson's approach. She worked hard on close-grained description of sun-

BARBARA FOLLETT

sets, lizards, aquatic plants, a red squirrel whose "pink tongue lapped the water much the way a cat's tongue does." She was obsessed with butterflies. Inspired by her summer world, Barbara also invented an imaginary world, Farksolia, and its language, Farksoo, poring over its grammar. Her father, whose lifelong project was a book on American usage (*Modern American Usage: A Guide*), was very attentive. Wilson even tracked down real card-catalog files to hold her growing store of Farksoo words.

Barbara didn't yet say it in her letters, but, nearing nine, she was obviously lonely. To be sure, she threw herself into the intensive projects she dreamed up—an advertisement for her parents' belief in sparing a child the curiosity-dampening distractions of ordinary school. Barbara wrote a long story about a cat mother's ingenious way of teaching her kittens to be self-reliant. She inventoried butterflies (no pinning, only temporary capture), first describing real ones, then inventing her own. Mr. Oberg later joined in, sending on elaborate paintings of imaginary butterflies she had described. Still, Barbara was restless, especially in "this vile apartment house," she wrote when the family moved from the outskirts into New Haven temporarily. Her father had taken a job at Yale University Press, but she wanted to be "oh, anywhere, everywhere except here!"

It was then, as 1923 began, that she posted the keep-out message on her bedroom door. Around the same time, she also wrote a blunter letter to her mother, relaying fierce annoyance on paper rather than in person:

> Talk about something! Get rid of your female friends who talk about nothing but their children, and your gentlemen friends who talk about nothing but books and colleges and automobiles. Or if you can't get rid of them talk about something really worth while. The worst part of this dull talk is that the listeners are interested!

She went on, lecturing her parents about the phoniness of their circle and the more serious topics they should take up. She would discuss Farksolia, the slaughter of trees, the beauties of nature, "and I would say a little about books and poetry. Not that I am putting an abuse on the books. I love books, but this everlasting talk about them all the time (and mostly not interesting ones at that) drives a sensible fellow mad."

Barbara didn't mind conveying that she felt like a butterfly caught in a net herself. She was plainly irritated with all the adults yet envious of her parents' friendships, suffocated by the self-conscious literary atmosphere yet unable to breathe without it, eager to be a rebel yet lacking a model for how to be other than—as she was in her note—a parent-like scold, urging more attuned awareness, more authenticity, more spontaneity. But Barbara knew where else to turn for venting; her rearing-by-writing truly had taken hold. She began a longer story than she had ever attempted. It was very much her own project, about a girl "so lonely that she went away to live wild," she wrote another adult friend. At the same time, it was also a quest to fulfill her parents' dreams of understanding the child soul. Here was yet another double bind, or a sense of redoubled purpose, or both: behind her closed door, Barbara was in fact on a family mission. She wasn't just aiming to meet a ninth-birthday deadline to present her work to her mother. She also put up the barricade so that she and her father would have privacy in which to peruse and perfect it together, part of the deep pleasure for her.

Wilson was impressed as his daughter read him installments of her forty-thousand-word creation—on which she tapped away for weeks, sometimes producing as many as four thousand words a day. He was also relieved to discover that "tawdry" urban apartment living hadn't squelched her nature-loving spirit. He surely recognized the classic theme, the childhood fantasy of escape. Barbara, with her nymph and fairy games, had been circling it for years in her writing, and her reading had featured it, too. But an adult friend's gift was especially well timed: Barbara received a copy of Barrie's *Peter and Wendy* that February, "one of the loveliest books that I have ever read," she wrote in thanks. "I don't see how you knew just exactly what I liked—I have always wanted to fly, myself."

She took wing with Eepersip Eigleen, whose flight from her parents takes her first to live amid the meadows, then by the sea, and finally in the mountains. Eepersip isn't an anarchic rebel. She works hard at her romantic outsider status: "For hours every day she practised running, leaping, dancing, and prowling, until she was as fleet as a deer and as soft on her feet as a lynx." Her parents aren't ogres, as Eepersip appreciates. Though they pursue her, they're also awed by her proficient wildness—"amazed at the way in which her dancing and leaping had improved." They yearn to have her back, but also can't help worrying that the price of capture may be too high. Eepersip discovers that the price of freedom is high, too, but she is willing to pay it.

Barbara ventured onto unsettling terrain in pushing Eepersip beyond heartwarming communion with nature. After her own escape, Eepersip returns to lure her little sister away from home to keep her company, but Fleuriss is scared of this leaping creature. Eepersip is too ethereal and unreliable for a smaller girl who needs the comfort of her mother. (Peter Pan is irresponsibly elusive, too, but he's also a rascal who captivates other children, and he calls forth Wendy's urge to nurture.) Eepersip grows more and more aloof. Lovely though the butterflies that encircle her are, she is slipping beyond the reach of human connection, into very cold regions. She ends up high in the mountains. A leaf-clad sprite now, Eepersip is stunned by a sunset as she stands on a snowy peak, before falling asleep in the frozen realm:

> In the sky Nature still flung about her colours wildly—fire was in the zenith, the long bank of clouds was vividly fringed with red-gold, and there to the south it changed to caverns of shadowed pink and strange violet. . . . Then one thrill and flame of gold spread about the whole earth; the snow at her feet was shadowy gold, and a pathway of it danced upon the air 'way to the horizon. It played upon each frost-feather; the eastern mountains were flushed with this soft gold.

Soon after, Eepersip turns into a fairy wood nymph invisible to all, "save those few who have minds to believe, eyes to see."

Actually, Fleuriss and that scene of mountain sublimity weren't in the pages that Barbara read to her father in early 1923, just before she turned nine. They appeared in the version Knopf published as *The House Without Windows and Eepersip's Life There* four years later, in February 1927, just before Barbara's thirteenth birthday. In a "historical note" about the book's provenance (which Wilson stressed was Barbara's idea rather than his), he emphasized preservation rather than evolution. Time had intervened but hadn't spoiled what he felt was a uniquely full, firsthand expression

> of what is in a normal, healthy child's mind and heart during that mysterious phase when butterflies, flowers, winging swallows, and white-capped waves are twice as real as even a quite bearable parent, and incomparably more important— the phase before there is any unshakable Tyranny of Things.

Here was a child's preadolescent vision rescued from "standardized" influences and revealed in its spontaneous, nature-loving essence. Readers of all ages, he felt, might learn from Eepersip.

The truth was more complicated, though a fervent child-ally like Wilson probably couldn't see it. Barbara's novella was a very mediated creation, which didn't make the product less interesting or the process less rewarding for her. After Barbara presented the original story to her mother, who was pregnant that spring, she got the plaudit that really counted—a chance to work it over with her father. He even proposed a private printing after careful revising. But a fire in their apartment building in the fall of 1923 destroyed the manuscript. After struggling to reconstruct her exact sentences, Barbara eased up and was pleased by how much better the new version was, especially since her new baby sister, Sabra, gave her a plot twist the heavily descriptive tale needed. And one of the best hikes Barbara had ever taken with her father—up Mount Moosilauke in 1925—gave her the vivid acme it needed, too.

By now the aim was no longer a private printing. Wilson had left Yale University Press to join Knopf, where his purview was a bigger public. Barbara wanted his attention. "Nothing ever happens unless you're here," she wrote her father, who was commuting and away more often. As the girl renaissance unfolded, Wilson's sights rose, and so did Barbara's. In early 1925, her story still in revision, she wrote Mr. Oberg that "Daddy and I have been correcting it, to make it as perfect as we can—and, when it is all corrected and copied on nice clean paper—it may be published." As she and her father focused on a final bout of editing in 1926, Nathalia's novel *The Sunken Garden* didn't escape the Follett family's notice. Knopf was surely watching the Daisy Ashford–inspired field, too. When Wilson submitted the manuscript to his bosses, the anticipation was intense. Barbara fell on the floor screaming with relief when, opening the gray Borzoi stationery, she read that Blanche Knopf liked her manuscript "enormously."

So did the critics. No unsettling maturity was going to stir up controversy this time (though in fact Barbara's parents supplied more bookish and fine-tuned collaboration than Clarence Crane could begin to manage). "We cackled over 'The Young Visiters' and whooped over Nathalia Crane," the critic and professor Howard Mumford Jones wrote in his review of *The House Without Windows*, under the headline "New Child Genius." He went on, "Fortunately there is no likelihood that Barbara Newhall Follett is going to suffer this indignity. She is too serenely a lyric artist. She has the Mozartian calm. She writes as though she were living in that serene abode where the eternal are. It is as it should be. That is where she lives and where she takes us."

The influential children's book reviewer Anne Carroll Moore disapproved of the homeschooled isolation and worried over the perils of premature publication and precocious professionalism, but Moore was the exception. A piece about the novel for young readers in *The American Girl* magazine advised that Barbara's vocabulary should be a model. Barbara's book was just what nostalgic adults needed, too. "There can be few who have not at one time or another coveted the secret, innocent and wild at the same time, of a child's heart," wrote the *New York Times* reviewer. "And here is little Miss Barbara Follett, holding the long-defended gate wide open and letting us enter and roam at our will over enchanted ground."

Jones was wrong, though, about the serenity. As Margery Williams Bianco, the author of *The Velveteen Rabbit*, pointed out, Barbara's fantasy of escape was bound up with "extraordinary single-mindedness and almost ruthless determination." Eepersip acted on both. Barbara clearly felt that her turn had come. Heralded as a voice of childhood freedom, she was now a teenager who wanted to actually exercise some clout—to push back against the adults on all sides. She wrote Moore, the reviewer, a testy letter: "It surely is very rash to slam down into the mud a childhood and a system of living that you know nothing about." Her focused hours at her desk gave her days outdoors, long summers, time for her violin as well as piano, and suited her perfectly, she informed Moore. She wrote what she pleased. At the same time, Barbara the writer whirled on her parents. She had a new passion—a less bucolic one—and dared them to thwart her pursuit of it.

"I am wild over PIRATES," Barbara wrote one of her correspondents, and she harangued her parents about acting on her enthusiasm, not just writing about it—though she did that, composing a forty-two-stanza ballad on the topic. She threatened to run away unless she was allowed to sail as a cabin boy on a schooner bound for Nova Scotia in the summer of 1927. Barbara took the planning in hand herself, consulting a nautical neighbor and scouting the New Haven wharf. *Treasure Island,* which she had first read at ten, remained a favorite. She may also have noticed a boys' spin-off of the girl-writer vogue, popularized by the son of the wealthy publisher George Putnam. In 1925 David Binney Putnam, twelve, wrote the first of a succession of books, in a direct boyish style for other boys, about glamorously adventurous trips arranged by his father—to the Sargasso Sea, Greenland, the Arctic, Africa, and more.

Barbara was impatient with the fairy-filled fantasy of escape and with her tame family, and eager for a very different follow-up to her first novel. She wrote letters to a friend while on the ten-day trip. Knopf quickly turned them into another book, *The Voyage of the Norman D., as Told by the Cabin-boy,* published not long after she turned fourteen in 1928. The memoiristic account got no lengthy working over with her father. This was her book, and it tacked this way and that, without Mozartian calm. In it, Barbara wrote as a self-conscious and confident teenager, half-mocking her "gay, piratical" romanticism but also proudly plunging into a real world that was utterly foreign. She mingled with shipmates, making a particular friend in barely literate Bill. Still the naturalist, she brought a newly human, often comic, perspective to her descriptions. "Some looked as though they were in a great hurry," Barbara wrote about a stream of jellyfish

> —as though they were gathering up their robes of state around them and hastening on; others were small, dainty, modest, and very scornful of the more splendid ones; some went sailing by, looking, for all the world, as though they were lost in a remote dream.

And then suddenly Barbara was upended. Shortly before the book's appearance, a letter arrived from her father, two days after her fourteenth birthday, telling her that he was leaving her mother. Wilson had fallen in love with a twenty-year-old secretary at Knopf and now portrayed his marriage to Helen as misery from the start. The child who had spun imaginative visions of fleeing abruptly became an abandoned adolescent. And as her devastated mother wrote a friend shortly after the news broke, Barbara had "worshipped her father in a terrifying way."

It's tempting to say, as Barbara soon did, that her father had worshipped her in a trifling way—indulged in child-focused fantasies of freedom, only to take flight himself, in search of new rejuvenation, when his lyrical girl and family idyll turned moody, unwieldy. At first Barbara appealed to him in the spirit of collaborative adventure he had reared her on. "This is the time of year when you are wont to have feverish spells of mountain-lure—why aren't you having them?" she wrote him. "I depend very much on you," she emphasized, using all of her metaphorical skills. "I trust you to give another heave at the capstan bars, to get the family anchor started toward the surface again. After all, you have the strongest shoulders for heaving of us all!" Barbara spoke for her sister, who "is not possibly able to grow up decently in the midst of this whirlpool." She confronted Wilson's girlfriend, who proceeded to tell Barbara that surely she wanted her daddy happy. Barbara lashed out at her: "I wouldn't stand up there, so extremely unashamed of myself."

And then, by the late spring, she gave up. Barbara "has changed terribly," a worried friend observed. But there was no mention of her turmoil in the version of subsequent events that Helen later recounted in a memoir called *Magic Portholes,* which Barbara worked on with her, this time editing her parent, not the other way around. It was an account of a literally outlandish plan to run away to sea, instigated by Barbara and signed on to by a mother distraught over her daughter's "bad condition spiritually." If Wilson could assert his freedom, so could they—and no scolding from him was going to stop Helen. "I believe there'll have to be a lot more iron in your control of her in the next two or three years," he had the audacity to write her in the summer, "or else she'll go completely to pot."

In the fall of 1928, mother and daughter set sail with their typewriters as part of their minimal luggage and with only a tenuous sense of how they would manage. They had Barbara's royalties and an advance for another book in hand. They also hoped Wilson would wire money along the way, though they weren't counting on it. They would sell journalistic dispatches as they went. Leaving Barbara's not-yet-five-year-old sister behind in the care of a friend, they were gone for almost two years. They made their way to the West Indies and then Tahiti and Samoa. They went on to Honolulu and the West Coast, earning some money by writing about their adventures. "To the world it is an extremely interesting educational procedure, and will be watched as such," Helen wrote a close friend. In truth, she confided, it was hell with, and often for, Barbara.

"A happy trip, a trip of gaiety and laughter and romance, all of these, but it was something more," Helen claimed as she promoted *Magic Portholes* four years later, celebrating her "playmate idea" of parent-child relations. "It was a piece of real continuity of those ten years which we had had before." Youth, she went on, was now sharing not just its imagination but "its unquestioning confidence in itself and its ability to accomplish anything in life." In fact, Barbara was unproductive and defiant, and Helen—with Wilson's call for "more iron in your control of her" now echoing in her head—felt scorned and powerless. Barbara did whatever she wanted. "I allow her to do so for any peace whatever," Helen confessed.

In this Neverland, nobody was a grown-up, but nobody was a carefree child either. The playtime the Folletts had so prided themselves on protecting and prolonging for Barbara was over— but where did that leave her at fourteen? "If you knew how extraordinarily wild I was," Barbara wrote from Tahiti to a friend, "you would get a good laugh out of it. Why, I make friends with the devil all the time." She even seems to have found herself being romantically pursued by an islander. Helen was panicked. Her daughter, whom she counted on as her coauthor, was supposed to be the gifted observer of exotic nature and island customs, not a rebellious participant. Barbara was disoriented, too. When Helen wrote to friends a couple of months later from American Samoa with news that "Barbara has gone to pieces," she was alarmed. "Her writing is not anywhere finished. She has lost interest in things, in living, in writing. She says, herself, she is 'homesick.'" Then Helen vented some pique, sounding like the put-upon teenager: "And it still seems incredible to me that it is Barbara who is dragging me back, and who is such a drag here."

In September of 1929, after arriving on the West Coast from Hawaii several months earlier, Helen left Barbara, now fifteen, with family friends to serve as chaperones and signed her up for junior college in Pasadena. Instead, Barbara fled. She headed north to join a friend she had met in San Francisco, planning to get work as a typist and write. The "girl novelist" runaway made national headlines. "I came away because I felt I had to have my freedom," she told the *Los Angeles Times* reporter who interviewed her after her arrest at a San Francisco hotel.

> I felt utterly suppressed, almost frantic, under the plans that had been made for me. I did not want to enter college nor live the standardized existence. I have never been to school in my life. Perhaps I might like it—I do not know. But this I know: I do not want to like it. . . . Why are older people crushing us this way? It seems to me I cannot wait six whole years until I am twenty-one in order just to be free.

To her mother, she had written from Pasadena as she left, "I want to be alone with my Disillusion or my Fairytale—as the case may be."

A decade earlier, in his *Harper's* article, Wilson had in passing acknowledged the risk that their vigilantly child-focused solicitude—which wasn't a license to run wild, he had stressed, but a spur to dream boldly with words—might lead to "a more painful disillusionment" with a dreary adult world. He never imagined how responsible he would be for propelling Barbara into that world prematurely—just in time for the Crash, it turned out. Hand-wringing by him, in any case, would have infuriated her. The last thing she wanted was to grant her father any more power over her fate—or to feel responsible for rescuing her mother either. Barbara was now impatient to chart a fearless path beyond her parents and their effete self-delusions.

Too impatient, it is possible to feel, looking back at what the next decade, a grim one for the whole country, had in store for her. Barbara's parents, in the name of sparing her any hindrances and being her "playmates," had for years subtly steeped their daughter in their romantic notions of imaginative girlhood—and then stopped. Off-kilter and in crisis, they gave up on guidance "at a very critical time in her life," as a worried family friend wrote, "when she needs to be associated with sane and well-balanced people." While Nathalia finished high school and lucked into the college education her mother and father had never had, Barbara balked.

But what she said she didn't "want to like" might have supplied the freedom she needed. By eighteen, she was tired of dull typing jobs. She had been feeling trapped since rejoining her mother and her sister, Sabra, in 1930, helping Helen get *Magic Potholes* done and keep the household going. Barbara noted that a college degree would be an asset in a terrible job market (overlooking another benefit: four years of paycheck-free time to read, a boon to any writer). Even so, the professor's daughter wasn't going to follow in those footsteps. She felt not "the faintest ray of desire or enthusiasm—in fact, I feel a decided antipathy."

Barbara wanted to be audaciously independent. She also tried to be clear-eyed—as her parents had never been—about the barriers, burdens, and obstacles that a free spirit had better be ready to deal with. The strain is evident in the pages she left and in the paths, and people, she pursued. "The only thing that makes me unhappy now is that my dreams are going through their death-flurries," she wrote in 1930 to an older writer with whom she had become friends during her California layover. Barbara doesn't sound sixteen.

I thought they were all safely buried, but sometimes they stir in their grave, making my heart-strings twinge. I mean no *particular* dream, you understand, but the whole radiant flock of them together—with their rainbow wings, iridescent, bright, soaring, glorious, sublime. They are dying before the steel javelins and arrows of a world of Time and Money.

A restless quest to keep sight of the gleam, and of its elusiveness, is there in the intense correspondence she began with an older sailor whom she had met on the schooner from Hawaii. He was a "bulwark, oasis, anchor—what-you-will," she said. "Mysterious, too, in his comings and goings, as the sea with its tide." By 1932 Barbara broke off what had become an epistolary romance, having found a less exotic countercultural kindred spirit on land and closer to her age. With a recent college graduate named Nickerson Rogers, she set off on mountain trips in New England and then adventures in Europe.

They married on their return, and both of them scrounged for jobs. As her twenties unfolded, Barbara welcomed his "calm poise" and steady progress at Polaroid in Boston, feeling more restless and stuck by comparison. "I am likely to weep and gnash my teeth with envy," she wrote a friend about her sister, Sabra (who went on, in 1961, to become the first female graduate student at Princeton). At fifteen, "she is happy, well poised, gets along with everybody . . . gets fun out of every situation"—a stunning contrast, Barbara noted, to herself at that age. Almost a decade later, she hadn't escaped secretarial work, but Eepersip's spirit stirred: Barbara made time for lessons in interpretive dancing.

She had stopped talking about her writing, but assorted unpublished stories, sketches, and a novel about a shipwrecked couple show Barbara struggling, again and again, to capture that radiance and the awareness of its transience. She arrived at moments of expressive brilliance, and got stymied by trite scenes and characters. Striking hints of originality appeared in brief scenes of ugliness and despair. But she hadn't yet outgrown her long girl-writer apprenticeship in wondrous beauty, and didn't dare look more closely.

In life, she also turned away. Overwhelmed at twenty-five by a marital crisis, her own this time, she left her Brookline apartment on the evening of Thursday, December 7, 1939. Barbara was never seen or heard from again.

CHAPTER 4

Performance Pressures

· 1 ·

"Your Child, Too, May Be a Shirley Temple," promised an article in the *Los Angeles Times* in July 1934. It was based on an interview with Gertrude Temple, "still a little dazed" by her daughter's swift rise into the ranks of top box-office draws, and it went on in a light vein to "Give Recipe for Making Super-Star Out of Lively Young-ster." First step: marry a banker named George and eat raw carrots, not candy, while pregnant. Make sure to give your growing baby wholesome fare soon as well—soup, cooked fruit, chocolate pud-ding or ice cream, no cookies. To encourage a "sense of rhythm and aid imagination," have her memorize nursery rhymes with mother and read bedtime stories with father. Above all, she should be sent to dancing school just as soon as she starts jouncing in her playpen, up on her tiptoes. No mother should delay on that crucial exposure. Ahead for your twirler, once spotted by talent scouts, lies a debut in a short film. Then a few small roles could be the prelude to the big break, a show-stealing song-and-dance number in a full-length feature. Suddenly famous, at barely five, she will sweep the whole family into a new world of wealth and attention along with her. Now the challenge, to be tackled "with fearful optimism," is to keep your little performer modest.

Gertrude, a shy beauty from the Midwest who had become a quiet Santa Monica wife, had read her share of such articles before and after Shirley was born. She knew what "mammas everywhere" wanted to hear. So did the reporter, who happened to be a woman. She was working in a genre by then familiar in Hollywood environs and never out of style since. It has thrived on lurid tales about very young showbiz stars, and more recently on subtler fare aimed at uneasy parents eyeing "the rug rat race": tips on handling the child-as-superstar—a precious family investment whose potential, touted at home, is to be promoted by well-timed, outsourced opportunities to excel every step of the way. (Your baby needn't be walking yet to qualify for early music classes—billed as good for baby brains and parent-child bonding, not just a sense of rhythm.)

In the midst of the Depression, the draw was obvious. The utter unlikelihood of producing "a super baby star of Shirley Temple caliber" only added to the democratic appeal. Because the odds against any success on the movie lots were so long, it was impossible to predict who would get lucky—and it was lovely to fantasize that such a rapid rise might be "phenomenally easy." The rush of aspiring stage mothers and their children to Hollywood had been gathering momentum ever since Jackie Coogan's big break in Charlie Chaplin's *The Kid* in 1921. One estimate claimed that as the talkies took off, a hundred children from all over arrived every fifteen minutes, hoping to be more than extras.

When Shirley struck gold, the moment was more propitious than usual. "Hollywood with the gong from the cleanup squad ringing in its ears . . . is making a desperate effort to locate more child stars," an article reported as the revised Motion Picture Production Code clamped down on unseemly fare in the summer of 1934. "Reasoning seems to be that stories about children will set things right." That was precisely the plot of Shirley's breakout film early that spring. In *Stand Up and Cheer!*, a Secretary of Amusement is appointed by the president to distract people from their woes. Thanks to the child entertainers he recruits to the stage, a country where "nerves are in the red" recovers hope, and the Depression vanishes. Shirley, almost six but billed as four, was the perfect emissary. In an era of virtuosic performing prodigies (Yehudi Menuhin was thronged after concerts), she was the vigorous democratic version. Superlative acting talents weren't required, but she had perfect timing, a great memory, and tenacity. As she tapped and sang, she exuded something even more alluring, in bleak times, than imaginative innocence. In her first full-length movie, as she proceeded to do in life, she projected utter confidence—in her own, and everyone else's, performance. And for the ebullient curly top, it seemed a breeze. "Oh, Shirley doesn't really work," says Jimmy Dunn, playing her vaudevillian father in *Stand Up and Cheer!*. (An absent mother was to become a staple in her films.) ". . . Look at her, she thrives on it."

On the opposite coast, a mother named Josephine Cogdell Schuyler didn't join the California-bound "flock of hungry locusts," in Hedda Hopper's metaphor. She was, however, following her version of Gertrude's recipe. Proudly self-exiled from her wealthy and racist white Texan family, she had made her way (via Hollywood and San Francisco's bohemian scene) to Harlem, lured by its renaissance. There she married a man named George who was not a banker. George Schuyler was a prominent black journalist, an editor at the socialist magazine *The Messenger* as well as at the weekly African American newspaper *The Pittsburgh Courier*, and a provocative columnist.

Josephine went well beyond a carrot-and-no-candy regimen. Long before getting pregnant, she had sworn by vitamin-rich vitality through nutrition. Her daughter, Philippa—born in 1931, three years after Shirley—was reared on a sugar-free and totally raw diet (which meant uncooked meat, too). Reciting poems with her mother and playing letter games on her blackboard with her father began early. Word of her spelling prowess at two and a half made its way to a film scout, in the form of an enterprising Pathé News reporter curious to see the Harlem marvel. He found an adorable child with, in George's words, the "dark liquid eyes of a fawn, and eyelashes like the black glistening stems of maiden hair ferns"—and skin the color of "lightly done toast."

Philippa's hue—the reporter had hoped for more like burnt toast—proved a deal-breaker for Pathé News. So did the parentage that produced it, as would have been true in Hollywood as well.

In the movie industry's campaign for social uplift and decency, the cleanup squad could find room for an *Our Gang*–style vision of integrated childhood, stocked with pickanniny stereotypes and naughty hijinks. But high on the list of the Motion Picture Production Code's prohibitions was any portrayal of "miscegenation," particularly between blacks and whites. Even Harlem, as the Schuylers were well aware, offered a wary welcome to marriages like theirs—which only spurred Josephine on. She had a truly ambitious Miss Fix-It role in view for Philippa. The fruit of her and George's rare union was a remarkable child. Philippa was a compleat prodigy in the making—precocious student, prolific girl writer, notable composer, and accomplished pianist, all rolled into one and wrapped in plucky public charm (and beauty) that got her called "the Shirley Temple of American Negroes." What better example of "hybrid vigor" could there be to confirm her parents' vision of "the permanent solution" to the nation's biggest problem of all? Philippa embodied the promise of interracial harmony.

A pendulum swing away from sensitive girl writers, Shirley and Philippa were troupers, too sturdy to inspire mere escapist flights of fancy. FDR got it wrong when he famously paid tribute to Shirley as a cheap opiate of the masses: "It is a splendid thing that for just fifteen cents, an American can go to a movie and look at the smiling face of a baby and forget his troubles." Her distinctive gift, rooted in her brash assurance, was shared by Philippa, who was more bashful: to remind grown-ups—in Shirley's case, those on-screen with her as well as her adoring audience—that woes had cures. Like prodigies in the spotlight before and since, only more so, both owed their allure not simply to exceptional talents. They were inspirational figures, harbingers of a future that could be very different.

Shirley, the ultimate Hollywood asset, and Philippa, the outsider, were worlds apart as they worked their morale-boosting, trouble-shooting wonder. But close to home, they each had what was almost always missing in the rags-to-riches, by-their-own-gumption tales that fueled the child star boom: a full-time Mrs. Fix-It. Gertrude and Josephine carved out (and got paid for) the role not of imaginative collaborator or mentor, but of omnipresent personal and professional manager. Even, or especially, the most promising stars needed businesslike intermediaries as they made their way in a fiercely competitive entertainment realm where the real codes bore little relation to the child-friendly displays. Not least, luck wasn't randomly distributed. As if Shirley didn't already get all the breaks, she also landed the most famous African American tap dancer, Bill Robinson, as her teacher. And a crucial ingredient in an endeavor that was anything but "phenomenally easy" got left out of that superstar recipe: mother and daughter had to have a great deal of confidence in each other. The real marvel is that in one of the pairs, the partners actually did.

· 2 ·

"There are two themes to my story," Shirley Temple told a Hollywood historian who paid her a visit soon after she published her memoir, *Child Star,* at sixty: "the great love I had for my profession and the great love I had for my mother." It was classic Shirley Temple, dispelling dark clouds—in this case, the inevitable suspicion that she had been the victim of a scheming stage mother and an exploitative film industry. Shirley presented a different view. Whether or not she was fully aware of it, the message of her five hundred pages—crammed with memories and details—is also classic Shirley Temple: all along, Gertrude was the comparative naïf, with an "ingrained awe of authority," and Shirley was the spunky, take-charge realist. Her version rings unexpectedly true.

The key to their success was that Shirley was ready to make the most of whatever deals came her way—even if the deals weren't "fair and square," as she sensed was often the case with the bigwig insiders (in Hollywood and elsewhere) who courted her. As long as Shirley felt sure in her relations with the two social outsiders who mattered most, she could stay sane—"at peace with myself," she said, ". . . no emotional hang-ups." Or to put it another way, she could draw on a deep sense of fun that sustained what was, after all, a lot of work. The main outsider, of course, was her mother. But she counted on someone else, too, the man who used the phrase "fair and square" (well aware of the rarity of such treatment), Bill "Bojangles" Robinson.

Gertrude Krieger had been seventeen, two years out of school and helping to support her family as a file clerk in Los Angeles, when she married twenty-three-year-old George Temple in 1910. He had quit school at fourteen, and was living with his widowed mother and siblings and working for the electric utility company. Gertrude was a dreamer, in her way, who had yearned to be a dancer. She was also a woman who didn't like leaving things to chance— though what she truly had a knack for was timing. In 1927, when her sons, Jack and George Jr., were twelve and eight, and George had recently become an assistant bank manager, she was restless in Santa Monica. Her two best friends had just had curly blond-haired daughters. As her thirty-fourth birthday approached, Gertrude decided she wanted one too. George was feeling flush enough to agree—and to get the tonsillectomy their doctor claimed upped the chances of fathering a girl. Along with eating carrots (good for instilling self-discipline in her unborn child), Gertrude sought out cultural experiences she hoped would leave their imprint on her fetus: art, literature, dance, music, movies. A bald daughter arrived on April 23, 1928, and a hint of blond curls soon appeared.

There were two themes to Gertrude's story for Shirley. "I wanted her to be artistic. I was determined that she should *excel* at something." The aims implied an accompanying subtheme. Gertrude—echoing the basic tenets of the no-nonsense behaviorist child-rearing expert of the hour, John Broadus Watson—was also determined "not to let my affection make me too lenient" or get in the way of teaching a self-sufficient daughter "not to be afraid of anything." Jack and young George were otherwise occupied, and soon the Crash curbed adult socializing. Gertrude seized her moment. She began dancing to music with Shirley a captive audience in her playpen and was thrilled when the baby "ran on her toes, as if she were dancing." Blessed with a great ear (utterly unlike her father), Shirley could hit the right notes when her mother practiced with her. She was also a deft mimic.

As her first phrase—"Don't do 'at"—indicates, Shirley wasn't always eager to obey. Her imitative phrase also suggests a penchant for bossiness on both her and her mother's part. Yet the two of them figured out a form of give-and-take that (mostly) dispensed with punishment and respected high spirits. "Love, ladled out in equal measures of encouragement and restraint," was how Shirley described Gertrude's formula, emphasizing that her mother, though strict, "seldom tried to dominate." As for the charismatic and feisty baby of the family, she didn't even need to try. Shirley fully appreciated her considerable clout, which only grew. "Secret best friends" with her father, she was a routine scene-stealer from her tolerant older brothers. Gertrude was vigilant, of course, but Shirley's lack of docility, however much it may have surprised her, didn't displease a mother whose own determination was more demure.

Gertrude had her eye on a new and approved route to excelling artistically. Though George had been spared the worst of the downturn, he was reluctant in 1931 to spend a dollar a week on lessons at the Meglin Dance Studio, a recent and already prestigious addition to a national dancing school boom. But Ethel Meglin knew how to pitch hard-pressed parents. She offered the "finest exercise to build up health and bodily vigor" and "an exceptional entrée into the entertainment field, with all its rich financial rewards." Gertrude emphasized the first part to George, who was wary of the Hollywood ambience.

As for the second part, mercenary ambition just wasn't Gertrude's style, according to Shirley. But professional-level performance opportunities clearly were on her agenda, and every student automatically became one of the "Famous Meglin Kiddies," participating in a revue during the week of Christmas at the Loew's State Theater in downtown Los Angeles. At three, Shirley was young (Mrs. Meglin generally took students at five), but Gertrude had her in good shape. Shirley gave her all in class, dancing with books balanced on her head. Gertrude sat knitting on the sidelines with the other mothers, getting her fill of talk about talent scouts.

Shirley wasn't plucked from the preschool crowd because she

stood out in the traditional, proto-adult way of prodigies—or in a lyrical, girlish way either. Quite the opposite. The day before Thanksgiving in 1931, when scouts from Educational Films Corporation arrived at Mrs. Meglin's to cast a series of *Baby Burlesk* shorts, Shirley's curls weren't fixed and her outfit was plain— Gertrude had been in a hurry that morning—and they were on their way out of class. A teacher called them back, only to have Shirley hide under the piano. She was repelled by one of the men, whose "moon-shaped, jowly, and moist-looking" face she still hadn't forgotten many decades later. But small size was a key requirement (for shorts featuring three-to-five-year-olds in oversize diapers doing mostly unsavory spoofs of movies), and she fit the bill. Lucky timing, in short, was crucial—even if Gertrude, writing to her mother, decided that "little old Shirley," with her jaunty cap and elkskin play shoes, had "evidently knocked them for a loop."

The pair were in turn knocked for a loop by a movie business that right away failed to conform to Gertrude's vision of developmental enrichment. After signing Shirley's contract for the burlesks, she wrote to assure her own mother that Shirley's "daily routine will not be upset very much," thanks to a good dramatic teacher, a nursery, and a kitchen in the studio. Gertrude quickly discovered the promises were hollow. She wasn't about to pull out, yet she remained wedded to her wholesome expectations—and she wasn't faking it. At any rate, Shirley never doubted that her mother truly had her best interests at heart, and a sense of Gertrude's "underlying streak of naiveté" empowered, rather than embittered, her as a girl.

Gertrude began managing—insofar as she could—a version of what legislators, as well as Hollywood moguls and unionizers, were strategically mandating: an experience on the movie lots that was, in the terms Gertrude favored, "a training ground for later life, a school where common virtues could be instilled and emphasized." The 1930s spelled the end of child labor, with an exception for underage movie entertainers. New Deal reforms included regulatory oversight to ensure (at least in theory) that young performers were engaged in educational work rather than merely onerous toil—and that their rewards were safeguarded rather than squandered by greedy elders.

Reality, of course, didn't match the lofty vows. "This business of being mother to a budding star is no joke," Gertrude wrote to her mother a month or so later. She had dragged a sick Shirley to the shoot of the first burlesk, *The Runt Page*, after the poor girl had battled a "raging cold" for more than a week and then, the day before the shoot, landed in the hospital with an eardrum in need of piercing. Gertrude had gone "almost crazy" with pleas for rescheduling, all for naught. But Shirley, "game little soul," got through the eleven-and-a-half-hour day, with the help of a couple of naps, and delivered her lines "as if nothing had happened." Gertrude, by contrast, was strung out, excited about the film's prospects, anxious about George's money worries, exhausted: "I think I look ten years older and have lost quite a little weight."

Without Shirley's phenomenal toughness, it is safe to say that their mother-daughter alliance would have gone nowhere. And both of them were acutely aware of that, which was essential to a sense of solidarity that Shirley characterized this way: "We each knew who we were, with or without each other." Shirley's home lessons in independence paled in comparison to the on-set training she got immediately, about which Gertrude was largely clueless. The *Baby Burlesk* star had to navigate a world of unfamiliar signals—lights, chalk marks, timing—and baffling terms ("bring in the dolly" raised her hopes), not to mention dangers.

When parents were ushered off the set and child welfare supervisors were shooed away for a coffee break, Shirley's bravery was brutally tested. An ostrich pulling her in a cart got spooked, and a lucky catch saved her from a bad fall. Undeterred, she was ready to ride an elephant, her next assignment. When a donkey tried to kick her, she ducked and then kicked him back. But even Shirley had her limits. Playing a missionary in the racist and most tasteless burlesk of all, *Kid in Africa*, which included a cast of black preschoolers, she had to exclaim, "These cannibals must be civilized!"—and watch in panic as the children raced right into a trip wire, installed to create more chaos in a jungle scene. Bloody mayhem ensued. She burst into tears.

Dealing with the adults, never mind animals and her cast mates, drummed in the sense that—much as she counted on her mother—she had better be able to fend for herself. "Kids, this is business," the director barked at his diapered cast. "Time is important. Don't waste it. This isn't playtime, kids. It's work." For those who didn't listen up, there was the "black box," a windowless sound room with a block of ice to sit on—perfectly designed to terrify, and to induce ear infections. Squeal to a parent, the kids were warned, and it was back on the cold seat for them. Shirley went ahead and told Gertrude, who credited the bizarre report to her daughter's overactive imagination. So Shirley, at all of four, came up with her own satisfying solution: pay attention and get it right the first time.

By the time Shirley, now five, stumbled into what proved her big break—getting cast at the last minute in *Stand Up and Cheer!* at the end of 1933—she was not fazed by much. On the two-day shoot, Shirley recalled that she "found the pressure exhilarating." Gertrude had been busy, not just coiffing her ringlets (fifty-six of them) but sewing a selection of dresses for Shirley's Fox Film handlers to choose from. (Her daughter needed her own clothes, Gertrude insisted, to be comfortable.) The two of them had gone over the script at home—before bedtime, as was their private, and patient, routine by now. "She reads and reads and reads," Shirley explained. "I talk and talk and talk." Gertrude was well aware that she didn't need to push. And her directorial staple was simple: "sparkle," which basically meant conveying natural expression with focused energy. "Just being herself," not acting, was Shirley's job, Gertrude firmly felt, in step with the general Hollywood prescription for young stars.

Yet arriving well prepared to do that was only the half of it. Proving, on the spot, to be resilient, resourceful amateurs as they made their way among the bumbling professionals was the more unusual skill the pair displayed already in their first bout of rehearsal and filming. When Shirley saw Jimmy Dunn sweating as he tackled some song-and-dance moves in his role as her vaudevillian father, she didn't hesitate to step in, leading him through the Meglin routine the studio decided to use. Meanwhile, Shirley herself had been left in the lurch, without the lyrics to her "Baby Take a Bow" number, though she had learned the tune. During breaks, she memorized them with Gertrude. She was crushed when her voice broke on the last word, but they had no time to agonize as they hurried off to lunch. Shirley tripped on the stairs and got a bloody lump on her forehead. Gertrude spit on a curl and used it as camouflage. Shirley was hustled back onto the set, feeling unhappily bedraggled—only to be entranced by the new tap shoes she had been loaned. Plus she truly loved to dance, and it showed. She had to lip-sync at the same time—a new task, but as a practiced mimic, she rose to it with ease. She never heard anything about her "flub," which everyone had decided was adorable. This child, Fox informed the Temples, had potential.

Shirley landed a contract in 1934 that awed the country: $1,000 a week for her, $250 for Gertrude. Between 1935 and 1938, she was the top box office star, dropping back to the top-ten in 1939. She helped save 20th Century Fox (the two companies merged in 1935) from near bankruptcy. At the height of her six-year Hollywood reign, she made more money annually than anyone in Hollywood besides MGM's Louis Mayer (and more than General Motors' president), $307,014 in 1938. She was photographed more often than anyone else on the planet, *Time* magazine reported in 1936. She received over three thousand fan letters a week. She moved mountains of merchandise—Shirley Temple dolls in all sizes, as well as dresses, soaps, watches, jewelry, sewing cards, hair bows, books. She endorsed products from Bisquick and Corn Flakes to Sunfreze ice cream and Vassar Waver hair curlers. In her prodigy domain—a child whose fame no grown-up could match—Shirley had only one predecessor: Jesus.

But what was it, in her case, that accounted for the acclaim? A puzzling question from the start, it became more vexed once she soared into the stratosphere. As Shirley said later, and perhaps her sharp-eyed younger self was aware of it, too, she "could sing,

SHIRLEY TEMPLE

dance, act, and dimple, but probably there were others around who could do equally well and far better in some categories." From the studio's perspective, that was an important part of the allure they were peddling: Shirley wasn't an anomaly. She was a natural who had a great time excelling at suitably wholesome endeavors and—this was crucial—conveyed that delight. The Hollywood publicists fudged her bio. A year got shaved off her age, to emphasize innocent vivacity, not precocity. Her Meglin Studio experience disappeared from her résumé. A cover story in *Time* was the conduit for the desired message, reporting that Shirley's "work entails no effort"—after describing a daily regimen that began at seven and ended at five-thirty.

Gertrude joined in, doubtless at Fox's urging, but she also believed that Shirley *did* love what she was doing, even if it was hardly the breeze that the world was given to think. "She just has a natural tendency toward acting. If it was hard on her, if she didn't like to do it, I'd take her out" was how Gertrude put it in an interview shortly after *Stand Up and Cheer!* opened. She sounded like Jimmy Dunn's hoofer character reassuring the bureaucrats that his daughter thrived on the routines, except that Gertrude added an educational twist, in step with the emerging developmental wisdom of the day. A drama teacher at Shirley's dancing school, she noted, felt "it would be wrong to discourage her as long as she enjoys it. She'd wilt, he said." At other times Gertrude suggested that what Shirley did wasn't acting at all, but "simply part of her play life."

If that was plainly wishful, Gertrude wasn't just airbrushing either. After all, the studio promptly decided to fit roles to Shirley's personality and capacities—one of which was, as Shirley put it, "a knack for projecting myself into make-believe situations without abandoning the reality of my true self." She was a sponge when it came to learning her lines, thanks not just to youthful brain cells but to her intense focus and a fierce desire to impress. At the same time, she was an upstart charmer quite unlike her somber mother. Shirley took real pleasure in her prowess and very soon was a savvy operator on the set. She didn't hesitate to give others cues, and she loved being the cut-up—a mix of pleaser, provocateur, and kid eager to have pals. She had a habit of wandering off to hang out with her favorites among the cast and crew, who were generally the least earnest.

The studio PR materials didn't accentuate this not-so-sweet-and-malleable side, but Shirley's roles were a clue to it. Though the girl on-screen got held up as an ideal of compliance whom other children should imitate, that wasn't the whole story at all. There was, as a critic noted, "something rude and rowdy" about her character that was also key to her appeal, especially to males. She played a wheeler-dealer, telling adults where to get off. The real Shirley modeled just that kind of cheekiness, and her power could be discomfiting. Adolphe Menjou, who starred as a disillusioned bookmaker transformed by her flirtatious charm and imaginative assurance in Shirley's even greater triumph of 1934, *Little Miss Marker*, emphasized her uncanny mastery. "This child frightens me. She knows all the tricks," he marveled, noting that she was an expert scene-stealer. ". . . Don't ask me how she does it. You've heard of chess champions at eight and violin virtuosos at ten? Well, she's an Ethel Barrymore at six."

But of course Shirley, the incarnation of can-do innocence, wasn't supposed to be a seasoned pro or a self-conscious celebrity, much less an exploited commodity. The mission to keep her "unspoiled," and at the same time to reassure her fans that she was getting special care, soon had everyone in knots, and Shirley nonplussed. A scene in her memoir has Gertrude, "agitated and talkative," sharing her anxieties about Hollywood's influence with Shirley herself—not exactly shielding her from studio machinations. Fox's chief of production, Winfield Sheehan, had just unnerved Gertrude with a warning from a child welfare supervisor that "there is no antidote to the corroding effect of Hollywood hubbub. It is impossible for children to remain impervious or unchanged." Eager to cow Gertrude into clamping down on Shirley, Sheehan declared that too much exposure to an admiring cast and crowds would swell her head and spell later maladjustment. He blew right past Gertrude's suggestion that growing self-confidence, not ego, was on display. "She can't get spoiled, Mrs. Temple," Sheehan lectured as Gertrude got more rattled. "She gets spoiled, it shows in the eyes." Gertrude didn't tear up in telling Shirley of the encounter, but she had earlier.

The upshot was a display of corporate, and cooperative, solicitude. A very New Deal spirit informed the studio arrangements elaborated in Shirley's contract: well-regulated security, portrayed in the press as the envy of any free-range child, was the touted priority. Shirley was the beneficiary of "a series of conferences between Mr. and Mrs. Temple and the Fox executives, all eager to safeguard the health of the child and keep her unspoiled," as an article put it. She had her own three-room bungalow on the studio lot to retreat to. There she met daily with a tutor, ate nutritional food without distraction, and took the naps she needed. She had a personal bodyguard and mandated vacations. She also had medical advisers who, with her mother, worked out a "system of relaxation" (which did not include watching movies, for fear they would taint her style).

This wasn't about pampering, the press liked to emphasize, or about curtailing childhood independence. Instead, here was a cutting-edge supervisory approach for all those interested "in rearing their children to be like prodigies." Not to be mistaken for indulgence, it offered a new and steady form of discipline. "Her routine of living," one account of Shirley's situation advised, "would make a very healthy child out of any baby who is normal, and a well balanced and trained little youngster as well." Another story about screen starlets judged the loss of "rough-and-tumble neighborhood play," and the risk of excess attention, a price well worth paying. "The average youngster on Main Street" would be lucky to have such close "care and chaperonage" by parents and state child welfare officials. Individual tutoring was a real advantage, and "the challenge of a job" gave the movie child rare character-building lessons. "Almost from the cradle it has been obvious to him, as it seldom is to the child supported by his parents, even in a moderately poor home, that effort 'gets you somewhere.'"

A vision was taking shape of a protected, and carefully directed, childhood in which play blurs into work (a very familiar notion by now). The Temples weren't paranoid in feeling vulnerable. Since 1932, the whole country had been following the Lindbergh kidnapping case with rapt anxiety, and the accused went to trial in January of 1935: among alluring potential hostages, Shirley surely ranked high. (In 1936 the Temples received an extortion threat—from a farm boy, it turned out.) Still, the studio deal was a far more coercive case of paternalistic control than advertised.

Shirley's arrangements meant she didn't get to share the studio schoolhouse with the other young actors. Her food was boring. Her lessons and rest times were tailored to filming schedules, not her needs. Vacations, given the mobs of fans, were impossible. For Gertrude and the family, barricaded behind the massive walls and electronic gate of a big new house in Brentwood Heights in 1936, constant studio and promotional business was now out of their hands. Perhaps Shirley can be forgiven, as the 1930s progressed, for behavior of just the sort her setup was purportedly designed to nip in the bud. Her voice coach later described audible tantrums from the studio cottage. He also reported that on a house call, Shirley demanded they play badminton first, whirling on her father when he suggested she start rehearsing: "Look, I earn all the money in this family. Don't tell me what to do."

Little wonder, too, that Gertrude was worried. Though Shirley, now nine, only dimly understood what was going on, her mother faced a crisis in 1937 that seemed to fortify the gumption that grounded both of them. Confronted with a medical scare, which called for surgery, an apprehensive Gertrude wrote to the old friend whom she had chosen as her maternal surrogate. Relations had already been tense with 20th Century Fox because she felt the studio wasn't giving Shirley roles that nurtured her growth. But with her friend, she wanted to discuss Shirley's continued thriving "as a human entity." "Any career child," she wrote, "is at a tremendous disadvantage," in need of inner bulwarks against "greed, selfishness, and flattery." Shirley had all that it took—patience, a sense of justice, tenderness, sensitivity, plus what Gertrude knew (though didn't say) she lacked herself, "a joyous spirit, full of pranks and teasing." Gertrude wanted to be sure those qualities were defended, not least Shirley's bold energy. Doing that had been a challenge for Gertrude—and not just because Hollywood made it hard. Again, she didn't say this, but Shirley intimated it: her mother had needed to overcome her own primness, and irrepressible Shirley helped her manage that. As she did in her letter, Gertrude mustered her clout to stand up for the feistiness that defined her daughter—and which, as it happened, was also a secret of Shirley's success.

During the two weeks that Gertrude was away in the hospital, Shirley never doubted that she would come home. But in the gloom, trying "to cope with the gaping hole caused by her absence," she sank briefly into "a swampland of confusion and helplessness." She wept every night with regret at taking her mother's love for granted and failing to convey hers. When a frail Gertrude returned, they rallied. Darryl Zanuck, the vice-president and head of production, decided to see how far Shirley could stretch (and to send her mother a be-careful-what-you-wish-for signal). To test Shirley's dramatic skills, he paired her with the legendary—and famously child-averse—director John Ford, "a blood-and-thunder mentor of hairy-chested males," Shirley the memoirist noted. In *Wee Willie Winkie* she was to play a valiant little peacekeeper in colonial India. The cards seemed stacked against her.

Except that Shirley hadn't just been coasting on cuteness so far by any means. Two years of honing her dancing skills with a legendary master of that art, Bill Robinson, had made her fearless in the face of daunting calls for excellence. The man whom Shirley considered the all-important mentor of her heart and feet had shown her (against lots of evidence, in life and in her movies) that demanding adults could be counted on to deliver serious, challenging fun. As Shirley described her meeting with Robinson at her cottage door early in 1935, it was a scene out of one of her movies. They started walking across the lot together, and when Robinson realized that Shirley was trying to catch up and hold his hand, he slowed down and took hers. It was the beginning of not just a partnership but an unusual friendship. She proposed that she call him Uncle Billy. He agreed, if he could call her darlin'.

Shirley had no idea what buttons she was pushing—but that was the point. According to Hollywood lore, Sheehan had summoned Robinson thanks in part to the director D. W. Griffith's remark that mixing blond-girl innocence with black characters would "raise the gooseflesh on the back of an audience." Robinson knew that he roused ire in Harlem by complying with Hollywood's racist rules, taking Uncle Tom roles and paying lucrative court to Shirley—but that wasn't his point. Bridling at the criticism, he trusted his scene-stealing powers on-screen to contribute to a mission he once described this way to a black reporter. "I am a race man!" he insisted. "I strive upon every turn to tear down any barriers that have existed between our two races and to establish harmonious relationship for all."

As a child, Shirley only gradually, and never completely, became aware of the Jim Crow realities that Robinson navigated in Hollywood and beyond it. But as soon as they began work together on *The Little Colonel,* a tale of family schisms set in the postbellum South, she made a thrilling discovery: he dealt with her as more of an equal than any other actor did—even though, or because, he was her teacher. Robinson took her seriously as a professional, rather than treating her as a pretty little "windup toy" that performed on demand (as even Gertrude could sometimes slip up and do). The singing and acting required by most of Shirley's roles expressly didn't call for feats of self-transformation. But tap-dancing "is an utterly unnatural skill," she emphasized in retrospect. Getting very good at it gave an ambitious girl the chance, with Robinson's one-of-a-kind guidance, "to elevate my ability to the height of my energy."

Unfazed that Shirley barely knew even the basics of tap, Robinson made the stair dance, which became the virtuosic centerpiece of the melodrama *The Little Colonel*, work brilliantly—and on short notice. The idea dawned late that Shirley, playing the family reconciler to Robinson's beloved family retainer, would join him in the routine that was his specialty. They were, Shirley liked to say later, the first interracial couple to dance on-screen in history—at a time when few dared do it off-screen (and when all on-screen physical contact between them had to be cut in the South). He deftly choreographed around the problem that childish body proportions make agile leg action hard, and came up with a trick to allow her to get more sound: she would kick the stair riser. Then they got busy. As Shirley later wrote, he was "imperturbable and kind, but demanding." His key advice was "Let's get your feet attached to your ears," and he showed her exactly what that meant. Proud of her powers of concentration and her zeal to nail things, she thrived on his high standards for precision and clarity. With him beside her, she couldn't get enough of the relentless practice that committed every move to muscle memory.

Perhaps because Robinson knew how it felt to be patronized as a naïvely cheerful hoofer whose feet just get to tappin', he imparted more than technique. He was the rare adult who actually gave Shirley a chance to practice a real version of the pieties she preached on-screen. Working with him, she discovered that hard-won mastery, enabled by a sympathetic and confident ally, can deliver self-respect and joyful fulfillment. Pulling off their routines, and achieving total synchrony as he carefully matched his moves to hers, was its own reward—"a final moment of elation in a long sequence totally devoid of drudgery." On-screen, too, Robinson's cool authority had a way of subverting a servant role that put him on a level with a child. In their next collaboration, *The Littlest Rebel* (a Civil War drama), he was again the only real grown-up anywhere in sight, ready to listen and to lead. He was the first black film character, a historian has remarked, responsible for a white one.

Wee Willie Winkie offered nothing like the challenge of tap dancing, but Shirley rose to the dramatic occasion (and proudly defied Ford's antichild prejudice in the process). Shirley is "growing up," the *New Yorker* film critic wrote, ". . . and there is a definite expansion of personality." Expansion of body, however, contributed to a drop in box office ratings as the 1930s ended. Good as her word, Gertrude and George bought out the rest of Shirley's 20th Century Fox contract when Gertrude saw no worthwhile work in store. Shirley had just turned twelve, and her mother's timing was right. As Gertrude said in a carefully crafted statement, her daughter needed a "life with other girls and boys of her own age, in school and during recreation hours, so that she will not develop an isolated viewpoint, which often brings on an unhappy outlook on life." Through the 1940s, Shirley dabbled in movies, but mainly she was a student at the exclusive Westlake School for Girls. Soon she became a popular wheeler-dealer there, too—not least with boys.

She didn't stick to Gertrude's tidy, happy script. Shirley, constantly called on during her childhood to rescue adults, was now in a hurry to claim her independence. At seventeen, she thought she was doing that when, in September 1945, over her parents' objections, she married twenty-five-year-old John Agar, the brother of a Westlake friend. George and Gertrude granted her only a small allowance as the couple moved into her renovated playhouse, hardly an ideal launching pad for a not-quite-ex-star and her insecure husband. Shirley signed a contract with David O. Selznick and was also loaned to other studios for several pictures, with mixed success. Agar drank and had affairs and, she later revealed, hit her.

By twenty, Shirley had a baby, but her marriage was beyond saving. Her film career was going nowhere.

Shirley filed for divorce at twenty-one in 1949. On a recuperative trip to Hawaii, she met Charles Black, a rare specimen—an American who had never seen a Shirley Temple movie. As they prepared to marry in 1950, she made a shocking discovery: her parents had run through her fortune. A decade earlier Gertrude and George had signed a pledge to hold half of their daughter's earnings in trust until she was twenty-one. It was a gesture in the spirit of the Coogan Act of 1939, which mandated that protection for child stars but didn't retrospectively cover Shirley. While shocking tales of greedy relatives fleecing young actors were stirring legislators to action, no one had worried about her—the epitome of well-tended talent.

Shirley and Charles took a vow of silence on the subject, "honoring family unity over material cupidity" (and deciding that George must have been duped). There she was, bailing out her elders again. But Shirley was also asserting a confident autonomy that she had developed early. And perhaps she had in mind Bill Robinson, who had died penniless in 1949. "There's no use in going through life as if you were in a funeral procession. After all, there's a lot of fun in it, so why grump and grouse?" he once told a reporter. "Why not dance through life?" His acolyte stuck with that outlook. Shirley Temple Black went on to work in television, ran unsuccessfully for Congress as a Republican, and was named ambassador first to Ghana and then to Czechoslovakia as Communism was collapsing, hardly luxury posts. As her early screen years might have predicted, she found her most fulfilling vocation in diplomacy.

· 3 ·

While Gertrude Temple was cramming her fetus with cultural enrichment in early 1928, the path awaiting Philippa Schuyler was being laid. Josephine Cogdell and George Schuyler got married on January 6, in thrall to each other and to a cause: challenging racial hypocrisies in the name of future racial harmony. George had just published a satiric takedown of "Our White Folks," which was causing a stir as the lead essay in H. L. Mencken's *American Mercury*. In his piece, George mocked those eager to proclaim "that the Negro is as good as they are—as if that were a compliment!—and to swear by all the gods that they want to give him a square deal and a chance in the world," while offering nothing of the sort. He also mocked the notion of a "natural aversion" to intermarriage: Why then the need for so many laws against it? Where George was caustic, Josephine waxed romantic, a daughter of the racist South who had dramatically disowned her heritage. The white race is "spiritually depleted," she wrote in her diary the week before she and George legalized their union. "America must mate with the Negro to save herself."

In her bond with George, Josephine heralded the square deal that would right the racial imbalance: "He needs to be cherished and inflated as I need to be pruned." She would "give him greater confidence in himself . . . make him certain of his superiority." Under George's firm hand, she would never "quit growing and solidify." But they shouldn't expect any outside help in their bold experiment, George warned the morning after their marriage, as he hurried out of town on an assignment. "Do you know, Josephine, we stand absolutely alone? We can't count on anybody," a remark she recorded in her diary. "The whole world is against us, the negroes as well as the whites?" Three and a half years later, they had company. Philippa arrived on August 2, 1931. She was just the youthful race-straddling recruit their cause needed—and a child-rearing project made to order for restless Josephine, who felt she had "dropped completely out of sight." It never occurred to her and George that in counting on their daughter to win over the world, they might be giving her—as they did in her diet—a very raw deal.

The child star craze had equal opportunity allure—ordinary, middle-class Shirley soared—and Hollywood fueled the promise of upward mobility with rags-to-riches plots that celebrated America's cooperative spirit. The Schuylers were well aware that Philippa tested any such storyline. But even before their baby began precociously talking, Josephine touted "extra vitality" as a biracial asset in the more competitive contest she faced: Philippa would have to prove herself a superior specimen, not just a sparkly girl. In Josephine's analysis of "hybrid vigor," heredity and history mingled. George, the key progenitor, brought emblematic black virtues to the mix. He provided "a splendid example of courage and endurance," having "from the cradle overcome the greatest difficulties without losing his sense of humor." Her own stock was a problem. As Josephine had recently written in an anonymous account of her racial awakening, she was the spoiled scion of a prosperous clan of ranchers and bankers who exemplified white folks' flaws: they were unjust bigots and joyless egotists.

Josephine professed to have discovered "the peace of humility" since her marriage, but joyless egotism ran deeper than she recognized. So did a proclivity to "go to extremes," one of the traits George ascribed to white folks—and he was rarely home to rein her in (not that he would have dared to try). Right after Philippa's birth, he went off to investigate the Liberian slave trade, and then kept up a frenetic pace of reporting and speaking: paying the rent in the Depression wasn't easy. Josephine leaned on the wisdom of the behaviorist John Broadus Watson (a protégé, like George, of Mencken's). Gleefully immoderate in his book *Psychological Care of Infant and Child,* he blamed "too much mother love" for creating emotional cripples, and he prescribed a formula in line with Josephine's nutritional zealotry. All toughness, next to no sweetness: that was Watson's secret to raising a sturdy child who could be steered to any vocation and would end up, he promised, an adaptable adult able to cope in an unpredictable world. Treat her like a small adult, he lectured parents. Be scant with praise and strict about routines. Avoid cuddling and kissing at all costs.

Where Gertrude Temple merely dabbled in the brusque parenting vogue, Josephine went overboard—in private. In public, she sounded if anything more laid-back than Gertrude when, in August 1934, she took a turn in the spotlight in a *New York Herald Tribune* article that reads like a parody of a Hollywood child-star profile. The newspaper sent Joseph W. Alsop (the future Washington columnist was then a twenty-three-year-old Harvard graduate) to 321 Edgecombe Avenue to watch as "Harlem's Youngest Philosopher Parades Talent on 3d Birthday." The headline continued, "Philippa Schuyler Spells, Draws and Then Rushes for Her Health Ice Cream." Also in a facetious vein, the accompanying photograph showed a small savage rather than a sage. In it, Philippa could almost be mistaken for one of the wary little cannibals on the set of Shirley Temple's most offensive *Baby Burlesk* short, *Kid in Africa*. She is semicrouched against a backdrop of foliage, naked except for a headband adorned with leaves. Her gaze is serious, and she betrays no trace of a smile.

Noting that her writer parents "sternly deny that she is a prodigy," Alsop wryly portrayed a child whose mother had clearly run her through her repertoire on other occasions. On the one hand, though he didn't put it like this, here was a higher-brow, and even more wholesome, young talent than the Shirley phenomenon. Where Hollywood's brand-new attraction dimpled and danced for a mass audience, Philippa twirled her globe and spelled:

> "I want my globe," remarked Philippa, emerging from behind her mother's shoulder and casting herself on the floor in an attitude of which Cleopatra in her best days would not have been ashamed. The globe was produced. With a small, but unerring, hand, with which she liked to cover each indicated locality, she pointed out the continents and countries suggested to her. Asia, India, Africa, Australia were picked out, and each time she spelled the name, making a little song out of Australia.
>
> "That's Ceylon," added Philippa, as a voluntary. "C-E-Y-L-O-N. And that's Madagascar. M-A-D-A-G-A-S-C-A-R."
>
> This seemed to call for a certain emphasis, so she turned round twice gracefully and rapidly on the rug, ending flat on her stomach.

On the other hand, Alsop hinted at the possibility that perhaps everything wasn't quite so effortless and unselfconscious as mother and daughter, both dressed in "bright silk pajamas," endeavored to convey.

But he only hinted. Philippa certainly didn't lack for energy, demonstrating her spelling prowess to "the accompaniment of violent kicking with both legs and considerable smiling." If her performance was getting a bit tiresome by the time she climbed on a chair for recitation time—some doggerel, "My Country 'Tis of Thee," Countee Cullen's "What Is Africa to Me"—it was also impressive, and she was adorable as she turned to her blackboard to write, draw, and do a few sums. Her mother didn't sound like a taskmaster. In describing her dietary regimen, Josephine emphasized fruit and fresh ice cream, not the raw meat part. Her teaching method, she said, was "to have no method," merely to indicate her own interest and leave it to Philippa to follow. Yet Alsop also observed that Josephine had very precisely calibrated her daughter's progress (eighth-grade level in noun spelling and fourth grade in verbs). Columbia University's psychology department, he took note, had been alerted.

Implicitly, the article raised a question that, in addition to being condescending and racist, was real: Was this pair perhaps trying too hard? A biracial child faced extra hurdles, and Philippa's started at home, where George, too, seemed to have forgotten one important way in which he believed black folks had it all over "Our White Folks." They, he had written, "have learned how to enjoy themselves without too much self-consciousness and exhibitionism." Josephine put Alsop's article in the scrapbooks that she and George had begun keeping since shortly after Philippa's birth.

At first the big albums had resembled a standard record of early milestones, advanced but mostly not outlandish—hesitant steps at about eight months, four recognizable utterances at fourteen months ("Jo," as she then called her mother, "Daddy," "God damn," and "How do"). For the often-absent George, the progress reports were welcome. Back home, he added his own note about the "exceptional sense of humor" of his one-and-a-half-year-old. George had gotten Philippa a blackboard when she turned one, and he and Josephine now joined in her intensive letter-learning games. They kept track of her amusing wordplay: Can you say, Philippa asked, "go crooked to bed"?

George, editing at *The Pittsburgh Courier,* notified the black press of her early exploits. By the time the mainstream press in the form of Alsop paid a visit to their precocious three-year-old, the fast-growing trove of memorabilia was becoming a more intensely parasitic and proprietary chronicle than any Hollywood fan club could gin up for a star. The scrapbooks, which the Schuylers planned to unveil when she was older, were a record of parental hopes and hubris as much as of Philippa's own progress. Shortly after inserting the Alsop clipping, Josephine added commentary, diary-style:

> Everywhere your Daddy goes people ask about you, having read of you. When I take you to the Library on 145th Street the lady librarian makes a great deal of fuss over you. It is very nice having an accomplished daughter. I glow with pride. If only we can keep this up, darling, maybe you can be a great personality in the world. I hope so.

In the scrapbooks, Josephine was also honest about tactics that she wouldn't have dreamed of revealing in public. She plainly felt the need to justify them to the older Philippa who would peruse the pages—and also to herself. "You are stubborn and self-willed and want to do things your way," she wrote in the fall of 1934, describing recent hard spanks. "While I am whipping you, you often put your arms around me and say most plaintively, 'Oh, Jody, don't you be bad to me. Oh Jody, please be nice to me.'" (Philippa didn't call her mother by the usual endearments.) Even Josephine half-recognized that her Watsonian rationale failed to add up: "I must teach you to adjust yourself swiftly to new situations (you do this well though) and to forget anger and forgive quickly (this you don't do)." Blind to her own impulse-control issues, Josephine applied the harsh hand she felt she herself needed, or at any rate desired. "Beat me and then love me," she had urged George, "and I'll be as docile as a lamb."

Betrayal, not beating, turned out to be George's mode of causing his wife pain, as Josephine discovered before long, but in a 1935 letter he was still in full worship mode. "Your respect for and confidence in and reliance upon me," he wrote her, were just the sustenance their union was supposed to provide. Philippa was if anything more blessed, George went on, though he was surely aware that Josephine veered between extolling her brilliant black child and fiercely pruning a daughter who mustn't be spoiled the way she, Josephine, had been. "You and Philippa are growing together like Siamese twins," he noted, thrilled by the development.

> She is going to be a facsimile of you with the exception that she is having a much better start in life. She can become anything under your tutelage. She has already become a wonder. I often speculate on what she will become and what glory she will reflect upon us. It is a wonderful thing to look forward to. I just know she is going to be a marvelously beautiful and intelligent woman. We must do everything to preserve her, like a hothouse flower, for she is a rare and exotic breed. There are few beings like her in the world.

Perhaps George, who generally derided such excessive fussing as white-folk nonsense, was hoping to soften Josephine's approach. (When he first spanked Philippa, Josephine wrote in the diary, it "almost killed him.") But he doubtless also knew that his wife wasn't to be deterred from her mission to turn out a hardy model of hybrid vigor for the world. A year earlier, Josephine had launched Philippa on a new track, eager to deflect suggestions that their preschooler was an overcultivated clone of her bookish parents. (Philippa had been churning out stories, sometimes ten a week, by hand and on the typewriter, which she was learning to use.) Since shortly before Christmas in 1934, Philippa had been very busy at their green upright piano. Josephine had engaged an African American graduate of Juilliard, Arnetta Jones, as her teacher.

Columbia University's Child Development Institute had noted, shortly before Philippa turned three, that "she excels chiefly in her capacity for sustained attention and ability to concentrate during prolonged periods." At the piano, as at her chalkboard, Philippa took off. Within a year, she had begun composing short pieces, too, telling stories in rhythms and notes. When she hurried up to the apartment one day to write "Men at Work" after watching a WPA construction project on the sidewalk, she didn't shy away from boldly dissonant tones. Not long before she turned five, Philippa was the youngest of seven winners in her first music competition, sponsored by the National Guild of Piano Teachers. She pulled off four required pieces with impressive agility for her age. She also performed five that she had written, and the judges discovered a gift that had eluded the NYU assessors who had recently tested her IQ at 180: perfect pitch. (Philippa's favorite song was her "Cockroach Ballet," about roaches feasting and then suffering a near massacre, with a few survivors celebrating.) Scores of her songs, printed up in a booklet by her parents, were unearthed in 2011 by the musician John McLaughlin Williams. He made an informal recording, pleased to discover signs of real growth in work that he felt surely reflected some exposure to contemporary music.

Philippa, with Jones as her teacher, now had a nonparental mentor. Josephine meanwhile was assuming the role of manager as she sought out musical venues to showcase Philippa's striking talents. The relationship that evolved between mother and daughter, though, was the opposite of Shirley and Gertrude's mutually confidence-boosting alliance. Perhaps emboldened by working with Jones, Philippa pushed her mother to "make a better rule about whipping me." Please, she urged as they wrote up resolutions on New Year's in 1936, "teach me some other way. . . . It doesn't make me want to follow the rules. It makes me think you can't love me as much as you say you do." Josephine, taking her cue from her daughter, devised new rules: deny pleasures (toys, meals) rather than inflict pain, all the while applying ever greater pressure to perform.

The new disciplinary regime hardly reassured Philippa, who was in turn discovering how to unnerve her mother. "You nearly scared me to death," Josephine scrawled next to a newspaper clipping about a recital in the spring of 1938. Philippa, not yet seven, was by then in school part-time but practicing and performing more and more (on amateur radio hours, too)—not to mention being a star participant in the New York Philharmonic Young People's Concerts annual notebook contests. (One of her commentaries on the season's series, thirty-six pages long and illustrated, won her a special prize at Carnegie Hall.) The May evening of that particular recital, Philippa was evidently exhausted. Josephine, who recorded the drama in the scrapbook, described her saying, just before going on stage, "'Jody, I want to do this but I don't believe I can make it' and smiling brightly." Josephine took it from there:

> "Good heavens! Why not?" "Well," still brightly, "I just don't feel like I can make it." "Look here!" I said sternly, "You have to make it. Of course, you can! Go on out there and show 'em!" You were a trooper! You showed 'em! You signed programs till your hands were weary. Next day I said to you: Don't ever tell me you can't make a thing again. You can make anything you prepare for. The time to think of that is weeks before and by more practice, which determines everything.

Philippa began to make a habit of balking as concerts approached, and a frantic Josephine recruited George to weigh in by mail. A girl looking for some unconditional love from her adored father wasn't going to find much in his chiding vote of confidence:

> You can do *anything* if you try hard enough and do as Jodie and Miss Jones say. I am very proud of you, darling, and I know that some day you will be a great person, especially if you will take advice without resentment or irritation. Practice makes perfect. You know that.

"Love was the thing that freed me from nagging uncertainty, allowing me to do my job better than the next kid," Shirley wrote in her memoir, evoking a child who felt bolstered even as she was buffeted by film industry demands. Philippa had a mother who was running the show and who felt she couldn't afford New Deal–style solicitude, or the pretense of it. No child welfare inspectors, waving labor regulations, were going to pay surprise visits to their Harlem apartment. Still, Josephine wanted to explain the relentless promotion and performance, and practice, in the scrapbook that Philippa would ultimately read. "I realize, darling, that these contests are often stupid and I know many educators disapprove of them," she began. "But here is why I persist":

1. George and Jody have nothing to give you save opportunity. And because we have refused to be conventional in our way of life, opportunity will not come to us unsought. We must seek the best for you, go out and get it or it will pass us by. We, and especially you, are a challenge to the set notions of America on race. These prejudices, erected to justify a diabolical system of exploitation of man by his fellow man, will not easily give way. Only genius will break them down, and that you have. So I take you about as much for the education of America as for the education of Philippa.

2. Aside from all this, it is good training in social conduct for you. You learn to meet new people in a friendly, charming fashion, to do your part under all circumstances. . . .

4. Finally, I heartily wish my parents had given me the kind of help I'm giving you. As I look back, I see how I longed to be important, to be taken seriously, to be given a way of life, pointed a road that was interesting. Instead, I was given money, social position and treated like a baby. I loathed it.

Her manifesto was far more forthright than Fox Film's pseudo-child-friendly contract, and deeply unsettling. Josephine didn't shrink from exposing the instrumental zeal behind elevating a child as an emissary of anything—whether racial enlightenment or uplifting (and lucrative) entertainment or a parent's thwarted dreams. In Josephine's case, all three were at stake. She didn't invoke the familiar defense of child-star labor either—that it was easy and educationally approved. She knew that a biracial girl couldn't win over a wary public with mere bubbly spirits. And lurking in Josephine's insistence on taking a hardworking child seriously was in fact a respect that Shirley, for one, yearned for.

Yet the effect, all but inevitable, was to erode Philippa's sense of autonomy. Not that the wider world could tell. At seven, Philippa thrived as she took composition and singing classes at the esteemed Convent Music School not far from their Harlem apartment. She also started spending several hours a day in fourth grade, the only black child at the Annunciation School, on the same campus grounds. ("If I just wanted to play games I could go to the park," Philippa had said in choosing it over a progressive school for the gifted. "But I want to learn something every day.") Assessing her "social relationships," her glowing school report described a "sunny, attractive child" who was "very mature . . . quite a favorite in the group." On the "mental hygiene" front, she was judged "fully secure in her home relationship, perfectly confident in her contacts with

PHILIPPA SCHUYLER

her child world." The faculty wished that Philippa could spend more time there.

The school's view was based, of course, on very partial exposure—which was precisely the problem. Ceding control of Philippa's training and development to other formative figures threatened Josephine's sense of importance and the Schuylers' project. A succession of piano teachers counseled against so much concertizing so soon, only to be fired or to quit when Josephine flouted them. So again and again Philippa lost her chance to forge a trusting bond with a teacher and to discover for herself, as Shirley had, the rewards of discipline and a sense of independence. Arnetta Jones was no Bill Robinson. But she and the other young women teachers whom Josephine lined up were impressive.

More important, they were dedicated to a child who was, as one of them put it, "just the most delicious thing" and "musically . . . like a sponge," with a phenomenal memory and extraordinarily strong, supple hands. Philippa adored them, too—yet "nagging uncertainty," in Shirley's words, undermined her. Josephine pushed; Philippa's audiences applauded; her teachers pushed back, eager to help her improve not just perform. Defensive about being corrected and desperate for unqualified allegiance, Philippa tested her teachers, not just her mother. With a dramatic flair she had picked up from Josephine, one day she accused a favorite teacher of not loving her (after some criticism of her playing). Philippa then rushed out, threatening to throw herself off the roof. Josephine rolled her eyes at what she said were mere antics. The teacher resigned on the spot.

Yet in the prescribed "friendly, charming fashion," Philippa continued to do her part in the world. Now almost nine, she played on "Philippa Schuyler Day" in June 1940 at the World's Fair in New York, which Josephine lobbied to have inserted into a packed schedule of specially dedicated days. (Bill Robinson was the only other black American so honored.) That same month, the Chicago-based *Quiz Kids* radio show debuted, and she was invited to "out quiz" the brainy young contestants, submitting questions. When *The New Yorker*'s Joseph Mitchell interviewed Philippa for a profile later that summer, he was captivated by her beauty and childish, riddle-telling verve. Her parents unobtrusively gave him a look at the scrapbooks they had been keeping, where he read of her incessant curiosity. "If there's any pushing done," Josephine told Mitchell as he left the apartment, "she's the one that does it."

When Josephine and George shared the scrapbooks with Philippa on her thirteenth birthday, she confronted fourteen portfolio-size folders that revealed her whole life to have been their scripted project. The timing couldn't have been worse, struggling as she already was to find her voice and place. She and her mother were just back from a "sabbatical" in Mexico. There Philippa had tackled her first orchestral composition, Josephine's new gambit for public attention. The piece, *Manhattan Nocturne,* was full of homesickness, the work of a girl who was feeling unmoored. Her mother had intimated that her beloved father, who had stayed behind to take care of the cats, was an unfaithful husband. En route to Mexico, Josephine hadn't taken Philippa with her to visit her family in Texas; her exile from that clan was clear. The scrapbooks exiled her from her own life. In the nightmares Philippa kept having, she yearned for suicide. She felt that she was no one, and she had nowhere to turn for solace. She had been left stranded without intimates—except for one, the mother who was sure that she had made Philippa into Someone.

In her loneliness, Philippa drove herself ever harder, reared to "do her part under all circumstances." The daunting obstacles that face any adolescent in the merciless world of concert performance were compounded for her. Now she recognized the "vicious barriers of prejudice" she was up against. "It was a ruthless shock to me that, at first, made the walls of my self-confidence crumble," she wrote later. "It horrified, humiliated me." The creative spur of turning to composition proved fruitful. Still, she suffered corrosive anxiety. She was newly aware "of the weighty importance of each concert."

The performance of her *Manhattan Nocturne* at a New York Philharmonic Young People's Concert in 1945 was greeted as a remarkable composing debut, "truly poetic, the expression of genuine feeling, a gentle, soft beauty and imagination," one reviewer wrote. For Philippa, almost fourteen, it was an ordeal that stirred up all "the uncertainties, confusion, anger, months of revision, hundreds of wee morning hours spent laboriously copying out scores and parts." The next year, shortly before she was to appear with the New York Philharmonic at Lewisohn Stadium as the soloist in Saint-Saëns's Piano Concerto in G and as the composer of the *Rumpelstiltskin* scherzo from her *Fairy Tale Symphony*, a new work, she told an interviewer: "I have to work now so that when I get older I'll be able to enjoy life really then." Her scherzo betrayed none of her travails. It was "expertly written," *The New York Times* judged, "with a broad melodic core that has genuine charm."

Philippa didn't let up on the work, and as she approached sixteen after a run of spectacular success, she seemed to relax. She even went on a few dates. Radiating beauty, she conveyed enjoyment and confidence as she talked to the press. Her *Manhattan Nocturne* and *Rumpelstiltskin* had won prizes and received premier exposure—played by the Boston Pops, and the Detroit, Chicago, and San Francisco Symphony Orchestras, along with the New York Philharmonic. Praise from the composer and discerning critic Virgil Thomson was just the kind that a maturing prodigy wants to hear. "She plays music, not Philippa Schuyler, even when she performs her own compositions," he wrote in the *New York Herald Tribune*. "And she gets inside any piece with conviction." He saw a "real gift for . . . saying things with music" in her *Fairy Tale Symphony*, which he found as interesting as the symphonies Mozart wrote at thirteen.

Philippa's rebound didn't last. In 1948 Josephine struggled to line up mostly black sponsors, hoping in vain for mixed audiences for the national tour she was busy arranging. "Do you know how many blacks took piano lessons because of Philippa?" the sociologist Hylan Lewis later said. Crossover allure, though, proved elusive. Josephine was also very worried about money, not just for Philippa's lessons but for the managerial salary she had been drawing for years. "You can make anything you prepare for" was a maternal mantra that gave Philippa plenty of room to torture her mother and herself. "She sits all day at the piano, won't eat," Josephine wrote George from the road. "Says she is too busy, or it makes her tired or sick to eat. She plays the scales over and over. . . . I am really low in spirit. There is no satisfaction in this for me when she is so cold and demanding, so irritable and exacting."

George's income had ebbed as he swerved rightward politically, but by 1949 he was worrying over Philippa's manic practicing and her single-minded pursuit of soaring goals. "Ten hours a day is entirely too much for anybody to work at music or anything else. . . . This is especially so where a person does *nothing else,*" he wrote to Josephine, who was increasingly estranged and often depressed.

> Philippa is ruining her girlhood with too serious application and other fool notions. She needs to have more optimism, hopefulness and buoyancy, and stop so much damn worrying about the future. It is especially silly at 18. Success is not a career or money, it is inner peace and smiling contentment and a minimum of grandiose illusions.

If George was hoping to exert any influence or enlighten his wife, he was way too late.

It was not the last time that Philippa came close to "breaking under the strain," as she put it. Her confidence shaken by more encounters with American prejudice, and her self-reliance eroded by her mother's insistent demands, Philippa "adjusted," she wrote. "I left." In 1952, the year she turned twenty-one, she embarked on a Caribbean tour without Josephine, who was soon urging her to return to play U.S. concerts. "STAYING. AM COMMITTED. PRACTICING EIGHT NINE HOURS DAILY. EXCEEDING WORK SCHEDULE. LEARNING PIECES," Philippa telegrammed in response. The American tour sponsor "CAN'T RULE MY LIFE. . . . CARAMBA. THATS BEEN TROUBLE. EVERYBODY WANTED MAKE ME PUPPET." It was the start of a peripatetic performing career abroad, which took Philippa to South and Central America, Europe, Latin America, and Africa over the next decade and a half. She plunged into mixed-race cultures, often barely skirting real danger amid political violence—and always practicing tirelessly. She found welcoming audiences, and also critics for whom her roiling style revealed more need than art. Returning home to face prejudice and maternal pressure firsthand, she would set off again.

An intrepid spirit, perhaps as much as particular talents, had marked out both Shirley and Philippa in childhood. Remarkably, neither of them lost it. Philippa lived for high drama, vainly seeking love and subsisting on little money and sleep as she struggled to assert her independence and forge an identity. Josephine never stopped hounding her, sending long letters when she was away, intruding on her daughter's ill-fated romances, too. "Do you realize what you are expecting of me?" Philippa, now almost thirty, wrote her in 1960.

> Are you aware of the pressures you put me under? Are you aware of the impossibilities you ask of me?
>
> To be a great pianist.
> To be a great composer.
> To be a great arranger.
> To be a great author.
> To be a great journalist.
> To always get marvellous reviews.
> To always pull off marvellous coups no one else could do.
> To get good photographs everywhere. . . .
> To always make money, and always keep within my
>   budget. . . .
> To always be a great beauty.
> This is beyond human capability.

Yet even as she and her mother continued to torment each other, Philippa refused to be constrained by perfectionist caution. That same year, in a quasi-memoir about her travels that had begun as a novel, she struck a very different note. She made a point of embracing "the turmoils, threats, hazards, uncertainties, of this age"—and of her own life so far. "I am not sorry that I was a child prodigy. There is so much to learn, and so little time in which to learn it," she wrote. A similar declaration of mettle had been Shirley's on-screen message, one that she had taken to heart in life. Philippa meant it, too, in the face of far more daunting lessons. She portrayed a young woman avidly taking risks, encountering strangers, crossing social boundaries.

"Youth is brave and wants to do battle," she insisted, a sentiment the prodigies in the previous pages all endorsed, in their own way. That included combat with elders, who tended to be crusader types themselves. Philippa was very much her parents' daughter even in her often embittered quest to chart a path beyond their vision of her as the biracial artist who would be a bridge between races. Not unlike the young Josephine in flight from Texas, Philippa was a radical shapeshifter, going so far as to shed her black lineage to try out a European onstage persona by the name of Felipa Monterro in the early 1960s. Following in her father's footsteps, Philippa flouted caution and convention as she fit reportorial writing into her travels. Her work included two books about Africa, which shared George's by now very conservative views and anti-Communist zeal. She wrote pro-war dispatches from Vietnam.

But she saw her country's blindness, too. Stunned by prejudice against black GIs and Asians in Vietnam, Philippa became more disillusioned than ever about American racial attitudes. She cofounded an organization to aid "half-castes" fathered by Americans. And she was determined to help evacuate children from a Catholic orphanage in central Vietnam to safety farther south. She had postponed her return to the United States several times, despite her mother's pleas, when the helicopter transporting her and a group of orphans went down in the South China Sea on May 9, 1967. Philippa drowned at thirty-five. Two years later, on May 2, Josephine committed suicide.

That future in which Philippa would "enjoy life really" had kept receding from her. When Shirley Temple discovered that she had been deprived of a fortune, forgiveness was her assertion of freedom. But Philippa Schuyler never escaped the sense that she was owed big, because she was. She could be exceptional, or else invisible: that was the brutal deal offered by a mother who failed to recognize a child's need to feel that she is lovable. A bigoted country confirmed a third option: however phenomenal she was, Philippa would be a perpetual outsider. When Josephine sent her grown daughter a benediction of sorts in the early 1960s, she had no idea how heartless it sounded—or how heartbreaking it would seem in retrospect. "We have tried to make you important. We have been as diligent and sincere on this end as you have on your end," she wrote Philippa.

> However, I can see why you are tired, it was a great ordeal, a tremendous task, which you carried out with great triumph and ingenuity. . . . YOU WERE PART OF HISTORY.
>
> Now, we can make this the end of all such attempts to capture public interest. . . . You have become a world figure. . . . Now, you can do as you wish with the future.

PART III

———————

REBELS

with

CAUSES

CHAPTER 5

Bobby Fischer's Battles

· 1 ·

Bobby Fischer, born on March 9, 1943, gave his single mother, Regina, a hard time starting very early. He wasn't easy on his sister either. Joan, five years older and unusually smart and responsible, was often left in charge. One rainy day when Bobby was six, she got tired of his fits at Parcheesi. The family had just settled into a cheap apartment on East Thirteenth Street in Manhattan after moving around the country during the previous half decade. At the candy store nearby, Joan bought a plastic chess set. She wasn't familiar with the game, but it seemed promising: Bobby liked puzzles a lot, and didn't like outcomes determined by a roll of the dice at all. Several years later, after they had moved again, to Flatbush—and Bobby had bounced unhappily among schools—his mother began walking him over to the Brooklyn Chess Club, where he would tug on the trousers of the club regulars. Never looking the men in the eye, Bobby would ask, "Wanna have a game?" And then he would set out to win. When he did, one grandmaster remembered, his eyes "flooded with maniacal glee."

In January 1958 Bobby, by then fourteen and a (lousy) student at Erasmus Hall High School, won very big. Three months after the Soviets' launch of *Sputnik* sparked educational panic in America, he became the youngest U.S. champion in a brainy game long dominated by the Russians. In "a football country, a baseball country," as Bobby later put it, his stunning rise was not immediately national news. On the television quiz show *I've Got a Secret* shortly after his triumph, he held up a mock newspaper emblazoned with the headline "Teenager's Strategy Defeats All Comers." Who was this gangly Mr. X, with dark circles under his eyes, notable for some sort of combative prowess and clearly uncomfortable in front of the cameras? The panelists took turns probing. Did his pursuit make other people happy? one of them asked. Bobby's answer— "It made *me* happy"—got a laugh out of the audience (in on the secret). The panel was mystified.

For viewers who might have lately tuned in to the *Quiz Kids* on TV (a brief stab at reviving the popular wartime radio show in a new medium), Bobby was a reticent contrast to the adorably ency-clopedic prodigies earning prize money to pay for college. What few words he said definitely didn't fit the adult-pleasing wunder-kind image cultivated over the course of the preceding half century either. Bobby, the antithesis of Shirley Temple in every way, may call to mind William Sidis—with the big difference that the wary loner in Brooklyn proceeded to become, of course, a huge success. More than that, Bobby insisted on calling the shots almost from the start and got away with it. His parent was the one who felt intimi-dated. That kids-are-boss power shift is likely to make Bobby seem not unfamiliar, particularly if your family life is scheduled around a young sports fanatic—though nobody could match Bobby's single-minded, unwavering focus. He was an unprecedented handful.

Regina was trying her best, however, to broaden her obsessive son's horizons. That was how Bobby got roped into appearing on *I've Got a Secret,* one of whose sponsors was Sabena Airlines. When nobody guessed his feat, he walked away with a prize in the form of two round-trip plane tickets to Russia. He was dying to see Soviet chess up close—to play their stars and visit the Young Pio-neer Palaces where the nation's, and world's, best young talent was incubated. Eager to expose her very bright children to foreign cul-ture and language, Regina was all for it. (Maybe Bobby would pick up new interests and buckle down at school, too.) But she couldn't possibly afford it, so she had wangled him a spot on the show. Now, with Joan enlisted as chaperone, the summer trip was on.

The Fischer family was right in step with Cold War zeal to play educational catch-up. At the same time, characteristically, mother and son were marching to their own drummers. That fall Congress passed the National Defense Education Act, a response to *Sputnik*-inspired fears that a streamlined Soviet system of top-down talent development threatened the strategic superiority of the United States. The time had come to boost federal support for college study of science, math, and foreign languages in particular. The following year Harvard's former president James Bryant Conant published *The American High School Today,* a best seller. An early champion of the SAT for a fast-expanding pool of college applicants, he urged greater academic rigor for gifted, test-acing achievers, along with general education for all.

The prewar message, sounded in different ways by prodigy promoters like Boris Sidis and Lewis Terman (and by Hollywood studios, too), had gotten through: young marvels, far from misfits, were ripe for newly systematic sorting and tending. Except Bobby bucked the trend in a well-timed way. Just when the meritocratic mission was catching on, here was a stubborn genius scripting his own rise off on the cultural margins. (No one would have imagined the weekend-consuming enterprise that scholastic chess has since become.) The democratic allure of a boy blazing a path into a field the enemy considered its own—not space, but chess—was hard to resist. What if this fiercely competitive young maverick could out-play the apparatchiks—without a Soviet-style machine assiduously training a cadre of high-ranked stars? The optics were exciting, even if the facts were potentially disconcerting.

In the corduroy pants, T-shirts, and cheap sneakers he always wore, Bobby with his blondish buzz cut and hazel eyes looked like an all-American boy. When a smile appeared, he seemed to beam. But that was mostly because a grin was rare, breaking through the scowl of a very prickly youth. Aloof arrogance, not dimpled confidence, was his signature. Unlike his prodigy predecessors, he stirred no concern that he might be subject to undue "forcing" by blinkered parents or mentors. Quite the contrary. Bobby, a forerunner of young computer-era upstarts, bucked authority. Inseparable from his pocket chess set, he said he needed no friends, and he bridled at adults—above all his mother—who presumed to hover or hound or just help. His IQ was sky-high, but he dismissed school as a place for "weakies" and a distraction from chess. He dropped out as soon as he could, at sixteen.

By then, Bobby had already made disruptive public scenes in the United States and abroad. His story, for all its rebel-with-a-cause allure, did not neatly vindicate a democratic approach to talent development, as the Soviets took pleasure in noting. Long before his paranoid retreat as an adult, Bobby's obstinate spirit and obsessive temperament spelled trouble—as well as spectacular accomplishments. His elders' attempts, such as they were, to encourage wider interests were a mixed blessing, too. And were their hearts really in those efforts anyway? This driven teenager, after all, looked like he just might be the one to rout the Russians. In any case, nudges toward well-rounded balance served only to fuel Bobby's monomaniacal focus—for good and for ill.

· 2 ·

Regina Wender Fischer exerted greater influence on Bobby than she recognized. She didn't, of course, choose the genes she passed on. She would have said her guidance, both as a role model and as a concerned mother, got ignored. More to the point, it routinely backfired: Bobby *did* take cues from her, and then typically proceeded to do the opposite. In his remarkably energetic defiance of help or direction, except on his own terms, the apple didn't fall far from the tree.

Shortly after he was born, Regina took up residence at the Sarah Hackett Memorial House for indigent single mothers in Chicago and promptly broke the rules: she tried to sneak in five-year-old Joan (who had been staying with her grandfather Jacob Wender in St. Louis during Regina's pregnancy). Regina then refused to leave and was arrested for disturbing the peace. A year earlier, when dire straits had led her to try placing Joan with a foster mother, she had run into trouble, too. The woman returned Joan and quietly reported Regina as a possible spy, her suspicions aroused by various items she found in a box of clothes—a high-quality camera and a letter from a leftist friend, among other things. The FBI opened a file on Regina. Agents keeping tabs on her got a copy of the psychiatric report that was ordered when she waived a trial after her Chicago arrest. The prognosis sounds discouraging: "Stilted (paranoid) personality, querulent [*sic*] but not psychotic. . . . It is difficult to see how she can unravel the complexities of her personal life. It is obvious that she will continue to refuse any agency or counsel."

The examiner underestimated her (and two decades of FBI surveillance, the extent of which she never knew, perhaps casts her paranoia in a different light). Regina, who stares out of photographs with dark-eyed intensity and gamine appeal, wasn't trying to unravel complexities. She was a remarkably restless woman who sought them out. Born in 1913 in Switzerland to Polish parents who were Jewish, she had grown up in the United States and speedily, if circuitously, graduated from college in her teens: she studied at three different universities. She headed to Berlin at nineteen to study some more, and met a German biophysicist, Gerhardt Fischer. She followed him to the Soviet Union, where he—evidently a Communist—was perhaps a Comintern agent. They married, and Regina began studying medicine in Moscow. Not long after Joan's birth in 1937 and before she finished her degree, Regina left and was en route to the United States in early 1939. Her husband, denied entry, ended up in Chile.

Regina bounced among cities and jobs, from schoolteacher to shipyard welder, taking whatever work she could get and often studying as well. (She ended up knowing six languages, several fluently, and she dabbled in Yiddish.) She paused long enough in Denver to have a brief liaison with a Hungarian mechanical engineer and mathematician teaching nearby, Paul Nemenyi. Bobby's birth certificate listed Fischer as his father (and Regina told a social worker her son was conceived during a rendezvous in Mexico with

her husband in 1942), but the evidence points strongly to Nemenyi. Regina apparently considered putting Bobby up for adoption
but couldn't bring herself to do it—or to settle down.

She kept the FBI busy. There were no subversive plots to
unearth, but just tracking her whereabouts was time-consuming:
Chicago, Oregon, St. Louis, California, Illinois, Arizona, Idaho
(where she officially divorced Gerhardt Fischer from afar in 1945).
Always scrounging for work and money, she turned to Jewish family agencies in various places for financial aid but not, it seems,
for counsel or other help with the children. Nemenyi weighed in
from a distance. In 1946 and 1947, according to the FBI records,
he told one agency that he "considered the subject to be mentally
upset and also described Robert as an 'upset child.'" To another
agency, he portrayed Regina as a "driving and aggressive person."
The social worker wasn't sure how to weigh his concerns, judging
him "somewhat of a 'paranoid type.'" (Clarissa and Henry Cowell's peregrinations forty years earlier, though the pair were similarly hard up, were an idyll by comparison.) All Bobby ever said
he remembered about these years was living in a trailer "out west."

Not long after they arrived in Manhattan in 1949, Joan resorted
to the chess set. She and her brother figured out the rules together,
but for Bobby chess wasn't an instant passion. Nor did he get the
sort of warm home support for playful exploration that can help
launch a youthful talent. Joan's interest flagged, and Regina, whom
Bobby then taught to play, was terrible at it. "My mother has an
anti-talent for chess," Bobby later said. "She's hopeless." Working
on her skills was not a priority, as Regina scrambled to earn a living and keep up her leftist political activities—and send her son to
summer camp. During either his first season out on Long Island,
when he was six, or the next one, Bobby stumbled on a book of
annotated chess games. For a boy with an evident antitalent for
friendship, it offered some comfort—but not enough. "MOMMY
I WANT TO COME HOME," Bobby wrote in big letters on a
prestamped and addressed postcard.

Regina had been looking for a cheaper rental in Brooklyn, and a
fight with the Tenants League in which she had been active precip-

itated a departure from Manhattan. (The FBI, never sure whether she belonged to the Communist Party, wondered if the fight got her expelled.) The chess set, minus some pieces, ended up in the closet of the apartment off Eastern Parkway where the Fischers moved in 1950. Bobby, cooped up and lonely, made a game of jumping off the bed (until the landlord complained). His Brooklyn school debut did not go well. Regina was in school herself, now juggling nursing classes with stenography jobs and her political work. At one point, as was noted in her FBI file, she picketed in defense of a "colored family" that had been forced out of a building. She was a member of a group called American Women for Peace and of the International Workers Order, too.

Regina sounds a lot like Mrs. Jellyby in Dickens's *Bleak House,* busy saving the world while her family foundered. Certainly neither peace nor order prevailed in her personal life, at least from what the FBI's neighborhood informants could tell. They variously described her as "antagonistic" and "argumentative," a litigious woman with a "suit complex." Someone else later said she was a "real pain in the neck." A more sympathetic source, who had evidently talked rather than merely tangled with her, reported that Regina was "an unstable, mixed up person who cannot settle on one objective. . . . She advised that the subject has moved about considerably and appears to encounter difficulty in everything she does."

That her son posed special problems was obvious to all—including Regina. Very unlike Mrs. Jellyby, she was doing her maternal best with few resources, and Joan, a conscientious honors student, could help only so much. By the time he reached fourth grade, Bobby had been in and out of six schools, unable or unwilling to engage with peers or seatwork, or homework, despite Joan and Regina's efforts. He was obviously very bright, so Regina tried a school for gifted children, where he lasted a day; he refused to go back. Bobby, small for his age but with an oversize will, was impossible to budge. For Christmas in 1950, he had asked for a new chess set. Almost eight, Bobby was soon as preoccupied as his busy mother and sister. He had found an all-absorbing way to tune out both their well-meant bugging and their absences.

In the most cerebral of games, he discovered an intricately rule-bound realm where a young mind can make phenomenal progress with no life experience. As fertile ground for prodigies goes, few pursuits supply better. Glacially though it moves, chess also rewards deep competitive urges, luring in the restless and the driven: there are more positional variations in the game than atoms in the solar system. Maybe by this stage, the fact that his mother and sister *weren't* interested served as a goad. For an uncooperative, uprooted boy who needed rules yet thrived on obstacles, the fit was obvious. "Thought that leads nowhere, mathematics that add up to nothing, art without an end product, architecture without substance": Stefan Zweig's appraisal of chess in his novella *The Royal Game* evoked the uncompromising purity of its allure.

Regina, having lived in Russia, surely appreciated the game's cultural lineage and aura, but mainly it bought peace in the apartment—and she was pleased that Bobby was no longer so stuck on comics. Right away, though, she worried about his isolation. Energetic organizer that she was, she wrote to the *Brooklyn Daily Eagle* (the newspaper that had made Nathalia Crane famous), seeking young opponents for "my little chess miracle," as she referred to him. Who knows what might have happened anywhere else, but Brooklyn was the chess-rich corner of the U.S. chess capital. In January 1951 the *Eagle*'s septuagenarian chess editor suggested she take her son to the nearby Grand Army Plaza library the following week, where several masters were holding a simultaneous exhibition. Soon to turn eight but still looking like a six-year-old, Bobby went with his new chess set in hand and found himself face-to-face with the pipe-smoking former champion of Scotland and New York State. "He crushed me," Bobby said out loud fifteen minutes later, and burst into tears.

Whether or not you credit the notion of a "crystallizing experience," the phrase psychologists have coined for early destiny-defining moments in some high-achieving lives, a defeat that might have been a deterrent for anyone else proved a catalyst for Bobby. Carmine Nigro, the newly elected president of the Brooklyn Chess Club, had been watching. He liked Bobby's sensible moves and his intense concentration. When Nigro learned Bobby had no father, he invited him to stop by the club any Tuesday or Friday night—never mind that children, the world over, were generally barred from such premises. Regina's effort to drum up peers had failed, but Bobby landed in peculiar company he found very congenial. His mother in tow, he proceeded to show up regularly and lose constantly.

H. G. Wells's caricature of the chessboard-obsessed breed as "shadowy, unhappy, unreal-looking men," however overstated, helps explain why things clicked. A field that took precocious talent in stride—then six-time U.S. champion Samuel Reshevsky, for example, had arrived as an eight-year-old prodigy from Poland in 1920—offered the right welcome for a boy like Bobby: gruff mentors lacking in interventionist zeal and overtly solicitous guidance. With little fuss, Bobby started going over to Nigro's house on Saturdays to share in lessons with his son Tommy, slightly younger and better at chess. (For Regina, often on weekend nursing duty, the new routine was a godsend.) The boys didn't become friends, but while Tommy bridled at paternal tutelage, Bobby bore down. He wouldn't have admitted he was doing it to please Nigro, and he probably wasn't. Leaving Tommy in the dust was perhaps an impetus. Sometimes Nigro took Bobby to Washington Square Park to face speedier players in the hustler scene there. In his first competition, early in 1952, Bobby emerged with a win and a draw.

That still left afternoons and non-chess-club evenings for a loner who before long was a latchkey child. ("I may get back after 3 to drop off groceries, and will then go back to study," Regina jotted in a note she left in the kitchen.) Bobby, by now an avid reader of chess books, became enough of a fixture at the Grand Army Plaza library that its 1952 newsletter included a captioned photo of him. When Joan or Regina returned to the apartment, they sometimes found him at the board in the gloom, the lamps not switched on. Bobby took refuge in his room when his mother had political friends over, as she often did. He went out several times with another visitor, a heavily accented and rumpled fellow: before his early death in 1952, Nemenyi stopped by on trips up from D.C. where, after a succession of short-term teaching stints, he had found a job as an engineer at the Naval Research Laboratory. Apparently at Regina's insistence, he didn't reveal his identity to Bobby. But a former prodigy himself (Nemenyi had shared first place in a national math and physics competition in Hungary as a teenager), he surely talked chess with him. And the man who had once been advised by a fellow émigré to mend his disheveled ways passed on a social nicety that Bobby always remembered. It's polite to break your roll before buttering it, Nemenyi told him when they were out at a restaurant together.

By the fall of 1952, Regina had found a small progressive school for Bobby, Brooklyn Community Woodward, where learning revolved around a student's special interest and, no less important from his point of view, you could "get up and walk around the room if you wanted." Bobby's IQ of 180 and an agreement to teach chess to other students won him a scholarship. It would be great to report that he sparked a chess fad, but he didn't. The thrilling development was getting picked for the school baseball team. Bobby, who lived mere blocks from Ebbets Field, now had another, more physical sport on his short list of interests. He mostly ignored his classwork, but his teachers were struck by his competitive zeal. "He *had* to come out ahead of everybody," whatever the game, one of them later told a reporter. "If he had been born next to a swimming pool he would have been a swimming champion." A photo of Bobby around this time suggests a boy quite pleased with his setup. He is sitting in the bathtub, a chess game in progress on a board laid across the tub and a milk carton by one hand. His other arm reaches up to touch a bare foot resting on his hair: Regina is nudging him to get out. He doubtless protests, but he is smiling.

Regina was worrying. Bobby had settled on one objective, just what his mother had trouble doing, and he pursued it with much the same zeal Regina dispersed among her various left-wing causes and her classes. (The FBI files note that Teachers College, yet one more place she studied, put her on a "special list" because of "her continued refusal to accept guidance and her attempts to change

BOBBY FISCHER

the . . . school curriculum to suit her personal whims.") She was all for studiousness, but Bobby was absorbed with his pocket chess set even at breakfast. Nigro lent him chess magazines. Teachers recalled his pockets bulging with copies of the Russian chess publication *Shakhmaty,* which Regina surely helped him begin to decipher—at least here was a new skill. Then he plowed on himself. He demanded she take him to Washington Square Park to play. Cowed, and probably guilty about leaving him alone so much, she obeyed.

Regina's efforts unwittingly followed what before long became a postwar talent development formula—pick up on a child's interest, and seek out high-caliber guides and enriching contexts. But stardom wasn't her aim, and the problem she hoped to solve had gotten worse. Chess drew Bobby out of the apartment, only to pull him into an obsessive, largely self-driven pursuit of specialization that meant he did ever less schoolwork—and that increasingly cut him off from the world. Now she set about trying to limit his fixation, yet her new undertaking carried the same risk. Bobby, who bore down harder in the face of impediments, was a self-made prodigy with a vengeance.

"For four years I tried everything to discourage him," Regina later said, "but it was hopeless." Carmine Nigro was not much of an ally in her mission, being a chess fanatic himself, although he had brief success in encouraging another pursuit. He gave Bobby accordion lessons until Bobby decided he couldn't spare the time away from chess. Regina somehow got Bobby to see a psychiatrist, Dr. Kline, in 1952. (How she afforded it is a mystery, too; she was struggling to put decent meals on the table.) But when asked why he spent so many hours at the board, Bobby was curt. "I don't know. I just go for it." Dr. Kline reassured Regina it was a phase. She turned to another psychiatrist, a chess master himself. He didn't predict an ebbing of the obsession—he admitted *he* hadn't shaken it—but told her that as passions go, chess was a worthy one and Bobby needed to find his own way.

His mother's mounting resistance helped ensure Bobby's intensifying persistence between the ages of nine and thirteen—just the surge of commitment that growing ranks of talent developers were soon insisting should be attentively encouraged. Bobby did it his way. Nothing dissuaded him, not being nagged by his mother or getting regularly beaten at the Brooklyn Chess Club. Both girded him for further battle. And then he began to win against his elders.

"When I was eleven, I just got good," Fischer later said, and the surge probably did feel as much like wizardry as the fruit of tenacity. In fact, Bobby was anything but a case of spontaneous mastery, or even of superspeedy takeoff. Congenital zealotry was key, and as was true for his prodigy predecessors, cultural timing proved unpredictably propitious. Bobby's hard-earned leap in skill happened to coincide with a thrilling external goad: in June 1954 Nigro took him to watch the Americans play the Soviet chess team for the first time on home turf, the largest chess event in U.S. history. He was rapt through all four days in the grand ballroom of the first hotel he had ever stepped into, the Roosevelt. He meticulously kept score as the Americans were trounced, 20–12. Bobby had discovered the best chess players in the world—the men to beat.

In the U.S. chess world, the Cold War overtones of the contest stirred professional envy more than political animus. Of course, the Americans didn't stand a chance, an editorial in *Chess Life* lamented. They were mere amateurs in a country that had no stake in the game. In the USSR, chess was a national mission, as *The New York Times* emphasized, too: "They are out to win for the greater glory of the Soviet Union. To do so means public acclaim at home, propaganda victories abroad." Since the mid-1920s the Soviets had been promoting chess as ideal training for the proletarian mind and, as a Soviet chess chronicler put it, "indisputable proof of the superiority of socialist culture over the declining culture of capitalist societies." After a brief interlude of American chess dominance while the Soviets were absent from the international Olympiads, in 1945 the Russians triumphed in a tournament played over the radio. U.S. strength dwindled in the late 1940s. A top player, Reuben Fine, quit to pursue his psychoanalytic career, and the former U.S. champion Samuel Reshevsky scaled back. In the USSR, meanwhile, the number of registered chess players grew to a million by the 1950s, and elite ranks surged.

A rising young Soviet chess talent had every opportunity on a path that would have struck Regina as ideal—the answer to all her problems with her headstrong, lopsided son. Bobby's future opponent for the world championship, Boris Spassky, who was six years older, was also the son of a single mother. She was so poor that she resorted to digging potatoes in Leningrad. As a lonely nine-year-old looking for entertainment, Boris spent the summer of 1946 watching games in a chess pavilion and fell in love, he said, with the white queen: "I dreamed about caressing her in my pocket." On his own, Boris found his way to the local Young Pioneer Palace, where he shared his passion with peers and entered a national system of expert instruction and competition.

He was taken under the wing of a senior chess coach who prescribed physical exercise (swimming and skating) as well as cultural exposure (opera and ballet), along with rigorous chess training. A steady dose of patriotic songs and ideological indoctrination rounded out the regimen. At eleven, Boris was still bursting into tears whenever he lost, but he was also bringing in the family paycheck: he earned a monthly state stipend higher than the average salary of an engineer. In the early 1950s, Boris moved on to other coaches. They taught him life skills—table manners, how to knot ties—along with chess strategy. By then they knew the ideological lessons weren't taking, but Boris mostly got away with his barely disguised disdain for the Party. By 1955, at eighteen, he had won the World Junior Championship.

That same summer of 1955, when Bobby was twelve, his chess regimen was a patchwork of his own making. He had no coach, but for several years he had been coaxed out of his shyness and exposed to new chess circles. Regina wanted to send him off to camp again, as she had for some part of every summer since he was six. He had come to at least love the chance to swim, but this time he refused. Nigro, who never expected to be paid, was ready to initiate Bobby into a new level of tournament play. Over Memorial Day weekend they drove to a Westchester County resort for the U.S. Amateur Championship. Bobby was nervous and tried to back out as they approached. Regina would have been overjoyed to hear him suggesting they instead make the most of the amenities, like tennis. Nigro pushed, sensing how much Bobby feared losing.

Bobby did fare badly. Nigro's advice, though, left an imprint on the player whose "fighting spirit," as Garry Kasparov has said, became a signature. He shouldn't expect to win every game, Nigro reassured him—just to play his best in each game. Or, as Kasparov summed up Bobby's version of the bromide, play "every game to the death, as if it were his last." At summer's end, he entered a tournament held in Washington Square Park that continued into the fall, sometimes crying when he lost (though he later denied it). He hung on, making his way up the ladder as a rainy chill set in, and placed fifteenth. Nigro would slip away and bring him back a burger, fries, and a chocolate shake. Never looking up from the board, Bobby ate. One day, half an hour after finishing his lunch, Bobby whispered, still focused on the board, "Mr. Nigro, when is the food coming?"

By then, Bobby had spent almost his entire summer at the

Manhattan Chess Club, the strongest club in the country. Founded eighty years earlier, it was a mecca for serious chess players, and Bobby's arrival there unfolded like a too-good-to-be-true screenplay. He and Nigro had been out rowing on the Central Park Lake; the boy, he felt, could use a change of scene, and his shoulders needed some beefing up. Spotting the plaque on the club's Central Park South building, Bobby asked to go in. He quickly defeated two opponents, attracting a crowd. The men who gathered were impressed at the way he could take in the whole board. Bobby's blitz games were enough to prompt one of the club's directors to introduce him to the president, a millionaire garment maker, who offered him a free junior membership. Bobby, the youngest member the club had ever admitted, quickly became a star in the weekly speed tournaments and moved out of the club's lowest group of players. The club regulars discovered this not-quite-teenager had phe-

BOBBY WITH HIS MOTHER

nomenal stamina, too. Bobby would arrive at the club in the early afternoon, and at midnight Regina picked him up (he cringed) for the subway ride home.

With the well-timed appearance of Nigro in his life, as much friend as teacher, yet with no systematic training, Bobby had cultivated an intense dedication to the game that rivaled the best-paid Soviet prospect's prescribed chess discipline—and that lacked any of the balance the Russians emphasized. In a picture Joan snapped in a subway car, probably after one of his long days at the club, Bobby is asleep with his head on his mother's shoulder. Regina is smiling, perhaps just a little uneasily. A woman seated nearby gazes fondly their way, with no idea what lies behind the sweet mother-son scene.

· 3 ·

On the July 4 weekend in 1956, Bobby won the U.S. Junior Championship and became the youngest chess master in history. He looked ten but was thirteen, and he knew how he intended to spend the rest of the summer: traveling on his own to meet the strongest opposition yet at the U.S. Open in Oklahoma City and after that at the First Canadian Open in Montreal. Regina resisted, and then gave up. He held a simultaneous exhibition to help raise money, and she found people for him to stay with. Bobby, chewing holes in his shirts as he played, tied for fourth in Oklahoma and second in Montreal (keeping the $59 Canadian prize for himself, not telling his mother).

By the fall he was a freshman at Erasmus Hall High School, but the only learning he cared about was happening a few blocks away. Jack Collins, a renowned player whom top U.S. talents sought out as a teacher, hosted a chess salon in the apartment he and his sister shared (complete with chess-piece-patterned upholstery and drapes). Bobby had first shown up at the door in June. Now he dropped by at lunch, in his free periods, after school—and accompanied Collins, who was wheelchair-bound, on outings, too, playing blindfold chess en route. Collins's learning-by-osmosis method was made for Bobby. When Regina dragged him home, he took books from Collins's extensive chess library with him. Hater of homework, he dove deep into research in his chosen realm—long before computers could instantly summon up centuries' worth of games. Bobby's herculean explorations of his predecessors complemented his upstart instinct to look beyond prevailing styles at the board. He was primed, starting very young, to see what others didn't.

On an unusually hot evening in October, ignoring the dress code of the elegant Marshall Chess Club off Fifth Avenue in Greenwich Village, Bobby appeared for the prestigious Rosenwald Memorial Tournament—his first all-masters outing—in a striped T-shirt. He played what was immediately heralded as the "Game of the Century," facing an opponent named Donald Byrne, a leading young player at twenty-six. Early on, Bobby offered up a knight—a move no one predicted but whose ingenuity the kibitzers quickly appreciated. And then, as his time was running low, Bobby realized that the extraordinary sacrifice of his queen could alter the entire game.

There were stunned whispers among the sweaty crowd of onlookers. Years later, Kasparov distilled Bobby's brilliance as an "ability to look at everything afresh." Already, while he was still more boy than teenager, his signature clarity jolted a chess elite that would go on to learn from Bobby that, again in Kasparov's words, "simplification—the reduction of forces through exchanges—was often the strongest path as long as activity was maintained." Seeing twenty moves or more ahead, Bobby proceeded to respond to Byrne with speedy calm, his long fingers propelling his pieces in unexpected directions and snatching his opponent's off the board.

The game eclipsed Samuel Reshevsky's victory at the tournament. Bobby's feat evoked comparison with America's most famous native chess prodigy ever, the Louisianan Paul Morphy. Many felt he had surpassed Morphy's legendary win at almost thirteen in 1850. Bobby continued to stun the chess world the next year. He won the U.S. Junior Open again in July 1957 and the U.S. Open a month later, the youngest person ever to manage that—and the only player to hold both titles at once. In January of 1958, taller and gawky now, Bobby emerged the upstart winner of the U.S. Championship. His cool ruthlessness was intimidating, though his well-gnawed fingernails and knuckle cracking (he had stopped chewing on his shirts) betrayed the tension. He played thirteen games against a very strong field without a loss. When his spectacular victory became clear, the "Mozart of Chess," as the *Times* called him, began to dance and jump around. But Bobby also sounded a querulous note. Upon being named an international master, he complained in a voice that was breaking, "They shoulda made me a Grand Master."

The growing acclaim for Bobby during his chess surge of the previous two years had been mixed with unease behind the scenes. Regina had continued to worry about his obsessiveness, though her ever-balkier teenager's success stirred a new ambivalence. She "lives in terror of him," an FBI informant noted, "but at the same time seems to 'gloat' over his publicity." Even for chess aficionados, well acquainted with single-minded eccentrics, Bobby's increasingly obstreperous style was unsettling. When he sat down at the board, he was a paragon of rule-abiding respect. Away from it, everybody could see that Bobby, for whom all the attention coincided with puberty, needed guidance. (Much the same, under very different circumstances, had been true of Barbara Follett— a celebrated author suddenly emotionally at sea—during her rocky mother-daughter voyage.) Yet nobody was better than Bobby at rebuffing unbidden attempts to provide direction. The anxious efforts to tame his intransigence—by his mother and by a motley chess entourage—were singularly inept, sporadic, and halfhearted. Whether subtler, or stricter, or steadier handling would have met with greater success is anyone's guess. And at what price, given a rare talent fueled by a defiantly individualistic temperament? That was the rub, especially since this was the United States, after all, not the USSR.

Lurking in the minds of apprehensive admirers was Paul Morphy, for reasons other than his youthful brilliance at the board. Bobby's 1956 anointment as his successor paid tribute to half of his legacy, as "perhaps the most accurate chess player who ever lived," in Bobby's words. But Morphy wasn't just the marvel who put the United States on the world chess map by triumphing over a European chess elite in 1858. He then quit chess in his twenties and became deeply paranoid before dying a recluse at forty-seven. Morphy also put madness on the American chess map.

For Regina, around 1957, proud though she was of Bobby's streak, recent publication of a monograph by the former-chess-star-turned-psychoanalyst Reuben Fine was a spur to give psychiatry another try. His *Psychoanalytic Observations on Chess and Chess Masters* opened with a nod to Ernest Jones's classic paper "The Problem of Paul Morphy," published twenty-five years earlier, and went on to pursue an Oedipal theme not irrelevant to the Fischer family. Chess, Dr. Fine declared, was a sublimated form of struggle with the father (the all-important yet weak king who must be checkmated). More useful was his division of chess greats into two groups: the "heroes," near-monomaniacal players surrounded by worshippers, and the "non-heroes," for whom chess was only a part of their life. The former, he noted, "showed considerable emotional disturbance." Regina—more anxious than ever to get her son on a well-rounded academic track, especially now that college was in view—phoned Dr. Fine. He would be dealing, she warned him, with a very unwilling patient.

To allay Bobby's astute suspicions, Fine agreed to invite him over to play chess in his family quarters—not the home office—in his huge Upper West Side apartment. The purpose wasn't psychological probing, he assured Bobby, and he began by sending him copies of his chess books to establish a bond and, at the same time, his authority. The disingenuous paternalism annoyed Bobby, who set the terms over their next six or so meetings. Dr. Fine couldn't win his respect without beating him, and being beaten prompted Bobby's fury. "Lucky," he seethed after every defeat. Flattering himself that there was at last some rapport and "hopeful that I might help him to develop in other directions," Fine one day asked a question about school. "You have tricked me," Bobby declared, and stormed off.

Bobby had seized his chance to confront a father figure—and a maternal accomplice—who played by deceptive rules. (No Oedipal gloss is needed to imagine how gratifying this must have felt.) Redoubling his commitment to dominating at the board, he continued his streak. Regina responded in her typically inconsistent yet fervent way. At first, she bore down in earnest on the school front. Languages were her specialty, and after Bobby failed a Spanish quiz, she exhorted focus while also urging the benefits of multilingualism for his chess travels, a savvy pitch. Regina started speaking Spanish to Bobby and tutoring him at home, and his grades soared. But soon she got swept up in his chess triumphs. After all, they made *him* happy. The "professional protester," as Joan once called her mother, now turned Bobby's career into a cause. Impatient over the lack of publicity and fund-raising, she wrote press releases and tried to get on television shows. She didn't seem to notice how much Bobby, mortified, resented the intrusions.

Bobby's peers, predictably, also hadn't managed to curb his growing insistence that, whatever the circumstance, he got to set the terms. When Bobby joined the Manhattan Chess Club, he had been the still boyish near-teen in a mostly older youth contingent, but soon they were acolytes, deferring to him and his hard-driving pace. On the trajectory from one victory to the next, Bobby became more imperious. A fellow participant in the 1957 U.S. Junior Championship tournament held in San Francisco described a fourteen-year-old master of shock-and-awe drama—except the intimidating act suggested a boy out of control. Bobby had missed the ice cream social beforehand, where there had been lots of talk about the reigning champion. Striding in late, his hair shaved short and his Levi's ragged, he ignored young fans as he headed straight for the director's table to find out what the winner would get this year. "I do not want another typewriter!" he raged on learning the first prize was a repeat. When another player mocked his assurance as premature, Bobby turned on him: "You don't know me."

Working up to his encounter with Gilbert Ramirez, the highest-ranked junior, Bobby repeatedly rebuffed Gil's invitation to play some speed chess in between his rounds. "Too weak," he muttered. But Bobby relented before the two of them, each with four victories so far, were to meet at the board. In front of a large crowd, he sat down for a brisk preview of things to come. They played twenty-five or thirty blitz games, and Bobby didn't lose or draw one. He spent less than a minute on each. "It's like angels are moving his hand!" said Miguel Najdorf, a leading grandmaster of the time who was among the spectators. Bobby won the real games, too, retaining the junior title.

Before heading to Cleveland to play (and emerge victorious) in the U.S. Open several weeks later, he killed time out west with Gil and some other boys who had played in the tournament. It was a rare occasion for bonding, which clearly did not go so well for Bobby. During a memorable fight on the drive across the desert, he bit Gil hard enough to leave scars. But Bobby was also doing his best to sound more calmly mature. Maybe someone had dared to offer him advice, though effective counsel had notably not been the pattern so far. "Yes, sometimes I did cry when I lost, but I don't cry any more," he had told the *New York Times* reporter Gay Talese before his summer conquests. "I'm thrilled about winning but I try to be nice to people. I don't know if older persons are embarrassed about losing to me, but I do not feel awkward about playing them—or beating them. I beat them, or they'll beat me."

In his monograph, Fine noted the Soviets' "determined effort to prove that in their society artists"—a category that included chess stars—"need not be the tormented prima donnas so often encountered in other countries, but can lead socially normal lives." If anything, Bobby was reinforced in assuming the opposite: that bucking normalcy was a privilege of path-breaking genius. Such heady hero stuff was not exactly helpful, especially for a highly temperamental and vulnerable teenager with years of nonstandard socializing already behind him. Carmine Nigro had moved to Florida in 1956, and he and Bobby never saw each other again. Even with Jack Collins, who gave him a home away from home, Bobby began making occasional digs behind his back. Bobby was always "ahead of any plans his elders had for him," noted Frank Brady, the founding editor of *Chess Life* who met him around this time and later became his biographer.

In any case, his elders' plans were not exactly clear or firm. The upper reaches of the chess establishment were concerned enough to convene a meeting. The governors' board of the wood-paneled Marshall Chess Club of course agreed on Bobby's phenomenal talent. The problem was his attitude. The club manager, Caroline Marshall—the widow of the former long-standing U.S. champion Frank Marshall, for whom rich patrons had originally bought the brownstone—had threatened to keep Bobby out if he didn't abide by its sartorial rules. Bobby paid no attention and provoked other sponsors with antics that were evidently far more disruptive. "Some of what he did was so outrageous it was decided maybe he had emotional problems," Allen Kaufman, a chess master who had known Bobby and who attended the meeting, later told a reporter (without offering details). Someone suggested consulting—whom else?—Reuben Fine. But a board member broached a quandary that hadn't occurred to Regina when she first asked for Fine's guidance: in Bobby, they might have a case of neurosis bound up with chess genius. Did they want to run the risk that successful therapy might derail the United States in its suddenly promising quest for a world champion? They did not.

Though he doubtless wouldn't have tolerated Soviet-style chess training, much less therapy, the mixed signals Bobby got during his chess and adolescent growth spurts arguably suited him too well. A conflicted mother and a muddled chess world—both filled mostly with permissive fervor on Bobby's behalf—gushed, and knew how to get out of his way. That helped inspire his focus and abet his young genius. But by the time they faced an ever more combative teenager whose rare gifts they revered—and had their own reasons for promoting—they were singularly ill equipped to deal. They squirmed, went behind his back, flinched, hoping for the best. And when the new U.S. champion, who turned fifteen two months after winning the title, was heralded by "not one word from the Government . . . silence from the authorities," as an outraged chess elder put it, a similar message got through to Bobby: you don't owe anybody anything.

Another message also registered, which no fifteen-year-old would handle well: keep winning, and you'll be owed big. As Bobby turned to face the world in 1958, America's great chess hope felt he had license to conceive himself a lone ranger, now on a global stage. The United States had finally gotten a satellite into orbit in late January, and the National Defense Education Act was in the works. But funding was not forthcoming for a prodigy in the Soviet national sport: Bobby was eager for a summer trip to the USSR before heading to Yugoslavia for one of the qualifying tournaments for the world championship. Government money hadn't been available for a spring visit to Moscow by a Texan piano prodigy, Van Cliburn, either. At twenty-three, he had just stunned the world by winning the Soviet Union's first International Tchaikovsky Piano Competition after adoring fans swooned, thrilled by his romantic Russian feel for their music. Starry-eyed Cliburn ("a boy, not a young man," his hosts judged) had swooned, too, enthralled by the country and its people. No wonder, perhaps, the Soviets were favorably disposed to Regina's suggestion that Bobby be invited to visit—and the U.S. government, nonplussed by the pro-Soviet effusions of one Cold War cultural emissary already, kept its distance.

Regina secured the airfare with the *I've Got a Secret* gambit, and the Soviets quickly found themselves with an anti-Cliburn on their hands. Bobby, too, was steeped in Russian prowess, but he aimed to do as he pleased. He and Joan arrived early, to give him extra time to "play against the best they've got," as he told a reporter. "Their style gets me. That's why I came here." He rebuffed the sightseeing his hosts had arranged, well aware that his mother had conceived of the trip as culturally enriching for him. His goal was immersion in the Soviet way of chess, and the chance to battle with the best. "We have to throw him out every afternoon," an official of the Moscow Central Chess Club said, initially charmed by Bobby's passion. "We don't know what to do with him. But he's a wonderful boy."

Soon Bobby asked when the games with their chess pantheon would begin, and was surprised to learn that the Soviets had no intention of trotting out their masters and methods. Exactly a century earlier, when Paul Morphy had taken his triumphant foreign tour, his trip had been marred only by the refusal of the top player (a Briton) to play a match. Bobby seized on the precedent, but he didn't have Morphy's "genial disposition, his unaffected modesty and gentlemanly courtesy," as *Chess Monthly* had described him. Bobby was furious. An interpreter perhaps misunderstood him when he said he had been served enough pork at meals, or else she transcribed Bobby's sentiments perfectly: "I'm fed up with these Russian pigs." Feeling insulted and betrayed by his chess heroes, he vowed eternal enmity. Bobby conveyed a toned-down version in a postcard to Jack Collins: "I don't like Russian hospitality and the people themselves. It seems they don't like me either."

Bobby returned home in the fall of 1958 from Yugoslavia, where he had become the youngest grandmaster ever and was lionized as a quintessentially American upstart, "laconic as the hero of an old cowboy movie," a reporter wrote. He draped a scarf he had bought for Regina around her neck and gallantly told her, "That's very Continental." But before long their apartment was too small for them both. She had begun petitioning and picketing the American Chess Foundation, which she felt was offering inadequate support to U.S. chess efforts. So was the government, which wasn't funding the Olympic team's trip to Leipzig in 1960. To Bobby's fury, she picketed in front of the White House and the State Department, and began a hunger strike for chess. Up-close-and-personal support didn't suit her so well, or him either, so Regina moved out to live with a friend in the Bronx. "It sounds terrible to leave a 16-year-old to his own devices, but he is probably happier that way," Regina wrote to another friend. "Maybe he is better off without my nagging him to get out for sports, etc, eat, get through his homework, go to bed before 1 am, etc. I am tired of being a scapegoat and doormat."

Regina ended up miles away, though they corresponded. She went to California to embark on a peace walk from San Francisco to Moscow and en route found a new husband, an Englishman. She at last finished her medical degree in East Germany and continued to keep the FBI busy tracking her political activism, now on the Continent, where she tirelessly protested against the Vietnam War. Bobby retreated to a filthy apartment that was all his, with chessboards next to each of three beds and the radio often on. It was his idea of bliss—and it was a barricaded existence. He had already devastated Regina by dropping out of Erasmus High. Bobby spent the rest of his teens brooding even more over his beloved game, playing and studying ten to fourteen hours a day. "Chess and me," as he later said, "it's hard to take them apart. It's like my alter ego."

Frank Brady, by then not the only acquaintance being kept at arm's length, offered a rare glimpse of his friend's absorption at seventeen. He lured Bobby out for dinner, and in an unusually expansive mood after devouring prime rib, Bobby tried to lead

Brady through some of his preparations for his next tournament. Out came the pocket chessboard. Like a magician revealing his moves in such sped-up motion that they remained a blur, Bobby set and reset pieces without a pause, re-creating moments in games that went back more than a century. His eyes fixed on the world he held in his palm, now murmuring to himself, Bobby never saw that Brady "began to weep quietly, aware that in that time-suspended moment I was in the presence of genius."

Soon, though, Bobby was in restless search of recognition and self-definition. Eager to discard the image of an "uncouth kid," he began wearing bespoke suits. He took to carrying around a blue box much bigger than his pocket chess set. Inside, though he kept it secret, was a Bible, which he was reading intensively. He had been impressed by the pastor of the Worldwide Church of God, a sect that blended Christian tenets and Jewish observances. Its emphasis on austere self-control suited him (and so did its suspicion of doctors). Bobby held on to his U.S. champion title again and again, undefeated in the tournaments. He made phenomenal showings against the best in international matches.

Yet Bobby was not a coolly self-reliant cowboy. He wrangled over rules and playing conditions, got riled up by opponents, and retreated from people who had thought they were his friends. The Soviets cast him as an uncooperative product of crass capitalism, "unintellectual, lopsidedly developed, and uncommunicative." The American chess world, too, now spoke out about the "colossal egotism" of an older teenager who had "managed to alienate and offend . . . almost everybody and anybody who might be in a position to help him in his career," as a former U.S. champion put it. Of course, Bobby had also been hearing for years now (from many of the same people) that he was in a class by himself. Perhaps that helps explain the monumentally immature snobbery on display in an interview with the writer Ralph Ginzburg in *Harper's* when Bobby was eighteen—further grist for everybody's and anybody's worst impressions.

Bobby took swipes at just about all of the company he had ever (uneasily) kept: women, Jews, high school teachers and students, Russian "potzers," phonies, cheap millionaires who scrimped on prize money, chess club riffraff, "barbaric" subway riders, his mother. "She doesn't know what she's doing. She ought to keep out of chess." He extolled his fancy clothes. Driven home by Ginzburg, he paused in front of his walk-up on a noisy, grubby Crown Heights block to describe his dreams of getting rich and living in a grand house, "built exactly like a rook," complete with "spiral staircases, parapets, everything." Ginzburg at least took note that Bobby "does not show malice" and included Joan's comment that her brother was "a boy who requires an extra amount of understanding."

When the magazine came out, an irate Bobby accused Ginzburg of misquotations. Whatever the particular inaccuracies (Ginzburg said he had destroyed the transcript), the interview was a cruel exposé of the broader truth: Bobby, for all his bluster, was deeply insecure, clueless about how to behave and convinced no one could be counted on. Young adulthood nearly at hand, he was sure only of what *he* was counting on. Yet the next year his vision of becoming the youngest world champion in history vanished. Bobby was devastated when he placed fourth in the tournament in Curaçao that decided the challenger for the world championship in 1963. In need of a culprit, he accused the Soviets of throwing games to each other to ease their way to the top. (There is a good chance they did collude, although they had no need to.)

As he entered his twenties, Bobby staked his identity ever more rigidly on being the ultimate nonteam player. He threatened to withdraw from international chess, charging that its rules favored the Soviets. After the unprecedented feat of a clean sweep of the U.S. Championship of 1963–64—not a single draw as he faced eleven top players—he kept his word. He didn't play in the qualifying tournament for the next world championship. Even his staunchest defenders in the chess realm were ready to conclude that a nation that didn't take the game seriously had perhaps gotten what it deserved. "Finally the U.S.A. produces its greatest chess genius," one chess veteran remarked, "and he turns out to be just a stubborn boy."

· 4 ·

"He is still very young; he is still capable of growing in many directions" was the more optimistic view of Bobby's friend Frank Brady, writing at the same juncture. Bobby was only twenty-one, and had recently blurted out that he wished "all this controversy"—by which he meant "all this about the Russians"—were over. Brady hoped it was a sign that he would soon be ready "to fulfill his immense promise, whatever the conditions." Bobby did rally over the next decade, but not by ceasing to demonize the Russians. As he had ever since boyhood, he clung to the self-image of the hero facing long odds and obstacles—in this case, the Soviet sabotage of his original championship dream. Bobby was more his mother's son than he ever recognized: even a solo crusader draws strength from a sense (however distorted) of having a larger cause.

As Bobby told it, he finally stopped stalling and showed up in Reykjavík in the summer of 1972 to play the reigning world champion, Boris Spassky, because he felt "an awful lot of prestige of the country is at stake." Now twenty-nine, he cast the contest as a political morality tale: "the free world against the lying, cheating, hypocritical Russians." Culturally, it looked like a battle between untrammeled genius and the totalitarian engineering of expertise. But in Iceland, as in Brooklyn, temperament in fact took center stage. It proved more important than any particular approach to talent development—and more recalcitrant than Soviet trainers or American admirers hoped.

In Reykjavík, Bobby and an independent-minded Spassky presented a spectacle of Cold War role reversal. Bobby was ready with fierce rhetoric, a stickler for rules even as he broke them, a master of mind games with his delays and ultimatums. He got marching orders from the government: Henry Kissinger prodded by phone (not that the match was a policy priority—détente was in full swing, and American officials simply hoped to avoid an embarrassing fiasco). Spassky, to his regime's displeasure, refused to make ideological speeches. His superiors were eager for pretexts to walk out. But Spassky's decision to go along with Bobby's demand to play in a closed room, away from cameras—a decision "taken on his own," his Soviet critics scolded in the postmortem—guaranteed that the match went on. Spassky waited and sweated through Bobby's antics for the chance to play chess against the best. After a surreally suspenseful two months of chess and drama, Bobby was a point away from the title as the twenty-first game adjourned on the last day in August. The next day Spassky phoned in his resignation. At the grand banquet two days later, Bobby was bored and pulled out his pocket chess set. Side by side at the head table, he and Spassky played out other possible last moves, none of which would have made a difference.

As "a propagandist for the free world," Arthur Koestler remarked of Bobby, "he is rather counter-productive." But Bobby proved immediately effective as a propagandist for chess in the dominant nation of the free world. Suddenly America's best-known sports celebrity, he was famous not just for his genius but for his fancy suits, the snits he threw, and his push for real prize money—not to mention the way he snatched up an opponent's pieces. He made the slow-moving game seem thrillingly aggressive with declarations like "the object is to crush the other man's mind. . . . I like to see 'em squirm." At the same time, the PBS chess master–turned–commentator in Reykjavík, Shelby Lyman, revealed "a gift for democratizing chess," Fred Waitzkin later wrote in *Searching for Bobby Fischer*. Lyman was a guide good at "clouding distinctions between ability and ineptitude." The moment was ripe for "persuading the United States that chess was within reach of all of us."

In the USSR, Spassky's loss elicited a fourteen-point plan from a sports bureaucracy intent on renewed rigor and more state resources for chess. In the United States, Fischer and his triumph gave a marginalized pastime associated with oddball brainiacs a big status boost. He inspired grassroots enthusiasm among all ages for a game long linked with unworldly, innately gifted eccentrics. Yet the man who had complained that chess got no respect in America soon made it clear he wasn't about to preside over, or profit from, the newfound zeal to popularize and professionalize the game. Rejecting deal after lucrative deal, Bobby turned his back on becoming another high-rolling sports star. "Nobody is going to make a nickel off of me!" he said, sensing potential exploitation in every offer.

What were he and his talent worth? In Iceland, Bobby had at last confirmed the answer he had dreamed of. He had given away most of his winnings to the Radio Church of God, which had predicted doom that very year, 1972. And then the world didn't end, and Bobby now reigned supreme. Yet he was a stubborn outsider who needed uphill battles. He demanded rule changes for the next championship, designed to spur more daring play and cut down on draws. When the international chess federation refused, he resigned his title in 1975.

Already in retreat, Bobby now dropped out of sight, into a life of near vagrancy and delusions of Jewish conspiracies—more radically adrift than William Sidis ever was, yet with an anchor: for years, Bobby depended on the full amount of Regina's Social Security checks, relayed to him by Joan, who deposited them for their mother. When he surfaced in 1992 in war-torn Yugoslavia and defeated Spassky in an unofficial rematch, he won a purse of $3.5 million. For a man now filled with anti-American animus, the chance to violate U.S. sanctions (and to spit on the notice prohibiting him to play) was perhaps a bonus. After an itinerant decade and a half abroad—emerging from obscurity one more time to hail the 9/11 attack—Bobby died of renal failure in Iceland in 2008.

If only Bobby's star power had persisted, went the refrain as American chess mania ebbed. Then the game could have secured its place as a well-remunerated, publicly venerated arena of exceptional achievement. Yet Bobby's early departure from the stage arguably helped save chess in the United States from becoming too, well, Russian: a streamlined, hierarchical enterprise aimed at precociously winnowing, honing, and systematically steering hyped young talent toward the rewards not just of expertise but of officially approved prestige and cultural privilege.

Instead, in an era when athletics are big business—and loom

large in competitive college admissions—the "sport of thinking" in the United States has held on to a certain purity along with its penury. The result is truer to Bobby's own spirit than it might at first seem. Against a backdrop of neo-*Sputnik* alarm in the 1980s, when the presidential commission's report ominously titled *A Nation at Risk* stirred panic about the state of American education, chess became pedagogically correct. It acquired cachet both as an elite extracurricular activity for private school students and as an innovative supplement in inner-city public schools. At one end, "chess parents" nursed proto-prodigy dreams, eager to seize on signs of a "knack" for the game as evidence of superintelligence. At the other, the goal was to engage at-risk students in a pastime that promised crossover academic payoffs. Proponents of all stripes cited studies correlating chess programs with better reading scores, problem-solving skills, critical and creative thinking (improvements of the sort likely to be found with just about any activity that gives kids extra attention).

Bobby hated school but certainly would have vouched for the power of chess to teach children, from tuned-out students to smart ones, a lot about learning. As he discovered early, the game requires focusing on how to focus—breaking down challenges and cultivating patience and persistence. Meanwhile, the neural plasticity that also makes children good language learners can propel gratifying progress at chess. Goaded ever onward by a rating system that shows them every increment of improvement, young players get hooked. With its blend of rigid rules and absolutist rankings on the one hand, and its infinite possibilities and competitive allure on the other, chess is ideally designed to spur what performance experts call "effortful training."

At the same time, Bobby would have said what the coaches of good school chess teams will tell you, too: don't bill the game to young players as a high-GPA goody-goody's pursuit, or as special education in disguise. And don't count on habits of effortful study in chess to inspire academic conscientiousness. Regina learned otherwise. Asked to name the crucial ingredients of chess prowess, Bobby gave a list—"a strong memory, concentration, imagination, and a strong will"—that omitted the brainy brilliance and math aptitude often associated with the game. Cognitive research backs him up, revealing that chess masters aren't distinguished by either. Nor, studies have found, do top players' phenomenal recall for chess combinations translate directly into other feats of memory: tested with random positions, or different material, they aren't likely to excel. The truth is that Bobby is the best—and the saddest—evidence that lessons learned at the board don't transfer seamlessly to school, or to life. The game's attraction, for those who get caught up in it, is rarely instrumental. "I just go for it," Bobby told the shrink. That love was a factor he left off his list, but it belonged at the top. Of all the touted pedagogical uses for chess, the indisputably effective one—it can sweep students up in a dizzying, demanding pursuit for its own sake, not its résumé potential—would surely have won his approval.

Bobby didn't mind being anointed "the greatest natural player in history," a tribute that reflects the mystique of innate genius long associated with chess. But he never tried to disguise how much self-driven nurture was involved—yet another corroboration of the latest research on high-level chess performance. "The ability to put in those hours of work is in itself an innate gift," Kasparov proposed. Or perhaps it was an urge that gathered force in a lonely boy in an empty apartment. Starting early, and summoning rare curiosity and energy, Bobby amassed an unmatched trove of combinations to deploy in unprecedented ways. He worked endlessly—in both senses: his dedication was unceasing, and his obsession was in the service of ends no one else should presume to dictate. That left his talent at the mercy, ultimately, of the many hurdles he set himself.

Nobody was going to force Bobby to defend his primacy at the board, fighting for the cultural superiority of the free world. It might have been liberating if someone had. In vain, Regina tried to appeal to his legacy beyond the board. "Don't let millions of people down who regard you as a genius and an example to themselves," she wrote him as he veered into anti-Semitism. But after so many years, she knew she couldn't set him straight. The best she could hope for was that Bobby still knew she wouldn't let *him* down, as in her own way she never did. "Remember," her letter went on, "whatever you do or whatever happens I am still your mother and there is nothing I would refuse you if you wanted or needed it."

CHAPTER 6

The Programmers

· 1 ·

As the spring semester of 1972 ended, a lonely fifteen-year-old college sophomore named Jonathan Edwards began spending as many nights as he could on the couch in a basement room of the electrical engineering department at Johns Hopkins University in Baltimore. At just about the same time, an eccentric high school junior named Bill Gates was quietly leaving home by the basement door every evening he could. His destination was the darkened office of a local Seattle company. Farther south, in what had recently been christened Silicon Valley, Steve Jobs, a pot-smoking and acid-dropping high school senior, was secretly scheming with his good friend to produce "Blue Boxes" that enabled free long-distance phone calls.

The real lure for all the boys was, of course, a bigger box: computers. As a Hewlett-Packard Explorers Club member, Jobs "fell in love," he recalled later, with an early, clunky desktop. The Lakeside Mothers Club at Gates's elite private school had bought time for students on the refrigerator-size Program Data Processor-10, only to watch anxiously as some of them became addicted. In that empty Seattle office at night, Gates and several friends were hunched over the teletype keyboard (with a chess board at hand to occupy them while programs were running). Jonathan Edwards, alone in his lair, was keeping his PDP-11 discovery to himself. That summer a *Baltimore Sun* article highlighting two "Hopkins Students Who Skipped High School" didn't mention what Jonathan was hooked on. Julian C. Stanley, the Johns Hopkins professor of psychology who helped speed him onward, didn't remark on it either.

The fact that parents and teachers had next to no clue about what the boys were up to was part of the thrill. It added to the allure of a pursuit that exerted a rule-bound fascination similar to the spell cast by chess—with one enormous difference. Computers had real-world clout. To revise Stefan Zweig's verdict on the self-enclosed realm of chess, the domain that had mesmerized Bobby Fischer: here was mathematics that added up to something, art with an end product, architecture with substance. The computer revolution was at hand. On this frontier, there was no clearly rated hierarchy of experts, much less a tradition of revered champions. The first hulking machines of the Cold War era belonged to a faceless military-industrial complex. Now computers were getting smaller, and the people obsessed with them had suddenly gotten much younger. Amid the antiwar protests, generational tumult, and technological ferment of the 1970s, a new category of teenage prodigies was emerging. They came bearing an insubordinate message with more far-reaching implications than Bobby's: they were nobody's protégés.

Unlike their prodigy predecessors, the adolescent boys lucky enough to get their hands on computers weren't mere precocious achievers of adult-level prowess. They were poised to be pioneers. They knew the powers they were honing would influence everybody, not simply impress their elders. They also dared to presume *they* would set the pace and the path. And lonely though programming work could be, they soon realized that their geeky peers, not their teachers or parents, would be their most important allies. "I knew more than he did for the first day, but only for that first day," said the math teacher who introduced Gates and his friends to the PDP hookup. After seventh grade, Joseph Bates, the other boy who went on to become a precocious Johns Hopkins student, took a summer noncredit college computer science course. A young math teacher at his school joined him. No one in the class could match Joe. Nerds in the eyes of cool kids and girls, these late social bloomers had parents and educators on edge. The boys mostly weren't out protesting "the machine." Machine-obsessed, they were inside, mysteriously programming. Where was this awkward yet arrogant male tribe—with its own underground life—headed?

By now everybody, young and old, takes the upstart-dropout-startup ethos for granted as a defining feature of the high-tech era. Your children know you can't keep pace with the apps they swear by, and if you have a coder up at all hours behind his closed door, good luck telling him that homework is more important. "The state of mind demanded by a world that quests after ever more rapid technical change is alien to anyone over forty," as Michael Lewis put it in *Next: The Future Just Happened* (2002). "The middle-aged technologist knows that somewhere out there some kid in his bedroom is dreaming up something that will make him obsolete." We have glamorized the misfit aura, too. Apple's "think different" ad campaign in the late 1990s made it a theme: "Here's to the crazy ones. The misfits. The rebels. The troublemakers. The round pegs in the square holes." But three decades before young computer adepts got branded and Lewis wrote about underage Internet subversives, the future was still unfolding. Inspired by a do-it-yourself ethos and countercultural ideals, a "personal computer movement" was building momentum.

For the elders of this unusual tribe, clustered on either coast, the prewar refrain about wholesome adjustment for prodigies was beside the point. They were the opposite of the mature mentor type, and proud of it. "Like infants discovering the world" was how the mathematician Seymour Papert described the group gathered in MIT's artificial intelligence lab in the 1960s. A decade or two (or three) older than the boys, he and his colleagues had been enthralled by their "all-night sessions around a PDP-1 computer." Hanging out at Stanford's AI lab in 1972, the journalist/futurist/ *Whole Earth Catalog* creator Stewart Brand celebrated "the youthful fervor and firm dis-Establishmentarianism of the freaks who design computer science." It was "the most bzz-bzz-busy scene I've been around since Merry Prankster Acid Tests," he wrote in his

Rolling Stone portrait of the "fanatics with a potent new toy"—
a toy that was "coming to the people." Nearby at Xerox PARC
(Palo Alto Research Center), Alan Kay (a former Quiz Kid) was
one of the "computer bums" determined to make that happen. The
little Dynabook he aimed to build was to be "usable in the woods,"
he said, by "children of all ages"—those avid, bold learners we start
out being, before school-bound labors kill the joy.

Brand paid tribute to the utopian pedagogy on the opening page
of the *Whole Earth Catalog* (subtitled *Access to Tools*): "A realm of
intimate, personal power is developing—power of the individual to
conduct his own education, find his own inspiration, shape his own
environment, and share his adventure with whoever is interested."
Children would become bold programmers instead of being pro-
grammed as if they were "bundles of aptitudes and ineptitudes, . . .
'mathematical' or 'not mathematical' . . . 'intelligent' or 'dumb,'"
Papert wrote later. For radical "Yearners" like him, impatient with
blinkered "Schoolers," the "informal learning of the unschooled
toddler or the exceptional child" was the model for all. Brand distinguished between "hackers" and "planners," and in the former lay
the hybrid ideal: preschooler meets prodigy—driven by exuberant
devotion not just to rules but to unruliness. "Remember this was
the 70s," Brand said in retrospect as he summed up the cognitive
style of the computer pioneers: "fuck around with it, mess with it,
try it sideways. That was what it was all about."

Julian Stanley, the advocate of skipping high school, was a math
guy from a different planet. The tall and gawky Georgian, nearly
fifty when he joined the Hopkins faculty in 1967, arrived fresh
from a fellowship at Stanford that had been "heaven"—but not
the high-flying computer freak kind. An educational psychologist
fascinated by psychometrics, he had chaired the College Board's
Committee of Examiners in Aptitude Testing; he had also served
on the Educational Testing Service's research committee. Stanley
swore by the postwar technocratic meritocracy that sorted and
labeled using measures of "schoolhouse giftedness" then stirring
debate. In Papert's terms, he was more schooler than yearner.

But even Stanley, a "'drybones methodologist,' virtually a fanatic about statistics" (his self-description), was primed for rejuvenation as he made the midcareer move to Hopkins. "Sick and tired" of the arid formulas, he was elated when, thanks to flesh-and-blood Jonathan and Joe, he stumbled on a new use for the SAT: give the math portion to middle schoolers, anoint the high scorers as precocious quants, and hurry the prodigies onward to Ph.D.'s. Stanley got busy fomenting what he later called a "quiet revolution" in education. His goal of accelerating a select few up a prestigious academic ladder was a stark contrast to the computer freaks' countercultural vision of Everychild-as-freewheeling-programmer, with "plenty of time for screwing around," as Alan Kay put it. In Brand's terms, Stanley was a planner, not a hacker.

Yet the categories proved too tidy to fit Stanley. Nor did the dichotomies suit his first radical accelerants, who proceeded onward to computing breakthroughs after serving as inspirations for what became a centerpiece of superachiever culture: the Johns Hopkins talent search and the Center for Talented Youth (CTY) summer programs, better known by now as "nerd camp." Jonathan and Joe may have started out looking more like the schooler and planner breed than their unchaperoned, and soon spectacularly successful, counterparts Jobs and Gates did. In fact, the pioneering computer prodigies on both coasts made the most of the meritocratic fast-track route *and* the oddball loner mystique.

At the same time, not getting carried away by either badge of distinction turned out to be a challenge for them all: a young upstart could be in too much of a hurry, too out of step with peers. Their successors also had to figure that out, among them Sergey Brin, a star CTY alumnus. So, in her own way, did a rare girl who ended up excelling in the boys' high-tech club, becoming (among other things) a MacArthur fellow and a cofounder of Google X. In 1987, the year Brin enrolled in a CTY session at fifteen, a teenager named Yoko Matsuoka arrived in Florida to pursue sports prodigy training, her "inner geek" under wraps: she was as eager not to be a dork as she was to be a bold standout. By then, the drawbacks of insular elitism had dawned on Julian Stanley, too. Two decades later, Silicon Valley wasn't yet dwelling on the downsides, but Jonathan was, having learned them the hard way.

· 2 ·

"It seemed to many persons then, including me, that this was a bold, perhaps rash, move," Stanley said later of the culmination of the Saturday pastime he dreamed up for Joe Bates soon after meeting the shy eighth grader with dark-rimmed glasses in 1969. You might say natural reflexes also kicked in: mentoring, for Stanley, meant measuring the aptitude of the boy whom a Hopkins colleague had flagged as a star in her summer computer course. He gave Joe test after test every weekend for months. He was eager for more specific insights than Lewis Terman's IQ assessment could supply, or than scores in the tippy-top percentiles of age-appropriate standardized tests could reveal. For Joe, who loved machines (his first word had been *bus*), the mechanical reasoning questions that cropped up were the most fun. For Stanley, giving College Board tests to a middle schooler delivered a special thrill. And when Joe scored a stunning 669 (out of 800) on the math SAT, Stanley felt sure he had found not just a rare talent but a rare tool for exposing it. The statistician sprang into action. Local high schools wouldn't accelerate Joe. His 642 and 772 on the two math College Board achievements (he did better on the harder one) and a 752 on the physics test inspired Stanley to ask the Hopkins dean to take a gamble and admit him.

Joe, who described himself in retrospect as a "calm and compliant kid" from a supportive lower-middle-class Jewish family in Baltimore, wasn't actually chafing. He had built circuits and learned programming for two glorious weeks the summer after sixth grade, thanks to a cousin at the University of Rochester computer lab. He had joined the eighth-grade math club at school on his return. He had lucked into being tutored (for free) by an idealistic young teacher who then enrolled in the noncredit computer course along with him. Now thirteen, Joe was taking college math

JOSEPH BATES

classes at night. He didn't lack for opportunities. By the same token, such a boy (a volunteer at the synagogue and a figure skater as well) was a good bet for Stanley's experiment. Plus Joe, though short, could pass for a college student: he was already shaving. His father began driving him to campus every day in the fall of 1969.

Joe's first year at Hopkins was indeed going superbly when, perfectly timed to stoke Stanley's excited sense of discovery, another thirteen-year-old boy came to his notice in 1970. "One swallow does not make a spring," he had reminded himself as he tracked Joe's progress, and Jonathan Edwards and his mother were clearly birds of a different, more ruffled feather. Evelyn Edwards, a reading teacher who had gotten wind of Joe's early admission, was a "very, very aggressive" lobbyist for a son whose obvious "maladjustment" (Stanley's words) also raised doubts. Jonathan, who had surged ahead in math outside of school, was miserably at odds with his classmates, a social outlier. But at thirteen, he scored even higher on the math SAT than Joe had, 716; he broke 700 on the math and physics achievement tests, too. Besides, stymied brilliance demanded attention more urgently than stable brilliance did. Stanley prevailed on Hopkins again. Jonathan, slight and still very much a boy, didn't blend in on campus, but he shaped right up. Stanley touted Jonathan's 3.75 grade-point average his first year and his own "conversion" to the fervent advocacy for off-the-charts children that had galvanized Lewis Terman before him.

"My life and career thereafter have never been the same," Stanley wrote shortly before he died in 2005. An anomalous event—an obviously extremely bright middle-school student acing a college entrance exam, and then thriving in college courses—had been replicated. Emboldened to feel that "the scientific method, in so far as it is a method, is nothing more than doing one's damnedest with one's mind, no holds barred," Stanley was not deterred by a sample of only two, both of whom had yet to graduate. He was excited by his SAT radar. It could, he was convinced, home in on rare math talent in an already select group of pre–high school students: those who clustered in the top several percentiles on the age-appropriate national standardized tests they took at school. Challenge them with a test like the SAT that had no "ceiling effects" for them, and otherwise hidden gifts would be revealed that could and should be speedily developed.

With a hacker's improvisatory zeal, Stanley wrote what he later described as the "shortest and probably quickest" grant application—barely five double-spaced pages long—proposing to "do something, I hardly knew what, to find and help such prodigies." He sent it to the newly established Spencer Foundation, which in 1971 was eager to disburse funds (and where he had a few friends on the staff). Stanley won a five-year grant of $266,100, with hardly a string attached. "As far as external controls, I didn't have any," he later marveled. "I could try anything I wanted to."

He was on the fast track, a step ahead of the federal government, which weighed in on gifted education a year later with typical bureaucratic caution, the top-down planner way. The Marland Report of 1972 was studiously all-inclusive in issuing the first official definition of "children of high performance"—students "with demonstrated achievement and/or ability in any of the following areas, single or in combination: 1) general intellectual ability 2) specific academic aptitude 3) creative or productive thinking 4) leadership ability 5) visual and performing arts 6) psychomotor ability." Congress appropriated a budget that was barely bigger than Stanley's, and it was for research and for the development of teachers, as well as for the first Office of Talented and Gifted. That meant training for grown-ups, not for gifted children.

The imposing name Stanley gave his project, the Study of Mathematically Precocious Youth (SMPY), promised research, but of an entrepreneurial, grassroots variety. He set out quickly, with several colleagues, to organize a talent search for students whose SAT math scores before they turned thirteen were 500 or above, matching or exceeding the average college applicant's. And that was just the start. "We decided we didn't find these kids just to admire them," as he put it, "but instead to help them." Stanley took his cues from the revered pioneers in the gifted field (which had become "very weak" in his view, he privately noted). He was inspired by Leta Hollingworth's educational efforts decades earlier on behalf of the supergifted group with IQs above 180, but he breezed by her concerns about possible social and emotional issues facing such children. Instead he invoked Terman's data on well-balanced genius. Stanley welcomed "the assurance that we were not going to find that our high scorers were burned out by twenty" as he kept his eye out for yet more recruits with truly sky-high scores who might hurry through college early. "Perhaps, if given the same opportunity," he reflected, "Gauss, Newton, and Einstein would have been even more precocious educationally." What the value added might have been, he didn't say.

Few talent searchers can resist dreams of spotting unusual, otherwise unheralded genius. In truth, though, Stanley's quest— which got its start in March 1972 and drew some four hundred eligible young SAT-takers—was structured to appeal to those already quite well served by a test-based status quo. That was partly why it proved so popular so quickly, growing sevenfold and becoming national in scope over the next fifteen years. Stanley talked about unearthing innately "exceptional math reasoners." But as he also acknowledged—and Joe and Jonathan demonstrated—the top performers had generally benefited from prior supplemental work outside of class to excel on college-entry tests so young. (Ten percent of the male participants who took the math SAT in his inaugural search scored 660 or above.) That in turn meant they were likely to have attentive parents, eager to enable extra math opportunities for their children—at any rate, for their sons. Several of Stanley's younger female colleagues took note that girls, far fewer of whom participated in the initial talent searches and made the cut, seemed to get less math encouragement. (Title IX, prohibiting discrimination based on sex by any educational institution receiving federal funds, was signed into law only in the summer of 1972.) As his searches quickly expanded beyond Baltimore, Stanley wasn't worrying about any lack of parental pushiness. "Fortunately," he remarked, "there always seems to be lurking in the background some envious mother who knows her child can do at least that well."

As for how to help his high scorers, Stanley and his colleagues were feeling their way in a pragmatic—yet also impatient—spirit. "Our intent is to supplement and complement school-based instruction," he later emphasized, "not supplant, criticize or 'invade' it." Above all, they wanted to find out how fast their mathematically precocious youths—and they, their promoters—could go. A month after the first talent search, twenty of "our 'prodigies,'" as Stanley called them, were enrolled in his first intensive math class. (The rare girls proved hard to retain, his colleagues found, deterred by math-demon boys they considered "little creeps" and by the stigma of seeming "different.")

It was the prelude to a flurry of experiments with, as he put it, a "smorgasbord of accelerative opportunities." After 18 hours devoted to Algebra I, most of the class of rising seventh graders performed as well on tests of the material as the top 40 percent of ninth graders who would have spent 135 to 150 hours. Stanley even ventured the stunt of bringing in seventy-five students and trying to teach them Algebra I in a day—and got a third of them through it. "But we decided we didn't want to play that kind of show-off stuff. That was not necessary. We would have Saturday classes and do things a little more leisurely and in intensive fashion." There was a reason he got the nickname Mr. Acceleration.

And though Stanley acknowledged it was a "clumsy phrase," there was a reason he coined "radical accelerants" to anoint the college-bound vanguard who scored around or above 700. Even, or especially, a "quiet revolution" needs publicizing, and the path of Stanley's pioneers exemplified his vision: bypass obstacles (stodgy high schools) and amass advanced credit and degrees—as fast and with as little fuss as possible, to avoid the "tragic waste of a rare national resource." Well before they had data, Stanley and his colleagues sped to the conclusion that he hoped to prove. "High test scores at an early age do not ... merely indicate 'developmental' differences of rate or sequence," he soon confidently pronounced. "They presage long-range, lasting differences in ultimate ability." The dearth of girls, not to mention minority students, didn't give him much pause.

Concerns voiced by other colleagues as they launched a Study of Verbally Gifted Youth in 1973 didn't slow Stanley down either. They raised questions about the overarching endeavor of early test-based spotting of mature promise. Might they be winnowing too narrowly, overlooking crucial harbingers of future creativity? "For example, skills such as idea generation and question asking may be required in combination with traits such as tolerance for ambiguity, persistence, and propensity for reflection." A score on an SAT, math or verbal, seemed notably inadequate to gauging such abilities and qualities—no easy feat to measure at all, especially in a preteen. But Stanley, dismissive of what he considered "vacuous talk about creativity," was ready with a rather brusque verdict on the nonmath side of the project: "Too many chiefs, not enough Indians, all sort of interested in different things—empathy, for example."

Cowboy gumption continued to thrive on the SMPY side, fired up by the view that the great math minds of the future lay in a rare few, singled out and steered onto their individualized paths right away. By 1977, Stanley had more than enough graduating radical accelerants at Hopkins to merit a story in *Time* magazine about his "mathematical wizards"—eight boys, three of them seventeen-year-olds, all of whom he was betting on for "original contributions." (Colin Camerer, an innovative behavioral economist at Caltech, went on to become perhaps the best known.) More teens were in the pipeline: in the wake of Joe and Jonathan, Stanley had enrolled seventeen boys by 1974. And his talent search had caught on. "Hundreds of seventh-graders have been pouring in from a wider and wider area to take his tests," *Time* reported.

As he had from the outset of the decade, Stanley sounded like a high-energy hybrid in touting his enterprise—part inventive upstart, part elitist technocrat. "We don't have any particular program," he told *Time*. "If you're gifted and motivated, we'll help you do anything that fits you." On the one hand, the young wizards were in charge. "Our goal," he declared elsewhere, is "to make them independent of us and independent of their parents as soon as feasible." On the other hand, they were being efficiently scripted to maximize their "most productive years" of research—"a precious human-capital resource," as colleagues later put it, to serve a high-tech era. Stanley was proudly hard-boiled about his emphasis, going so far as to say at one point, "We're not a talent *development* group. We're a talent utilization one." A numbers guy to the core, Stanley had his stars' stats by heart. He could recite their middle school feats on the math SAT, the grades they had skipped, their early college matriculation and graduation dates. He could list their stellar GPAs and advanced degrees. Later on he could report exactly how old, or rather young, they were when they received their professional laurels. He said he sometimes felt like the book of *Guinness World Records.*

Those different things—empathy, for example, and social and emotional issues generally—didn't lend themselves to the litany. In fact, Stanley seemed to be counting on a certain impervious immaturity to speed his protégés along smoothly. "Scientists are stable introverts," he said of his group in the *Time* article, as though his math recruits already belonged to the guild. "They are not highly impulsive and tend to act rationally." Stanley went on to invoke empirical evidence that mathematically precocious boys are backward when it comes to peers, in particular girls. "This has been a great asset in the early-entrance program because it gives them more time to study." (Stanley's own experience didn't exactly match up: parting from his girlfriend and his best friend when he skipped *fourth* grade, he once said, had left him "discomfited socially" for several years.) One of his seventeen-year-old Hopkins graduates, who had arrived on campus as a barely high school–age kid, indicated that calmly forging ahead did not come as naturally as Stanley suggested. "I try to appear as normal as possible," he told the

Time writer. "If you go around broadcasting that you're a weirdo, then people look at you like you're a weirdo."

· 3 ·

The academically tractable profile that Stanley described would have surprised Steve Jobs and Bill Gates, not to mention their parents. One of Stanley's own pioneers didn't fit the mold either, not that Stanley took particular note. Pleased to report that Jonathan Edwards's "'maladjustment' disappeared completely" upon his arrival at Hopkins, Stanley was soon busy tending to other recruits. And Jonathan himself, now fifteen, sounded like a gung-ho radical accelerant as he shared his plans with *The Baltimore Sun* after his sophomore year in 1972. He would plow straight on to a Ph.D. "Given that you have the raw ability, the secret, if there is any, is that you have to adapt," he explained. "You have to get used to what's expected of you." Except that, as Jonathan was also well aware, conforming to adult plans was just what members of his baby boom generation were loudly announcing they did *not* have to do—and grown-ups had better get used to it.

In fact, not unlike Gates and Jobs, Jonathan had already had practice pushing back, and ahead, in a less-than-cooperative way. Long-haired teenagers who took to the streets in generational rebellion weren't the only ones calling the shots. So were young oddball academic standouts, beneficiaries of a child-focused postwar parenting ethos of a newly solicitous sort. Steve got the message very early from his adoptive mother and father that "they were willing to defer to my needs." They let him know he was special (as school testing confirmed), and if he was a troublemaker (his antics included setting off explosives in kids' lockers), he needed greater stimulation, not punishment. If he needed to escape bullying, as he did when he skipped fifth grade, they would scrounge to buy a new house in a better school district. And if he bullied his parents—as he did, particularly about college plans when the time came—well, that was part of the bargain. The catalyst he really counted on was a close buddy more obsessed with computers than even he was, Steve Wozniak.

The Gateses' experience was a more uptight, upscale variation on the theme. Bill (called Trey by his parents and friends) was the middle child in his close-knit and well-connected Seattle family. He was precocious and socially aloof and, by eleven, constantly battling his mother. She and his father resorted to counseling for all three of them. The therapist's verdict after a year: Mary Gates would have to readjust because her son wasn't going to. She and Bill Gates, Sr., backed off, and they dispatched their scrawny and not exactly endearing almost-teenager to Lakeside School—where he proceeded to do what he pleased, an extreme version of the sort of quirky student the staff prided itself on attracting in the 1960s. Among other things, he felt perfectly free to pay very little attention to what his mother cared a great deal about: where he would go to college and whether people looked at him like he was a weirdo. Finding a few equally offbeat friends who shared his tech fervor—Paul Allen in particular—proved crucial.

Jonathan was a lonelier outlier than either Jobs or Gates, and certainly than Joe, his fellow radical accelerant at Hopkins. The misfit spirit of Bobby Fischer's family may come to mind, thanks not just to Stanley's wary diagnosis of Evelyn Edwards as "very, very aggressive" but also to Jonathan's own assessment of his family as "not socially well-adjusted." Atheist New York intellectuals transplanted to a Bible-belt suburb of Baltimore, his parents didn't mingle and showed little interest in getting their son or his younger sister involved in sports or neighborhood life. During a polarized era, their response as urban liberals stranded in a conservative setting was to focus more fiercely on not blending in.

Jonathan's father, Lionel, was an electrical engineer of few words. As a reading specialist, Evelyn put her passion for learning into practice. She went to night school to learn logic, determined to tackle the *Principia Mathematica*. Their extraordinarily bright son was a sponge, immersed in math and science—and science fiction. As Jonathan later put it, he "drank the Kool-Aid" in a science- and genius-worshipping household. He welcomed the opportunities his parents found for him, while feeling marooned at school, despite stumbling into oases of engagement there. His fifth- and sixth-grade teachers let him work on solo projects, even teach classes. In junior high, he lucked into an attentive math teacher who arranged for him to take high school geometry. By the time he met Dr. Stanley, Jonathan had made his way through algebra, trigonometry, and calculus outside of regular school—taking courses at, among other places, Harford Community College, where his father taught.

Unlike Joe, who was cooperative and quiet, Jonathan had made a habit of blowing off schoolwork that bored him. "I know I could do very well in them if I wanted to," he told *The Baltimore Sun* of the classes he had ignored, "but I didn't want to." Not that "goofing off and [becoming] a disciplinary problem" saved him from being shunned as the brainy boy. Venting anti–Vietnam War sentiments didn't win him cool points with his peers either. At home, the response wasn't to clamp down but to seek professional advice. A consultation with a New York psychologist, recommended by Jonathan's aunt, evidently didn't leave his mother feeling they could just ride out the phase. No wonder she seized on Stanley's experiment with Joe. Jonathan remembered his mother half-joking—years before Columbine, of course—that "if I hadn't gone to college I would have blown up my school." For her part, Evelyn was at her wits' end.

She was surely relieved to hear her disaffected rebel speak like a grade-conscious adult-pleaser as he hit puberty and the halfway mark at Hopkins: "You really have to be great," Jonathan the rising college junior declared, "not just make C's but A's." At the same time, being his mother and a teacher, she was perhaps not altogether surprised that a more complicated story soon surfaced. Jonathan had started out as a fourteen-year-old commuting student whose avid interest excited professors. He felt he had been "let loose in wonderland," he said in retrospect. Just how loose, though, got elided in the brisk account Stanley later offered, which had Jonathan zooming from an initial stellar GPA onward to pathbreaking computer work in the banking field when he was barely in his twenties—proof, in this telling, that top-down academic channeling worked like a charm.

The truth was that Jonathan got mesmerized by computers along the way, pulled onto a track that led nowhere Stanley could fathom. Nor could Gates's and Jobs's parents and teachers—or, for that matter, the boys themselves. "People imagine that programming is logical, a process like fixing a clock," Ellen Ullman, a rare woman pioneer among the baby boom coders, has written. "Nothing could be further from the truth. Programming is more like an illness, a fever, an obsession. It's like those dreams in which you have an exam but you remember you haven't attended the course. It's like riding a train and never being able to get off"—even if other people are eager to pry you away from the machine and lure you back into human company. For Jonathan, the fact that nobody was tugging was a mixed blessing.

The irony was that having been hustled into college early, he was left more completely to his own devices than Jobs and Gates were out west. Gates described himself becoming "hard core" at roughly the same time—seeking out computer access "day and night"—to his parents' alarm. As he began tenth grade in 1970, they managed to impose a nine-month hiatus, during which Bill "tried to be normal, the best I could," though it didn't last. Picking back up with his Lakeside programming cadre, he and his friends shifted focus, newly intent on "monetary benefits," as one of them wrote in his journal, rather than merely "educational benefits." Down the coast, Steve left total tech immersion to reclusive Steve Wozniak, several years older. Jobs branched out, discovering a niche in a hipper geek crowd among the high school seniors, drawn to books and drugs along with electronics; he also landed a girlfriend. But Jonathan hadn't latched onto anyone, including Joe. For his part, Joe found wonky socializing at Hopkins (only newly coed) just about his speed—relieved not to have to deal with a crazier high school scene.

Jonathan, who had taken an introductory programming course his freshman year, instead began spending hours alone in the basement room where the electrical engineering department had a

PDP-11, a later model of the computer that had launched Bill a few years earlier. In retrospect, he described encountering the manual and feeling that he barely needed a guide to begin exploring: "It was just obvious. It was as if I'd already read the book." Living at home, Jonathan now set off for Hopkins at five in the morning during the summer of 1971. He wanted to squeeze in all the time he could at the teletype keyboard of what was called a minicomputer—which it was, compared to the huge mainframes that emerged in the 1950s. Soon he had persuaded the "double E" chairman to give him a key to the department library, where Jonathan often slept on a sofa rather than waste precious hours in travel.

In contrast to Gates's parents, the Edwardses did the opposite of trying to curb their son's monomania. When Jonathan, not yet fifteen, asked if he could live alone on campus as a sophomore, they agreed. Looking back decades later, a father of three himself, he was stunned that his parents—and his professor—approved the plan. Where did he eat? How did he cope? What, if any, advice did he get from Stanley? He couldn't remember. (Regina Fischer, having left Bobby at sixteen by himself in the family apartment, couldn't quite believe she had taken such a step either.) The hours with the PDP-11 expanded, his solitude unbroken by the Go and chess games the Coke-drinking Lakeside diehards enjoyed together while programs were running. Jonathan recalled collaborating with assorted graduate students on a space war game at one point, but he was still a skinny kid lacking in social confidence, who felt he had little in common with older students on campus. (In his memory, Joe was in a different league, too, with a girlfriend—though Joe hadn't in fact yet dared to date.)

Programming, as Jonathan reflected with the hindsight of middle age, didn't so much supplant other relationships as provide a desperately needed substitute. "An act of taking dictation from your own mind" is how Ullman has summed up the process of navigating "between the chaos of human life and the line-by-line world of computer language." Jonathan emphasized the allure of getting out of his head, exploring ways to share what lay within it. This "romantic view," he acknowledged, might seem a jarring perspective to apply to a hypercerebral teenager who felt inept at making emotional connections. But it was the struggle to communicate, he had gradually come to understand, that helped drive his curiosity and creativity in a "new medium of expression, never seen before." Software in the early 1970s, before anyone had much "idea how it work[ed], what its parameters" were, presented itself not just as a new science. It was an artistic frontier—a "blank canvas," an "intellectual sculpture" to be discovered. Stanley's formula of well-timed adult guidance in the acquisition of mathematical reasoning skills, and degrees to go with them, missed the essence of the experience. For Jonathan, personal turmoil—both intellectual and emotional—turned out to be crucial, and anything but simple.

JONATHAN EDWARDS

Jonathan evoked a state of enthralled absorption, with the machine itself in the role of mentor, one without office hours or a kindly manner. The computer wasn't a solicitous intermediary. It was a strict interlocutor and ally—and before long, if things went well, the computer was at the programmer's beck and call. "You're like a god in your own private universe, abstract world," Jonathan said, conveying the heady power that can be obscured in what looks like mere dry code. "It works, or it doesn't—more often doesn't, because you make mistakes." Debugging and doggedly proceeding, on "a machine that can *do* things," made for a process at once unforgiving and rewarding. "Turn a kid loose in this new universe where they can create things—it's intoxicating like writing novels," he said, "only they're dead but this can make things happen." He emphasized the intense pleasure in it, "especially if you don't find pleasure elsewhere." Start when you're young and flexible enough, and the pursuit readily becomes a compulsion.

"As in art, you have an inner voice that tells you how to sculpt this giant thing. You get a picture of a complex thing and you create it—and it talks back to you," Jonathan said of a creative process that was rule bound but *not* self-enclosed. "It's almost a personal relationship. You can get lost in it," he explained, describing the allure of work that supplied a reciprocity he struggled with in life. "It's a non-human world good for someone who hasn't focused on sending emotional signals back and forth, but logical ones. The best programmers are not engineers but would-be artists." They are also, he emphasized, would-be lovers and intimate friends, daunted by the challenge of expressing those desires. "You don't find friendly, socially extroverted people good at it," Edwards had concluded. Why burrow into the formidable complexities of non-social circuitry if warm-blooded bonding comes easily to you? The real programming standouts, he insisted, have been driven to their mastery by social hurdles they feel they can't handle.

In his junior year, hormones kicked in as he turned sixteen, and Jonathan's wonderland became a darker, disorienting place. The bowl haircut in his *Baltimore Sun* photo was gone. He made the move to the long-hair-and-wire-rims look and gave dating a try. But he was small and still younger than his Hopkins classmates, and hopelessly ill at ease. What Jonathan could blur by being belligerent in middle school, he now had to face head-on: he was, he felt, a social failure. By high school, Gates the pipsqueak know-it-all had allies and enjoyed a guru aura. With Paul Allen, he began parlaying computer skills into business opportunities. Jobs, the erstwhile loner, now had his cool countercultural crowd, as well as his partner in tech adventures, Steve Wozniak, holed up with electronics journals.

Holed up himself, Jonathan was unhappily isolated—and restless. The year before, "interested in logic and big ideas," he had added philosophy as a second major and begun hanging out with a graduate student in the department. Through him, Jonathan gravitated to a "circle of potheads," his phrase, and got caught up in the scene that Jobs had discovered before setting off for college. "The whole sex, drugs, and rock and roll thing messed me up for a long time," Jonathan said—a derailment, in his eyes, where Jobs saw enlightenment. For Steve, the "fusion of flower power and processor power," as Jobs's biographer put it, primed him for an open-ended route as high school wound down. A hipper rebel than Bill (who duly applied to Harvard), Steve let his parents know he considered Stanford too staid: "The kids who went to Stanford, they already knew what they wanted to do. They weren't really artistic." Questers applied to Reed College, and when Steve headed there in 1972, the mantra on the back cover of the *Whole Earth Catalog* he brought along summed up his ethos: "Stay Hungry. Stay Foolish."

And by extension, don't stay the college course just because your elders want you to—or just because, in Jonathan's unusual case, you've already sped along the fast track toward specialized expertise before most kids have even begun their applications. (Jobs lasted one semester, and didn't reenroll.) On his seventeenth birthday, in the fall of 1973, his senior year, Jonathan dropped acid. He then withdrew from the term. In 1974 he left Hopkins, despite pleas from Dr. Stanley and his parents.

Convinced that "making some big change seemed necessary," Jonathan first tried a comparatively small one. In the fall of 1974, he enrolled at MIT as a special student, planning to take the two classes he needed to finish up his Hopkins degree. He was eager to find kindred spirits. And MIT's Artificial Intelligence Lab looked like a cutting-edge place to pursue graduate studies—which Joe, as it happened, had just embarked on in Cornell's computer science department in 1973. With his B.S. and M.S.E. in hand and his eighteenth birthday in view, Joe was counting on earning his Ph.D. in two years.

But for both of Stanley's pioneers, the superexpress academic approach had hit its limits. When Joe didn't pass all his qualifying exams at Cornell, freezing up in part of the orals, he spent the summer paralyzed by anxiety yet clueless about the source. Insight came only with the help of a psychologist: Joe's failure, which was how he saw it, shattered his self-image and left him feeling judged, convinced his parents and friends no longer loved him. Stanley, with whom the Bates family spent some time at the beach that summer, joined others in reassuring Joe that nobody counted on faster progress than *he,* Joe, wanted. Radical acceleration was meant to be an experiment, not a daunting set of expectations. Inclined at first to leave Cornell, Joe decided to carry on at a slower pace. Jonathan didn't last at MIT. Turned off by the academic politics, he said, he dropped out as the spring semester of 1975 arrived. Flouting credentials, though haunted by the sense that he needed to make some contribution, Jonathan quit with just one more course left to fulfill his B.A.

As Stanley's Study of Mathematically Precocious Youth took off in the mid-1970s, his first two specimens—now the age of ordinary college freshmen—weren't quite the models he made them out to be. They were *more* off the charts. He had dreamed up a talent search with the goal of hastening advanced training for brilliant math minds that might otherwise get slowed down and drift off course. But the boys proved readier to set their own (unsteady) pace and direction than Stanley could have guessed when he sprang them from high school. He hadn't foreseen the disruptive catalyst that college would offer: the computer. He didn't figure on cultural unrest either. Joe was ambushed by the pressure of what felt more like a race than he had realized, not ideal for someone still figuring out his identity—and fixated on big ideas: his dissertation, finished by the end of the decade, explored whether machines (never mind fast-tracked boys) can be made into creative mathematicians. For Jonathan, the accelerated experience provided fodder for the sense that academia perhaps wasn't a congenial place for intellectual rebels after all.

"An alien, a Martian plopped down," was how Jonathan described himself in retrospect. Stanley, like Lewis Terman before him—and Boris Sidis and Leo Wiener—had hoped to rescue young math wizards from that lopsided outsider image. But what if they made it clear they didn't exactly want or need rescuing?

What if brainy nonconformity, rather than the mark of an American loser and loner, could be a sort of badge of honor—a basis for community? Other than Silicon Valley, Jonathan could hardly have plopped down in a more welcoming place than Cambridge and its environs, where cultural and technological ferment was happening well beyond tidy college quads. Martian qualities like Jonathan's were a ticket of entry to a realm less hierarchical than the ivory tower and less hermetic than a basement.

Five decades earlier, Norbert Wiener (whose book *Cybernetics* claimed a spot in the *Whole Earth Catalog*) had found a refuge from stuffier Harvard down Massachusetts Avenue at MIT. Now Jonathan escaped from MIT to a burgeoning tech world in the Boston area in need of computer obsessives like him. He began full-time work at one of the many software companies springing up, Technology Management Incorporated (TMI)—in step with Gates, who spent the summer after his restless first year at Harvard in 1973–74 working on mainframes at nearby Honeywell. Jonathan had moved into the new Cambridge Zen Center, where studying under a Korean master "prodded me to grow up," he said in retrospect—a tamer verdict than Jobs probably would have rendered on his meditational journeys, which since his departure from Reed had taken him to India. Yet for Jonathan, too, the "mathematical, Spartan feel" of the discipline clarified horizons. He felt poised to make "big, philosophical decisions" as he ventured forth into the real world. At TMI, he found a different rigor. Jonathan also found an exhilarating freedom on the frontier of computerized business, which offered "the room for the wild stuff," the arena for "breaking the rules."

Discovering his technological mission had entailed a more wayward path than Stanley had imagined. At just about the point in life when college students are expected to declare a major, Jonathan "decided that computers were where I was going to make my mark." If the urgency to do that weighed on him, and it did, leaving the academy felt liberating. In January 1975, the new issue of *Popular Electronics* introduced a kit for building a personal computer called the Altair 8800: the future conjured up at the start of the decade by hacker pioneers like Alan Kay and prophet-publicists like Stewart Brand had arrived. Bzz-bzz busyness, and business, spread beyond AI labs. Prodded by Paul Allen, Gates ditched his Harvard work (to his parents' distress). The two of them spent feverish weeks coming up with a version of BASIC that worked on the Altair. Looking at the specs for the microprocessor, Steve Wozniak got the idea for what became the Apple I, and Jobs saw the financial promise. The revolution was under way.

TMI's province was minicomputers, newly affordable for small and midsize businesses. TMI's superstar, it was obvious within mere months, was Jonathan. Still in his teens, he became the technical leader of a project to build one of the first electronic money transfer systems at Citibank, paving the way for automating many business processes. He was drawn to a romantic image of himself as a Tom Swift figure out of the books he had loved as a boy: a young outsider-turned-inventor transforming the world of industry. He, unlike Joe, hadn't given Julian Stanley academic credentials to recite. Instead, Jonathan took a certain pride in not having even a high school diploma, and in 1980 he cofounded a software firm, IntraNet. He hadn't ceased feeling lonely or worrying, as Joe did, too, "that if I made one mistake, I was ruining or dashing this incredible potential." Yet computers, Jonathan said as he looked back, "gave my kind a way to live."

· 4 ·

"By 1979 we of SMPY were nearly exhausted from our efforts," Julian Stanley reported. He was also proudly stunned by the results. "It usually takes a viable idea twenty years to get in circulation, if it ever does," he noted, but his talent search had spread nationwide in barely a decade. His startup was ready to go public, so to speak—thanks, as he had recognized from the outset, to a "propitious *zeitgeist*." Mr. Acceleration's real secret lay in not being too far ahead of the curve. Meritocratic pressure had been on the rise since the mid-1970s, as colleges stepped up the competition for top students, and applicants did the same for spots at top colleges.

A Nation at Risk delivered a dire educational prognosis in 1983, the same year *U.S. News & World Report* issued the first of its annual college rankings, fuel for the escalating admissions race. Stanley's timing was perfect when he entrusted younger colleagues at Johns Hopkins with a project: institutionalizing his enterprise.

The Center for Talent Development, as it was soon named, launched its first residential summer program in 1980. A growing array of college campuses began hosting the three-week sessions. They offered Stanley's signature fast-paced coursework to eligible students, those who scored 500 or above on the math SAT, and now also the verbal part, before turning thirteen—the top one in one hundred, he estimated, of their age group. Not quite as pricey as "the typical French camp or fat camp or tennis camp," Stanley remarked, the endeavor quickly spawned similar enterprises based at Duke, Northwestern, and the University of Denver. A new priority, overlooked in his portrayal of his radical accelerants as "stable introverts," had emerged: to "encourage participants to be far more interactive socially." Prodding from adults hardly seemed called for. "It was a wonder beyond any experience I might have imagined," remembered an early summer program participant who later returned as a computer teacher, and he wasn't referring to his blitz course in astronomy. "I was surrounded by a fellowship of geeks."

But what about girls? That was a "hot topic," Stanley noted with little of the enthusiasm CTYers might have expressed. He was annoyed to find the gender disparity among high math scorers attracting media attention, partly due to his own new "personal project, if not a passion": identifying more tippy-top math stars like Jonathan and Joe, the one-in-ten-thousand rarities. While CTY administrators were adding over-500 verbal scorers for a more coed mix of campers, Stanley narrowed his focus to a "700–800 on SAT-M Before Age 13 Group"—which proved overwhelmingly male. By 1983, he and a collaborator had turned up a total of 260 eligible boys and 20 girls. That a gap existed came as no surprise. (The broader search, with the lower math cutoff, had turned up twice as many boys as girls.) Its size, though, delivered a jolt. Even a math-phobe could calculate the gender ratio: thirteen to one.

Stanley, quite sure that innate differences were at work, didn't appreciate the heat from the women's movement. The fraught issues "need to be investigated by other people," he grumbled in 1984. "I'm getting awfully tired of the strident feminist who says, 'Why don't you do more?'"

More, if that meant anointing ace math test-takers on the verge of puberty as a genius club bound for greatness, might not work so well with girls as with boys in any case. For Sergey Brin, enrolling in a CTY program the summer he turned fourteen must have seemed like an obvious step. It offered the blend of fast-track study and brainy bonding favored by his Russian-Jewish father, Michael Brin, a fierce math professor at the University of Maryland—and by Sergey, too. Six when he arrived in the United States from Moscow in 1979 with his family, he had become a cocky cut-up and computer guy by middle school, eager for any occasion to advance (and advertise) his math precocity. Brin later described himself as a beneficiary of the Montessori approach: free-range learning for kids until they turn twelve and then, "because of the hormones that boys have, you actually need to send them to do hard labor in their teens. Otherwise, their mind gets distracted." The key was "to maintain focus, even through these difficult years," he felt, and he joked that old-style farm work was out.

And co-ed peer fun was in, CTY administrators understood, not that they scripted it or anticipated the social dynamics. By the time Sergey signed on for his three-week dose of academic intensity in 1987, CTYers had come up with their own formula. The summer immersion featured a quirky extracurricular culture that no parent would find described in the official promotional material. A favorite ritual was a rendition of "American Pie," followed by a group chant, "Die! Die! Die! Die! Live! Live! Live! Live! Sex! Sex! Sex! Sex! More! More! More! More!," at the end of the weekly dances that were now part of geekdom. The zaniest campers—the guy, say, with the orange jumpsuit and outré attitude—could count on being the cult heroes they probably weren't back at school. But for a math girl with bold aspirations, the quest for break-the-mold allure was still daunting, even at CTY nerd camp.

When Yoko Matsuoka traveled to Florida at fifteen in the fall of 1987, her destination was high-powered tennis camp. She was a Tokyo sports prodigy who had devoted her phenomenal energy to excelling on the court, eager to find a way to be more than a dutiful middle school wonk. (If she had read the *Time* cover story on "Those Asian American Whiz Kids," out in late August of '87, the quote from a high school teacher in New York's Chinatown wouldn't have surprised her: "Now they think all we know how to do is sit in front of a computer.") Every good girl in Japan was supposed to be an ideal student, so at eleven, introvert though she was, she had decided on an alternative. The only child of two athletic parents, fervent fans of the "bad boy" tennis star John McEnroe, Yoko had seen a different route for an ambitious upstart like her. Her idol excelled, but he was a rebel type, too. Among his many feats, that attitude especially inspired her, not that she dared overtly embrace it.

Elite talent development in tennis (as in girls' gymnastics) was on the rise by the mid-1980s, and Japan caught the wave as well. The surge in resources was the youth sports equivalent of the "wealth of facilitative options" that, as Stanley later noted, was fast replacing the "dearth of special, supplemental, accelerative educational opportunities we encountered prior to 1971." In 1978 a coach named Nick Bollettieri had opened a brutally rigorous tennis academy in Florida. Soon renowned for its stellar roster of junior players, the "tennis factory" model inspired global imitators. Every day at three o'clock, when classmates at her all-girls Catholic school in Tokyo trooped to *juku*, or "cram school," Yoko boarded a train to a tennis clinic in the suburbs for hours of conditioning and drill. Every night she returned home at ten-thirty without having eaten dinner. She rose at six-thirty the next morning to hurry off to school. For Yoko, tennis was the focus, but she loved helping fellow students finish their math homework from cram school the day before. She didn't put it this way, but here was her chance to show off academically—math came easily to her—without being a goody-goody grade-grubber at all.

Yoko rechristened herself Yoky upon her arrival in the United

States, where finding her place yet distinguishing herself presented a new set of challenges. She had come to attend Bollettieri's newly expanded academy in Bradenton, Florida. Before an afternoon of boot-camp-style training at the large spread, the tennis stars spent a morning at the local public schools. Yoky, initially a shy exchange student with shaky English, said barely a word in her classes for three months, but teachers took note that she was ahead in math and physics. In what little spare time she had, she focused on burnishing her language as well as social skills by watching *Family Ties* and, later,

YOKY MATSUOKA

The Cosby Show. She picked up the idea that a wacky "airhead" image was the American girl's secret to avoiding peer ostracism and getting attention. Being a jock also definitely gave her a boost.

Yoky still wasn't ready to make math and science interests a priority. At any rate, she wasn't ready to do so publicly, and she didn't have to. By now Stanley himself had decided that radical acceleration was unnecessarily "flamboyant," thanks to that new "wealth of facilitative options." As she settled in, Yoky could avail herself of advanced placement unobtrusively. Back in Tokyo, she had balked at being just another dutiful girl grind. Now she was aware that being a girl geek in the United States was just too weird to be cool. Midyear, when she dared to start talking, she was stunned to find that her peers "think that I'm actually cute"—and she wasn't about to jinx it. "Come on, this is crazy!" she felt, and shrugged off the academic distinctions that came her way. She saw her friends' raised eyebrows when signs of nerdy high achievement slipped out. Tenacity and prowess on the tennis court, though, served her perfectly: a source of popularity but also of purposeful autonomy.

The freedom she felt from the constraints of tame schoolgirl life in Japan was thrilling. Yoky was determined to stay in America when her year was up, and her parents gave in—on the condition that she apply to a more academically rigorous private school. Her tennis aspirations still high, Yoky sought out a first-rate athletic program as well and ended up at a private school near Santa Barbara, California. Stanley would have approved of her pace and the improvising that enabled it. After exhausting the school's math offerings, Yoky was tutored a couple of times a week by a professor from nearby Santa Barbara City College. The next year she took almost all her courses there, while finishing up a few high school requirements and toiling away at tennis—and keeping up the ditzy-girl-jock persona among her peers.

But her persistent refusal to fully embrace math-star status might well have puzzled Stanley (especially since daughters of Asian-born-and-educated parents predominated in the still small but steadily growing female cohort in the 700M group, and they were a big share of girl CTYers, too). His entire mission, after all, presumed that early membership in the company of supertalented math minds was a welcome spur to excel. It certainly was in the case of Sergey Brin, singled out as special well before his CTY summer. For a brash boy with "more nerdy interests than most of my peers," as he put it later, the imprimatur of precocious math star served to elevate rather than isolate him as he, like Yoky, took college courses in high school. It served him well as he sped on to the University of Maryland. He got his B.A. in three years in 1993, just before he turned twenty, with honors in math and computer science, and he headed to Stanford for a Ph.D. with more graduate courses already under his belt than peers from Harvard or MIT could boast.

For Yoky, not that she summed up the situation in quite these terms, the mantle of math brilliance—with its aura of innate giftedness, its elitist spirit, its presumption of single-minded focus and foreordained career direction—didn't fit right. While she juggled tennis matches, problem sets, and different career dreams every week (medicine, nutrition, physics, math, engineering, professional

tennis), she had always known one thing she didn't want: to be anybody's idea of just the good girl on a predictable, adult-approved
path. When she arrived at the University of California at Berkeley,
a scheduling dilemma forced a decision: if she planned on taking
labs, she would have to miss tennis team practices. She opted for
labs, but it was a jock-inspired idea—a mechanical "tennis buddy"
she had daydreamed about years earlier—that got her excited about
robotics. Yoky chose an overwhelmingly male-dominated major,
electrical engineering and computer science. Outside of class, she
kept up the airhead style and skirted mention of her field (feeling
that it was like saying, "Oh, I'm one of those men who don't wash
their hair and smell bad and don't dress well"). She made sure not
to be caught carrying a textbook, vanishing into the library at exam
time.

In retrospect, Yoky sometimes lamented the stress of masquer-
ading: she hadn't felt exactly liberated to "embrace her inner geek"
early on. More often she celebrated the multitasking that her "dual
life" taught her, and the multidisciplinary interests she had carved
out time for. Well before she found herself at Google, the contours of her path and Sergey's converged. At Stanford, with lots
of graduate coursework already behind him, he now had time for
some diversifying, California style—learning to sail, Rollerblad-
ing, trying out trapeze arts and gymnastics. His father inquired at
one point "if he was taking any advanced courses." Sergey's answer:
"Yes, advanced swimming." Tech entrepreneurship invited sampling, too, at a university actively encouraging it by the 1990s; an
ideal collaborator, Larry Page, soon joined the computer science
department. Sticking to the advanced-degree route, endorsed by
Michael Brin with a fervor that Julian Stanley shared, had lost its
allure for Sergey. "I tried so many different things in grad school,"
he said later, having left without a Ph.D. "The more you stumble around, the more likely you are to stumble across something
valuable."

In Yoky's case, finding a way to seem, and feel, girl-like and not
grindlike brought real rewards. She avoided getting locked into a

particular academic groove before she was ready—a feat of self-definition that ended up fueling high confidence as well as social openness. She also deftly navigated an obstacle to high achievement that had begun to interest psychologists in the mid-1990s: stereotype threat. When people internalize the negative expectations associated with a group to which they belong, they proceed to underperform on tests or other challenges. Girls get lumped as bad at math; nerds, presumed good at math, get labeled as flops with the opposite sex. (Jonathan Edwards knew the burden of that assumption.) Both girls and nerds often get tarred with a reputation for a blinkered lack of creativity, of bold and charismatic "attitude."

The clout of sports, and her undercover approach to math, helped Yoky escape all of that. It wasn't until she got to MIT as a graduate student in 1993 that she could address more directly the gender and peer pressures in male-dominated high-level math and computer pursuits. When she filled out a nametag with "airhead" instead of "Yoky," her mentor (the pathbreaking roboticist Rodney Brooks) advised what she had begun to recognize herself: it was time to highlight, rather than hide, her idiosyncratic course. That turned out to mean being more than a pioneer in neurobotics, the multidisciplinary realm where her tennis buddy schemes led her. She delved into neuroscience, cross-fertilizing fields in a quest to create a brain-linked artificial hand with human dexterity to help the disabled.

For Yoky, dropping the antic-girl act also meant cultivating a different, cool-girl geek image. Named a MacArthur fellow in 2007, and by then an associate professor at the University of Washington in Seattle and the mother of three, she often found herself an ambassador of sorts. She didn't pretend to have easy answers as she addressed a younger generation of girls with STEM leanings. You still risk being considered a social loser, she sighed—and she didn't recommend her airhead strategy. Still, she thought her path could be instructive. Plenty about it was. You needn't be, as she had made sure not to be, conspicuously singled out as a preteen math wonder. Early sorting processes like SMPY unwittingly convey that math is only for geniuses. In fact, anointment as a precocious quant may backfire, eroding resilience: girls, Yoky noted, are more prone than boys to take occasional lousy grades as verdicts on their potential.

She emphasized collaboration and the goal of using technology to help people directly, interests she figured other women shared with her. And she looked back on her tennis obsession as a real asset, not just for jock prestige. The early focus essential to the serious pursuit of sports—or music, Yoky also suggested—could prove more useful than pulling off prodigious math feats. At the same time, juggling different talents and social groups was good practice for coping with the fate that hard-driving women better expect: an extra-heavy dose of competing demands. The year before Yoky headed south for a sabbatical year at brand-new Google X (a Silicon Valley swerve away from academia that eventually led her to Apple, which she left in late 2016), she shared thoughts in a 2009 interview on Cogito.org, a website sponsored by the Center for Talented Youth. Among other things, she described the hectic pace of a life that was anything but solitary, either in her busy lab or at home chasing her kids around.

Julian Stanley, though no longer alive to read the interview, would surely have saluted her. He had died at eighty-seven in 2005, by which time girls made up nearly a quarter of the 700M group (now called the Study of Exceptional Talent), a tripling over the course of two decades. Back when he had rather brusquely left it to others to "do more" to help girls catch up to the boys in his select club of superhigh math scorers, he hadn't known what to expect. But Stanley had always been an undaunted and impatient improviser, and so was Yoky. Ready to do what she could to make a dent in an intimidating boy-geek culture, she also urged girls to be bold interlopers. "I am very interested in changing this trend over time, somehow, but it will take time with concrete role models," she told Cogito. "So my advice is to not worry about it and JUST DO IT."

· 5 ·

Standing out and speeding ahead, yet not ending up too isolated—or too insular: Jonathan Edwards had those challenges very much in mind as he approached his fifties, the age Julian Stanley had been when he embarked on his mission to cultivate a math-minded elite. Over the decades since his IntraNet startup, success for Edwards had been inseparable from struggle. Against the odds, he felt, he lucked into family life: in 1991 he married a woman he once described as "all heart" to his "all brains." They went on to have three children. After "many years of toil and tears," he and his partner sold IntraNet in 1998 for stock worth $49.1 million.

His Tom Swift stage behind him, Edwards was still an uncredentialed outlier. In 2002 he found a niche at MIT as an unpaid research fellow in the Computer Science and Artificial Intelligence Lab's Software Design Group. Half a decade earlier, in 1997, Joe Bates, a full-time professor at Carnegie Mellon, entered the business world: he founded a company using AI to create newly rich interactive drama in video games for children, featuring characters who seemed to have feelings and awareness. In 2005, now the CEO of another company, he tackled a bold hardware project still under way a decade later—a superfast, less accurate chip, which he felt held the key to a new leap forward in AI, as well as to advances in other sciences and in augmented reality.

Edwards would never be socially at ease, he knew by now, or free of the pressure to leave behind an "intellectual legacy." He had found an urgent question that consumed him—how to radically simplify the programming of software applications, which had become extraordinarily intricate. Edwards's paradigm-challenging mission was itself daunting, and in 2015 he was still experimenting. With his "vision of bringing programming to everyone," he wasn't thinking small. His quest went against the grain of the geek hierarchy in which he had risen so young and so fast. He left MIT in 2015 for a stint with the Communications Design Group, newly created by Alan Kay, who had dreamed up the Dynabook for "children of all ages" forty-five years earlier at Xerox PARC. "Our nerd culture embraces inhuman levels of complexity," Edwards wrote on his blog, *Alarming Development,* in 2016.

> Mastering mind-boggling complexity is our mutant super-power. It is our tribal marker. Complexity is the air we breathe, and so it is invisible to us. Simplification will only come from outside this culture. To disrupt programming I first have to reinvent it for a fresh audience of non-programmers.

Edwards chafed at the hypermeritocratic elitism he saw on all sides, constraining boldness and openness. In conversation half a decade earlier, he had sighed at the MIT graduate student scene, packed with "brilliant, compulsive achievers . . . like Olympic athletes," with no life, no youth. Back in the 1970s, when the computer revolution had just begun, young "outliers and freaks like myself," he said, had felt free to try "wild stuff," to veer off appointed paths and break rules. Living in the affluent Boston suburb of Wellesley, he worried over the competitive stress in his children's lives, too. He didn't wish his youthful misfit miseries on his daughter and two sons, but he didn't want them caught up in what he called "the achievatron thing" either.

That was his phrase for a whole culture of studiously calibrated achievement, starting early and culminating in a cutthroat college admissions process at top-tier schools. Jonathan, with Joe, had been a kind of harbinger, and CTY, however unwittingly, had encouraged the downward creep of accelerated, adult-directed credentializing for student superstars. In an online forum for former participants called RealCTY, such complaints got an airing. For the alumnus who had extolled the "fellowship of geeks" in the early 1980s, CTY's remarkable growth and success jeopardized what had felt special. He lamented the spread of a "get-ahead" attitude, students "moaning about transfer credit and placement issues." Younger alumni on the site reproached the staff for stifling the best and most important part of the experience: peer communing and craziness outside the classroom.

As two honorary forerunners of CTY, Edwards and Bates were

eager to share a Julian Stanley association with their children, but acceleration held little allure. When his eldest made the cut for a summer program, Edwards was pleased that his son had zero interest in fast-track math and happily gravitated to offbeat courses (existentialism, literature of the fantastic). Jonathan hoped his children would soak up what he had missed out on—learning "how life works, [how] to be balanced," how to bond. Bates, though still haunted by how easy it can be for any kid to "absorb as normal the notion that everything should happen fast," was glad when his daughter wanted to enroll in a CTY session. He was always telling his two children what he felt he had been told a little too late: proceed at the pace *you* want. In fact, he said, "I'm sure they're sick of hearing it." But in an ideal world, Joe thought, every student would have the chance to do just that. Amid the great variety of minds out there, his own didn't strike him as particularly rare.

Stanley's pioneers—the boys he had so eagerly steered onto the established academic path while their computer-obsessed counterparts on the West Coast were forging ahead without much adult supervision—had ended up looking and sounding, if anything, more like the outsiders. Jobs and Gates had thrived on their combative alliances with friends, flouting guidance from their elders. Impatient arrogance had quickly become a trademark. (The professor who supervised Harvard's computer lab, where Gates had been at all hours before he dropped out, described him as "an obnoxious human being . . . not a pleasant fellow to have around." At Atari, where Jobs worked after dropping out of Reed, he let older employees know that he considered many of them "dumb shits.") They, like Sergey Brin and Larry Page later on at Google, helped fuel what Ellen Ullman called "the cult of the boy engineer." Theirs was a hacker world renowned more for being a ruthlessly competitive hothouse than a free-ranging enterprise.

Silicon Valley was, of course, hearing plenty about how "the culture of programming unfairly excludes" some groups, Edwards wrote on his blog. "More power to them," he said of the underrepresented aspirants clamoring "to join the programming elite and get a spot at the startup trough." But in his view, a "bigger issue with far greater importance to society" demanded attention. A potent toy, as Stewart Brand had called the computer decades earlier, had "come to the people." The dream that the computer would prove a truly liberating tool for all had not. "The bigger injustice is that programming has become an elite: a vocation requiring rare talents, grueling training, and total dedication," Edwards declared, his reclusive young self surely in mind. "Normal humans are effectively excluded from developing software," he felt, but including them was the cause that now drove him. Wryly anointing himself "a Mad Computer Scientist," he had emailed several years earlier that "my goal in life since an early age has been to leave behind me one good idea," and speed had long since ceased to be the point. "A new way of programming will be it, or nothing."

PART IV

———————

MIRACLES

and

STRIVERS

CHAPTER 7

The Mystery of Savant Syndrome

· 1 ·

Bill Gates has been informally diagnosed with it. So, after the fact, have Newton, Mozart, Yeats, and Wittgenstein. The label gets applied to Bobby Fischer, obsessive and unable to look anybody in the eye. Reclusive William James Sidis, with his trolley fixation, is a candidate, too. And Jonathan Edwards raised this possibility in retrospect: maybe Asperger's syndrome, not just off-the-charts mathematical skills, helped account for his sense of being so out of step. Of course, he had grown up well before the autism spectrum disorder—called by some "the engineers' disease"—claimed a place in the 1994 revision of the *Diagnostic and Statistical Manual of Mental Disorders,* psychiatry's authoritative guide. Nearly twenty years later, in 2013, the Asperger's label was officially dropped. But high-functioning autism had come trailing an aura of precocious genius, along with painful social cluelessness, and that aura was here to stay. The very bright yet remote "little professor" profile had become, as a journalist put it, "a signature disorder of the high-tech information age." The diagnosis, rooted in descriptions published in 1944 by the Viennese pediatrician Hans Asperger, seemed to be everywhere—a portent of struggle, surely, yet also perhaps of unusual potential. Hadn't Asperger said that "for success in science and art a dash of autism is essential"?

An unsettling experience, or some version of it, no longer belongs to obscure lore: a wriggly toddler, obsessed with numbers and letters, is already spelling out words—when he isn't intently lining up his toy cars or melting down at loud noises. Perhaps he begins to seem even harder to engage than usual. Or a teacher or relative remarks that he isn't really interacting with other kids. A parent's something-isn't-quite-right feeling intensifies. It is time to turn to, where else, the Internet. Venture beyond UrbanBaby and there, awaiting discovery, is a new term that might help explain an avid, and cuddle-averse, code-breaker: "Is my child an autistic savant?" Dr. Darold A. Treffert, a soft-spoken Wisconsin psychiatrist in his eighties who has been called the "godfather of savant research," was surprised by how often visitors to his website sent that question to his inbox as the new millennium got under way. Hopes and fears about what a child will grow into, or out of, can take sudden swerves.

An expert consultant on the multi-Oscar-winning *Rain Man* (1988), Treffert had banished the old *idiot* prefix and helped spread an awareness of a disorienting phenomenon: remarkable gifts emerging in tandem with profound neurological problems— and "without lessons or training," he marveled. In the film, Dustin Hoffman's Raymond Babbitt, fidgety and uncommunicative, could count spilled toothpicks at a glance and multiply big numbers very fast. Neuroscientists and psychologists, though stymied by a sample size too small for rigorous study, were fascinated. Musical gifts (including absolute pitch), artistic flair (generally hyperrealistic), calendrical agility (naming the days of the week on which particular dates fall), computational virtuosity: the startling skills, accompanied by astonishing powers of memory, seemed to be disproportionately associated with autism.

Treffert had a new prefix for those who burst forth with more than "splinter skills." They were "prodigious"—the rarest subcategory of already rare savants, who would count as prodigies even if they had no disability. Soon enough his informal global inventory of prodigious savants could boast a bona-fide American prodigy, a preteen with a reedy voice and an innocently intent Harry Potter face. His name was Matt Savage, and by the time Treffert met him, he had been hailed a "Mozart of jazz." Born in 1992 in Boston and given an autism spectrum diagnosis three years later, Matt emerged as the perfect poster child for the newly capacious vision of savant gifts, not that anyone told him the term. Matt, easily overwhelmed by a clamorous world, loved multiplying large numbers, performing calendrical stunts, amassing facts—the telltale memory-based, repetitive sort of talents that cropped up in roughly one in ten people on the autism spectrum. But his real fervor was directed elsewhere. Starting at six, Matt had made remarkably rapid progress on the piano. He was soon jamming and composing at a sped-up tempo, too. A CD of his pieces, which he performed with a jazz trio, was out by the time he was seven.

For savants, precisely that kind of creative and improvisational work had been presumed out of bounds, yet here was an autistic child with a near spontaneous gift for it. Even "normal" musical prodigies rarely manage such feats of invention—and when they do, *Mozartian* is almost always the adjective that gets bestowed. In the case of another prolific young composer who found himself in the spotlight, it was inevitable. Jay Greenberg, born half a year before Matt, shared the Harry Potter look—thick eyebrows and glasses, and an intense gaze that didn't quite engage. He also displayed similar sensory hypersensitivity and what seemed like effortless musical wizardry. The boys didn't share a genre: before he turned ten, Jay was busy transcribing classical orchestral works straight from his head onto paper—among them a haunting Brahmsian *Overture to 9/11*. By contrast, tuning in to people proved a struggle for him, yet Jay also didn't share an autism diagnosis with Matt.

Without one, Jay was a prodigy who, however anomalous his brain might be, didn't officially belong to a prodigious savant category that would always be tiny but was growing slowly as awareness of the phenomenon spread. Treffert's unusual club soon had another member, whose mother had found her way to his website. Jacob Barnett was six years younger than Jay and Matt. As a toddler in rural Indiana, Jake had retreated into autistic silence, only to reemerge and surge ahead in math and science, astronomy in particular. He displayed phenomenal powers of recall and, barely out of kindergarten, began discussing Kepler's laws. Jake could also play back tunes and do calendrical computing, his mother discovered before long. Surfing the Internet together, they looked for kids like him. When they came upon other savants, he eagerly displayed similar skills. She called Treffert, who predicted further surprises.

Whatever the distinctions among the prodigious boys might amount to, these children were—glaringly, unmistakably—different. And at the turn of the millennium, that otherness wasn't explained away or played down or defined up (by, say, a term such as *radical accelerant*). Jake's academic leaps thrilled his parents less as a sign that he was speeding ahead than as evidence that he could avoid derailment: terrified when he had shut down as a toddler, they dreaded that ever happening again. Unlike their prodigy predecessors, Matt and Jay were quite obviously not on a fast track to popular renown, or cutting-edge inventions, or vast fortunes (or likely to be swept up in an unanticipated wave of competitive interest, as Bobby Fischer had been). Their musical obsessions were hardly trendy—not that the small boys noticed. And their parents didn't much care. Above all, they were intent on helping their hard-to-reach children engage somehow.

Propelled by sudden inspiration and rapt concentration, these strange young minds in turn moved parents and mentors to transcend conventionally ambitious dreams and refocus: look at how the unusual gifts could work wonders *now*. Avid testers like Julian Stanley had emphasized measurable mastery and a future-focused trajectory. In their defiantly idiosyncratic ways, so had tech-inclined upstarts from Bill Gates to Jonathan Edwards. By contrast, these prodigies highlighted the mystery of inborn talents. Even if the made-for-prime-time saga of uncanny virtuosity and effortless progress wasn't the full story for Matt or Jay or Jake, as it surely wasn't, here were gifts that had blossomed so far without competitive pressure. A tidy or speedy script for long-term success wasn't on hand either. The boys and their families—as well as the experts probing for affinities among prodigious savants, "regular" prodigies, and the rest of us—were playing it very much by ear.

· 2 ·

You could say that inside just about every well-rounded young wonder touted in the twentieth century there had been a lopsided, often lonely rarity trying to get out. Autistic prodigies at the turn of the millennium succeeded—and then some. The boys invited the kind of awed appraisal that had greeted (and soon grated on) the nineteenth century's most famous shut-in child, Helen Keller, and her teacher, Annie Sullivan, christened a "miracle worker" by Mark Twain. He also called her Keller's "other half." The pair's emotionally entwined, pedagogically intense alliance was indeed crucial—and would have been impossible without Keller's "soul-sense." That was her phrase for the acute empathy that served as her special radar. Matt Savage and Jake Barnett experienced the opposite: "mind blindness," the inability to extrapolate the mental states of others that is a signature symptom of autism. And if Jay Greenberg had any aptitude for social intuition, he kept it well hidden. The prodigy ideal of readily engaged standouts and deeply attuned mentors—an ideal so often observed in the breach—was obviously irrelevant.

Both the boys and the adults on whom they depended could hardly have been more disoriented—which is not to say they were unfocused. Acutely sensitive to stimuli, fixated on details, reliant on strict regimens and repetitive behavior, cut off from conventional expectations: the profile fit Matt and Jake starting very young. A version of it also fit their mothers, caught up in the all-consuming mission of doing their best to deal with children who weren't merely out of step with peers, as Jonathan Edwards had been. Their sons seemed barely to register others. Meanwhile, Jay's parents coped with a situation Bobby Fischer's mother had known well: a hard-to-handle, exceptionally intelligent little boy on a track of his own, soon prompting calls from teachers. "So a problem child?" asked an interviewer from *60 Minutes* in 2004. "Very problematic," Jay's mother replied. Yet there was also a silver lining of sorts. The extreme isolation could be a spur to learning, as Annie

Sullivan had noted in Helen's case. "She has one advantage over ordinary children, that nothing from without distracts her attention from her studies."

But first comes the challenge—presented by ordinary and extraordinary children alike—of spotting the something within that might direct youthful curiosity and help develop raw capacities. Prodigies generally make that task astonishingly easy, very early, as Jay certainly did. On *60 Minutes,* his mother, Orna Weinroth, an Israeli-born painter, implied a sudden epiphany. Out of nowhere Jay at two began drawing cellos, she said, and soon they morphed into notes on a staff. "This child told me, he said, 'I'm gonna be dead if I am not composing. I have to compose. This is all I want to do.' . . . And when a child that young tells you where their vision is, or where they're going, you don't have a choice."

Actually, "Bluejay," as Jay called himself, hadn't taken flight quite so spontaneously. Living in Chapel Hill, North Carolina, where Jay's father, Robert, was teaching linguistics at the university, the Greenbergs enjoyed regular chamber music gatherings, sometimes in their own living room. Jay was transfixed (he got to see and hear cellos up close) as he was nowhere else. Naturally his parents paid eager attention to that messy musical notation of his. And when Jay had filled many notebooks by the age of six, the Greenbergs could turn, thanks to their musical network, to a Juilliard professor and composer named Samuel Zyman for advice.

Matt and Jake, by contrast, are testimony to how obscured those inner interests and aptitudes can be, and how difficult—and crucial—tapping into them may prove. Who knows whether they may be developed into an exceptional talent, but they just might serve as a basic conduit to the world. Or could, if not for a catch-22: autistic children supply at best garbled signals to guide their elders. Matt was chattering away and reading at eighteen months, and counting Cheerios in his high chair. His parents—Diane Savage, then a computer programmer for a company in the Boston area, and her husband, Larry, a chemical engineer who worked in IT at Raytheon—took pride in their precocious son. At the same time, they couldn't ignore Matt's hand-flapping, his failure to make eye contact, his aversion to touch and to all kinds of sounds, even the swishing of windshield wipers. He would throw fits over rituals gone awry. (Matt's bedtime routines, jotted down for his grand-mother, filled a legal-size page.) The Savages, who in the early 1990s knew next to nothing about autism, felt they had an expla-nation for their brilliant boy who demanded quiet, except when he wailed at a noisy world: "He's so busy learning things, he can't deal with the sensory side of things was our theory," Diane said. But Matt's brief foray into Montessori preschool—he lasted two days before being "officially expelled," as she put it—tested the theory. Something just wasn't right, and Diane, a woman used to getting results, now needed answers.

With Jake, the discordance was more dramatic, as his mother, Kristine Barnett, chronicled in her 2013 memoir, *The Spark: A Mother's Story of Nurturing, Genius, and Autism.* Before he turned two in the spring of 2000, he was a giggly, easygoing toddler who wrestled with his dad and was a wizard with words. He talked early and recited the alphabet backward and forward. He memorized DVDs (not just in English: he liked switching the language selec-tion). He read along with a CD-ROM of Dr. Seuss. But gradually he ceased to speak or respond. Kristine, who poured her abun-dant creative energy into directing a lively day care center in their garage, watched him gaze for hours at plaid fabrics and patterns of shadows. He would spin in dizzying circles, stare at his hoard of flash cards, shrink from physical contact. At least he didn't throw fits. Michael, Jake's father and a Target employee, kept saying it was just a phase. But articles about autism were everywhere now, and Kristine's mother, struck by one, dared to suggest they had bet-ter find out what was wrong.

For both the Savages and the Barnetts, a diagnosis delivered a reverse epiphany. They, unlike the Greenbergs with Jay, got no sud-den insight into what their sons desperately wanted to do. Instead, it now hit them how much they, the parents, were going to *have* to do—and how little they, or perhaps anybody, understood what was happening in those young heads. "Your son," Diane was stunned to hear when she took Matt, now three, to be evaluated at Boston

Children's Hospital, "has pervasive developmental disorder with hyperlexia. He's perseverative and echolalic and speaks in a Gestalt manner." Her multisyllabic talker, Diane now realized, was imitating more than communicating. Churning through books, Matt wasn't following the plots. The experts proposed the then newly minted Asperger's label. Six years later, Kristine received the same verdict when a battery of in-home assessments revealed that along with radically skewed skills, Jake had a superhigh IQ. Unaware that Asperger's was on the dreaded autism spectrum, Kristine was briefly buoyed—and then a second evaluation before he turned three put him into the "full-blown autism" category.

In both families, the diagnoses coincided with the arrival of new babies—barely noticed by their big brothers but guaranteed, or so it soon seemed, to overwhelm already daunted parents. Matt's sister was a difficult infant who went on to present her own set of developmental issues. The Barnetts' second son, diagnosed with a dire neurological disorder called reflex sympathetic dystrophy, was in acute pain and danger. Yet the cascade of humbling burdens inspired, if anything, unprecedented helicoptering zeal. Convinced there was no time to waste in fighting back against fatalistic predictions for sons like theirs, Diane and Kristine redoubled their focus on their firstborns, while their husbands stepped up to deal on other fronts.

The maternal approach, at the outset, was lockstep-parenting-according-to-the-experts of a sort that could make the most Ivy League–obsessed overschedulers look like slackers. "We research the hell out of everything. That's our scientific approach," explained Larry, who quit his job to manage the intricate family logistics. (He took up financial investment work from home.) Diane, who left her job as well, immediately turned for advice to the autism crusader then on the cutting edge. The very night she got back from Matt's evaluation at Children's Hospital, Diane called Bernard Rimland, the founder of the Autism Research Institute, not expecting him to pick up. It was late, but he did.

The Savages put Matt on the DAN! (Defeat Autism Now) protocol, the array of dietary strictures and other treatments that Rimland had begun promoting—the cure, in his view, for a biomedical disorder caused by toxins, nutritional issues, and immunological problems. Matt's sensitivities, his parents felt, quickly improved. He wasn't easy to get through to, but they put his hyperlexia to use: often unresponsive to verbal directions, Matt couldn't resist reading written notes. He also underwent Auditory Integration Training, another experimental treatment for autism gaining popularity in the early 1990s. And Diane choreographed an intensive weekly regimen of carefully vetted therapy sessions (occupational, physical, speech, behavioral) for him, plus a roster of parent support group meetings and conferences for her.

Every interaction with Matt had an "ulterior motive," she said. Even what looked like downtime at home was hardly a respite. The purpose of their games was to help him overcome social barriers, learn new behaviors, acquire the basic life skills he lacked. But Diane had rewards at the ready, too, to keep him on task with the retinue of specialists. She couldn't order enough math workbooks and puzzles as treats for a boy who could tell her, and did, "My mind is made of math problems." At the nearby autism preschool collaborative the Savages joined, Matt and his parents learned a lot from a wonderful teacher's positive strategies, and by luck she moved on to the public kindergarten at the same time as Matt did. Still, Diane was exhausted, and Matt, now six, seemed to be slipping. Bothered by sounds again, he acted out more.

A half decade later, out in Middle America, the Barnetts were several steps lower on the income ladder than the Savages, and their son was drifting further toward the low-functioning end of the autism spectrum. For Kristine and Michael, state-funded professional services for children with autism were the affordable resource at hand—a special education realm by now more systematized than the cure-focused vanguard at the core of Diane's tailor-made treatment plan. Jake was signed up for the full range of therapy that Indiana's First Steps program offered children with developmental issues until they turned three. "The calendar on the kitchen wall was so jam-packed that nobody but I could read the microscopic handwriting I used to cram it all in," Kristine noted.

Doing further research, and pestering (her word) therapists who had become friends, Kristine wanted to do more. She was spurred on, and scared, by the persistent contrast between the eager mayhem of her day care kids and the mute disengagement of a son who had once tumbled among them. Kristine and Michael added forty hours a week of "applied behavior analysis" work with Jake, later shifting to a less drill-oriented and more child-initiated "Floortime" therapy (which was just as time-intensive). And when First Steps services ceased, and a summer loomed before state-funded developmental preschool began, Kristine got even busier. She devised more sensory-rich activities to keep Jake from losing ground, enlisting high school volunteers to help.

But she could tell Jake wasn't really tuning in, and after starting to communicate by pointing at cards with pictures—a big step—he made little progress. He did, though, surprise her. At a toy store one day, after listening to various music box tunes, he proceeded to play them all on an electric roll-out piano mat by the cash register. She also couldn't help noticing that during the activities he did on his own time (what little there was of it), "his focus was ferocious," and the results could be startling. That summer Jake was obsessed with Kristine's knitting basket. He pulled out yarn and wrapped it all around the kitchen. Instead of a "terrible, tangled mess," she was stunned to find he had woven intricate multicolored webs.

What the two of them needed, it dawned on her, were breaks from the constant work of therapy. Kristine began scooping Jake up, along with a box of Popsicles, for short nighttime outings to a nearby country pasture—plain old childhood fun. He still barely acknowledged her presence, but he was obviously transfixed by the stars, even if he couldn't tell her that. Several months into their "dates," he once actually blurted out a "night-night" at bedtime. So Kristine was crushed as she watched the relaxed boy of those summer moments regress when he began heading off on the bus to spend his days in developmental prekindergarten.

· 3 ·

However tirelessly they followed the experts' regimens in the early years, neither Diane nor Kristine was about to settle for mere repetitive structure and drills. ("Did you get in your hours?" was the refrain among parents with autistic children.) Their best guides, as they did their utmost not to forget, were the boys right in front of them—each stuck at a difficult point. Matt, struggling with sensory overload at six, and Jake, who seemed miles from being kindergarten-ready: both had their mothers feeling stymied, discouraged by the narrow emphasis on the basic skills their boys lacked. Their maternal reflex, which helped them forge on, was to shift the focus to gifts they were sure lurked within.

"I always believed that even when he was hard to reach, there was a shining star in there," Diane later told a CNN interviewer eager to hear about Matt. Her goal: "we just had to find a way to get to it." The rhetoric of unshakable faith in an inner light ran through Kristine's book, too, an amped-up echo of Annie Sullivan's insistence on kindling Helen Keller's interests, bucking straitlaced pedagogy in the process. "I knew my child better than any expert could," Kristine wrote. "And I saw a spark in Jake. Some days, true, there was only the faintest glimmer."

Framed this way, manic helicoptering became something more like heroic liberating. The top-down micromanaging was supplanted, or at any rate richly supplemented, by bottom-up empowering. Where lore had it that Helen Keller suddenly awoke to the possibilities of language as her teacher spelled into her hand at the water pump, the child-driven drama with these boys was different: discovering and encouraging *their* special language was a quest that kept adults on their toes. That was true for Jay, too. A child of few words, he needed his parents as intermediaries more than as interveners, since his composing fervor readily drew well-positioned facilitators. Jay first met Samuel Zyman, the Juilliard professor who was also a composer, on a visit to New York City when he was six or seven. Small talk and eye contact never happened,

Zyman recalled, but they engaged through music. The notebooks Jay had been filling for years revealed piano sonatas influenced by remarkable insight into how Beethoven wrote his. And when Jay stopped in on a rehearsal of Zyman's guitar concerto, he leaped at the chance to turn pages as Zyman played the orchestral part on the piano. After one run-through, Jay's comments on the piece showed he grasped its structure and harmonies in ways that floored Zyman.

When he was six, math-minded Matt stumbled on his power to make very gratifying sense of a new realm of patterns—thanks to more active help from his mother than she generally took credit for. (Diane was wary of a stage-parent stigma.) A second round of Auditory Integration Training that year did more than make sounds bearable for Matt. Diane and Larry, upstairs in their Sudbury house, were stunned to hear him downstairs playing "London Bridge" and other tunes on a rainbow-keyed Little Tykes xylophone piano that came with color-coded music. This was the same boy who had

gotten upset whenever Diane, trained on the piano as a child, tried to play. (The exception was when he asked for "Peanuts," by which he meant the TV show theme song, or "fast," which meant the third movement of Beethoven's *Moonlight Sonata*.) Now she showed him middle C on their big piano, pointed out how the Little Tyke music sheets matched up with the keys, and explained the way octaves worked. For Matt, whose fascination with numbers and ratios had lately spawned an obsession with roller coasters (he loved reciting their speeds and other

MATT SAVAGE

specs), it all made sense. He quickly figured out the piano's eighty-eight-note language of sound.

Matt later said he was pretty sure he had skipped around in the beginner piano books that Diane promptly pulled out of the closet, where she had been saving them for the day when her children were ready for lessons. She and Larry described him racing straight through them all. Diane once again hurried to the phone. A local piano teacher who came highly recommended (and who, Diane said wryly, sighed when she heard yet another parent touting a gifted child) agreed to meet Matt. His perfect pitch, sight-reading skill, ability to play back what he heard, and astonishing memory—plus his restless energy—left her in no doubt: here was a "special situation," in Diane's words.

As Matt careened between piano and couch, knocking over plants en route, he made remarkable—if unruly—progress in their weekly lessons. When he chafed at being told to play the notes on the page, rather than the ones he thought sounded best, his no-nonsense teacher was firm. Classical pianists, she said, stick with scores. Jazz pianists, his ever responsive mother mentioned, get to improvise. Though Diane and Larry knew little besides that about jazz, Matt remembered they at some point played Miles Davis's *Kind of Blue* for him, and it made a big impression—for a quirky reason: with numbers always very much on the brain, he recalled happily noting several tracks in the nine-minute range (three out of five, as it happens).

An event that made a big impression on his parents happened a year later, one lovely summer day at a crafts fair in Maine when he was seven. As Diane liked to tell the story, the family strolled past a jazz band warming up in a tent, and Matt yanked free of her grasp. He climbed onto the piano bench, asking to play, and when the surprised sax player proposed a blues tune in the key of B-flat, Matt proceeded to chime right in. In truth, as Diane had "to admit sheepishly," *she* was the one who had asked whether the band could play a song with Matt. He would never have reached out that way, and she was just hoping to fend off a tantrum as she tried to extricate him from the tent. But she wasn't embellishing, she stressed, in saying he had never played anything like that before. The sax player ran after them, urging jazz lessons for Matt. Diane, as usual, got right on the phone. This time she called the precollege program at the New England Conservatory. At the audition, held two weeks later, Diane said Matt astonished the faculty.

Faced with a truly boxed-in boy, Kristine emphasized that she was no mere behind-the-scenes facilitator in the unfolding of Jake's powers. She was a "fighter," ready to do battle against a blinkered educational system prone to underestimate children's potential. If a boastful tone crept in, and it did, Kristine's immodest confidence ("I came to see my maternal intuition as a compass pointing true north") and her crusading gumption ("the over-the-top 'muchness' of my schemes was a big part of the way I worked") also drove her crucial decision. She pulled Jake out of state-funded developmental preschool, convinced he was shutting down out of boredom. The boy who clutched his alphabet flash cards (which his teachers told Kristine not to let him bring to school) wanted to learn, her intuition told her. Why should he be destined for stagnation in special education? Never mind grand expectations, her hope was to help pave his way into mainstream kindergarten.

At home, she now carved out time for activities Jake loved and was great at (like puzzles), not just for practice in what he couldn't do (like sit still next to another child)—and at three he began talking again. That didn't mean conversing. Still, Kristine was listening closely to his litanies and realized he wasn't just reciting numbers but adding them, as well as reading and remembering everything. And she saw that Jake, once fixated on his flash cards, now constantly dragged around a college astronomy textbook she had bought at the local Barnes & Noble when she had found him sitting on the floor glued to it. But Kristine couldn't forget about those social skills if he was going to have a shot at kindergarten. So she reached out to other families by email, hoping to add a few other children with autism to the mix. Her goal was a group experience that would suit Jake better than just mingling with her day care crowd seemed to.

When she heard back from one exhausted parent after another, all conveying that she was their "port of last resort," Kristine scaled up her scheme. She founded a charity. Twice a week in the evening, after vacuuming the day care space, she ran "a highly unorthodox kindergarten boot camp." Similarly fervent parents followed her lead in welcoming, rather than squelching, a common symptom in their autistic children: intense and persistent interests. Whether those preoccupations did, or didn't, "match up with some so-called normal template for child development" wasn't important. With Jake's beloved astronomy textbook and their summer stargazing in mind, Kristine arranged an outing for him to see Mars through a telescope at the planetarium on the campus of nearby Butler University, which was holding a special program.

Jake couldn't wait, though on learning that their tickets included a lecture and slides, Kristine had second thoughts—not that he was disruptive or prone to tantrums. But Jake insisted, and rather than squirming, he piped up when nobody else responded to the professor's question about why Mars's moons were elliptical in shape. What size were the moons? Jake asked. Told they were small, he suggested that gravity doesn't exert enough force on them to pull them into spheres. In Kristine's account, "the room went silent," and she was overwhelmed. On the drive home, he couldn't stop talking about the solar system. What struck her as much as her own wonder at the revelation of Jake's passion was "the awe and veneration" shown by others in the audience. They "had been inspired, transported to a better place, and they'd been delivered there by Jake."

Kristine's tone conveyed a humility all too rare in hovering parents, who so often presume that young minds are simply there to be steered. Jake "hadn't been missing after all," she realized, just because he was unreachable. Unhindered, he had been busy working: his repetitive behavior, much as some autism researchers speculated, reflected detail-oriented curiosity rather than being merely a self-soothing habit. "Rage to master" was a relevant phrase coined by another psychologist, Ellen Winner, who concluded that a fiercely self-propelled drive was what set a true prodigy apart from a superindustrious high-achiever. "Nobody was telling Jake *how* to learn," Kristine wrote, "because nobody thought he could. In that way, autism had given Jake a bizarre gift." At the same time, Kristine's reverential version of events had the too-good-to-be-true gloss that the original "miracle worker," more than a century earlier, had noted could be more uplifting than useful. It "rubs me the wrong way" was Annie Sullivan's response to an "extravagant" early report that heralded selfless labors (hers) and phenomenal feats (Helen's). "The simple facts," Sullivan went on, "would be so much more convincing!" Yet the facts of these one-of-a-kind cases could also be confusing. As Jay, Matt, and Jake now surged ahead, they confounded mentors, along with parents, at just about every turn.

· 4 ·

"What would you do if you personally met an eight-year-old boy who can compose and fully notate half a movement of a magnificent piano sonata in the style of Beethoven, before your very eyes and without a piano, in less than an hour?" Bowled over, Samuel Zyman posed that question about Jay. He agreed with the Greenbergs that the "best academic, musical, and social environment for him to develop to his fullest potential" wasn't obvious. Send him to Juilliard, Zyman concluded—not that even an incubator of musical talent like his conservatory offered a Jay-appropriate track. But Jay was off in his own remarkable orbit in any case: that was Zyman's message, which he spread not just at Juilliard, where Jay enrolled as a scholarship student in the precollegiate division at ten, but also on *60 Minutes* two years later.

The outward contours of Jay's musical trajectory certainly had been unorthodox so far. He had started cello lessons at three. He then tackled the piano on his own, though filling those notebooks with music, not practicing an instrument, was his priority. By seven, he was learning all about theory and composition—and forging a real bond—with a music graduate student in North Carolina. Steadily composing, Jay took violin lessons in Macedonia, where he lived with his family the year he turned ten in December. But Zyman's emphasis, amplified by *60 Minutes*, was on Jay's *inward* creative pathway. He compared Jay to "the likes of Mozart, and Mendelssohn, and Saint-Saëns" in his brilliant compositional fluency at such an early age. Jay's feats of rapid auditory and visual conceptualization and memory, Zyman said later, outstripped anything he had encountered in other young composers busy writing similarly sophisticated music. Watching Jay enter the bassoon part of a piece into the computer, measure after measure, without even a glance at what the rest of the orchestra was doing, had stunned him. "It's hard to convey what that means," Zyman said. "Who can do that?"

At the behest of *60 Minutes*, a pale and serious Jay did his best to elaborate on the theme of spontaneous creation. "It's as if the unconscious mind is giving orders at the speed of light," he said. "I just hear it as if it were a smooth performance of a work that is already written, when it isn't." The camera caught him sounding neurologically informed. "Multiple channels is what it's been termed," Jay went on, explaining that his "brain is able to control two or three different musics at the same time—along with the channel of everyday life." The camera also caught him looking socially ill at ease. That ordinary-life channel didn't seem to be coming in so loud and clear, as indeed how could it for a child so absorbed in solitary pursuit of those musics? An awkward game of catch with another boy—a bit of B-roll footage—showed Jay in need of guidance on where to put his thumb in the baseball mitt. By contrast, adjustments were rarely called for in the pursuit that truly counted for him. "No, I don't really ever do that," Jay said when asked about revising a piece of music. "It just usually comes right the first time."

But the remarkable musical fluency that helped pave Jay's way into New

JAY GREENBERG

York's elite musical precincts didn't guarantee a seamless experience once he got there. "I was an unwelcome arrival at Juilliard's doorstep in 2002" was Jay's wry version of events in retrospect. Zyman's savant-like billing of him and the ensuing media coverage raised eyebrows. So did Jay's bridling at the mandatory ear-training classes, which the school considered necessary discipline even for an adept like him. Where Zyman had hoped that "being surrounded by other super musically gifted kids would help him," Jay's reticence came across as arrogance. (Zyman knew otherwise: his son briefly went to the same Upper West Side magnet public school as Jay did, and they connected over other intellectual interests.) And though Jay grasped musical theory as if he were wired for it, Zyman marveled, examining his own work was a different story, as another leading faculty member discovered in working with him.

"We had real problems at the beginning," remembered Samuel Adler, a revered composition teacher and an eminent composer. (He was a former child prodigy himself, born in 1928 in a hospital in Mannheim, Germany, adorned with a plaque noting that Mozart had once lived in a house on that spot.) Jay was hesitant even to show his pieces, and then "everything I said . . . he said 'no, that's how I heard it.'" Adler didn't dispute that music came "pouring out" of Jay, or that what he could hear in his head, and then put down, was highly unusual. It was an augury well worth attending to: "A person who can do that and grows into that can be an excellent composer." But such eruptions were generally, he noted, a gift of immaturity: as a young musician, "you think you can do the whole thing . . . because you're not discriminating." It's easy to believe "every note is sacrosanct." Yet the key to fertile invention, Adler emphasized, was a dogged refusal to be satisfied, a constant self-questioning—hardly encouraged by "this business of having somebody say to you, oh, you're the next Mozart."

Adler had experienced firsthand the stern school of deflation. His father, a composer, had ruthlessly curbed his fledgling work (as, of course, Mozart's father had not: Leopold had his son churning out pieces). And Adler felt deeply in debt to the "terrifying teachers" he had found in Aaron Copland and Paul Hindemith, who goaded him to self-criticism. "Let it gush out for a while" was Adler's more permissive philosophy, "but also know that it's been done." With Jay, he concluded there wasn't going to be a "break-through critiquing his own music." So during two and a half years of weekly lessons, they worked together on technique instead. Adler was relieved to see Jay throw himself into exercises in different styles: "He was truly terrific and this gave me great hope that he had it in him to grow." Not that the way ahead—as Adler had seen from decades of work with students whose childhoods had been prodigiously focused on musical mastery—was smooth. "I think all these very talented people have some kind of problem in communicating, which I don't think is a bad thing, by the way," he reflected. "It's just that they are not quite in this world."

Nor was Adler, Jay might have told him, quite in *his* world. Adler evidently never guessed that what he called gushing, Jay experienced as a "spurt of productivity and growth," as he wrote later in notes on some of the pieces from this period. However uncomfortable and uncommunicative Jay may have been at Juilliard, his three years there were full of ferment for him as a composer, starting in late 2002 with his *9/11 Overture*. Whatever sound bites a reclusive boy gave television interviewers, Jay relied on more than bolts from the blue. His avid listening, and Adler's tutelage, lay behind a burst of work that included a viola concerto, a quintet for strings, and a sonata for cello and piano. And Jay did know how to critique, or at any rate ruthlessly reject, his own musical creations. On the way to finishing that sonata in 2004—his first work involving a cello soloist—Jay had thrown away several "unfruitful attempts over the years." The boy whose first written notes had looked like little cellos was determined to write a "particularly remarkable" piece for the instrument. It wasn't until he was almost thirteen that he was finally satisfied.

· 5 ·

"Genius is an abnormality, and can signal other abnormalities" was the blunter verdict of Samuel Adler's Juilliard colleague Veda Kaplinsky, a renowned piano teacher and for years the head of a pre-collegiate division full of off-the-charts students. Speaking with Andrew Solomon about prodigies for his book *Far from the Tree,* she went on in the clinical vein that Lewis Terman had hoped to banish but that Matt and Jake's parents knew well: "Many gifted kids have A.D.D. or O.C.D. or Asperger's. When the parents are confronted with two sides of a kid, they're so quick to acknowledge the positive, the talented, the exceptional; they are often in denial over everything else." What Kaplinsky didn't say, but Matt and Jake discovered as they forged ahead, was that the reverse situation—autism undeniably in the foreground, outsize abilities a surprise—could be a lucky break of sorts, strange and unlikely though that may sound.

"Teach the talent" was the Savages' and the Barnetts' refrain as they pushed back against the deficit-focused regimen prescribed for children with autism. Darold Treffert's surmise that "Matt comes with software installed—the musical chip" might suggest that a mere flick of the switch was all it would take. But Matt, prone to tuning out the world and throwing tantrums of frustration, offered daily reminders that talents are part of complicated emotional and cognitive packages. Even a mother who shared his perfect pitch and knack for playing pieces by ear, as Diane did, had to face that there was plenty in Matt that she couldn't fathom or aspire to fine-tune. (Children afflicted with mind-blindness can help make adults humbler about their own insights into others' heads.) If anything, the little she and Larry knew about jazz might have given them pause: here was a form of music rooted in improvisational collaboration. For a boy like Matt, as impervious to social signals as he was alert to rule-based patterns, jazz hardly seemed an obvious match. Yet that was also precisely its allure. The aim above all was to keep him from spinning off into his own fixed and lonely track.

At the New England Conservatory, the Israeli-born pianist Eyran Katsenelenbogen found lessons with Matt exciting and exhausting. The effortless brilliance of his new student (who focused better if he sat on his teacher's lap) wasn't what stood out most. Katsenelenbogen was struck more by the stark imbalance in

Matt's abilities, "some . . . that are very far ahead and some that are very far behind," and in his proclivities as well—true for all of us, but extreme in Matt's case. He could hear chords and do big calculations in his head yet wouldn't go to the bathroom alone for fear of the flushing noise. At the piano, Matt's right hand was light-years ahead of his left. He surged through pieces, Katsenel-enbogen recalled, "like a scanner, moving quickly and getting a lot of information." Introduce him to bebop style, and "he went home and in two weeks he came back with knowledge that would have taken someone else years" to pick up—not because he followed a herculean practice routine. Yet ask Matt to rework a passage, and he was devastated. "That sentence was horrible to him," Katsenel-enbogen said. "That translated to him as 'You're no good.'"

On his own, though, Matt loved repetition. "I used to play a lot of the same melodic lines in the right hand over and over to see how long I could do it," he recalled at twenty-one. He obsessively worked through Jamey Aebersold's play-along jazz CDs of famous tunes, and Diane kept him stocked with volume after volume. His parents also bought him jazz albums, and he "could just listen to them over and over," too. Diane and Matt were busy on other fronts as well. He had begun messily writing out songs. ("Bouncy," with odd time signatures, was how he described his favorite composing mode.) Diane scouted prospects for ensemble playing, since he was too young to do that at the conservatory.

The nearby Acton Jazz Café hosted laid-back jamming sessions on Sundays. She headed over and put Matt, now eight and still tiny, on the list to take his turn. His blue sneakers didn't reach the pedals, and his head wasn't visible above the piano. But after he had played Ellington and Gillespie standards, the applause was loud—and he liked it. Before long, Diane had lined up two café regulars to form the Matt Savage Trio: John Funkhouser, a bass player now on the Berklee College of Music faculty, and a drummer and music teacher named Steve Silverstein.

She had lucked into collaborators with the sensitivity and patience to engage a boy who "wouldn't make eye contact . . . [and gave] the impression he was thinking of something else, that there were at least two streams going on at any time," Funkhouser remembered. Matt needed stability that pick-up groups wouldn't have given him. The paid gigs soon multiplied—thanks to an article about him in *The Boston Globe* after an early trio performance and then a *20/20* appearance, along with other media interest in autistic talent. Though Matt "wasn't that far along" technically, Funkhouser said, his "prodigious . . . ability to keep the form" was there from the outset. Matt "would be playing and looking around the room, seeming to pay no attention to what he was doing on the piano," or what his sidemen were up to—but the clueless style was deceptive. Matt, Funkhouser felt, had the improviser's gift "right out of the gate." He "was able to keep track of where he was, without fail," never losing his place on the original melodic path as he soloed at the keyboard, "even when he was only nine years old." (Funkhouser noted that he himself had mastered the skill only when he was a grad student, in his mid-twenties.) "I just understood jazz theory really intuitively" was how Matt put it later. "And I liked to do everything as fast as possible because slow is boring."

Synchrony with people was another story. For his sidemen, the trick was to work at Matt's tempo and tap into what engaged him. Funkhouser, who felt as much like an uncle as a mentor, recalled the breakthrough moment when Matt really tuned in to *them*. During a rehearsal, he had been "taking laps" (as they called his habit of restlessly circling the room), seeming barely to acknowledge Funkhouser's suggestion for a new way to play a piece. Then, for the first time, Matt incorporated the change when he sat down at the piano—and was eager to stick with it. Matt remembered how *un*intuitive the collaborating felt. "Everything visual comes to me naturally, and also everything mathematical," he reflected. "But just the interaction aspect of things is a whole other different world—especially in music, where everyone understands things through hearing and talking, which is a whole other thing for me, even though I love music so much." Funkhouser and Silverstein left their bandleader to devise his own introductory patter with the audience, and Diane didn't butt in either. Early on Matt rambled at the mike, often trailing off in a "Well, anyway . . . ," more cheerfully spacey than self-conscious. Gradually he found a sweetly stilted, humorous style that gave him obvious, and contagious, pleasure. The medium was the Savages' persuasive message: Matt's gigs, rather than being exploitative exposure, unlocked new ways to communicate.

So did his work with the legendary Charlie Banacos, which couldn't have been better timed. Matt, now eleven, joined the ranks of students—an illustrious group—for whom the charismatic teacher's individualized approach was transformative. Banacos, a pianist and composer himself, homed in on a musician's distinctive neurological profile and tailored his training to that. "They really clicked," Funkhouser said, noting that Matt "grew by leaps and bounds, way beyond me . . . especially in his reading ability, and his ear" during his six years with Banacos. Matt felt he was seriously focusing on his technique for the first time. And he credited Banacos with conveying "life lessons," and lots of "silly jokes," along with the arduous intricacies of jazz. Banacos didn't just work with Matt on the piano and ear exercises that were his pedagogic specialty. They read and talked about Aesop's fables, too.

By then, the Savages had moved to a farmhouse in southern New Hampshire, feeling that both of their children needed the flexibility of homeschooling. Outdoor freedom seemed a good idea, too. "We definitely did extreme things for our kids," Larry said of their new life, growing produce and raising organic grass-fed beef and chickens. Matt sounded wistful in retrospect about moving away from peers (he had begun to make friends in the Sudbury elementary school) and sighed at the long commute to weekly lessons with Banacos (almost two hours each way). But he also confirmed his mother's assessment: he didn't feel isolated— a geography buff, he thrived on the trio's busy touring, and he and his sister joined in local homeschooling activities. Not least, he loved the tranquility of farm life, happily playing with the barn cats when his parents shooed him away from the piano. Winter meant downhill skiing, which he could do midweek without crowds.

For Matt, the quiet proved productive. If his preteen tunes were predictably derivative, as Funkhouser observed they were (Matt, looking back, called them "clichéd"), "he evolved very quickly from everything being the same to exploring lots of different musical territory in a rudimentary but impressive way." His technique continued to improve. He lucked into jams with jazz luminaries like McCoy Tyner and Bobby Watson. A piece in *Time* about Matt's debut at the Blue Note in Manhattan in 2003 highlighted the growing sophistication of his peripatetic style, shifting "between softly gliding passages and furious fantasias with his arms whipping up and down the keyboard." Matt's output, not just his melodic verve, drew notice: five CDs, Larry's handiwork, by the age of eleven. Impressed by the breezy brilliance at the piano, *Time*'s critic also recognized the struggle, quoting a youthfully buoyant Matt looking ahead: "'Autism,' he says, 'is like a huge wall, and if you reach the top of it, you're on your way.'"

Closer up, Funkhouser was struck by Matt's remote affect in performance and a jaggedness in his musical approach. Was it the autism at work, he wondered—or maybe the influence of Matt's hero Thelonious Monk? It was hard to tell. A year later, the title of Matt's sixth album, *Cutting Loose*, suggested newly mature expressive horizons, though as the lead tune revealed, he was also still very much a numbers guy. "Infected with Hemiola," Matt called the song. In the liner notes he explained that he was referring not to a disease but to "a musical term meaning that you play phrases from one time signature when you're actually in another."

What creative leaps might lie ahead? Matt had a tantalizing refrain at the ready when interviewers asked. "What I love about jazz," he continued to say, now with years of intensive therapies and half a lifetime of lessons behind him, "is that you can break the rules and be free." But the real liberation for Matt so far was that the adults in his life were focused on the more prosaic, yet no less prodigious, progress that had already happened. By twelve he had made "huge strides emotionally," his parents and his sidemen agreed, and his music had been crucial.

A similar teach-the-talent approach kicked in with Jake, whose mother—like Matt's, and Jay's as well—found herself dealing every day with evidence of "a turbocharged working memory, advanced powers of visual-spatial cognition, and an extraordinary attention to physical detail." Kristine ticked off classic autistic (and prodigy) traits in her inventory of Jake's core capacities. (Given Jake's musical aptitude and Matt's math and pattern-recognition acuity, you might almost wonder whether they could have swapped paths if the catalysts had been different.) "As long as Jake could get a good dose of serious astronomy," Kristine reported, he was better able to handle social and emotional hurdles in mainstream kindergarten and beyond. But maintaining a balanced perspective, her memoir revealed, was no easy matter for parents.

On the one hand, Kristine prided herself on being a spirited, unspoiled woman from the heartland who had always loved kids (she now had a third son) and knew better than to burden childhood with worshipful expectations. "If I had stopped and let myself bask in the awe of Jake's amazing abilities—if I had stopped to ponder how unusual he really is—I don't think I could have been a good mother to him." Jake wasn't, she wrote, one of those systematically buffed kids "from a private school in Manhattan." He was a boy whose needs prompted her to improvise. So she went ahead and asked if he could sit in on astronomy classes at nearby Indiana University–Purdue University Indianapolis (IUPUI) after school some afternoons. He thrived in the courses, which didn't make her a Pygmalion. She wasn't one of those joylessly dutiful parents always "trying to 'fix'" their children's autism, either. Kristine emphasized that, through it all, she was a mom who never forgot about "play and ordinary childhood experiences." She made sure their house became a video game hub in the neighborhood. (Jake was the resident ace.) Youth soccer and Little League mania might be out of reach, but Saturdays were for hacking around on fields with balls, not for science fairs or Math Olympiad study sessions.

On the other hand, Kristine could and did get carried away. It was that "over-the-top 'muchness'" of hers at work (undiminished, despite the hardships of severe illness and a brutal recession experience, with Mike out of work and her day care nearly empty). But Jake was fortunate not to be the sole focus of the commotion that ensued. With her typical missionary zeal, and with more low-functioning students now enrolled as business picked up again, Kristine decided that families with autistic kids needed what she wanted for Jake: a place for weekend athletics, with no one keeping score and parents relaxing together on the sidelines. She threw herself into plans for a sports center, Jake's Place—even as she also got caught up in ambitious new academic plans, and dreams, for Jake.

Thriving as a drop-in at IUPUI, Jake by ten hadn't merely found his way to the savant website. He had made it onto the gifted-education-network radar. More to the point, his mother was soon on the experts' wavelength. Kristine, who had begun her memoir as a champion of gut maternal instincts, now started to sound like a superachievement specialist. Soon she was armed with a heady new diagnosis—their son was "profoundly gifted"—and less attentive to her internal compass. Jake was invited to apply to an early-college program, and the pair went into overdrive, dragging an initially dubious Mike along. Jake aced a battery of tests and proceeded to binge on AP exams while Kristine enrolled him in Mensa, the high-IQ club. His interview for the accelerated program went badly (Jake got distracted, scrambling to pick up coins that fell out of his pocket), and he was judged too immature to manage more than three credit hours, which meant only one math class the first semester.

JACOB BARNETT

The setback left him with lots of time and, in Kristine's telling, proved the catalyst for a leap of maturity that couldn't help
but strain credulity. Jake didn't merely dive into online coursework.
Soon, as he pursued his own ideas, a "creative fugue state was his
primary reality," she wrote. Jake at eleven found himself, Kristine
announced, in the throes of upending Einstein's theory of relativity
and, if *his* theory held, on the road to a Nobel Prize. She cited as her
authority a Princeton astrophysicist whom she emailed, worried
that Jake might be getting lost as he scribbled equations all over his
whiteboards, as well as the windowpanes, late into the night. It was
the counterpart to a Mozart moment, which the professor, Scott
Tremaine, in fact aimed to gently undercut. Though Kristine failed
to notice, he diplomatically did *not* stoke the miracle rhetoric in
his emails back to her and to Jake. Instead he sent Jake a list of relevant books. His implicit message to Kristine was one she had earlier endorsed herself: fueling kids' interests needn't—shouldn't, she
had said—mean conveying inflated expectations. Jake had learned
an impressive amount so far, Tremaine wrote her, noting that his
theory involved "several of the toughest problems in astrophysics
and theoretical physics. Anyone who solves these will be in line for
a Nobel Prize."

Like Jay and Matt, Jake was in for a brief blizzard of media
exposure (*60 Minutes* couldn't resist another superaccomplished
boy). But by then he was happily enrolled in the Honors College
at IUPUI, where the attentive dean was often called "Mama Jane"
and did her best to help him, at thirteen, fit in with older students. And the savant perspective spared him the worst of the classic prodigy treatment. As Matt's jazz life had, Jake's story inspired
optimism instead of the doom-tinged voyeurism that had sent
young Norbert Wiener a century earlier into depression. Gone was
the fraught vista of future disappointment. Whatever failures, or
feats, might lie ahead, Jake's precocious gifts had already helped
rescue him from isolation. Ideally, they could pave the way for a
maturity of richer social and emotional connections. Kristine,
though she went overboard with the Einstein comparison, saw up

close what counted most for her small man on campus, who was now a teenager. "The biggest change," she noted, "is that Jake is finally capable of real conversation."

· 6 ·

With the arrival of adolescence and shadows on their upper lips, none of the boys was exactly a chatterbox. But all three were ready to talk back, in different ways. Jay (who had a habit of quietly humming musical phrases during pauses in conversation) needed his own chance to dispel the Mozart effect—the glow not just of effortless, but also of crowd-drawing, musical genius. By 2006, when he graduated from high school in New Haven at fourteen, the tricky business of shielding him while also promoting him had been in the hands of ICM Artists for several years. His agent there was trying to make the most, but not too much, of ripe early moments for a young composer before he had to face the "hazardous transition to maturity," in the words of *The New Yorker*'s music critic Alex Ross, who knew what lay ahead for even the most remarkable talents in a marginalized classical music world: "the disappointing realization that modern American culture has no space for a composer hero."

The rarity of his experience was now dawning on Jay. Prime chances to hear his work played live—invaluable, and infrequent, for an orchestral composer—kept turning up and were hard to turn down. His recording debut was on a major label ("a validation" that, as a profile of Jay in *The New York Times* noted, "a classical composer may never live to see"). In 2006 Sony Classical released a CD of two of Jay's pieces: his Fifth Symphony, played by the London Symphony Orchestra, and his Quintet for Strings, performed by the Juilliard String Quartet and the cellist Darrett Adkins. The *Times* review, itself another unusual validation, highlighted "verve in the rhythms and invention in the harmonies; the tunes catch the ear. Movement by movement and start to finish, the architecture has a sturdy logic that does not preclude surprise." A year later Jay sat in the front row at Carnegie Hall for the world premiere of his

Violin Concerto, commissioned for and played by the virtuoso, and former prodigy, Joshua Bell.

Visibly ill at ease as he faced the audience to take his bow, Jay resisted the role of ingratiating wunderkind offstage, too. He wanted to counter the "divine inspiration" aura encouraged by his *60 Minutes* appearance three years earlier, when he had spoken of whole pieces arriving in his head. He tended to hear themes, he explained, but the links among them became clear only later; "at the age of 12," he drily noted, "I was not exactly the most articulate of individuals around." Which was not to say that now, at the age of fifteen, he showed much interest in becoming more communicative. "I really don't spend much time interacting with other people," Jay told a questioner eager to know what his peers made of his musical work. And asked about what he was trying to convey in the concerto, he resorted again to sardonic-laconic mode: "I don't know. I never figured that out." But Jay felt he had figured out one thing: that a postponement of publicity "for about 10 years" might have served him well. "I'd have to start out getting pieces played at schools and universities and benefits and the like—like normal composers," he said. "And then eventually when my talents are better formed have all the commissions and interviewers coming in."

Jay—who had supplemented high school with Latin, philosophy, and music composition classes at Yale—proceeded to spend a couple of gap years pursuing music as well as other interests (writing, tae kwan do, and photography among them). By the time he headed off in 2009 to study music at Peterhouse College at Cambridge University, the lack of self-critical distance on his musical creations that had worried Samuel Adler certainly was no longer a problem, if it had ever been one. Jay sounded coolly underwhelmed by his past work, not least his Fifth Symphony. And he was clear-eyed as he described a future goal, "to reach the point where I'm using sounds in such a way that there's no other way it could've been composed, but at the same time it's not predicable or boring." It might elude him for more than a decade or, he added, perhaps a lifetime.

Yet that lack of interaction, Jay's mode up to his midteens, now seemed to bother him in ways that it hadn't before. Earlier, his aloofness had served almost as a shield. Being cut off from "emo-listening, hip-hop-dancing, ironically 'American Idol'-analyzing classmates," as Alex Ross had put the plight of young classical composers, had so far spared Jay the kind of musical pressures that young Mozart faced. And early on, he had seemed almost impervious to the publicity he got, which could have been far more intrusive. (Ross in particular had been studiously circumspect in noting the promise of such a young composer.) Abetted by protective enablers, from his parents to Samuel Adler, and by an iPod stocked with musical heroes, Jay had made the most of creative isolation and concentration—states all too rare in our clamorous e-world and deeply congenial to a people-avoidant boy.

Now, though, Jay felt a need to reach out, not that he'd had much practice. He started a Facebook page devoted to an irregular series of "notes," mostly about music, where in sardonic-plaintive style he expressed a desire for contact. "Thus, no longer can I remain entirely aloof from my listeners (I'm sure there are *some* . . . probably . . .)." Or from living musicians, whose work on the "cutting or the bleeding edge of music as I know it" he was eager to track down. Or from popular music, which he was interested to try incorporating into his pieces. Or from performing artists, if the ruthlessly winnowed selection of his work that he now considered "worthy" was ever to get heard, not least by him on more than his computer. "So, although I'm aware very few people actually read this blog, I'd like some recordings. Please?"

At the same time, Jay began to do what even—or perhaps especially—a former prodigy has every right to do, however all-powerful and fruitful his childhood passion has seemed. He wavered and wondered about trying another path. Was he studying music, he asked in one of his Facebook notes, just because he could do it well and with ease? Should he really be listening to his "inner scientist"? Jay didn't change course at Cambridge or stop composing. As he had in New York, he took long walks "conducting in my head," and he wondered what the locals made of him: "I imagine they just think I'm drunk." But not long after his return to the

United States, he left again and went even farther away. His father was appointed a dean at the University of Auckland, and Jay—who had stopped writing his Facebook notes and hadn't been responding to his agent's calls about occasional commissions—followed along with the family. Like many another driven superchild turned twentysomething, perhaps he was still trying to decide what he wanted to do. Nobody else, his disappearing act suggested, should presume to predict where he might end up.

Matt and Jake—who as autistic outsiders had been practicing social interaction for years—pushed back in another spirit. They forged ahead on prestigious inside tracks. (So had Helen Keller, determined "to go to Radcliffe, and receive a degree, as many other girls have done.") Matt, who had completed high school work a year early and had been collecting ASCAP Young Jazz Composer awards along the way, enrolled at the Berklee College of Music in Boston in the fall of 2009. The only accommodation Diane sought there was a well-located dorm room. She wanted to make sure he could decompress between classes. Drilled by his mother in social and laundry strategies during his gap year, Matt threw himself into navigating more than musical challenges when he arrived.

He picked up on every cue he could—how not to dress (shorts and a T-shirt), how not to interpret his classmates' cool lingo (literally), how not to view professors who showed up late and ill prepared (too impatiently). Meanwhile, Matt was circumspect about signaling his autism. Downplaying it as "almost a gimmick" that had garnered attention for his youthful talents, he also quietly acknowledged that "communicating with friends" was still an issue. He helped a Boston Conservatory committee that was planning music programs for children on the autism spectrum, and he toured for autism benefits, but at club gigs the topic rarely came up.

In 2011, on the release of his ninth album, *Welcome Home*, Matt performed at Dizzy's Club Coca-Cola, Jazz at Lincoln Center with the renowned alto saxophonist Bobby Watson. The only hint of unworldly savantism was Matt's way of gazing around the room as he played. Then again, Watson wandered around between solos, so for anybody who didn't know Matt's diagnosis, here were two quirky jazzmen at work. Still slight at not quite nineteen, Matt addressed the audience with a faintly awkward smile and into- nation that made him seem very young. His theme, though, was experience. Dressed in a dapper black button-down shirt over black pants, he talked about his recent years on the go—shuttling among New York, Boston, and New Hampshire—and about figuring out where he might be headed. "That's a tune all about the decisions— how it's tough sometimes," he riffed about "Inner Search," ending with the positive take he had learned from Charlie Banacos. "But out of those times can come great music." Matt's brilliant tech- nique was on display, and he shaped the set to culminate with his most ambitious piece yet. In the five-part *Big Apple Suite,* he made impressive use of his signature bounce, along with inventive chord work, striking melodies, and newly reflective moods.

After graduating from Berklee in 2013, Matt braved the Big Apple full-time to get his masters in performance at the Manhat- tan School of Music (MSM). The degree included a good dose of composition, too, and on a Sunday in May 2014, as his first year ended (final exams started the next day), he excitedly prepared for a concert at Small's Jazz Club in the Village. It was Mother's Day, but Diane wasn't there in the cavelike venue. For Matt, the real occasion was his twenty-second birthday and the chance to play new work with a couple of classmates as sidemen and other MSM friends in the audience. Matt pivoted virtuosically from keyboard to piano and back, joking that he might slip some Justin Bieber into his long medley *Epic Standards.* And he went on to bridge pop and classical worlds with his latest pieces.

From "Go On," a trio that built on a four-chord vamp inspired by pop tunes, Matt turned to "Rebuilding," another trio, this one written for an assignment in a very challenging class devoted to jazz styles and analysis. Based on a Bartók theme, it was Matt's venture away from "straight-ahead jazz," as he put it, incorporat- ing twentieth-century classical music and the complex methods his teacher had introduced. "It's a journey from chaos to order," Matt explained the following year, when he also featured it at his mas- ter's recital, again in a pairing with "Go On." This time his parents were in the audience. So was the head of the McCarton School for children on the autism spectrum, where Matt had been teaching music several times a week to students whose blend of distractibility and intense focus he knew well. "It's all about attention span" was his hard-earned pedagogical insight.

As for what lay ahead, perhaps a quick look back at William Sidis is in order. A century earlier he had graduated from Harvard, having endured ordeals that a prodigious savant label would surely now spare anyone even remotely like him. He announced his intent to live "in seclusion"—and stuck to it. Matt headed to Boston after graduation, ready to take a break from New York City, which could feel "chaotic," he said. An orderly journey was not exactly in view—when is it for a young artist? But retreat was the last thing on his mind. At twenty-three, he returned to old haunts to play gigs and compose, while holding down a half-time job teaching music to students on the spectrum. Soon he had started a funk band, and was working on a new solo recording. Neither Matt nor his parents expected that he should by now have "arrived." While his father admitted to worrying that Matt never seemed to slow down and relax, Diane saw the flip side. "He's been developing all this time, not just until he was ten and eleven," she said. "He's making gains. . . . I hear it every time he calls."

Jake was almost fourteen—an eager college student who had lately also become part of a physics research group at Indiana University–Purdue University Indianapolis—when he had an onstage moment to share some thoughts about his path so far. In 2012 he took a very twenty-first-century-style developmental step: he gave a TEDxTeen talk. By now he had dropped his backward-baseball-cap look in favor of shaggier hair. Pacing in front of the PowerPoint screen in his flip-flops, he did his best to be, as the genre demanded, heartfelt and hortatory without being too wonky. "Suppose you guys are all doing your homework . . . and you're doing great on your homework, you're getting great prizes, you're getting fabulous prizes," Jake said to his peers in the audience, his voice rising. "You're doing it all wrong!" Forget being the top scholar, getting the 4.0 GPA, making the dean's list. If you really want to contribute, Jake had a TED-tailored mantra at the ready: You need to stop learning and start thinking, in your own unique way, and then you'll start creating. From Isaac Newton (barred from Cambridge University by an outbreak of the plague), he segued to his own story of being stymied by school (bored in special ed, barred from college for a semester by childish klutziness). "What did I do? Did I stop learning and just start playing video games and stuff? NO!! I started thinking about shapes." Having so far skirted one of his mother's favorite words, *passion,* he couldn't resist closing with the classic exhortation to his peers to find theirs.

Whether he knew it or not, Jake was echoing the most successful TED talk of all time, the education adviser and speaker Ken Robinson's plea to upend traditional pedagogy and let children's curiosity and strengths take the lead. But Jake issued his call to inhabit your own head with the authority of someone who knew, in very unusual ways, what that meant. Helen Keller, notably enough, had taken up the same theme in *The Story of My Life.* Arrived at Radcliffe, which she had revered as "the wonderland of Mind" and considered proof of prestigious arrival, she "soon discovered that college was not quite the romantic lyceum I had imagined. I used to have time to think, to reflect, my mind and I. We would sit together of an evening and listen to the inner melodies of the spirit." Nostalgic for the peace of nondistraction, Keller regretted that "in college there is no time to commune with one's thoughts," and anticipated Jake's refrain. "One goes to college to learn, it seems," she wrote, "not to think," which didn't stop her from doing both.

The savant paradigm, associated though it is with the idea of spontaneous giftedness, delivers a rather different insight: children's minds are their own to shape—yet even prodigies can rarely do that fruitfully alone. Fine-tuning with a glorious future in view misses the point. Childhood needs protecting, and the wonderland, as Keller put it, better be in the unfolding. Jake at fifteen lucked into a veritable lyceum, and his family was ready to move to Waterloo, Canada, to keep him company. In 2013, to quote his immensely proud mother, he "became the youngest person ever accepted into the Scholars International program at the Perimeter Institute for Advanced Physics, the second-highest-rated institution for the study of theoretical physics worldwide." Perimeter, founded in 1999 by the founder of BlackBerry, had designed the master's-level program to draw young math and physics talent from around the world with its intensive curriculum. Tuition, room, and board were free—crucial for the Barnetts.

There was more: blackboards everywhere (should the urge to brainstorm strike), pass-fail grading, no exams, and a focus on group work. The Perimeter Institute director who had dreamed up the scholars program, the South African theoretical physicist Neil Turok, pushed back against the Lewis Terman tradition. "It's the outliers, the oddballs, the unusual kids who often have the most to offer," he liked to stress. "And our whole system has turned into a factory," he said of the status quo. "We crank people through—certificates, qualifications, degrees—and stultify, don't reward creativity and unusual ideas." Which wasn't to say that Turok was ready to romanticize misfits or endorse grandiose visions. He was wary of hearing (as he often did) people "who come to you and say 'I'm going to make the next unified theory, or I'm going to show Einstein is wrong.' That sends all the bells off the wrong way, because at that point in your development you really don't know enough to make claims like that."

What a prodigious savant in midadolescence needed, Turok appreciated, was the kind of leeway that any driven young high-performer can use. "My main job with Jacob is, where possible, to take the pressure off him," he said as the institute's new recruit arrived. "I tell him, 'You're here to play and have fun. We don't have any expectations. Don't put pressure on yourself. Your enthusiasm is your biggest asset; just protect that.' We'll see where it goes."

All three boys had been lucky recipients of versions of that message ever since they were small—and they hadn't been very clued into other people's expectations anyway. In Jake's case, as in Matt's, the burdens of autism brought an ironic benefit: the presence of grown-ups in their lives who, however determined they were to front-load intensive training for their children, quickly discovered the limits of being in a goal-driven hurry. If the boys' gifts could help them engage with the world as they grew, that was progress. And if the most basic lesson they and their parents and mentors learned from one another was undaunted curiosity about what might lie in store, that marked a real advance, too.

CHAPTER 8

Tiger Parents, Super Children

· 1 ·

In October 2009, the glamorous Chinese pianist Lang Lang stood on the stage at Carnegie Hall next to a small Asian-American version of himself. Marc Yu, who had been named a Davidson Institute for Talent Development fellow four years earlier, had acquired more than front teeth since then. Now ten, he had the moussed, mussed hair and red socks of an acolyte. He had just finished a performance with Lang Lang of Schubert's Rondo in A Major for four hands, part of a *Lang Lang and Friends* program that featured several other young protégés. Marc had displayed his musical mastery. He had also clearly been practicing the flourishes of his idol, famous for conveying passion—"my hallmark," as Lang Lang put it—in more than just his sound at the piano. The swaying body, floating hands, mobile face: Marc had absorbed the repertoire. When Lang Lang handed the microphone to Marc, whom he had met three and a half years earlier, he knew he could count on the California prodigy to say something imaginative. To Lang Lang's question about how it felt to play in Carnegie Hall, Marc replied, "It's one of those magical places where the gods live, or fairies. And I would love to come back."

Everyone knows the joke about how to get to Carnegie Hall: practice, practice, practice—the route Jay Greenberg had skirted, and a goad Matt Savage hadn't much needed as he progressed (unlike most children on piano benches, as parents often discover). Marc had made toil his mantra ever since being named a Davidson Institute fellow—"You should play Game Boy less, and you should practice more"—but the message of this buoyant evening was the transporting power of music. The program, with a cast of performers who were all of Asian descent, featured twenty-seven-year-old Lang Lang as a catalyst of the remarkable surge in classical music vitality under way in China. The virtuoso spillover was transforming U.S. conservatories and stages, and with his newly launched Lang Lang International Music Foundation, he aimed to ride—and help guide—a wave of prodigious young talent around the world. Awakening an audience, a new generation of music lovers, was on the agenda, too. The theme was not perspiration. Lang Lang's website summed up his signature aura. "If one word applies to Lang Lang, to the musician, to the man, to his worldview, to those who come into contact with him, it is 'inspiration.' It resounds like a musical motif through his life and career."

In fact, a second, rather different word—*competition*—was also at the heart of Lang Lang's story, which was a world away from savant sagas. Music offered Matt a route from social isolation to gratifying interaction. Striving to be set apart was the theme of Lang Lang's ghostwritten memoir, published in 2008 in two versions, *Journey of a Thousand Miles: My Story* and a youth edition called *Lang Lang: Playing with Flying Keys*. The odyssey that had brought Lang Lang to *his* Carnegie Hall debut at eighteen in 2001 had been driven by the phrase "Number One." Throughout his childhood in rank-obsessed China, he said, the words "never left my consciousness, at least not while I was playing." Lang entered his first piano contest at the age of five, and his father, Lang Guoren, made it clear that winning was essential—that day and for years to come. In China's cutthroat, hierarchical musical world, one high-stakes challenge after another lay ahead: it was the most old-fashioned of prodigy gauntlets, presided over by all-powerful grown-ups. The preteen computer or chess geek could flout parental desires and standards, but not the miniature musician. Doing merely well, a small boy glued to the piano was never allowed to forget, would sabotage the ultimate goal.

Spiky-haired, flamboyantly emotive Lang Lang was the last sort of model or mentor you would expect to emerge from such unremitting pressure to excel. He was a physical, not just a musical, rebuke to "the robot stereotype," as one reviewer put it—the notion "that Asian musicians are all technique and no feeling, precision without soul." He was, in short, the man for a moment when a rising China and a recession-stunned America were both second-guessing their talent development traditions. Never mind geopolitical rivalry, currency battles, trade imbalances. The classical music realm, with a global dynamo like Lang Lang in it, offered a vision of a hybrid East-West approach to extraordinary achievement: a convergence of Chinese-style rigor and expressive American vigor—each asset vaunted by a culture also well aware that it could use a dose of the other virtue. Vibrant creativity, after all, surely called for both. And Lang Lang supplied an ideal extra ingredient, a dash of rock-star-rebel allure.

"The Lang Lang Effect," the *Today* show called the fallout in China, where his flashy prowess was credited with spreading the well-known national zeal for piano training. As any Chinese parent could have told you, learning an instrument was a high-prestige extracurricular pursuit, with the added benefit of promoting academic excellence. (The disciplined focus ideally paid off in school, and the best young musicians might get a boost in a college race dominated by the dreaded entrance exam, the *gaokao*.) As any Chinese kid could have told you, there was no choice but to comply—and now a world-famous idol had given lessons cachet. An aura of fun and hero-worship was just the upstart appeal a generation of stressed-out young grinds could use.

Meanwhile, the United States was primed for the opposite emphasis. Americans had mostly gotten over the "Mozart Effect" fad of the 1990s, which promised a cognitive boost for babies exposed early to classical music CDs—sweat-free enrichment. A more demanding formula for exceptional performance had lately become a cultural catchphrase, thanks to Malcolm Gladwell's pitch for the research behind it in his best-selling *Outliers: The Story of Success* (2008). Starting with a study of elite violinists, the psychologist K. Anders Ericsson had surveyed pianists, chess players, athletes, and others to come up with what Gladwell coined the "10,000 hour rule." That was the quota of "deliberate practice"— effortful work, starting early and sustained assiduously—required for outstanding accomplishment by anyone in any field. Talent, Ericsson boldly concluded, was beside the point.

"The scientific formulation of the American dream," another psychologist called the rule. Gladwell heralded the "magic number of greatness," using the same adjective that Marc had reached for as he spoke up at Carnegie Hall. In his introduction to the youth edition of Lang Lang's memoir, the conductor Daniel Barenboim also invoked enchantment. "Dear Children of the World," he began, eager to celebrate musical uplift for all and to downplay the daunting reality of practice-filled hours. "Being a musician is important, and it is very serious," Barenboim wrote, "but it is also a lot of fun." The young Lang Lang, he promised, "most likely was very much like each and every one of you"—and still is, in spirit. He "has remained a child in the sense that he never ceases to wonder at the magic of music."

But had he ever actually had a childhood? Prodigies had always prompted versions of that worry, and they still did. (What parent, surveying children's ever more crowded extracurricular schedules, doesn't share it?) In truth, Lang Lang's pages told a darker story, and that night Marc could have done the same, not that anyone would have guessed, except his mother. The yearned-for musical pinnacle might be a habitat for fairies. A child's path to it, both pianists knew, was anything but.

Two nonmusicians—both daughters of Chinese immigrants, as it happened—knew it, too, and set out to explore the duress children experience on the path to exceptional achievement. One was a psychologist at the University of Pennsylvania named Angela Duckworth. She gave the effort-vs.-talent debate a jolt with a co-written article in 2007 that appropriated the term *grit*, which she defined as "perseverance and passion for long-term goals"—a not-so-magical internal ingredient of success. The other was a parent, and a Yale Law School professor, named Amy Chua. She added a decidedly un-fun external element to the effort-over-talent paradigm: coercive pressure. In a tell-all account of pushing her two daughters toward virtuoso heights on the piano and violin, she hid none of the conflict that roiled their household. When *Battle Hymn of the Tiger Mother* came out in early 2011, it caused a furor.

This was progress, perverse though that may sound. The uncensored adult insights, along with Lang Lang's timely inside story (Norbert Wiener had been more than twice his age when he published *Ex-Prodigy*), finally put the biggest mystery of all front and center: What motivates a child to pursue off-the-charts mastery, which is guaranteed to be anything but easy, even for a prodigy? The age-old debate over whether talent is the product of nature or nurture was unlikely ever to end. (Juilliard's Veda Kaplinsky had a comeback for both sides: talent is like sex in marriage—if it's good, it's 10 percent, and if it's bad, it's 90 percent.) But at last, more pressing questions were getting the explicit scrutiny they deserved.

So were the too-simple answers of the past, which had variously celebrated prodigies' "reserve energy," eager curiosity, imaginative spontaneity, spunky confidence, and undistracted focus as the special fuel that propelled them. Just as important, very young prodigies, Marc among them, were having their say—even when it wasn't what their elders wanted to hear. How, when, and why do children—who could be socializing, playing video games, exploring this or that passing interest—muster the kind of solitary, strenuous, tedious, time-consuming effort that spurs them onward in a particular pursuit? And at what price, however fruitful their fervor may seem at first?

· 2 ·

"To me, the most shocking thing about grit," Angela Duckworth said in a TED talk in 2013, "is how little we know, how little science knows, about building it." Her own Chinese father seemed to have hit on one tactic, not that she was about to endorse it. He repeatedly told her, she wrote in her book *Grit* three years later, "You know, you're no genius!" Amy Chua's father goaded rather differently. When she won a history prize but not the best-all-around-student award in the eighth grade, he warned her, "Never, never disgrace me like that again." Lang Lang's father made such paternal prodding look tame, yet when he spelled out the grit-based philosophy that guided him, he could have been speaking for them all—fathers and daughters, Marc Yu and his mother, and lots of other Americans, too, especially readers of *Outliers*. "You may face a competitor who has more talent than you," Lang Lang recalled his father explaining. "You can't control that, though I believe you have all the talent and creativity you need. But you *can* control how hard you work. You can make sure that you work harder than anyone."

His father's actions, though, conveyed a far less psychologically correct message, and did so more bluntly than even the most zealous prodigy promoters in early-twentieth-century America would have dared: "*I* can control how hard you work" was the presumption. "*I* can make sure that you work harder than anyone else." Lang Guoren's proprietary authority was a variation on the immigrant striver's credo familiar to Boris Sidis and Leo Wiener: in effect, he and Zhou Xiulan, Lang Lang's mother, had stumbled into a new country in 1976 when the Cultural Revolution ended.

The traumatic decade had shattered families and aspirations, his to be a musician (he played the *erhu*, a two-stringed Chinese fiddle) and hers to be a dancer or actress. Three years later, the one-child policy was in place. Lang Lang's mother and father joined a generation of parents who, not surprisingly, focused on the futures of their "little emperors" with an intensity that pushed traditional Confucian tenets of "family education" to extremes. The race was on to dedicate every parental resource and self-sacrificial impulse to ensuring that a child's progress was not thwarted as theirs had been. The utmost filial piety and tenacity, it went without saying, were due in return.

Filial autonomy was simply not part of a picture that, at least to an outside observer familiar with the latest Western expertise, looked all wrong. The approach violated just about everything psychologists were beginning to think might help motivate children to stick with the hard work of honing a talent—and, ideally, go on to become creative adults. Exposure to music came early for chubby Lang, born in 1982 in the northwestern industrial city of Shenyang. So did fearfully intense pressure to please, applied by his first teacher, who was his father. Lang Guoren had practiced doggedly to earn a short-lived job in the Air Force orchestra, and Zhou Xiulan, imaginative and beautiful, worked as a telephone operator. Together they had saved up enough money to buy a cheap piano in 1984 for a toddler whose ear for radio tunes they took as a sure sign of talent. They crammed the upright into their small room in the artists' barracks. Now they, like just about every family there, had their child busy learning an instrument. Lang, a shy preschooler yet also a show-off, was thrilled—and on edge: playing under the judgmental eye of his stern-faced father, already fanatically determined that his son would excel, was anything but relaxing. What moments his adored mother could seize for snuggling with Lang—"a sensitive child," she stressed to her husband—were brief. Lang Guoren would order their son back to the piano bench, scolding that "all this sentiment makes him weak."

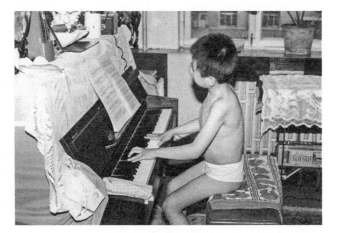

LANG LANG

Plenty of would-be virtuosos move on, as Lang did, to "real" lessons around the age of four (nine at the latest), though few parents display Lang Guoren's zeal to secure the highest-caliber teacher already at that stage—and then to butt heads with her. In Zhu Yafen, he discovered a great teacher, only to adamantly resist her pedagogical wisdom. Her style was to emphasize "the importance of balance between mastering technique and musicality," she explained later. She also advocated moving beyond China's "competition-oriented attitude to one of comprehensive knowledge." And especially with a young boy as emotionally connected to music as she felt Lang was by nature, she counseled against precisely what Lang Guoren urged: harsh pushing. Uncomprehending, he kept up his demands on his son to practice more hours, memorize more quickly, and enter every contest, where "winning, winning, winning" was all that counted and slipping up would be catastrophic. A pat on the back, which Lang Guoren always gave him before he stepped on stage, was the only demonstrative touch Lang knew from his father (until, at ten, he asked him to put his arm around him in the cold bed they shared).

No wonder the prospect of kindergarten had Lang feeling scared and off-balance. His confidence was tied up in external plaudits and a rigid practice regimen: a photo of him at the piano after his first competition victory at five (he played a very difficult Kabalevsky variation very well) shows a little boy already fond of big hand flourishes. With peers, though, he felt awkward. His parents, no surprise, let him stay home instead, practicing for hours—with a tape recorder (his idea) to prove that he was hard at it. Zhou Xiulan, who worked nearby, checked in on him. Lang Guoren, who had since become a police officer, bore down on him with the "unchallenged power" that was a Chinese father's prerogative. When a setback came, Lang, now seven, was distraught, tearfully screaming at the judges who had ranked him seventh in a competition, "It's not fair! You cheated me." Back home at the piano, he was increasingly in the grip of a two-word obsession: *Number One, Number One.*

"Achievement motivation," the experts call such success-driven striving, noting that a relentless focus on extrinsic rewards can lead to a blinkered fear of failure and then to burnout—dangers beyond the ken of Lang Guoren, reared on traumatizing turmoil himself. He was ready for any sacrifice, which he felt gave him the right to presume that his son was, too. As Lang turned nine, his teacher agreed the time had come to move on to Beijing's Central Conservatory of Music, the next step on the arduous path to international renown. The external obstacles were staggering. Only twelve out of two thousand young applicants to the conservatory would make it through an ostensibly meritocratic contest, which in fact was a bribe-greased system opaque to outsiders. The emotional upheaval was devastating, intensified by Lang Guoren's brutal denial of family distress. Zhou Xiulan, now the sole breadwinner, had to stay behind in Shenyang. She couldn't reveal her grief at the rupture, and Lang's anguish met with dismissal and fury. Lang Guoren flung his distraught son's favorite toys out the window.

A newly desperate energy possessed Lang, now alone with his taskmaster in huge and alien Beijing. "When I played the piano, I was happy, my father was satisfied, and I felt my mother's presence nearby. When I wasn't playing the piano, I felt that everything was lost." In their unheated apartment, he practiced manically, his hands almost numb, but on the bench he was warmer than he was in bed. And then Lang's new teacher, whom Lang Guoren was counting on to be their stringent ally, proved irrationally sadistic beyond even the harshest Chinese pedagogical standards. Professor Angry, as Lang called her, set contradictory goals in every lesson and berated him for his failure to fulfill them. Lang Guoren, panicked, insisted on compliance. Overwhelmed by senseless dictates, Lang felt betrayed as well as bereft.

He was right to. One day his teacher dismissed him for reasons neither father nor son could possibly have guessed. Lang Lang, she said, was "a lost cause." Actually, as they found out only later, some backstabbing conservatory applicants (also from Shenyang) had fed her rumors that Lang Guoren was involved with criminals. Lang's father snapped. "Die now rather than live in shame!" he shrieked at his son when Lang returned from school the next day.

Lang Guoren commanded him to swallow a bottle of pills, and was ready to throw him off the eleventh-floor apartment balcony and then die himself. The mania subsided only when Lang began pounding his hands into the wall—desperate to destroy what his father had always told him to protect. "I hate my hands, I hate you, I hate the piano," he sobbed, while his father implored him to stop. ". . . I'll never practice again. I'll never touch the piano for as long as I live."

Lang's beloved teacher in Shenyang had warned against sabotaging his pleasure in music. American psychologists newly curious in the 1990s about the motivational mysteries of talent development might have said *I told you so*. A father blind to parent-child boundaries and obsessed with grueling exertion; a deep family schism over emotional nurturing; a skewed focus on narrow competition at the expense of early exploration; an impossible teacher, backed by an implacable parent, at a key turning point in training—any, never mind all, of these difficulties could derail even a child impelled by an inner "rage to master," the psychologist Ellen Winner's phrase for the inborn zeal that she felt distinguished a true prodigy.

Intensity was essential to developing a gift, but undiluted pressure could destroy sustained commitment. For talented teenagers, particularly in the arts, fruitful drive thrived on enjoyment, not just challenge; Mihaly Csikszentmihalyi, a leading figure in positive psychology, probed that balance in research with colleagues. For adult artists and innovators, the psychologist Howard Gardner observed, the ability to "make some kind of a raid upon their childhood" helped fuel creativity. If incessant goal-focused demands for precocious mastery had quashed playful curiosity and risk-taking, imaginative resources might well not be there to draw on. Lang, not even a teenager yet, seemed depleted already by his ordeals. "I was ten years old," he announced in his memoir, "but I had never had a childhood that was anything but a miserable effort at trying to be an adult."

Except Lang hadn't flamed out. After four months "stuck in hell," neither touching the piano nor uttering a word to his now abject father, he was back at work. Ambushed by hate and plunged into depression, he had been saved by his own deep love of music: that is the official message of a memoir designed to transcend a daddy-dearest screed and spread the "magic of music" spirit. But the facile uplift misses the more distinctive drama that emerges from Lang Lang's account, with its child's-eye view. In taking readers inside the big, fuzzy head and the lonely heart of the boy he had been, his pages evoke a hidden struggle for filial autonomy, under way from the start. They reveal unexpectedly fraught internal forces propelling his zeal to improve his skills. You couldn't call it typical childish fun. At the same time, well before the Beijing blow-up, Lang had been finding freedom—to defy his father and begin to define himself—through his endless labors at the piano.

Given the ebulliently extroverted Lang Lang brand, it comes as a jolt to learn how solitary his days were, and how essential that was to his progress and to the need to forge his own sense of purpose. The Chinese context is crucial. That competitive mantra (*Number One, Number One*) was a culturally approved challenge, not just some crazy paternal imperative. The command to grind away had the aura of a summons to glory for Lang Lang, who prided himself on the drive to win that "was in my blood . . . *is* in my blood." And Western classical music, because it *wasn't*, exerted special allure. Mozart (number one, his father told him) beckoned to Lang as "a golden boy who danced from one birthday party to another." At seven, Lang could picture the bright keys on the new piano that was first prize in a contest he entered, and he wouldn't let up. That same year he began talking with his mother about her struggles during the Cultural Revolution, when she was given no chance to shine because she was the daughter of despised landlords. Excelling for her sake clearly counted immensely for Lang. So did her, and his teacher's, tributes to his sensitivity.

Clarity of expectations and feedback, and a sense of emotional commitment to a larger cause: a child pursuing music in China didn't lack for either of those spurs to advancement. But Lang's own imagination—a world Lang Guoren knew nothing about— held the more immediate, intimate secret to sustaining his concentration as he practiced for hours, doggedly toiling over hard passages. The catalyst had come very early, and later on Lang Lang loved to evoke it in his musical missionary work with children. It's obvious why. As a toddler, just when the piano arrived in the apartment, Lang watched "The Cat Concerto" episode of the *Tom and Jerry* cartoon on the family's little black-and-white TV. He sat riveted by the tuxedoed cat whose performance of Liszt's Hungarian Rhapsody no. 2 becomes a manic duet/fight with a mouse.

Tom's playing awakens Jerry, asleep inside the grand piano. The mouse gets right to work on revenge. Snatching away piano keys, setting a mousetrap for a stretchy finger, Jerry ratchets up his attempts at sabotage. Fabulous acrobatics follow as the music goes on, not missing a beat—though a few jazzy ones get added. "I understood at a very early age that not only was making music great fun," Lang Lang reported in the didactic mode of *Playing with Flying Keys*. ". . . It told me secret stories, and they were mine alone to hold in my imagination." For a boy whose prize toy was his collection of Transformers—robotic action figures that can change shape—cascading pranks were an ideal counterpoint to that relentless mantra roll in his head. The same theme of protean adventure was at the heart of Lang's other favorite cartoon, about a Chinese mythological hero called the Monkey King, a protector of monks and children whose virtuous work left plenty of room for mischievous metamorphoses.

Yet there was also a subtext. Tom and Jerry's silly game is frenetic and violent, the way cartoons often can be: the pair plays through pain, plenty of it. And they share the most daunting of goals—no slipups. Though at the end Jerry takes a bow in a trim tuxedo, Tom has emerged a tattered, exhausted wreck. Looking back, his relationship with his father very much in mind, Lang Lang recognized the grimmer implications in the antic partnership. The duet/fight had the potential to "turn a child's play into an obsession." Extreme immersion in the piano could verge on an escapist addiction for a child desperately missing his mother, and wishing that time and space could contract, which is just what fervent focus can make them do.

But he mostly grasped at the theme of resilience. A boy who spent a lot of time alone was always making up stories to keep himself company. For Lang at the piano, faced with musical challenges, the storytelling helped keep him practicing, hour after hour. Lang was ready to chase, fall down, chase again, seeing how fast he could go, "even if my hands grew tired and my fingers began to ache"— and even as his father hounded him to do more, always reminding him of some imminent performance. The higher the pianistic hurdles, the more of a heroic battler Lang became in his stories, and he knew he could count on his cast of companions. Monkey King was an imaginary friend who would never desert him.

Lang didn't put it this way, of course, but he had carved out space for a version of the "autotelic experience"—absorption in an activity purely for its own sake, a specialty of childhood—that Csikszentmihalyi discovered was essential to "flow." The deeply satisfying experiences of flow, the psychologist wrote in his best-selling 1990 book by that title, "usually occur when a person's body or mind is stretched to its limits in a voluntary effort to accomplish something difficult and worthwhile." The prize always beckoned, but Lang was finding ways to get lost in the process. It was more about intensity than serenity. And then came the times when the straining gave way to a sense of surrender, which brought with it a flawless rendition of a troublesome passage.

Lang's internal script was ideal for the kind of productive, not merely repetitive, practice that can spur real progress. For a tense, competitive child who was cut next to no slack, his stories also helped him to rebound from criticism, to make use of a teacher's suggestions. He was devastated when he lost the competition that was supposed to deliver the new piano with its shiny keys. But before long the stuffed yellow dog, a despised consolation prize that Lang kicked when he was struggling with a piece, joined his loyal, private corps of supporters.

That "voluntary" in Csikszentmihalyi's formulation is important, and becomes more so the older a child gets and the harder the performance challenges prove to be. A teacher out to crush him, a father ready to kill him: for Lang in Beijing, to say that coercion—inner and outer—overwhelmed volition is an under-statement. But strange though this may sound, the crisis that led Lang, the year he turned ten, to do battle with a chastened father was a very lucky break, literally. Before the turmoil of puberty, he viscerally experienced—and defiantly expressed—an independent identity. It helped that one day early in his bitter boycott of the piano, he stumbled on an ally from the outside world. In their Beijing neighborhood, Lang made friends with a fruit vendor, younger than his father, who became a champion—a living recruit to his imaginary cohort at just the right moment. It was also crucial that Lang's classmates at his regular Beijing school coaxed him to resume accompanying their choir. Lang kept that a secret from his father. He was still punishing Lang Guoren, newly aware of how much power he wielded and how much the piano mattered to *him*, never mind his father.

When they reconciled, the terms were different. Too young for potentially self-sabotaging adolescent rebellion, Lang was old enough for a very healthy assertion of ego. He could see then, not just in retrospect, that "my father and I shared an obsession. His drive was great, but so was mine, and I knew that I needed him." They were never going to be a mellow pair, but they had each faced fears of utter disaster—the end of their quest, and the loss of control and of trust. The prospect terrified them both, which redoubled their zeal, now seasoned with some realism about the politics of the competitive system. A new teacher's counsel that Lang should calm down and stop "chasing the music" proved help-ful. So was the arrival of Lang's slacker cousin, a gifted clarinetist whom Lang Guoren could more accurately berate for laziness—and who made Lang feel more proudly industrious.

What one researcher has termed a "midlife crisis" common to prodigious young musicians—when intuitive imitation leads on to, or doesn't, a more reflective sense of direction—wasn't yet over by any means. But Lang had made cognitive and emotional leaps, even as his father refused to let up. Lang placed number one among the twelve chosen for the conservatory. Still small and pudgy at twelve, he triumphed at his first international competition, feeling a confident lightness, especially in Liszt's "Tarantella," and outshining government-favored rivals.

There was reassurance in the stark rigor, in the knowledge that "the path to success in China was unambiguous: you had to beat out everyone else in every contest you entered." And, though Lang Lang the memoirist never said this, surely he'd had in mind the reward beyond all rewards if he succeeded: reunion with his mother. At the same time, he described getting worked up into a "feverish state" as the competitive hurdles intensified with the arrival of his adolescence. Now Lang faced Westerners, too, steeped in the classical tradition as he worried he wasn't. He was unable to relax, desperate for prizes to validate his talent, convinced that he had "to practice ten hours a day to stay sane." An epiphany on hearing a fellow competitor, a blind Japanese pianist several years older, helped him find a new release of feeling as he performed. "He wasn't trying to capture the emotions," Lang realized as they played for each other, sharing not competing; "he *became* the emotions." To grasp at inner poetry while meeting the most exacting of external demands: Lang struggled with the tensions. His perfectionist compulsion could feel like a trap—and yet it had taken him so far.

Without those competition victories, his path to the United States would have been unimaginable. Lang arrived as a scholarship student, now fifteen, at the Curtis Institute of Music in Philadelphia in 1997. If his Beijing breakdown had proved to be well timed, so was his breakout—a bout of un-Chinese youthful turmoil—in the United States. Lang Lang's rebellion was tame compared with Yo-Yo Ma's more than two decades earlier, when the cello prodigy battled the Asian family discipline that felt so at odds with the American push for self-discovery.

"I was meshuga," Ma said of his teenage self in a *New Yorker* profile, buffeted—and broadened—by "conflicting messages coming from within, from parents, from school, from career." Lang's dose of clashing values was sudden and concentrated. In Philadelphia, he was juggling an utterly new world, a new language, a local high school and rowdy classmates. He faced a new childish freedom and a new mature autonomy, and a new concept for a "practice-crazed" young pianist—balance. At Curtis, he encountered a very alien conservatory ethos as he got down to work with his teacher, Gary Graffman (a former prodigy himself), who weaned Lang Lang off competitions and eased him out of Lang Guoren's fierce grasp. To make real progress at this point, "it can't be about the prize," Graffman told him, aware of what a radical conversion this was for a Chinese-trained teenager. "Simply concentrate on the music, not where the music will take you."

Graffman was also helping him to "think culturally," Lang Lang said in conversation years later, his eyebrows rising as he thought back to the personal and musical excitement he had felt. Where Yo-Yo Ma portrayed his "meshuga" phase as a prolonged revolt against discipline and a floundering quest for self-direction, Lang Lang evoked an efficiently facilitated crisis. In America's upstart energy and individualism, he found thrilling alternatives to conformity. He cursed his father out publicly, dramatizing who called the shots now. At the same time, Lang faced a scary question as he awaited his moment in the performance spotlight: "If I were not preparing for some contest, where would I find motivation?"

Filling in for André Watts at seventeen, playing with the Chicago Symphony at the summer Ravinia Festival, launched his career, which brought with it the real if enviable problem of overdrive. When a hand injury forced a monthlong hiatus soon after his Carnegie debut, he had to push through his panic at not practicing. Lang Lang the memoirist made the psychological turning point sound all but effortless. In a matter of weeks, with the help of teachers and other Americans now in his life, he found relief from his compulsive grind and discovered rewards in friends, books, girls, Frank Sinatra. The quest for East-West synergy surely wasn't quite that smooth, but Lang had journeyed in the easier direction, from rigor to vigor.

"Was I ever really a normal teenager?" Lang Lang wondered, a doubt that young fans of the coolest piano superstar in the world might not have guessed he had ever entertained. As his memoir wound down, he wasn't about to dwell on that question. "Maybe not, but I also wasn't crazy. The piano is a beautiful thing, but during that month I learned that it isn't the only beautiful thing." Lang Lang—now a twentysomething star with an inspirational brand to promote—was eager to share a convivial, companionable vision of talent development utterly different from his childhood regimen. He preached what his small self hadn't practiced: "You don't have to sacrifice everything to be a musician." The pianist who had labored under the fiercest of fathers stepped forth as the high-fiving and fun-loving young mentor whom children—like Marc Yu—dreamed of. Such a relationship answered Lang Lang's needs, too, the writer Andrew Solomon sensed when he met up with him and Marc in the summer of 2008 after they had played Schubert's Fantasie in F Minor for four hands at the Proms, in London's Royal Albert Hall. Solomon was struck by "Lang Lang's avuncular gentleness with his protégé; I had never seen him so vulnerable."

Lang Lang institutionalized the role through his global music foundation, launching a Young Scholars program that celebrated stellar mastery as the antithesis of a lonely, grueling, narrowly competitive quest. To judge by their bios, the inaugural scholars onstage with him that night in 2009 at Carnegie Hall had been winnowed with that in mind. Musical virtuosity was their focus—and as at conservatories, students of Asian background disproportionately made the cut year after year—but they also checked the versatility box: along with hours of piano practice, they squeezed in hockey, novel-writing, and swim team, too.

The new honor (no money attached) was a summons to become even busier—in a socially engaged spirit, like their mentor's. During their two-year tenure, they would do more than expand their peer and professional networks through intermittent chamber music and orchestral experiences and master classes. Lang Lang anointed them ambassadors of classical music. Enlisted to "play it forward," his variation on the pay-it-forward theme, they would showcase their talents at, among other places, strapped U.S. public schools selected to participate in one of the foundation's other initiatives: an effort to develop a keyboard-based music curriculum for low-income kids unlikely ever to have lessons otherwise.

What naturally didn't get said at the school ribbon-cutting events was that for pianists at Marc's level, sustaining musical progress presented daunting financial challenges of its own—among many other pressures. Balancing the demands of performance and practice with the life of an ordinary student could seem logistically impossible. As a model and mentor, Lang Lang offered musical opportunities, credentials, and camaraderie—and a darker caution than he perhaps realized. Passion and perseverance had the power to fuel brilliant performance, but were also bound up with pain and sacrifice. (The Chinese have a term for such arduous discipline, "eating bitterness.") For parent and prodigy alike, as for Tom and Jerry, who was pushing whom blurred and changed in bewildering ways. But adults could take note: the grit that ultimately counted was beyond their grasp.

· 3 ·

Shortly before stepping on stage in 2009 for his Carnegie Hall debut with Lang Lang, Marc sat down with a CBS interviewer. He didn't talk about gods, or fairies, or magical places—that was the comment he had ready for his postperformance moment at the microphone. Marc picked up instead on the earthbound theme he had made his refrain for several years, as he shared up-to-date talent development insights along with his musical feats. "All you have to do is practice every day, and when you grow up you are a virtuoso," he had said with a snaggle-toothed grin at age seven in a documentary. How many hours a day? someone was always asking him. "As much time as an average kid would spend in front of the TV," he had cheekily explained, his accented English a giveaway that he was steeped in his mother's Cantonese, not cartoons, at home.

Now Marc sounded more subdued. "My technique is much better than one year ago," he quietly observed. His interviewer, rather than pausing for details, hurried on to the predictable can-you-believe-you've-made-it-to-Carnegie-Hall question. The response wasn't quite the undaunted message the old, or rather younger, Marc would have delivered. "It's like looking at the moon and how am I going to get there?" he said with typical expressive flair. He then half-sighed, "And the answer is always what my mother said, 'Practice.'"

For her part, Chloe Hui's refrain so far, to all who asked, had been that "practice!" was precisely what she never needed to urge her son to do. At five, Marc was already clamoring to devote himself to pieces he knew Lang Lang had mastered as a boy. He pushed to take up the cello, too, inspired by his other idol, Yo-Yo Ma. Chloe, a soft-spoken beauty who had yearned for music lessons growing up in Macau, felt *she* had been playing catch-up almost from the start. She had joined relatives in San Francisco at seventeen in 1989 and studied film in college. During a postgraduation job as a blackjack dealer in Las Vegas, she met Marc's father, a Chinese-American foreign securities investor. They soon married, and Marc (to whom Chloe gave a thorough in utero exposure to classical music) was born in January 1999. Three years later his parents divorced, and his father left the country. Awed to discover that Marc had perfect pitch, Chloe had by then sought out piano lessons for him.

In an interview, Marc quaintly summed up the situation like this: "When I was three, I asked my mom, may I become a concert pianist? She said yes." (Whether accurate or semi-apocryphal, such an exchange would have been unimaginable between either of the other single-mother-and-son pairs in these pages: Clarissa Cowell didn't believe Henry needed her permission, and Bobby Fischer bridled at asking Regina's consent for anything.) Marc was enchanted by music and memorized all the pieces in his piano book after his first lesson. In no time, he had acquired enough finger technique to reveal the kind of expressive gift that, Gary Graffman has noted of early talent spotting, a teacher can pick up on even in a simple lyrical phrase. Chloe reported that soon Marc was at the piano for four to five hours every day—often more, if he was absorbed in learning a piece: an off-the-charts level of practice for anyone at his age. She sat in on his lessons and supervised his practicing (a standard approach with young students of his caliber). She also told of waking up early to go over new music and her notes on what his teacher had said. Marc described getting out of bed in the middle of the night to work on a new passage, playing softly so he wouldn't wake up his mother. By day, he wriggled on the piano bench, of course, and joked with his teacher at his lessons—until he got serious. If a passage needed rephrasing, Marc picked up on the suggestion immediately, then explored and nailed the improvement. As notable as his ear and fledgling musical insight, in short, was his exuberant tenacity—whether he was entranced by riddles or

by Rachmaninoff. "I don't know where he begins and she ends," his kindergarten teacher observed of Marc and Chloe. "But he's definitely a driven little boy."

Irrepressible Marc perfectly embodied a temperamental asset that purists on both sides of the talent-effort debate, newly attentive to motivation, were by now ready to emphasize. Ellen Winner had endorsed

MARC YU

the notion of an innate "rage to master" in her book *Gifted Children: Myths and Realities* in the mid-1990s. Adults couldn't match that kind of focus and phenomenally compressed pace, she had concluded, nor could they force it in a child. Two decades later Winner's appearance in 2007 with Marc in a National Geographic documentary called *My Brilliant Brain* coincided with the debut of the less romantic term *grit,* for stick-to-itiveness that seemed to be only partly genetic and far more widely distributed. In her article in the *Journal of Personality and Social Psychology* that year, Angela Duckworth played up its importance to long-term success rather than to precocious accomplishment. But it was never too soon, she suggested, to "encourage children to work not only with intensity but also with stamina"—whatever their gifts, since her data indicated that grit and talent were unrelated, or even perhaps inversely related. Duckworth knew she was getting ahead of the science, but she couldn't resist a prescriptive leap: grit, the key to putting in hours of deliberate practice, could itself grow with practice.

Research wasn't likely to clinch it, and as a supremely cooperative duo, Marc and Chloe blurred the grit/innate rage-to-master difference in any case. They defied images of dogged Asian competitiveness in the process. If Winner was right that Marc needed no prodding, she also hastened to emphasize how much guidance and support self-driven young dynamos like him nonetheless did require (as Matt Savage's parents would testify). Chloe and Marc gave every sign of a deep synchrony that eluded prodigious savants and their parents, as well as Lang Lang and his father—and, as it happened, Amy Chua and her two daughters. The grit-focused music training well under way in that family generated lots of yelling and other signs of tension. Chua's husband and fellow Yale Law School professor, Jed Rubenfeld, a bemused bystander, noted tooth marks on the piano in their big New Haven house. Sophia, their superconscientious pianist, vented stress more quietly than did her younger sister, a natural on the violin. Lulu shredded music and shrieked in protest against her mother's tyrannical enforcement of "the diligent, disciplined, confidence-expanding Chinese way," which Chua promised would produce bold strivers—not "soft, entitled" American-style dilettantes (and definitely not "weird Asian automatons").

Chloe, with Marc chiming in, also proudly contrasted fervent dedication like theirs to the serial dabbling encouraged by American parents. But their more hardscrabble and harmonious story served to affirm a faith in child-driven—not parent-dictated—excellence and enlightened pedagogy. Given a tepid welcome by her in-laws in the Los Angeles suburb of Monterey Park after her divorce, Chloe and Marc were hardly low-impact additions to the household. Their piano went in the garage, as did they, for hours. So they became regulars at a nearby park, lugging along his cello for plein air practicing—and Marc squeezed in some outdoor fun as well. There on the hillside with Chloe, playing Handel on his cello when he was five, Marc also got a lucky break. He was spotted by the sales associate of the Pasadena Symphony, who gave the two of them comp seats when he discovered they were far too strapped to be subscribers.

Marc eagerly joined the audience—and found an audience. The symphony's staff, including the assistant conductor, was captivated by a child who was so rapt (he pored over scores), so fervent (Marc was obsessed with Handel's *Messiah*), so talented (by ear, he could name all the notes of any chord he heard, in order). Marc played with remarkable feeling as well as facility, and all his practicing didn't dampen his friendly ebullience in the slightest. Adulation, however, wasn't what such a prodigy-parent pair, subsisting on child support from Marc's father, needed. His new fans knew enough to at least try to resist fawning over a precocious star. What Marc did need was an intensive, and very expensive, education. At six, he landed a generous scholarship at L.A.'s Colburn School of Music. There both his piano and cello teachers had the added job of keeping him humble when a front-page *Los Angeles Times* story about him, followed by his Davidson Institute fellowship, suddenly brought lots of media inquiries and performance opportunities.

In America Marc faced nothing like the "unambiguous" path to virtuoso success that had structured Lang Lang's early years in China. In any case, Chloe had ruled out competitions because Marc disliked them. Nor did she have the perks of privilege that Amy Chua took for granted as she juggled her daughters' private school demands and music schedules, and secured special teachers: ample income, an academic's flexibility, Ivy League clout and connections. And even Chua, a dynamo, was swamped. Marc proudly said, "My mom is my manager." Chloe (who had decided to home-school him, which ruled out her returning to work) quietly said she felt like an overwhelmed improviser. "First, and foremost," she added later, she was "his protector," yet their mostly ad hoc approach also meant they were constantly on edge. An old-fashioned patron would have been welcome. Instead, Marc got caught up in a swirl of celebrityhood, which Chloe eyed eagerly—but also warily—as a route to sponsorship of a sort.

Marc, unlike Jay Greenberg, loved his talk show and performing experiences—and he was thrilled when Lang Lang, having heard from Jay Leno that he had a devoted acolyte in Marc, met him on a trip to L.A. in 2006 and they bonded. But Chloe, familiar with traditional Chinese disapproval of overpraising, also knew the risks of the prodigy circuit. The pitfalls of identifying genius early didn't go unnoticed by the Davidson Institute's founders either. In the wake of Lewis Terman and Julian Stanley, Bob and Jan Davidson saw to it that their carefully chosen fellows didn't use the spotlight to parade God-given specialness or downplay the grit essential for success. Instead, the fellowship application as well as the award festivities were occasions to discuss passion and persistence, obstacles and failures, and the importance of supportive allies. Without explicitly saying so, Chloe followed suit, anticipating Lang Lang's "play it forward" theme. Marc didn't merely stir awe with his facility and real feeling at the piano. (He had by now dropped the cello.) He was a small spokesman for a pedagogically, and cross-culturally, correct mission.

Prodigies before Marc had been held up as examples, displaying their mastery, but children themselves had rarely been the exhorters—which in Marc's case meant spreading the latest tenets of metacognitive wisdom that he had been reared on. In theory, at least, the exercise was helpful to him, too. He conveyed what the psychologist Carol Dweck in 2006 called a "growth mindset," rather than a "fixed" one. He didn't boast about his brilliant way with Mozart's Piano Concerto no. 15, but instead begged for harder pieces. He gave priority to process over prizes, skirting competitions—though he was zealously competitive with himself: early on he refused to play anything that seemed remotely childish (even as he doted on his stuffed pig collection).

Marc emphasized the pull of constant work and learning. "I want to achieve incredible things. That's why I practice a lot," he explained, which didn't mean he simply surged forward. He hit snags, but you "can't give up too easily," he said. Diligence, Chloe added, demanded stubbornness. Effortlessness—Csikszentmihalyi's "flow"—didn't really come up, though Chloe spoke of the joy that music brought Marc. Duckworth later described puzzling over the relation between flow and the "not-so-fun-in-the-moment exertion" of deliberate practice. She even staged a debate between Csikszentmihalyi and Anders Ericsson that she hoped would settle the matter. It didn't. Duckworth called for more research and in the meantime floated a hypothesis. Deliberate practice—using constant feedback to master a skill just out of reach—was an action, she proposed; flow was an experience. Gritty people didn't just do more of the former. They also enjoyed more of the latter—when they were performing, not trying to improve.

Marc certainly gave the impression that performance—which wise teachers warn can stunt progress if begun too early and done too often—was a source of real pleasure, not of perfectionist pressure. Playing Schubert with Lang Lang in *My Brilliant Brain* was a dream come true (and the two continued to meet up whenever Lang Lang's schedule permitted). Chloe, who was intent on finding teachable moments in travel abroad, chose performances that were occasions for Marc to give back, not just to showcase his gift—hoping that he in turn might be the beneficiary of others' largesse. His participation in a benefit concert for victims of Hurricane Katrina joined the list of other doings on a website Chloe now maintained. Marc played to raise money for poor children, and he made appearances at schools and on radio broadcasts (both American and Chinese) to spread music appreciation to youth. He played at a world summit on innovation, at a benefit for the victims of the Sichuan earthquake, at a U.S.-China strategic economic dialogue, at a celebration of young Chinese-American leaders. They were on the road, Chloe said, more than they were at home.

All this virtuous persistence, so far, gave no sign of eclipsing passion. "The thing is," Marc said, you "have to love music." He couldn't have sounded more grateful to his mother and his mentor for opening doors. "I think with an ordinary mom," he said, "I never would have played with an orchestra." And thanks to his idol, he had an exciting new goal as of 2007: that year, Lang

Lang invited Marc to join him in 2009 for their Carnegie Hall duet. Lang Lang also recommended a new teacher, an eminence at the Shanghai Conservatory of Music, as an alternative to Juilliard, which Chloe had looked into for Marc. Starting the summer of 2007, she wedged the literally outlandish bimonthly commute into their already crazy travel schedule. The time had come for the arduous technical work that Marc, now eight and a half, hadn't tackled with his American teachers at Colburn, who had encouraged his musicality.

Ahead of schedule, Marc's midlife crisis as a musical prodigy was beginning. Neither he nor Chloe needed Lang Lang's life story (not yet published) in order to recognize the escalating tensions. By the following year (when the memoir appeared), the similarities were striking—and so was a big difference. Marc faced his own Professor Angry, but he and his mother talked back to him, and they talked to each other. Marc, the superdiligent student who had worked through a dozen pages of a piece when his Colburn teacher assigned him one page, now confronted demands that were formidable even for him. "It was so much abuse, verbally and emotionally," Chloe said, remembering the lesson when the teacher had thrown a CD, impatient that Marc hadn't yet signed with a record label. (He had gotten an offer, Chloe said, after the lovely 2008 performance of Schubert's Fantasia in F Minor with Lang Lang at the Royal Albert Hall, but she had felt it was premature.) "If I've been teaching fifty years and nobody has gone mad," she recalled the professor taunting, "you should be okay. How come an American boy can't take training like that? How come my Chinese students can do it?"

Chloe figured that Marc, and she, could take it, given the stamina both of them had mustered so far. "In the future," she had boldly predicted to Andrew Solomon, "Marc will be telling people, 'I'm American-born, but trained in China.' China will love him for that." But their China-bound quest for East-West synergy went against the grain in a way Lang Lang's America-bound journey hadn't. Chloe and Marc both felt drained, not newly anchored, and he got to decide his course. What Marc didn't say as he sat down with the CBS interviewer in the fall of 2009 at Carnegie Hall, because he wasn't yet completely sure, was that he and his mother had recently walked to his Shanghai professor's studio for the last time, both of them in tears.

Their old synchrony was no more. Marc had always been spiritedly stubborn. Nearing eleven, and feeling embattled (and jet-lagged), he had begun to balk under rising pressure. Chloe was deeply conflicted. "I don't want to hear the word *pushy* used about me," she had told Solomon in 2008. In retrospect, though, she acknowledged that Marc hadn't been the only one propelled by a rage to master. "He was showing a lot of passion and motivation. I push him even harder, because he shows me how much he can do, and I believe he can do even better," she reflected. "But I also believe it has to come from him." Now Marc was telling her it didn't, and she was listening. "I wish I had been born a normal boy and you were a normal mom with a nine-to-five job and I went to a normal school," Marc said once, and then more than once, "Mom, I'm not sure I want to do this anymore." Chloe had watched grimly intent Shanghai parents who felt they couldn't turn back—who ordered up beautiful suits, a tailor told her, for graduation performances that were all too likely to be the students' last outings on stage. Chloe realized that she was relieved, if also devastated, to hear Marc voice doubt.

The decision was wrenching, "the toughest time of our lives," Chloe said two years later. Well aware that the transition to "normal" wouldn't be easy either—Marc hadn't been in a classroom for years—she sought out the antithesis of old-style pedagogy. In the fall of 2010, Marc began sixth grade (on a generous scholarship) at a very progressive private school for gifted students in Hillsborough, California. Proud of "its distinctive inquiry-based interdisciplinary studies, constructivist project-based learning, and its pioneering work in social emotional learning and design thinking," the Nueva School was too close to Silicon Valley to be laid-back. But for decades the school had emphasized "reflection [as] an essential practice for learning." As a priority for a recovering prodigy and his mother, it would be hard to improve on "patience with ourselves as we think about what was and look forward to what could be." Though Marc had a rocky start socially (he and Chloe were regulars in the counselor's office as they both got used to a radically new life), he pronounced school, and his first sleepovers, "so exciting!" Taking conducting lessons in L.A. and intermittently checking in with a piano teacher, Marc was practicing on his own, much less intensely. Chloe was working on not shouting advice from the kitchen. "Shut up, Mom!" he would yell back. "I know what I'm doing! I'm the pianist."

Before they went on summer vacation in 2011, Chloe finally read Amy Chua's best-selling *Battle Hymn of the Tiger Mother*, which had left parents across America gasping and gossiping at school gatherings and on soccer sidelines, in supermarkets and at dinner parties, ever since it had appeared six months earlier. Shockingly honest about her tactics, Chua had gone public with the kind of exposé usually staged by prodigies themselves, later in life. She outed Chinese-style family pressure in pursuit of children's high performance, "an inherently closet practice" in the United States, she noted. At the same time, she blasted the queasy hypocrisy of American-style hovering: parents who panicked over missteps and signs of stress in their kids, all the while programming them to overshoot every benchmark of success.

Sounding nothing like a dour scold in the Lang Guoren mold, Chua wrote as a self-mocking iconoclast, an over-the-top "music mom" in a culture of mere soccer moms—not that she actually saw her girls on their way to soloist careers. She was "huggy" and goofy with them. She also bossed and cruelly derided, and dictated grueling practice schedules and zero slumber parties. Her daughters were huggy back and also explicitly hostile ("you're diseased") as they sped along. Chua's hyper regimen ran on a hybrid spirit—far more openly coercive than helicopter parenting and far more openly combative than classic Asian parenting.

Chua's pursuit of excellence wasn't simply about stamina or grit. Upstart drive was, somewhat paradoxically, what she aimed to drum into girls blessed with meritocratic credentials in their cradles. (They could all but coast into the Ivy League on their parents' coattails, thanks to legacies at Princeton and Harvard and faculty pull at Yale.) So Chua was ready—in fact, eager—to explode the filial piety so important to her forebears. She took bold satisfaction in doing what no prodigy-promoting predecessor would have dreamed of: broadcasting a defiant child's bitter rebellion. Helen Follett had made sure to hide just that, writing a book that portrayed her voyage with Barbara as a daughter-driven adventure, rich in intergenerational bonding, not the embattled ordeal it was.

Three-quarters of a century later, showcasing a fierce struggle for autonomy was more than acceptable. Add pugnacity to stunningly polished precocity, as well as perseverance and passion in pursuit of long-term goals: the blend just might amount to a secret sauce, for East and West. Near the end of *Battle Hymn of the Tiger Mother*, when Chua let Sophia ease up on the piano after acing her recital in a Carnegie Hall auditorium, Lulu staged her revolt. Now thirteen, she reamed Chua out in the middle of Red Square—"I HATE YOU. . . . You've wrecked my life . . . You're a *terrible mother.* You're selfish. You don't care about anyone but yourself. What—you can't believe how ungrateful I am? After all you've done for me? Everything you say you do for me is actually for yourself." She cut back on the violin and took up tennis instead, ordering her mother to butt out. "I don't want you controlling my life."

Chloe had been avoiding the book and shrugging off the jokes parents made in passing about her possible tiger-mom tendencies. The school year over, she turned to Chua's memoir. She immediately sat down and read it again with Marc, who was now twelve. "We cried over each other's shoulders," Chloe wrote in an email, "thinking of what we've gone through." (For readers in China, Chua discovered on her book tour, catharsis was a more common response than outrage.) In a phone conversation after they had returned from vacation, Marc said he could hear his own household in the Chua-Rubenfelds'—"all the yelling, screaming," Chloe added, "lots of pushing, resisting." For her, it was still raw. Marc seemed to be mustering that key to learning—reflection. "When I was younger," he said, "I was more like Sophia," who insisted she had been spurred on less by Chinese-style duress than by her own discipline. "Now that I'm a teenager, I'm getting more like Lulu. I'm more rebellious and more resentful."

Marc, though, wasn't ready to lash out at his mother. "I am and will always be grateful for the sacrifices she made for me," he took care to say. For now, he was also evidently having better luck keeping regrets at bay than Chloe was. Thinking back on their partnership, so intense and insular, she was swamped by second-guessing. "To play professionally has a big price tag on it, a tremendous amount of pressure," she knew, and she had helped apply it. Yes, Marc had made choices, unlike kids in China. Still, the Shanghai conservatory scene made her rethink warnings she had heard all along. "Isn't it too risky to put everything on one child and focus so narrowly on the piano and nothing else?" She had to ask herself, she acknowledged some months later, whether at times she had "compromised my own values to keep Marc's success intact." She and Marc had made a habit of speaking openly about the rigors of a quest like theirs, but not the darker dilemmas. Chloe wanted to be honest about the turmoil now—not that she would have been capable of masking it with comic archness, in the *Battle Hymn of the Tiger Mother* vein.

Amy Chua never really had to doubt that her daughters would have plenty of options, and stellar CVs, even if she failed in her mission to add musical precocity to their list of accomplishments. To counterbalance her guilt, she could always tell herself that lessons in grit would stand her girls in good stead. Plus they had at least had each other's company (and their father's sympathy) in their misery and fury. She heard them fiercely whispering about how crazy she was, when they weren't saying it to her face. Chua invited them to speak up in the memoir's "coda," as she struggled for a way to close the book. They weren't inclined to help, but Sophia put a key question to her: Was she after truth or a good story? Sophia was ready with a wise response to her mother's predictable answer. "That's going to be hard," she told Chua, "because the truth keeps changing."

Chloe felt that she'd "had a prodigy dropped into my lap." Lacking resources, she had worried constantly about how best to meet such a "big responsibility." At this point, she had no idea where the story was headed. Marc right now was glad, at last, *not* to be thinking, and talking, about long-term goals. "I feel deprived of being able to grow up and have fun like other kids," he said bluntly. "But I also feel very privileged to have had all the experiences I had that other people never get to," he added more gently, especially "traveling to different places." Having found his way to that typical, and rarely trouble-free, place—middle school—he was getting his bearings. Lang Lang wrote that he had needed a mere month, at the age of seventeen, to discover that piano "isn't the only beautiful thing." Marc, who was getting a comparative head start on a whole new track, already knew it was a lot more complicated. But some things hadn't changed—for now. Given a five-page writing assignment, Marc produced twenty pages. "I like homework," he said. "I just do."

Epilogue

Prodigies, being rarities, by definition belong to the realm of anecdote rather than data. For precisely that reason, they invite fascinated scrutiny—and dismissal, too. Write them off as freakish geniuses or phenomenal rote-learners embarked on peculiar life courses, and you can gloat over their failures and treat their feats as irrelevant to the rest of us. An anti-elitist impulse to do just that can be bracing. Yet the stories in these pages are proof of a different kind of egalitarian urge as well: to view prodigies as off the charts in a more inclusive sense—not as children beyond the normal in either a miraculous or a readily measurable way, but as children whose off-the-beaten-track experience may help expand the cultural map of human potential and achievement. The effort to push those boundaries is still very much a work in progress, and prodigies deserve credit for doing their best to keep us humble. However their stories unfold, they vividly remind us of what we so easily forget: that every child is a remarkable anomaly, poised to subvert the best-laid plans and surprise us. Even a devoted number-cruncher like Julian Stanley, who set great store by case studies too, heralded the view that "each child is a complex and conscious organism, not a mere unit in a statistical sample."

The stories gathered here highlight what children do ineluctably, and quickly—they change. The accounts, taken together, also raise a question about continuity: How much have perspectives on prodigies really evolved since Norbert Wiener and William Sidis set off for Harvard? A century after Leo Wiener and Boris Sidis riled Americans by touting their pedagogical secrets and phenomenal sons, Amy Chua at Yale offered a reprise, featuring her more conventional superdaughters. The tiger mother's guiding tenets echoed the Russian émigré fathers'. Start the talent-building process very early; assume the child is sturdy and full of energy; expect feats of mastery; value family loyalty above youthful autonomy or popularity with peers. The immigrant striver's credo retains its power, as alarming as it is inspiring, for outsiders and insiders alike in America. Yet the whole package doesn't apply neatly to all the prodigies down the decades by any means. In these stories, continuity goes hand in hand with constant, and fruitful, controversy.

The stark nurture-over-nature faith at the heart of the credo has been tested again and again, beginning with Henry Cowell and his supporter Lewis Terman. More important, the parent-knows-best confidence that drove it has been tested, too, first by remarkable girls in the interwar years. And as America's meritocracy shifted into high gear after World War II, the prodigies in these pages started wielding clout more overtly.

It's worth noting the unintended consequences at work. A national system for the early sorting and streamlining of talent was of course Terman's dream come true—yet one result, on display in these stories, was new interest in prodigies as balky and lopsided outliers, just what Terman had aimed to prove young wonders were *not*. Bobby Fischer, defiant at every turn, was followed by upstart computer geeks who didn't just drop out of college against their parents' wishes. Well before that, they surged ahead of adults, mastering tools and preparing to shape a future their elders hadn't even imagined. Autistic savants were still further beyond others' ken. Incongruous talents like Matt Savage's and Jake Barnett's— a reminder of how hidden gifts can be—have inspired an incongruous response. The competitive-race paradigm so familiar to ambitious parents doesn't really apply. Instead, the quest is to nurture fierce interests in hopes of opening up otherwise obstructed childhoods—a crucial first step, whatever the future might hold.

Meanwhile, the different tenets of the credo, which have kept arising in various forms in these stories, have also kept raising questions that shift over time but never get settled. How impressionable, for good and ill, are very young children as they discover and pursue their talents? Barbara Follett and Nathalia Crane entranced and disturbed their elders to an unusual degree, and concern about tainted innocence persists. How much toil does fast-paced mastery actually demand, and what price might it exact? Philippa Schuyler and Shirley Temple gave the lie to claims of stress-free early achievement, and by the time Marc Yu emphasized his tireless practicing, the blurry line between passion and obsession (in child and adult) couldn't be ignored. When precocious children get anointed as exceptional, what benefits and burdens ensue? For Julian Stanley, as for Terman before him, early winnowing promised a brisk and well-guided path to future distinction. Yet for Jonathan Edwards, as for Henry—and even more strikingly, for Matt and Jake—obstacles and waywardness proved crucial. Where does a child's motivation come from, and what sustains it? Lang Lang and Marc offered disconcerting answers, and they were hardly the first to do so.

Not far from the surface of all these debates lie key questions about children's autonomy. They go hand in hand with confusion about the role that peers play, or don't, in young lives devoted to extraordinary achievement. Adults in the earlier stories didn't worry much about social mingling. From Norbert through Shirley, the children scrounged for whatever company they could get, which included older nonparental accomplices. Isolation spelled trouble, as it did for children from midcentury onward, too. Think of William, Barbara, and Philippa, stranded with two overinvested parents who brooked few intermediaries. And then think of Bobby in his filthy apartment and Jonathan on his own at Hopkins, as well as Marc, whose bond with Lang Lang proved fleeting.

The same adults who were inclined to dismiss peers as distractions also downplayed the prospect of independence. In stories that unfold in the earlier decades, the notion that a "midlife crisis" awaits nearly every prodigy at or near puberty didn't really occur to grown-ups. They were focused on precocious leaps, not on an inevitable turning point when children become acutely conscious of their distinct identity. Parents and mentors presumed that momentum would propel a young marvel onward through adolescence. They tended to gloss over the fact that immature absorption in a pursuit has to give way to newly committed, self-aware exploration—or else to some sort of break or scaling back. But for Gertrude Temple, with a daughter in a child-star industry fixated on baby-faced appeal, the arrival of a crossroads was too conspicuous to ignore.

She stepped forth with a version of what is by now conventional developmental wisdom. Demoralized by new career pressures on her almost-twelve-year-old, she prepared a well-timed retreat for Shirley to an exclusive California private school. In her public statement, Gertrude cited her daughter's need for a "life with other girls and boys of her own age, in school and during recreation hours, so that she will not develop an isolated viewpoint, which often brings on an unhappy outlook on life." For Shirley, of course, the transition wasn't nearly as pain-free as her mother suggested—and hoped. Hanging out with teenage peers presents its own difficulties (not to mention risky opportunities); relinquishing the arduous, yet also ego-gratifying, work of honing gifts isn't easy either. For all the children in these pages, whether they scaled back or stepped up the already intense dedication to their remarkable talents when adolescence arrived, the inevitable swerve into ex-prodigyhood was a struggle.

Seventy years after Gertrude made her move, Chloe Hui—demoralized by ever-rising career pressures as she and Marc shuttled to and from Shanghai—had found a place at an exclusive California private school for her eleven-and-a-half-year-old in 2010. Buffeted by relief mixed with regret, she lacked Gertrude's I'm-in-charge-here confidence. Meanwhile, Marc, unlike Shirley, could feel that he had been a full partner in the decision to veer onto a nonvirtuoso path. (Gertrude hadn't consulted her daughter about the plans.) With a century of prodigy stories in mind, I was primed to see welcome change. Marc fit the most old-fashioned of prodigy profiles—the frail-necked musical performer apprenticed to his instrument when he was tiny and soon taken on the road. Yet both he and his mother also stood out for trying to make the most of cumulative talent development insights. Chloe knew better than to count on seamless adjustment. As for Marc, who among his predecessors in these pages would have been so sure, while still so young, that he would prevail if he pushed back—in need of a chance to try being, of all things, less rather than more unusual?

On the brink of adolescence in 2011, he had appeared to be headed in a promising direction after missing out on "normal school" as a little boy. To be sure, the sociable and flexible Nueva School experience was, for Marc, totally unfamiliar. Landing in America's now thriving proto-prodigy culture—even in its progressive, rather than full pressure-cooker, form—guaranteed its own share of challenges. But he had been eagerly finding his place. So half a decade later, the news that Chloe and Marc, who was now seventeen, were both struggling with depression and anxiety pulled me up short. That their relations were rocky went with the teenage territory. But I had let myself anticipate a story of productive push and pull, of high-spirited versatility—not the bleak update I heard. "So much has happened that is so intense, so extreme, I never expected it," Chloe told me in the spring of 2016.

Her unease was acute as we sat together. At the same time, her willingness to be open about their misery seemed in keeping with what I remembered. So did Marc's readiness to take his separate turn to think aloud. And two themes familiar from prodigy stories before theirs were, it was clear, here to stay. The first is that lessons and predictions about unusual lives—whether the extrapolations are grandiose or cautious—almost never pan out as expected. The second is that pretending otherwise has become ever less tenable: facing up to jolts—from brief upsets to big shocks—is all but unavoidable, as prodigies seize chances to speak up and parents become readier to voice doubts. "I was following my heart, wanted to do everything I could to help him. I had no idea it would end up like this," Chloe said. She hoped the latest developments in their lives might shed light for others: "There are lots of Marcs out there, getting pushed. There are lots of Chloes."

More than half of Marc's lifetime ago, the two of them had resisted the prodigy-tale tradition of airbrushing a child's goal-directed race toward a pinnacle of exceptional fulfillment, fame, or fortune (or all three). Progress, they frankly admitted, entailed strenuous labor—and a boy might decide to slow down. Now their sad updates didn't simply conform to the cautionary conventions of the genre either. Grist for Schadenfreude wasn't the point. Setbacks and conflicts, as every story before theirs also reveals upon close inspection, are all but inevitable and complicated. Precocious paths, even those studded with thrilling achievements, are rarely free of worried second-guessing by grown-up and child.

Ambivalence has a way of mounting rather than subsiding as the youthful years go by: Why the hurry, starting so early, to nurture future-oriented consistency and promote narrow proficiency in children? What makes prodigy stories useful parables about childhood is their power to remind us, with unsettling vividness, that the same children whose signature traits may seem so fixed are also constantly in flux. And no parents, anxious though they tend to be about imparting an influence, should worry about leaving an imprint. All parents make some dent. But even (or especially) the most assiduous talent developers among them can't begin to guess what the mark will be, given the vagaries of life and luck.

Chloe was wrestling with that conundrum. Marc "had such a gift, and I just wanted to help him to focus. I never thought that such intensity would surface in other things." But now it "plays itself out in very difficult ways with friends and family," she said. At school, she reported, Marc's social blundering invited bullying and spelled girl trouble. Feeling isolated, the boy who used to fixate on a musical problem now obsessed over what he considered total failure. He could see only dire extremes, Chloe worried. He was falling way behind in his work while his classmates in eleventh grade began the college scramble. At home, Chloe, who had remarried, described an unhappy (and convoluted) blended-family scene, with

Marc declaring himself an outcast. As for the past, he would tell her he had "one hundred percent bad memories" of his upbringing. It was a struggle for him, she felt, to summon good ones—certainly in talking with her. Her own view of those years, she noted, grew darker and darker the more the two of them suffered in the present. Now she looked back and indicted herself as "a very pushy, obsessive person." ("He doesn't fall far from the tree," she remarked.) If only she had seen the perils, as well as the potential, in the zeal they shared.

I had second thoughts about having asked Marc to meet with me and imagined that he might well change his mind. But he didn't, seeming to welcome a reprise of one part of his former life: an adult asking him to talk about the challenges he faced—and not expecting him to give just the burnished version. Chloe had prepared me to encounter a teenager miserably trapped in black-and-white thinking. Marc, still boyishly slight and now wearing cool dorky glasses, conveyed the opposite. What he said suggested a deeply conflicted view of his trajectory. However difficult he found grappling with his past to be, he also conveyed a desire *not* to reject it. Was he downplaying his real despondency in order to offer a perspective that he knew others would want to hear? Or was he articulating mixed feelings that he didn't share with his mother because he needed to punish her?

If Marc wasn't sure himself, that was perhaps because both were true. "I would choose the same path, if I had it to do again, looking back now, aware of the impact, both negative and positive," he said right off—just the kind of gray-toned picture Chloe would have loved to get from him. The assessment also had a for-the-record ring, and I couldn't tell how heartfelt the positive side of Marc's ledger was. Thanks to his musical career, he said, he was good at talking with adults, not least teachers. Piano was still a "big passion," as he put it, but practicing and performing had become "pretty relaxed, when and what I want." At school, Marc said he liked showing off at the keyboard, and his prowess was an entrée to working with other musicians in the jazz and rock bands. Marc had begun composing and mentioned a scene he had written for a possible musical about—"this is going to sound very autobiographical," he noted with a wry smile—"a kid who's having trouble with bad situations." He had also taught himself to transcribe (aided by his perfect pitch), aware that it could be a social asset. "All the popular kids can sing and play the guitar," he observed wistfully. Occasionally transcribing songs for them was the closest he came to connecting with that realm.

Marc sounded dutiful as he professed that his past had given him "a great appreciation of things" he felt his peers took for granted, like the opportunity to go to such an unusual school. What he really wanted to talk about were the painful legacies, in particular the corrosive feeling that he hadn't measured up. By that, he didn't mean regret at having dashed the high hopes—his and others'—that he would return to Carnegie Hall. In his view, he had failed in a quest that seemed far more important, and that he had been ill prepared for: to carve out a place for himself beyond the virtuoso track, while still feeling special and powerful, as every kid yearns to. "I always expected things to go my way. If I wanted it, I worked hard enough, I got it, and people loved me," he said. "That's no longer true, and I feel I exist in the shadow of popular kids."

In retrospect, the expectations that guided his childhood looked almost enviably simple, Marc reflected. Excelling at the piano had been the aim, and all-consuming though the challenge was, "I was so excited about performing that I didn't really grasp the reality of the struggle." The pressure to practice was intense, but "for what I was trying to do, it was what's needed," he remarked, ". . . and back then half of the time I didn't think it was too intense." Marc wanted to emphasize how invested he had been, how swept up. He didn't realize his mother was anxiously counting on him as the source of their income. He wasn't focused on feeling unmoored by their constant travel, and he didn't dwell at first on the loss of his relationship with his idol. Lang Lang had faded out of their lives around the time that his foundation geared up, which was also when Marc's Shanghai lessons, recommended by Lang Lang, began to sour.

By comparison, Marc said, the many pressures of his subsequent life felt overwhelming. Being normal, in its way, turned out to take as high a toll as being exceptional. He was expected to do well in his classes, and also to find time for the piano. He was supposed to be a good sibling after being "an only child around whom everything revolved," and to handle difficult family dynamics after such an intense bond with his mother. Navigating middle school social challenges had mostly confounded him, and the sense that "no one at school really gets me" left him feeling stranded in high school.

But Marc didn't want merely to wallow. His unusual path, he thought, had given him "a wider perspective than other kids have"—not that he had arrived at a balanced view of himself or of what he had been through. Of course he hadn't; the work of shaping an identity has its own mysterious pace. "All this focus on the piano," Marc felt as he looked back, had eclipsed chances for forging a stable family and close friendships. A dire verdict was tempting: To sum up his past as an ordeal engineered by others had a dark simplicity. But Marc rarely settled for what comes easily. He wasn't about to write off a childhood full of fervor and remarkable feats. Desolate though he often felt, and sounded to Chloe, he seemed to understand how helpful it would be to claim his musical odyssey as his own—and as a singular accomplishment. Tapping into that sense of agency was likely to take lots of practice.

Norbert Wiener, familiar with depression, had learned what Marc, along with plenty of other prodigies, also discovered: early feats of achievement and the intense anticipation they inspire may well help to fuel a child's growing sense of autonomy, but can also skew it. Stubborn drive and open-ended curiosity make all children not just avid rule-learners but also rule-breakers. When mastery comes quickly, what at first feels like playful and purposeful empowerment may become shadowed by anxiety, blocking the engagement with a wider world that helps gifts and creativity flourish. Parents may end up paying a similar price, becoming more enmeshed in children's lives, or more embattled, than they ever intended. The same adult-level powers that set prodigies apart have a way of stirring hopes that may lead, as Andrew Solomon puts it in *Far from the Tree,* to "a tragic misunderstanding of where one human being ends and another begins."

But as Wiener found—as did plenty of ex-prodigies in his wake—doom is not foreordained by any means. Disappointments and difficulties are unavoidable, though. That reality of childhood is writ large in the stories of off-the-charts children. When Wiener wrote down what he considered a prodigy's crucial entitlement, he purposely laid out modest terms: the "chance to develop a reasonably thick skin against the pressures which will certainly be made on him and a confidence that somewhere in the world he has his own function which he may reasonably hope to fulfill." Wiener was silent on the theme of success. He offered no facile cures for stress. What he emphasized was respect for a child's sense of his or her own separateness. In an overachiever culture of hovering adults and social-media-saturated youths, that last piece of advice may sound the most unfamiliar of all, and be the most valuable.

The young upstarts who helped usher in the computer revolution after Wiener's death were geeks busy bucking adult guidance and writing their own scripts in ways he couldn't have envisioned—and would have envied. Proud oddballs, they have also enjoyed a surge in status that would have stunned Terman and that Stanley hadn't counted on. The tech pioneers got the best of both worlds, reaping meritocratic rewards yet also breaking the rules when they chose. Their precocity couldn't be mistaken for mere accelerated mimicry; innovative mastery came early.

Of course, the worship of fast-track nonconformity they inspired has had unintended consequences of its own. The blinkered elitism that has accompanied the "achievatron" ethos, as Jonathan Edwards labeled the hypercompetitive striving that he lamented, might well have given Wiener pause, too. His childhood experience made him skeptical of insular clubs, whether of Boston Brahmins or prodigies. At the same time, as an ungainly half-man and half-boy, he understood that a feeling of contributing to something bigger counted for more than being brilliant. Prone to dark lows, he also never forgot how elusive that feeling of creative fellowship could be.

In the meritocratic race that continues to intensify, it is the stories of prodigious savants like Matt and Jake—autistic children whose aura recalls otherworldly marvels of long-ago lore—that come closest, surprisingly, to embodying the unillusioned spirit of Wiener's counsel. Experts and others invoke the savant phenomenon as evidence that unsuspected talents may lie hidden in the brains of all of us. Many also cite autistic achievements as proof of just how crucial the dedication of families, teachers, and others is to the blossoming of any gift. Less often remarked on, but as important, the prodigious savant paradigm calls attention to the child as *other*—a small person in his own world, endowed with mysterious powers and puzzled by many things, whose way out and forward is anything but obvious.

A century ago, Wiener's father enlisted his son in the cause of portraying off-the-charts childhoods as well-rounded idylls, the crucible for future greatness. To take autistic prodigious savants as guides is to go very much against that grain. Their predicaments suggest an alternative perspective on youthful gifts, and on how and why they are worth nurturing. From this vantage, children are still figures who fascinate, yet now they can also be counted on to confound adult expectations early and often. The fixation on future distinction recedes. Instead, the emphasis shifts to encouraging as rich an experience of childhood normalcy as possible, and appreciating the many mundane personal qualities and capacities that enable it. Early development of a special talent, commonly praised for instilling rigorous discipline and focus, acquires a different value. The pursuit of an intense interest may help children overcome fears that might otherwise grow, self-doubt that could box them in. Excited engagement gives minds and bodies new ways to respond, interact, communicate.

All too often, the impulse to herald youthful talents risks inspiring swelled heads and raising sky-high hopes that are likely to be disappointed. But adopt the viewpoint of the hypersensitive and remote child, and of the family hoping to help him or her feel less overwhelmed by the world, and the impulse to champion a child's singularity becomes an opportunity: a chance for someone to begin developing both a thicker skin and a feeling that "somewhere in the world he has his own function which he may reasonably hope to fulfill." That benediction of Wiener's conveys not just wise pragmatism but, perhaps most important, patience. Resilience and assurance, without which gifts may prove useless, grow slowly.

Back when I first met Marc at six and he was doing his best to stump me with riddles before his music lessons, I was eager for him to get to my favorite, but he never did: Why did the little boy throw the clock out the window? In any case, as I thought about it in retrospect, the punch line—because he wanted to see time fly—was all wrong. The last thing prodigies, or any other children, need to feel is that the clock is ticking on their talents.

Acknowledgments

Writing about America's preoccupation with speedy achievement turned out to be slower work than I had hoped. In the course of it, I learned a lot about a virtue much touted in these pages: patience. I mean other people's deep reserves of it. If prizes were awarded for that, combined with unflagging displays of interest, my family would be covered in ribbons. The most profound gratitude usually gets saved for last, but I'll flout patience and put it first. Over many years and many dinners, my husband, Steve Sestanovich, listened and guided with a confidence in the project that has made all the difference. He read and took his pen to every draft and never doubted that the book would get done. Our children, Ben and Clare, never ceased to be curious about what *Off the Charts* might, someday, say. I couldn't have hoped for better catalysts or companions.

I'm especially grateful to the people who have made the second half of this book possible, carving out time in their very busy lives to talk with me. Jonathan Edwards, Joseph Bates, and Yoky Matsuoka shared thoughts and memories, both about the children they had once been and the parents they have since become. Lang Lang somehow squeezed a conversation into an impossible schedule, and made a family photograph available. While the furor over *Battle Hymn of the Tiger Mother* was in full swing, Amy Chua and Sophia Chua-Rubenfeld spoke candidly about their experiences.

With the younger people whose cooperation has been so crucial, a slow pace has had its advantages. When I first read about Matt Savage, his parents, Diane and Larry, wisely felt their preteen needed less exposure, not more. But by the time Matt headed to graduate school, they and he went out of their way to be available and helpful. Several visits with Matt in New York were highlights of my work. His bass player, John Funkhouser, contributed the thoughtful musical and personal perspective I needed. I was also very glad to have a chance to speak with Matt's teacher Eyran Katsenelenbogen. I welcomed the wry self-portraiture Jay Greenberg conveyed by email. His agent Charles Letourneau's insights, as well as my interviews with his Juilliard teachers Samuel Adler and Samuel Zyman, broadened my view. My meeting with Marc Yu and Chloe Hui more than a decade ago helped inspire this book, and I deeply appreciate the trust they've shown from the beginning.

Writing about child prodigies and related subjects for *The New York Times Magazine* and *Slate* was a crucial part of exploring the field and shaping the book. I counted on Alex Star and Meghan O'Rourke for their editorial guidance on those pieces. In the process, I also learned a great deal from various experts, among them Ellen Winner, Howard Gardner, David Henry Feldman, Dean Keith Simonton, Jan Davidson and Bob Davidson, David Lubinski, and Darold A. Treffert.

I've benefited from various library collections and the generous help of many people in the course of my research. The Institute Archives and Special Collections at MIT granted permission to consult and quote from the Norbert Wiener Papers, and the MIT Museum provided a photograph. I owe a large debt to Dan Mahony, whose online archive of materials by and relating to William James Sidis was invaluable. Stephen Bates shared his very thorough research on Sidis. Leon Hansen kindly made a photograph available. Courtesy of Houghton Library, Harvard University, I've cited a letter from William James.

I spent rewarding time reading through the Henry Cowell Papers, archived in the Music Division of the New York Public

Library for the Performing Arts, and thank the David and Sylvia Teitelbaum Fund, Inc., for permission to quote from them. Christopher English Walling allowed me to cite material about Cowell from the Anna Strunsky Walling Papers, held in the Yale University Library, the Manuscripts and Archives division. The Department of Special Collections and University Archives at the Stanford University Libraries supplied material from the Lewis Madison Terman Papers.

The Rare Book and Manuscript Library at the Columbia University Libraries provided access to the Barbara Newhall Follett Papers and the Helen Follett Papers. Stefan Cooke gave me permission to quote from the former and to use a photograph. I relied on his annotated collection of Barbara Follett's letters, *Barbara Newhall Follett: A Life in Letters,* published in 2015, and on his website. Richard, Roger, and Michael Meservey graciously approved my use of Helen Follett's writings. Kathie Pitman shared her research on Nathalia Crane, and other advice, with me. The Brooklyn Public Library staff provided help as I perused the archives of *The Brooklyn Daily Eagle* for articles about Crane. I'm grateful to the Schomburg Center for Research in Black Culture, and the Manuscripts, Archives and Rare Books Division of the New York Public Library, for days of fruitful research in the Schuyler Family Papers. Thanks in particular to Miranda Mims. Karen Hilliard Johnson gave me permission to quote from the material. Kathryn Talalay's biography of Philippa Schuyler was enormously helpful.

A FOIA request elicited a fascinating trove of material in the form of the FBI's file on Regina Fischer. Frank Brady's biographies of Bobby Fischer were essential, and he kindly made two photographs available. The Spencer Foundation gave me access to the transcript of Julian Stanley's contribution to the Spencer Foundation project, an oral history, 1981–1985, housed at the Columbia Center for Oral History. Jordan Ellenberg's perspective on the Study of Mathematically Precocious Youth was extremely useful, as were our email and phone exchanges. Tim Cawley made time to discuss his experience filming *From Nothing, Something: A Docu-*

mentary on the Creative Process. I count myself lucky to have had the chance to speak with Gary Graffman about Lang Lang and piano training in China and the United States. Ariela Rossberg, the education manager of the Lang Lang International Music Foundation, filled me in on its mission.

As I was finishing up, I was excited to meet another astonishingly talented young pianist, a high school freshman named Avery Gagliano, then in the throes of deciding how music would fit into her life. Fitting Avery into the book didn't work out, but she and her mother, Ying Lam, helped me think about an all-important transition.

Friends contributed in different ways. Early on, Megan Marshall and Emily Yoffe had useful suggestions. Emily Abrahams was always ready to lend an ear (and at the end, with Ruth Abrahams, an eye). Robert Wilson offered thoughts on a chapter. So did Stephen Bates. Mary Jo Salter, Judith Shulevitz, Alex Star, Margaret Talbot, and Dorothy Wickenden each read versions of this book in its entirety; I can't thank them enough for providing incisive and generous editorial input along the way.

Amy Weiss-Meyer sprang into action to help with fact-checking and notes at the end, just the careful collaborator I needed. Janice Wolly answered my copy-editing questions. With Todd Portnowitz steering the manuscript through the production process at Knopf, as well as tracking down photographs, I knew I was in great hands. My agent, Sarah Chalfant, gave me unfailing encouragement and wise advice from start to finish. And no one could have guided *Off the Charts* to its conclusion more eagerly and astutely than Ann Close, my editor, did. I might still be at it without her.

Notes

Prologue

ix **a six-year-old named Marc Yu:** Marc Yu, visit with author, July 13, 2005.

ix **"stop wasting our brightest young minds":** Jan and Bob Davidson with Laura Vanderkam, *Genius Denied: How to Stop Wasting Our Brightest Young Minds* (New York: Simon & Schuster, 2004). See also the Davidson Institute website for its mission to "serve profoundly gifted young people 18 and under. Profoundly gifted students are those who score in the 99.9th percentile on IQ and achievement tests." "About Us," http://www.davidsongifted.org/About-Us.

x **"She is still composing":** *The Ellen DeGeneres Show,* February 21, 2006.

x **"I don't know":** *Your L.A. with Janet Choi,* KTLA, August 23, 2006.

x **"You should play Game Boy less":** Ann Hulbert, "The Prodigy Puzzle," *New York Times Magazine,* November 20, 2005.

xi **"The possibilities are extraordinary":** Jeffrey Bernstein in *My Brilliant Brain,* a three-part National Geographic series filmed in 2006, when Marc was seven, and released in 2007.

xi **honing youthful potential ever earlier:** Garey Ramey and Valerie A. Ramey, "The Rug Rat Race," National Bureau of Economic Research Working Paper 15284, August 2009.

xii **"grit," the latest lab-tested talent development secret:** See Angela L. Duckworth, Christopher Peterson, Michael D. Matthews, and Dennis R. Kelly, "Grit: Perseverance and Passion for Long-Term Goals," *Journal of Personality and Social Psychology* 92, no. 6 (2007): 1087–101.

Duckworth's book, *Grit: The Power of Passion and Perseverance,* was published by Scribner in 2016.

xiii **"yesterday's news"**: Madeline Levine, *Teach Your Children Well: Parenting for Authentic Success* (New York: HarperCollins, 2012), p. 12.

xv **"the public ever hears of"**: Norbert Wiener, *Ex-Prodigy: My Childhood and Youth* (1953; reprinted Cambridge, Mass.: MIT Press, 1964), p. 4.

xvi **"Next to God comes Papa"**: Maynard Solomon, *Mozart: A Life* (New York: HarperCollins, 1995), p. 11.

xvi **"miracle, which God has allowed"**: Ibid., p. 5.

xvi **"the understanding about the balance of power"**: Phyllis Rose, *Parallel Lives: Five Victorian Marriages* (New York: Vintage, 1984), p. 7.

PART I
NATURE VS. NURTURE

Chapter 1. The Wonder Boys of Harvard

Where not otherwise indicated, biographical details are drawn from Amy Wallace, *The Prodigy* (New York: E. P. Dutton, 1986); Flo Conway and Jim Siegelman, *Dark Hero of the Information Age: In Search of Norbert Wiener, the Father of Cybernetics* (New York: Basic Books, 2005); and Norbert Wiener, *Ex-Prodigy: My Childhood and Youth* (1953; reprinted Cambridge, Mass.: MIT Press, 1964).

3 **"The first thing my April Fool's boy wanted"**: Sarah Sidis, "The Sidis Story" (1950). Her account is available on sidis.net, the W. J. Sidis Archive and the Boris Sidis Archive.

4 **one of the first**: "Wonderful Boys of History Compared with Sidis," *New York Times,* January 16, 1910.

4 **"with the aid of a crayon"**: "Boy of 10 Addresses Harvard Teachers," *New York Times,* January 6, 1910. The article misstates Sidis's age—he was eleven, not ten.

4 **"the most brilliant man in the world"**: S. Sidis, "The Sidis Story."

5 **"the individuality, the originality"**: Boris Sidis, *Philistine and Genius* (Boston: Richard G. Badger, 1919), accessed on sidis.net.

5 **"10,000 hour rule"**: Malcolm Gladwell, *Outliers: The Story of Success* (New York: Little, Brown, 2008), pp. 39–40. As Gladwell notes, K. Anders Ericsson and colleagues employed the term "deliberate practice" (p. 288). See K. Anders Ericsson, Kiruthiga Nandagopal, and Roy W. Roring, "Giftedness Viewed from the Expert-Performance

Perspective," *Journal for the Education of the Gifted* 28, no. 3/4 (2005): 287–311.

5 "I congratulate you": William James to Boris Sidis, September 11, 1902, William James Papers (MS Am 1092.9 (3775)), Houghton Library, Harvard University.

6 Einstein's revolutionary papers of 1905: John S. Ridgen, *Einstein 1905: The Standard of Greatness* (Cambridge, Mass.: Harvard University Press, 2005).

6 "men with much money": Jerome Karabel, *The Chosen: The Hidden History of Admission and Exclusion at Harvard, Yale, and Princeton* (Boston: Houghton Mifflin, 2005), pp. 41–42.

6 "new immigrants": Ibid., pp. 47–48.

6 "What will become of the wonder child?": "A Savant at Thirteen, Young Sidis on Entering Harvard Knows More Than Many on Leaving. A Scholar at Three," *New York Times,* October 17, 1909.

7 "was not forced": "Harvard's Four Child Students and the Fathers Who Trained Three of Them," *Boston Sunday Herald,* November 14, 1909.

7 "I tried at one time": Wiener, *Ex-Prodigy,* p. 139.

7 he went to the gym every day: "Harvard's Four Child Students."

7 "greasy grind": Karabel, *The Chosen,* p. 21.

8 "Parents Declare Others": "Harvard's Four Child Students."

8 "up to the human race": H. Addington Bruce, "Bending the Twig: The Education of the Eleven Year Old Boy Who Lectured Before the Harvard Professors on the Fourth Dimension," *American Magazine,* no. 69 (1910): 690.

8 "Philistine and Genius": His speech was later published, first as a short book in 1911 and then in a revised edition in 1919.

8 "could be overwhelming": Weiner, *Ex-Prodigy,* p. 18.

9 "with thin necks": Isaac Babel, *The Collected Stories,* ed. Nathalie Babel, trans. Peter Constantine (New York: W. W. Norton, 2002), p. 61.

9 "lightning calculators": H. Addington Bruce, "Lightning Calculators: A Study in the Psychology of Harnessing the Subconscious," *McClure's Magazine,* September 1912, p. 590.

9 "perform vast sums": "The Boy Prodigy of Harvard," in Edward J. Wheeler, ed., *Current Literature* (New York: Current Literature, 1910), p. 291.

9 "Mere 'reckoning machines'": Bruce, "Lightning Calculators," p. 593.

9 "liberal-minded citizen": B. Sidis, *Philistine and Genius.* In *The Prodigy,* p. 104, Wallace cites Sarah Sidis's memoirs, in which she quotes

Boris saying, "We set our poor little musical prodigies to practice six hours a day so they may delight roomfuls of people. We don't seem to care that we make them educated boobs."

9 **suffer a depressive crisis**: Bruce L. Kinzer, *J. S. Mill Revisited: Biographical and Political Explorations* (New York: Palgrave Macmillan, 2007), pp. 28–39.

9 **"willing to give the necessary trouble"**: John Stuart Mill, *Autobiography of John Stuart Mill* (New York: Columbia University Press, 1924), p. 24.

9 **"children's needs of the concrete"**: Tom A. Williams, "Intellectual Precocity: Comparison Between John Stuart Mill and the Son of Dr. Boris Sidis," *Pedagogical Seminary* 18 (1911): 91.

9 **"minds are built with use"**: Wallace, *The Prodigy*, p. 20. In *Philistine and Genius*, Sidis wrote that "the beginning of education is *between the second and third year.* It is at that time that the child begins to form his interests. It is at that critical period that we have to seize the opportunity to guide the child's formative energies in the right channels."

9 **"the psychology of suggestion"**: Bruce, "Bending the Twig," pp. 690, 694.

10 **"reserve energy"**: B. Sidis, *Philistine and Genius*.

10 **"That is the key"**: Bruce, "Bending the Twig," p. 695.

10 **"learn by [rote]"**: "The Most Remarkable Boy in the World," *New York World Magazine,* October 7, 1906, p. 3.

10 **"the child who thinks best"**: "The Secret of Precocity," *Literary Digest,* July 15, 1911, p. 101.

10 **"one of the absurdities"**: A. A. Berle, *The School in the Home: Talks with Parents and Teachers on Intensive Child Training* (New York: Moffat, Yard, 1915), pp. 18–19.

11 **"the impossibility of man's being certain"**: Norbert Wiener, "The Theory of General Ignorance," p. 1, notebook in Norbert Wiener Papers (hereafter NWP), MC 22, Box 26C, Folder 421, Massachusetts Institute of Technology, Institute Archives and Special Collections, Cambridge, Mass.

13 **"element of *élan*"**: Wiener, *Ex-Prodigy*, p. 74.

13 **"house of learning"**: Ibid., p. 62.

13 **"shaggy uncomformity"**: Ibid., p. 27.

13 **"a greater challenge"**: Ibid., p. 66.

14 **"a poet at heart"**: Ibid., p. 74.

14 **"the blessedness of blundering"**: "Harvard's Four Child Students."

14 **Making children "work out problems"**: H. Addington Bruce, "New

Ideas in Child Training: Remarkable Results Obtained in the Education of Children Through New Methods of Some American Parents," *American Magazine*, no. 72 (1911): 292.

14   H. "Addlehead" Bruce: Norbert Wiener to Bertha Wiener, November 10, 1914, NWP, MC 22, Box 1, Folder 9.

14   "No casual interest": Norbert Wiener, *I Am a Mathematician: The Later Life of a Prodigy* (Garden City, N.Y.: Doubleday, 1956), p. 18.

14   "He would begin the discussion": Wiener, *Ex-Prodigy*, p. 67.

14   "often ended in a family scene": Ibid., p. 68.

15   "I relearned the world": Conway and Siegelman, *Dark Hero of the Information Age*, p. 14.

15   "unorthodox experiment": Wiener, *Ex-Prodigy*, p. 92.

15   "brains and conscience": Ibid., p. 93.

15   "schoolroom behavior": Ibid., p. 94.

15   "a sense of roots and security": Ibid., p. 99.

15   "calf love": Ibid., p. 101.

15   an upbeat send-off for a prodigy: "The Most Remarkable Boy."

16   "prim and quaint": Ibid.

16   "The most important thing": S. Sidis, "The Sidis Story."

16   Sarah Mandelbaum herself: On Sarah Mandelbaum Sidis's education, see ibid. and Wallace, *The Prodigy*, pp. 9–13.

16   "like all normal little fellows": S. Sidis, "The Sidis Story."

17   At home, Billy at five months: Sarah Sidis, "Book of Methods," eighteen-page unpublished manuscript, University of Miami Archives, accessed on sidis.net. See also S. Sidis, "The Sidis Story."

17   Boris supplied Billy with calendars: "The Boy Prodigy of Harvard," in Wheeler, ed., *Current Literature*, p. 291.

17   Sarah watched bemused: S. Sidis, "The Sidis Story."

17   Sports held no interest: Ibid.

17   At breakfast: "An Infant Prodigy," *North American Review*, no. 184, April 14, 1907.

18   "Aha, you forgot": S. Sidis, "The Sidis Story."

18   "expounding the nebular hypothesis": E. H. C., "A Phenomenon in Kilts," *Boston Transcript*, November 16, 1906.

18   he balked at math: Bruce, "Bending the Twig," pp. 692, 694.

18   a new logarithmic table: "Harvard's Quartet of Child Prodigies: Unique Problem for Psychologists in Education of Young Sidis and His Three Companions," *New York Times*, January 16, 1910.

18   "He soon told me": S. Sidis, "The Sidis Story."

19   "skipping and dancing": E. H. C., "A Phenomenon in Kilts."

20   **pick up the pace:** Kathleen Montour, "William James Sidis, The Broken Twig," *American Psychologist*, April 1977, p. 268.

20   **"Our undisciplinables":** Ronald Steel, *Walter Lippmann and the American Century* (Boston: Little, Brown, 1980), p. 13.

20   ***"wisdom,* even any common sense":** Montour, "William James Sidis," p. 273.

20   **"I was certainly no model":** Wiener, *Ex-Prodigy*, p. 132.

20   **"utterly without self-conceit":** Magazine of the *Boston Sunday Herald*, November 7, 1909.

21   **One informed listener:** Wiener, *Ex-Prodigy*, pp. 131–32.

21   **"Is that any plainer now?":** Wallace, *The Prodigy*, p. 59.

22   **"such a mind should find":** Ibid., pp. 55–56.

22   **"Marvelous Griffith":** "Farmer a Rival to Harvard Prodigy," *New York Times*, February 19, 1910.

22   **"weakened recently by overstudy":** "Sidis, Boy Prodigy, Ill," *New York Times*, January 27, 1910.

22   **"new and better system":** "Topics of the Times: Young Sidis Suffers a Breakdown," *New York Times*, January 27, 1910.

22   **"though not cruel":** Montour, "William James Sidis," p. 273.

23   **"nervous patients":** Wallace, *The Prodigy*, p. 85.

23   **"persons who are hobby ridden":** "Dr. Sidis to Cure Hobbies," *New York Times*, January 17, 1910.

23   **twirling his hat:** Katherine E. Dolbear, "Precocious Children," *Pedagogical Seminary* 19, no. 4 (December 1912): 465.

24   **"drift into national degeneracy":** These quotations from the 1911 edition of *Philistine and Genius* can be found in Doug Renselle, "A Review of Boris Sidis' *Philistine and Genius,*" http://www.quantonics.com/Boris_Sidis_Philistine_and_Genius_Review.html#TOC. See chaps. 5 and 15.

24   **"bent on repelling, offending":** "Philistine and Genius," *New York Times*, June 25, 1911.

24   **"pulled down upon his stout head":** S. Sidis, "The Sidis Story."

24   **He graduated cum laude:** "Harvard A.B. at 16," *New York Times*, June 14, 1914.

24   **"mentally . . . regarded by wise men":** "Harvard's Boy Prodigy Vows Never to Marry," *Boston Herald*, n.d. All the quotations from Sidis in the rest of this section are from this article.

25   **"manufactured man":** Mill, *Autobiography of John Stuart Mill*, p. 109.

26   **"freak of nature":** Wiener, *Ex-Prodigy*, p. 119.

27   **"nearly completely a man":** Ibid., p. 106.

27   **"severely lacerated self-esteem":** Ibid., p. 76.

27   "doubt as to whether": Ibid., p. 116.

27   "prodigy comes to realize": Ibid., p. 117.

27   "a gentlemanly indifference": Ibid., p. 140.

28   "black year of my life": Ibid., p. 151.

29   "consciousness of belonging": Ibid., p. 145.

29   "confused mass of feelings": Ibid., p. 152.

29   "My only want is": Norbert Wiener to Bertha Wiener, c. October 1910, NWP, MC 22, Box 1, Folder 4.

30   honing rabbinic learnedness: Wiener, *Ex-Prodigy*, p. 133.

30   "What is the Egyptian word": Norbert Wiener to Leo Wiener, c. January 1911, NWP, MC 22, Box 1, Folder 4.

30   "Give it to him!": Norbert Wiener to Leo Wiener, c. February 1911, NWP, MC 22, Box 1, Folder 4.

30   It was "devastating": Wiener, *Ex-Prodigy*, p. 159.

31   "How is your work?": Norbert Wiener to Leo Wiener, c. May 1911, NWP, MC 22, Box 1, Folder 4.

31   drawings he sent as postscripts: See, e.g., Norbert Wiener to Leo Wiener, October 2, 1910, October 16, 1910, November 4, 1910, and November 30, 1910, NWP, MC 22, Box 1, Folder 4.

31   "filial servitude": Wiener, *Ex-Prodigy*, p. 163.

31   "he is so young": "Harvard Boy Ph.D. to Study Abroad, His Father Plans," *New York American*, March 8, 1913.

31   "Just Missed Becoming": "Just Missed Becoming a Great Merchant," *Boston Daily Globe*, December 27, 1914.

32   he dropped out in his third year: Stephen Bates, "The Prodigy and the Press," *Journalism and Mass Communication Quarterly* 88, no. 2 (Summer 2011): 379.

32   he was "kidnapped": William James Sidis, "Railroading in the Past," accessed on sidis.net

32   in flight from his parents' "protection": He puts "protection" in quotes and describes himself as "scared of his own shadow." Ibid.

33   William got good news: Roscoe Pound to William James Sidis, April 30, 1923, Roscoe Pound Papers, Harvard Law School Library. See also Bates, "The Prodigy and the Press," p. 379.

33   "mentally abnormal": "Commonwealth vs. William Sidis," April 25, 1923, Roscoe Pound Papers, Harvard Law School Library.

33   "I just want to work": Wallace, *The Prodigy*, p. 196.

33   his most ambitious endeavor: William James Sidis, *The Animate and the Inanimate* (Boston: Richard G. Badger, 1925). See also Wallace, *The Prodigy*, pp. 156–60, for a letter from Buckminster Fuller to Gerard Piel, February 27, 1979.

33 **dragged back into the limelight:** See Bates, "The Prodigy and the Press."

33 **It was written by James Thurber:** Jared L. Manley, "Where Are They Now? April Fool!" *New Yorker*, August 14, 1937, pp. 22–26.

34 **active in defense of pacifism:** According to Wallace, he proposed using the term *libertarian* for the limited-government cause. Wallace, *The Prodigy*, p. 238.

34 **"defeated—and honorably defeated":** Wiener, *Ex-Prodigy*, p. 134.

34 **unable to overtly rebel:** "Deprivation of the right to judge for myself and to stand the consequences of my own decision," Norbert wrote, "stood me in ill stead for many years to come. It delayed my social and moral maturity, and represents a handicap I have only partly discarded in middle age." Ibid., p. 140.

34 **"physically strong":** Leo Wiener to Bertrand Russell, June 15, 1913, NWP, MC 22, Box 1, Folder 5.

34 **"horrible fog":** Norbert Wiener to Leo Wiener, October 18, 1913, NWP, MC 22, Box 1, Folder 5.

35 **"an iceberg":** Norbert Wiener to Leo Wiener, October 25, 1913, NWP, MC 22, Box 1, Folder 5.

35 **"Do not work too hard":** Leo Wiener to Norbert Wiener, May 24, 1914, NWP, MC 22, Box 1, Folder 8.

35 **"I have occasionally taken":** Norbert Wiener to his parents, April 1914, NWP, MC 22, Box 5, Folder 7.

35 **"loafing":** Norbert Wiener to Bertha Wiener, June 17, 1914, NWP, MC 22, Box 1, Folder 8.

35 **"fine, especially fine":** Leo Wiener to Norbert Wiener, May 24, 1914, NWP, MC 22, Box 1, Folder 8.

36 **"It may seem a step down":** Wiener, *Ex-Prodigy*, p. 253.

36 **"or control and communication":** Subtitle of Wiener's *Cybernetics: Or Control and Communication in the Animal and the Machine* (Cambridge, Mass.: MIT Press, 1948).

36 **Cybernetics laid crucial groundwork:** Doug Hill, "The Eccentric Genius Whose Time May Have Finally Come (Again)," Atlantic .com, June 11, 2014.

36 **"sired, inspired, or contributed to":** Conway and Siegelman, *Dark Hero*, p. xiii.

36 **"the children's machine":** Seymour Papert, *The Children's Machine: Rethinking School in the Age of the Computer* (New York: Basic Books, 1993), p. vii.

37 **"struggles in a half-understood world":** Wiener, *Ex-Prodigy*, p. 5.

37 **"rigorous discipline and training":** Ibid., p. 290.

37 "chance to develop a reasonably thick skin": Norbert Wiener, "Analysis of the Child Prodigy," *New York Times Magazine,* June 2, 1957, p. 34.

Chapter 2. "A Very Free Child"

Where not otherwise indicated, biographical details are drawn from Michael Hicks, *Henry Cowell: Bohemian* (Urbana: University of Illinois Press, 2002), and Joel Sachs, *Henry Cowell: A Man Made of Music* (New York: Oxford University Press, 2012).

38 "I noticed his eyes were staring": Anna Strunsky Walling, "Henry Cowell, Fifty Years a Composer," p. 4, Anna Strunsky Walling Papers, MS 1111, Box 34, Folder 406, Manuscripts and Archives, Yale University Library.

39 "There was never a deviation": Ibid., p. 3.

39 "He says, 'Choo-choo say,'": Clarissa Dixon Cowell, "Material for a Biography," Henry Cowell Papers (hereafter HCP), JPB 00-03, Box 74, Folder 1, Music Division, New York Public Library for the Performing Arts.

39 "I find much in Henry": Ibid.

39 "an artist of unusual talent": Hicks, *Henry Cowell,* p. 56.

39 "Lad Shows Signs": Anna Cora Winchell, "Lad Shows Signs of Real Genius," *San Francisco Chronicle,* March 6, 1914, p. 5.

39 "Youthful Wonder Has Charm": "Youthful Wonder Has Charm of Genius," *Daily Palo Alto Times,* January 23, 1914.

40 A former brainy boy: Henry L. Minton, *Lewis M. Terman: Pioneer in Psychological Testing* (New York: New York University Press, 1988), pp. 3–9.

40 "especially prone to be puny": Barbara Stoddard Burks, Dortha Williams Jensen, and Lewis M. Terman, *Genetic Studies of Genius,* vol. 3, *The Promise of Youth: Follow-Up Studies of a Thousand Gifted Children* (Stanford, Calif.: Stanford University Press, 1930), p. 474.

40 "mob spirit": Boris Sidis, *Philistine and Genius* (Boston: Richard G. Badger, 1919), preface.

40 For his starter sample: On Terman's own children, Fred and Helen, see Joel N. Shurkin, *Terman's Kids: The Groundbreaking Study of How the Gifted Grow Up* (Boston: Little, Brown, 1992), p. 16.

41 "a very free child": Hicks, *Henry Cowell,* p. 32.

41 "Both his father and I disapprove": C. D. Cowell, "Material for a Biography." Quotations in the following two paragraphs are from the same source.

42   "like a zither with a keyboard": Henry Cowell, "Some Autobiograph-
     ical Notes," typescript in Adolf Meyer Papers, Alan Mason Chesney
     Medical Archives of the Johns Hopkins Medical Institutions.

42   "the development of initiative": C. D. Cowell, "Material for a Biog-
     raphy."

42   In her diary she marked: Ibid.

43   "not a single unpleasant sound": Ibid.

43   "the long deferred literary life": Harry Cowell to Clarissa Dixon
     Cowell, January 12, 1901, HCP, JPB 00-03, Box 3, Folder 16.

44   "I cannot play because": C. D. Cowell, "Material for a Biography."

44   "Henry showed no strong impulse": Ibid.

44   "all the children I played with": Sachs, *Henry Cowell*, pp. 25–26.

44   "crushing all children": Hicks, *Henry Cowell*, pp. 20–21.

44   "at least enough of it": C. D. Cowell, "Material for a Biography."

45   "Groping Among Educational Methods": Ibid.

45   "who feel no special voluntary interest": Ibid.

46   an "impassioned" six weeks: On Clarissa as Henry's teacher and their
     journey and arrival in Iowa, see ibid.

46   sent his father a song: Harry Cowell to Henry Cowell, September 9,
     1907, HCP, JBP 00-03, Box 3, Folder 19.

47   "getting fitted into my own place": Clarissa Dixon Cowell to Harry
     Cowell, quoted in Sidney Cowell memoir, HCP, JPB 00-03, Box 76,
     Folder 5.

47   a curious novel about: Clarissa's novel was *Janet and Her Dear Phebe*
     (New York: Frederick A. Stokes & Co., 1909).

47   he was composing music: Henry Cowell to Harry Cowell, n.d., HCP,
     JPB 00-03, Box 18, Folder 5.

47   enjoying them "like a baby": Henry Cowell to Harry Cowell, May 5,
     1909, HCP, JPB 00-03, Box 18, Folder 6.

47   "He loves a land": Clarissa Dixon Cowell to Harry Cowell, quoted in
     Sidney Cowell memoir, HCP, JPB 00-03, Box 76, Folder 5.

47   "I have had enough of New York": Henry Cowell to Harry Cowell,
     May 5, 1909, HCP, JPB 00-03, Box 18, Folder 6.

47   "I wish that he had had": Harry Cowell to Clarissa Dixon Cowell,
     May 12, 1909, HCP, JPB 00-03, Box 3, Folder 23.

48   "Sweet peas, phlox": Henry Cowell to Harry Cowell, July 25, 1910,
     HCP, JPB 00-03, Box 76, Folder 5.

48   San Francisco streetcar transfers: Sachs, *Henry Cowell*, p. 32.

48   "The plant business was never worse": Henry Cowell to Harry Cow-
     ell, July 29, 1911, HCP, JPB 00-03, Box 18, Folder 6.

48 **having urged his father:** Henry Cowell to Harry Cowell, January 23, 1911, HCP, JPB 00-03, Box 18, Folder 6.

49 **"Hour by hour she listened carefully":** C. D. Cowell, "Material for a Biography."

49 **"She is a big soul":** Sachs, *Henry Cowell,* p. 85.

49 **"As a boy of a dozen years":** Lewis M. Terman, *Intelligence of School Children* (Boston: Houghton Mifflin, 1919), pp. 248–49.

50 **"schoolhouse gifts":** Joseph S. Renzulli, "Reexamining the Role of Gifted Education and Talent Development for the 21st Century: A Four-Part Theoretical Approach," *Gifted Child Quarterly* 56 (2012): 150.

50 **first revision of Binet's test:** On Terman's revising work, see Minton, *Lewis M. Terman,* pp. 46–51.

50 **"the brightest child to whom he had ever given":** C. D. Cowell, "Material for a Biography."

50 **Even Henry boasted to his father:** Henry Cowell to Harry Cowell, January 29, 1912, HCP, JPB 00-03, Box 18, Folder 7.

50 **"Although the IQ is satisfactory":** Terman, *Intelligence of School Children,* pp. 246–47.

50 **"only two things considered":** Lewis Terman, notes, HCP, JPB 00-03, Box 96, Folder 3.

51 **"Henry Cowell was a very Ordinary man":** Lewis Terman, notes, dated February 1912, HCP, JPB 00-03, Box 96, Folder 3.

51 **"St. Agnes Morning":** Liner notes for *Songs of Henry Cowell,* https:// www.dramonline.org/albums/songs-of-henry-cowell/notes.

51 **"Always he has worked mostly alone":** C. D. Cowell, "Material for a Biography."

51 **"the dirtiest little shrimp":** Hicks, *Henry Cowell,* p. 70.

52 **"Adventures in Harmony":** Ibid., p. 44.

52 **"hungry ocean in the human soul":** On Henry's music for *Creation Dawn,* see ibid., pp. 49–52.

52 **"the steadying hand of instruction":** Walter Anthony, "In the World of Music: Opera Star Will Sing in Concert," *San Francisco Chronicle,* July 26, 1914.

53 **the blunt view:** Hicks, *Henry Cowell,* p. 57. The quotes are from Redfern Mason, "Work of Merit at Concert of Local Society," *San Francisco Examiner,* March 6, 1914.

53 **"useful to modest talent":** C. D. Cowell, "Material for a Biography."

53 **"but reasonable discipline":** Winchell, "Lad Shows Signs of Real Genius."

53 "Whether anybody can teach this lad": Anthony, "In the World of Music."

53 He served as a conduit: Minton, *Lewis M. Terman*, p. 112.

54 "gone . . . far along his own lines": Hicks, *Henry Cowell*, p. 67.

54 "dissonant counterpoint": Alex Ross, *The Rest Is Noise: Listening to the Twentieth Century* (New York: Picador, 2007), p. 521.

54 "There is a new race": Ibid.

54 "You know how well": Henry Cowell to Clarissa Dixon Cowell, October 31, 1913, HCP, JPB 00-03, Box 18, Folder 7.

54 "Oh, but he was a splendid comrade!": C. D. Cowell, "Material for a Biography."

55 "Everyone here composes": Henry Cowell to Russell Varian, December 1916, in Hicks, *Henry Cowell*, p. 75.

55 the institute "cads": Henry Cowell to Ellen Veblen, November 22, 1916, HCP, JPB 00-03, Box 18, Folder 10.

55 "the Keyboard Terror": Ross, *The Rest Is Noise*, p. 147.

56 Terman published the Stanford revision: Minton, *Lewis M. Terman*, p. 48.

56 some sixty children in the Bay Area: Ibid., p. 95.

56 the future Nobel Prize–winner William Shockley: Joel Shurkin, *Broken Genius: The Rise and Fall of William Shockley, Creator of the Electronic Age* (London: Macmillan, 2006), pp. 12–13.

56 "string piano": Hicks, *Henry Cowell*, pp. 110–11.

56 He aimed to supply data: On Terman's postwar effort to expand his influence and on *Genetic Studies of Genius*, see Minton, *Lewis M. Terman*, pp. 95, 100, 110–15. Terman described the origins and growth of his research in Lewis M. Terman, ed., *Genetic Studies of Genius*, vol. 1, *Mental and Physical Traits of a Thousand Gifted Children* (Stanford, Calif.: Stanford University Press, 1925), pp. 5–17.

56 confident sense of specialness: Mitchell Leslie, "The Vexing Legacy of Lewis Terman," *Stanford Magazine*, July–August 2000.

57 selection bias: Ann Hulbert, "The Prodigy Puzzle," *New York Times Magazine*, November 20, 2005.

57 roughly fifteen hundred students: Terman, *Genetic Studies of Genius*, vol. 1, p. 39.

57 "the widespread opinion": Ibid., p. 634.

58 85 percent of them had skipped grades: Ibid., p. 285.

58 "the majority of gifted children": Leta S. Hollingworth, *Gifted Children: Their Nature and Nurture* (New York: Macmillan, 1926), pp. 136–37, 148.

58 By now an outspoken eugenicist: Minton, *Lewis M. Terman*, p. 147.

58 "The great problems of genius": Terman, *Genetic Studies of Genius,* vol. 1, p. 641.

59 "The title is not meant to imply": Burks, Jensen, and Terman, *Genetic Studies of Genius,* vol. 3, p. 4.

59 a peculiar effort to link: Catharine Morris Cox, *Genetic Studies of Genius,* vol. 2, *The Early Mental Traits of Three Hundred Geniuses* (Stanford, Calif.: Stanford University Press, 1926).

59 Eight-year-old Goethe's literary work: Ibid., pp. 162, 217.

59 "persistence of motive and effort": Ibid., pp. 217–18.

60 "so harnessed to the organized pursuit": Leta S. Hollingworth, *Children Above 180 IQ: Origin and Development* (Yonkers-on-Hudson, N.Y.: World Book, 1942), pp. 237–38.

60 "rapid rise to international fame": Burks, Jensen, and Terman, *Genetic Studies of Genius,* vol. 3, p. 324.

61 Even in music, the field best known: Ellen Winner, *Gifted Children: Myths and Realities* (New York: Basic Books, 1996), p. 278.

62 "One would hardly be justified": Burks, Jensen, and Terman, *Genetic Studies of Genius,* vol. 3, p. 452.

62 "'Mother,' she said one day": Lewis M. Terman and Jessie C. Fenton, "Preliminary Report on a Gifted Juvenile Author," *Journal of Applied Psychology* 5 (1921): 178.

62 "heterosexual adjustment": Hicks, *Henry Cowell,* p. 139.

63 "cultural defense": Ibid., p. 141.

63 Terman's twenty-five-year follow-up volume: Lewis M. Terman and Melita H. Oden, *Genetic Studies of Genius,* vol. 4, *The Gifted Child Grows Up: Twenty-Five Years' Follow-Up of a Superior Group* (Stanford, Calif.: Stanford University Press, 1947), pp. 311–52.

63 "itself to me in a flash": Sachs, *Henry Cowell,* p. 73.

64 "I was bristlingly modernistic": Hicks, *Henry Cowell,* p. 145.

64 But his wide-ranging influence: Sachs, *Henry Cowell,* pp. 510–13.

64 the thirty-five-year update: Lewis M. Terman and Melita H. Oden, *Genetic Studies of Genius,* vol. 5, *The Gifted Group at Mid-Life: Thirty-Five Years' Follow-up of the Superior Child* (Stanford, Calif.: Stanford University Press, 1959).

64 "my 1,400 gifted 'children'": Minton, *Lewis M. Terman,* p. 252.

64 "There are many intangible kinds": Terman and Oden, *Genetic Studies of Genius,* vol. 5, p. 145.

65 William Hewlett and David Packard: Shurkin, *Terman's Kids,* p. 224.

65 Fred also lured William Shockley: C. Stewart Gillmor, *Fred Terman at Stanford: Building a Discipline, a University, and Silicon Valley* (Stanford, Calif.: Stanford University Press, 2004), p. 311.

65   made him a pariah: Shurkin, *Broken Genius,* pp. 212–25.

65   "the group has produced": Terman and Oden, *Genetic Studies of Genius,* vol. 5, pp. 150–51.

65   "Two weeks ago today": Lewis Terman to Henry Cowell, July 24, 1956, HCP, JPB 00-03, Box 15, Folder 26.

66   "I don't know when I have received": Lewis Terman to Henry Cowell, August 9, 1956, HCP, JPB 00-03, Box 15, Folder 26.

PART II
DAUGHTERS AND DREAMS

Chapter 3.   "A Renaissance of Creative Genius in Girlhood"

69   her father, Clarence: On Nathalia's parents, see Nunnally Johnson, "Nathalia from Brooklyn," *American Mercury,* September–December 1926, p. 59.

69   She beat time with her foot: James C. Young, "Child Poet Explains Her Lines 'Just Come,'" *New York Times,* November 22, 1925.

69   "When she is writing": "Girl Undismayed by Authorship Fuss," *New York Times,* November 16, 1925.

70   "Nobody may come into this room": Barbara Newhall Follett, *The House Without Windows and Eepersip's Life There* (New York: Alfred A. Knopf, 1927), p. 53. An ebook is available at https://sites.google.com /site/thehousewithoutwindows/download-books. Page numbers are from the PDF version.

70   "renaissance of creative genius": "A Girl Who Is Famous in Two Continents," *Current Opinion* 70, no. 5 (May 1921): 671.

70   "America has rushed into": Louis Untermeyer, "Hilda and the Unconscious," *Dial,* August 1920, p. 186.

71   decidedly not "parshial": Daisy Ashford, *The Young Visiters or, Mr. Salteena's Plan* (New York: George H. Doran, 1919), p. 25.

71   Prodigies thrive on receptive culture: See David Henry Feldman, *Nature's Gambit: Child Prodigies and the Development of Human Potential* (New York: Teachers College Press, 1991), pp. 11–15.

71   "All the mother's darlings in the country": Squib from *The Pittsburgh Press,* June 2, 1926.

72   "drawing its substance directly": Untermeyer, "Hilda and the Unconscious," p. 188.

72   "How beautiful!": Amy Lowell, "Preface," in Hilda Conkling, *Poems by a Little Girl* (New York: Frederick A. Stokes, 1920), p. xii.

72   **daughters of parents who were book lovers:** Even Opal Whiteley, who claimed she was an orphan brought up by unbookish people, said her real parents had left her crucial books that—along with nature—were her teachers.

72   **a generation reared on *Peter Pan:*** Lisa Chaney, *Hide-and-Seek with Angels: A Life of J. M. Barrie* (New York: St. Martin's Press, 2006), p. 230.

73   **"off to Tahiti":** Untermeyer, "Hilda and the Unconscious," p. 190.

73   **her "songs":** Johnson, "Nathalia from Brooklyn," p. 53.

74   **He suggested she send them:** Ibid.

75   **"child would ever submit any work":** Nathalia Crane, *The Janitor's Boy and Other Poems* (New York: Core Collection Books, 1974), p. 75.

75   **"little, long-legged, bright-eyed child":** Edmund Leamy, "Nathalia Crane, Fourteen Years Later," *America*, March 20, 1937, pp. 571–72.

75   **" 'The History of Honey' ":** Crane, *The Janitor's Boy*, pp. 53–54.

76   **"rhythmical, lilting production":** Ibid., p. 75.

76   **"The Janitor's Boy":** Ibid., p. 3.

77   **"My candle burns at both ends":** Edna St. Vincent Millay, *A Few Figs from Thistles* (New York: Frank Shay, 1921), p. 9. The first edition appeared in 1920.

77   **"lack of childishness":** Annie Wood Besant, "The Youngest of the Seers," *Theosophist Magazine* 46, no. 2 (1925): 647.

77   **"I sat down on a bumble bee":** Crane, *The Janitor's Boy*, p. 27.

78   **"The work was alternately juvenile and mature":** Louis Untermeyer, *From Another World: An Autobiography* (New York: Harcourt, Brace, 1939), p. 290.

78   **"nothing except that she is":** Quotations from Benét are from Crane, *The Janitor's Boy*, pp. xi–xiii.

79   **"Looking shyly out at the world":** "Seltzer Will Modify His Claims of Foreign Honor Given Nathalia Crane," *Brooklyn Daily Eagle*, November 11, 1925.

79   **"Literary Storm Center":** *Brooklyn Daily Eagle*, December 6, 1925.

79   **"I am an ancient lady":** Nathalia Crane, *Lava Lane and Other Poems* (New York: Thomas Seltzer, 1925), p. 40.

79   **"I am as much mystified":** "Publisher Urges Test," *Brooklyn Daily Eagle*, November 9, 1925.

80   **"A poet is continually trying":** "Untermyer [*sic*] Tells Why He Believes Nathalia Has the Gift of Poesy," *Brooklyn Daily Eagle*, November 17, 1925.

80   **"how a child can absorb so much":** "Child Poet Picks Big Words from Air," *New York Times*, November 17, 1925.

80   Words "just come": Young, "Child Poet Explains."

80   "They always fit": "Child Poet Picks Big Words from Air."

80   "Nathalia, tell us what you know": Johnson, "Nathalia from Brooklyn," pp. 55–56.

81   "born upon the back of a menu card": "Markham v. Prodigy," *Time*, November 23, 1925.

81   He diagnosed Nathalia's father: Clement Wood, "Nathalia Crane's Poems Credited to Father in Clement Wood's Analysis," *Brooklyn Daily Eagle*, November 22, 1925.

81   spare his daughter the ordeal: "Nathalia Crane's Father Again Refuses Scientific Test of 12-Year-Old Poet," *Brooklyn Daily Eagle*, November 20, 1925.

81   dismissed the idea: The journalist George Currie would later write that, after having dinner with the Crane family, he concluded that Nathalia's "vocabulary was that of a studious old granny, and that just when she was babbling something boringly puerile out would pop something amazingly grown up." George Currie, "Passed in Review," *Brooklyn Daily Eagle*, January 27, 1936.

81   "The following is our way": J. M. Barrie, *The Little White Bird* (London: Hodder & Stoughton, 1913), p. 110.

82   "The windows were never opened": Untermeyer, *From Another World*, p. 289.

82   the "new father" type: Ann Hulbert, *Raising America: Experts, Parents, and a Century of Advice About Children* (New York: Alfred A. Knopf, 2003), pp. 100–115.

82   "prematurely aged by lingering traces": Johnson, "Nathalia from Brooklyn," p. 58.

82   "The Cranes were at their best": Untermeyer, *From Another World*, p. 289.

82   "I read them for hours": Young, "Child Poet Explains."

83   "this gifted girl": "Girl Poet Receives Scholarship Here," *New York Times*, September 27, 1925.

83   "moulded by well-meaning teachers": Untermeyer, "Hilda and the Unconscious," p. 190.

84   Nathalia responded like a pro: Nathalia Crane to Louis Untermeyer, September 22, 1925, Louis Untermeyer Papers, Special Collections, University of Delaware Library, Newark.

84   "In the darkness who would answer": Crane, *The Janitor's Boy*, p. 17.

84   "Through the wizardry": Nathalia Crane, *The Sunken Garden* (New York: Thomas Seltzer, 1926), p. 11.

85   **a Kiplingesque poem:** "Miss Crane's Poem on Lindbergh Wins," *New York Times*, October 25, 1927.

85   **she had written six books:** By then, she was the author of *The Janitor's Boy, Lava Lane, The Singing Crow* (1926), *Venus Invisible* (1928), and two novels, *The Sunken Garden* (1926) and *An Alien from Heaven* (1929).

85   **Though nonplussed by her "phantasmagoria":** Untermeyer, *From Another World*, p. 296.

85   **In Nathalia's strange poem:** Nathalia Crane, *Pocahontas* (New York: E. P. Dutton, 1930), pp. 20–21.

85   **Another scholarship:** Leamy, "Nathalia Crane, Fourteen Years Later," p. 572.

85   **"attention . . . toward the college entrance exam":** Nathalia Crane, speech at convention of Camp Fire Girls, January 2, 1936.

85   **She quietly kept up:** "Too Much Sweetness Kills Poems, Says Nathalia Crane," *Washington Post*, August 13, 1934. "I work at them more now," she said of her poems, "and I do a great deal more revising and correcting than I used to."

85   **"Nathalia at 22":** "Nathalia Crane Mourns Passing of Boro Landmarks," *Brooklyn Daily Eagle*, January 26, 1936.

86   **"by turns unusually graceful":** From Louis Untermeyer's foreword to Nathalia Crane, *Swear by the Night* (New York: Random House, 1936), p. 5.

86   **"clairvoyant illumination":** Ibid.

86   **"It may be an erratic genius":** Ibid.

86   **Nathalia had puzzled Untermeyer:** Untermeyer, *From Another World*, p. 298.

86   **The reviews of one:** See Paul H. Oehser, "The Minor Muse," *Washington Post*, December 2, 1939.

87   **a long poem, set partly in hell:** Nathalia Crane, *The Death of Poetry: A Dramatic Poem in Two Parts: And Other Poems* (New York: Monostine Press, 1942).

87   **"reverence for life":** Email message to Kathie Pitman, April 20, 2002.

87   **"Remember you're mine":** Helen Follett, August 23, 1914, Helen Follett Papers (hereafter HFP), Box 7, Folder 4, Rare Book and Manuscript Library, Columbia University Library.

87   **a storybook about birds:** Helen Follett, November 2, 1914, HFP, Box 7, Folder 4.

87   **"Only—one does not know":** [Roy] Wilson Follett, August 11, 1914, HFP, Box 7, Folder 4.

88 "war, I suppose, has made us": Helen Follett, September 1917, HFP, Box 7, Folder 4.

88 "caught on to the reading game": Helen Follett, November 1917, HFP, Box 7, Folder 4.

88 Each claimed credit: Helen Follett, "Education via the Typewriter," *Parents' Magazine*, September 1932, p. 22; Wilson Follett, "Schooling Without the School," *Harper's*, October 1919, p. 701.

88 "piece of machinery": H. Follett, "Education via the Typewriter," p. 54.

89 her first typewritten letter: Ibid., pp. 22–23. See also W. Follett, "Schooling Without the School," p. 701.

89 "educational scheme . . . as practically sound": H. Follett, "Education via the Typewriter," p. 54.

89 "Schooling Without the School": Wilson quotes are from W. Follett, "Schooling Without the School," p. 700.

90 "no shilly-shally affair": Helen Thomas Follett, "Education à la Carte," *Pictorial Review*, July 1929, p. 2.

90 "All the doors and windows": H. Follett, "Education via the Typewriter," p. 24.

90 "to be a bore to *me*": H. Follett, "Education à la Carte," p. 2.

91 "Let's say something in words": Helen Follett, p. 10 of typed manuscript in Barbara Newhall Follett Papers (hereafter BNFP), Box 5, Folder 1, Rare Book and Manuscript Library, Columbia University Library.

91 "the consuming passion": W. Follett, "Schooling Without the School," p. 704.

91 "As for me": Helen Follett, p. 10 of typed manuscript in BNFP, Box 5, Folder 1.

91 Holdo Teodor Oberg: Stefan Cooke, ed., *Barbara Newhall Follett: A Life in Letters* (Farksolia, 2015), p. 12.

91 "Mention the exquisiteness": Homeschooling notes from January 9, 1923, BNFP, Box 6, Folder 4.

91 "masses of stuff": Barbara Newhall Follett, "In Defense of Butterflies," *Horn Book Magazine* 9, no. 1 (February 1933).

91 evidence of ample reading: W. Follett, "Schooling Without the School," p. 703, and B. N. Follett, *The House Without Windows*, p. 55.

92 wrote a magical fantasy: For an excerpt from Barbara's story, see Stefan Cooke, "About Barbara Follett," *Farksolia*, February 15, 2012, http://www.farksolia.org/about-barbara-follett/.

92 "little battered typewriter": B. N. Follett, "In Defense of Butterflies."

92   **proper copyediting and proofreading style:** B. N. Follett, *The House Without Windows,* p. 54.

92   **When his students were reading Dickens:** Harold Grier McCurdy, ed., in collaboration with Helen Follett, *Barbara: The Unconscious Autobiography of a Child Genius* (Durham: University of North Carolina Press, 1966), p. x.

92   **"my native element":** Barbara Follett to Edward Porter St. John, July 3, 1925, BNFP, Box 1, Folder 4.

92   **"comrade of trail and river":** B. N. Follett, *The House Without Windows,* p. 54.

92   **"I want as long as possible":** Barbara Follett to Edward Porter St. John, February 4, 1923, BNFP, Box 1, Folder 4.

93   **"dressing up in a green dress":** Barbara Follett to Holdo Teodor Oberg, October 16, 1922, BNFP, Box 1, Folder 1.

93   **"pink tongue lapped the water":** Barbara Follett to Edward Porter St. John, October 22, 1922, in Cooke, *Barbara Newhall Follett,* p. 34.

93   **Mr. Oberg later joined in:** Barbara Follett to Holdo Teogor Oberg, April 19, 1923, BNFP, Box 1, Folder 2.

94   **"this vile apartment house":** Barbara Follett to Edward Porter St. John, February 4, 1923, BNFP, Box 1, Folder 2.

94   **"Talk about something!":** Barbara Follett to Helen Follett, early 1923, in McCurdy, *Barbara,* pp. 41–42.

94   **"so lonely that she went away":** Barbara Follett to Edward Porter St. John, February 4, 1923, BNFP, Box 1, Folder 2.

95   **"tawdry" urban apartment living:** B. N. Follett, *The House Without Windows,* p. 54.

95   **"one of the loveliest books":** Barbara Follett to Mrs. Coleman, February 4, 1923, BNFP, Box 1, Folder 2.

95   **"For hours every day":** B. N. Follett, *The House Without Windows,* p. 8.

95   **"amazed at the way in which":** Ibid., p. 10.

96   **"In the sky Nature still flung":** Ibid., p. 49.

96   **"save these few":** Ibid., p. 52.

96   **"of what is in a normal, healthy":** Ibid., p. 56.

97   **"Nothing ever happens":** Barbara Follett to Wilson Follett, July 18, 1925, in Cooke, *Barbara Newhall Follett,* p. 145.

97   **"Daddy and I have been correcting it":** Barbara Follett to Holdo Teodor Oberg, February 7, 1925, BNFP, Box 1, Folder 4.

97   **Nathalia's novel *The Sunken Garden:*** The typescript of a review of *The Admiral and Others* by Peggy Temple mentions *The Sunken Garden,* BNFP, Box 5, Folder 2.

97	**Barbara fell on the floor screaming:** Barbara Follett to George Bryan, mid-April 1926, BNFP, Box 2, Folder 22.

97	**Blanche Knopf liked her manuscript:** Blanche Knopf to Barbara Newhall Follett, April 14, 1926, BNFP, Box 2, Folder 18.

98	**"We cackled over":** Howard Mumford Jones, "New Child Genius," *World*, n.d., BNFP, Box 3, Folder 3.

98	**Moore was the exception:** Cooke, *Barbara Newhall Follett*, p. 224.

98	**Barbara's vocabulary should be a model:** May Lamberton Becker, "Barbara Follett Writes a Book," *The American Girl*, June 1927, p. 51.

98	**"There can be few":** Henry Longan Stuart, "A Mirror of the Child Mind," *New York Times*, February 6, 1927.

98	**"extraordinary single-mindedness":** Margery Williams Bianco, "New Horizons: *The Voyage of the Norman D.*," *Saturday Review of Literature*, June 9, 1928, p. 943.

98	**"It is surely very rash":** Barbara Follett to Anne Carroll Moore, March 28, 1927, BNFP, Box 1, Folder 7.

99	**"I am wild over PIRATES":** Barbara Follett to Edward Porter St. John, January 20, 1927, in McCurdy, *Barbara*, pp. 87–93.

99	*Treasure Island,* **which she had first read:** "Magic Portholes History," n.d., HFP, Box 3, Folder 8.

99	**David Binney Putnam:** See, e.g., "Boy Is Author at 12," *New York Times*, July 23, 1925; David Binney Putnam, "Greenland Ho!," *Youth's Companion*, August 26, 1926; "Putnam to Explore Arctic in Summer," *New York Times*, April 25, 1927; "Game Hordes Await Boy Scouts' Safari," *New York Times*, June 10, 1928; "Boys' Expedition Sails for Iceland," *New York Times*, June 20, 1931.

99	**"gay, piratical" romanticism:** Barbara Newhall Follett, *The Voyage of the Norman D., as Told by the Cabin-boy* (New York: Alfred A. Knopf, 1928), p. 93.

99	**"Some looked as though":** Ibid., p. 143.

100	**he was leaving her mother:** Cooke, *Barbara Newhall Follett*, p. 273.

100	**misery from the start:** Helen Follett to Anne Meservey, n.d., probably June 12, 1928, in Cooke, *Barbara Newhall Follett*, p. 289.

100	**"worshipped her father":** Helen Follett to Oxford Meservey, April 1928, HFP, Box 1, Folder 1.

100	**"This is the time of year":** Barbara Follett to Wilson Follett, March 7, 1928, in Cooke, *Barbara Newhall Follett*, pp. 274, 276–77.

100	**"has changed terribly":** Helen Follett to Oxford Meservey, April 12, 1928, HFP, Box 1, Folder 1.

100	*Magic Portholes:* McCurdy, *Barbara*, pp. 103–4.

100 "bad condition spiritually": Helen Follett to Oxford Meservey, April 12, 1928, HFP, Box 1, Folder 1.

100 If Wilson could assert: Helen Follett to Anne Meservey, November 20, 1928, HFP, Box 1, Folder 1.

100 "I believe there'll have to be": Wilson Follett to Helen Follett, August 5, 1928, HFP, Box 1, Folder 2.

101 "To the world it is": Helen Follett to Anne Meservey, September 12, 1928, HFP, Box 1, Folder 1.

101 "A happy trip, a trip of gaiety": "Magic Portholes History," p. 28.

101 "playmate idea": Helen Follett, interview by Cal Warton, "Herald Headlines," *Boston Herald,* February 28, probably 1933, HFP, Box 6, Folder 1.

101 "It was a piece of real continuity": "Magic Portholes History," p. 28.

101 "its unquestioning confidence in itself": "Adventurer in Life and Education," brochure for William B. Feakins, Inc., HFP, Box 6, Folder 2.

101 "I allow her to do so": Helen Follett to Anne and Oxford Meservey, November 9, 1928, HFP, Box 1, Folder 1.

101 "If you knew how extraordinarily wild": Barbara Follett to Ellen Meservey, February 28, 1929, BNFP, Box 1, Folder 8.

101 romantically pursued by an islander: Cooke, *Barbara Newhall Follett,* p. 422.

102 "Barbara has gone to pieces": Helen Follett to Anne Meservey, May 10, 1929, HFP, Box 1, Folder 1.

102 The "girl novelist" runaway: "Girl Novelist Held in San Francisco," *New York Times,* September 21, 1929.

102 "I came away because I felt": Floyd J. Healey, "Freedom Lures Child Novelist," *Los Angeles Times,* September 21, 1929.

102 "I want to be alone": Barbara Follett to Helen Follett, n.d., BNFP, Box 2, Folder 22.

103 "at a very critical time": Ralph Blanchard to Anne and Oxford Meservey, 1929, HFP, Box 1, Folder 5.

103 "the faintest ray of desire": Barbara Follett to Alice Dyar Russell, March 12, 1931, BNFP, Box 1, Folder 9.

103 "The only thing that makes me unhappy": Barbara Follett to Alice Dyar Russell, June 16, 1930, in McCurdy, *Barbara,* p. 107.

104 "bulwark, oasis, anchor": Barbara Follett to unnamed man, October 4, 1930, in McCurdy, *Barbara,* p. 126.

104 "calm poise": Barbara Follett to Alice Dyar Russell, November 1, 1938, in McCurdy, *Barbara,* p. 141.

104 "I am likely": Ibid.

104 But she hadn't yet outgrown: "What I rebel against is—is—well, giv-

ing in to ugliness, that puts it in a nutshell," says Barbara's protagonist in a draft of her shipwreck novel, *Lost Island,* p. 141, BNFP, Box 4, Folder 1.

Chapter 4. Performance Pressures

Where not otherwise indicated, biographical details are drawn from Shirley Temple Black, *Child Star: An Autobiography* (London: Headline, 1989), and Kathryn Talalay, *Composition in Black and White: The Life of Philippa Schuyler* (New York: Oxford University Press, 1995).

106 **"Your Child, Too, May Be a Shirley Temple"**: Alma Whittaker, "Your Child, Too, May Be a Shirley Temple," *Los Angeles Times,* July 1, 1934.

107 **"mammas everywhere"**: Ibid.

107 **"the rug rat race"**: Garey Ramey and Valerie A. Ramey, "The Rug Rat Race," National Bureau of Economic Research Working Paper 15284, August 2009.

107 **"a super baby star"**: Whittaker, "Your Child, Too."

107 **"phenomenally easy"**: Rosalind Shaffer, "The Private Life of Shirley Temple, Wonder Child of the Screen," *Chicago Daily Tribune,* September 9, 1934.

107 **a hundred children from all over**: Norman J. Zierold, *The Child Stars* (New York: Coward-McCann, 1965), pp. 56–57.

107 **"Hollywood with the gong"**: Rosalind Shaffer, "Hollywood to Do More Films About Children," *Chicago Daily Tribune,* July 8, 1934.

107 **"nerves are in the red"**: From *Stand Up and Cheer!* (1934), directed by Hamilton McFadden.

107 **Yehudi Menuhin was thronged**: Marie Winn, "The Pleasures and Perils of Being a Child Prodigy," *New York Times Magazine,* December 23, 1979, p. 143.

108 **"Oh, Shirley doesn't really work"**: From *Stand Up and Cheer!*

108 **"flock of hungry locusts"**: Jeanine Basinger, *Shirley Temple* (New York: Pyramid, 1975), p. 24.

108 **via Hollywood and San Francisco's bohemian scene**: Carla Kaplan, *Miss Anne in Harlem: The White Women of the Black Renaissance* (New York: HarperCollins, 2013), p. 100.

108 **"dark liquid eyes of a fawn"**: Talalay, *Composition in Black and White,* p. 14.

108 **a deal-breaker for Pathé News**: Ibid., pp. 46–47.

109 **any portrayal of "miscegenation"**: See the MPPA's Production Code of 1930, http://www.artsreformation.com/a001/hays-code.html.

109 **a wary welcome to marriages**: Kaplan, *Miss Anne in Harlem,* p. 86.

109 "the Shirley Temple of American Negroes": "The Shirley Temple of American Negroes," *Look,* November 7, 1939, p. 4.

109 "hybrid vigor": Talalay, *Composition in Black and White,* p. 13.

109 "the permanent solution": Kaplan, *Miss Anne in Harlem,* p. 87.

109 "It is a splendid thing": Anne Edwards, *Shirley Temple: American Princess* (New York: Berkley Books, 1989), p. 63.

110 "There are two themes": Aljean Harmetz, "What Makes Shirley Run, in Her Own Words," *New York Times,* October 25, 1988.

110 "ingrained awe of authority": Temple Black, *Child Star,* p. 54.

110 weren't "fair and square": Ibid., pp. 123–25.

110 "at peace with myself": Ibid., p. 62.

111 "I wanted her to be artistic": Basinger, *Shirley Temple,* p. 100.

111 "ran on her toes": Anne Edwards quoted in an undated article in *Parents Magazine,* p. 11.

112 "Don't do 'at": Temple Black, *Child Star,* p. 7.

112 "Love, ladled out": Ibid., p. 62.

112 "seldom tried to dominate": Ibid., p. 46.

112 "Secret best friends": Ibid., p. 52.

112 "finest exercise to build up health": Ibid., pp. 5–6.

112 mercenary ambition just wasn't Gertrude's style: Ibid., p. 12. Temple Black tells, and dismisses, the story circulated by Hal Roach that Gertrude Temple tried several times to get Shirley an audition for *Our Gang* but never made it past the front desk.

112 "Famous Meglin Kiddies": Diana Serra Cary, *Hollywood's Children: An Inside Account of the Child Star Era* (Dallas: Southern Methodist University Press, 1998), p. 201.

113 *Baby Burlesk* shorts: See Temple Black, *Child Star,* pp. 12–14, for the quotations in this paragraph.

113 "daily routine will not be upset": Ibid., p. 15.

113 "underlying streak of naiveté": Ibid., p. 49.

113 "a training ground for later life": Ibid.

113 The 1930s spelled the end: John F. Kasson, *The Little Girl Who Fought the Great Depression: Shirley Temple and 1930s America* (New York: W. W. Norton, 2014), pp. 58–59.

114 "This business of being mother": Temple Black, *Child Star,* p. 15.

114 "We each knew who we were": Ibid., p. 46.

114 "bring in the dolly": Ibid., p. 19.

115 "Kids, this is business": Ibid.

115 "found the pressure exhilarating": Ibid., p. 34.

115 Her daughter needed her own clothes: Edwards, *Shirley Temple,* p. 41.

115 "She reads and reads and reads": Philip K. Scheuer, "Being Mama's

Little Elfy One of Those Things Child Prodigy Must Put Up With," *Los Angeles Times*, May 6, 1934.

115   "sparkle": Temple Black, *Child Star*, pp. 20–21.

115   "Just being herself": Ibid., p. 188.

115   **When Shirley saw Jimmy Dunn:** Ibid., p. 34. Dunn even credited Temple with rescuing him from "his own personal and private depression." Grace Kingsley, "Jimmy Dunn Credits Recent Good Luck to Shirley Temple," *Los Angeles Times*, December 23, 1934.

116   her "flub": Temple Black, *Child Star*, p. 35.

116   the top box office star: Basinger, *Shirley Temple*, p. 79.

116    $307,014 in 1938: Zierold, *The Child Stars*, pp. 71–72.

116   photographed more often than anyone else: "Cinema: Peewee's Progress," *Time*, April 27, 1936.

116   She moved mountains of merchandise: Lorraine Burdick, *The Shirley Temple Scrapbook* (Middle Village, N.Y.: Jonathan David, 2001), pp. 10, 34; Kasson, *The Little Girl Who Fought the Great Depression*, pp. 5, 137–49.

116   "could sing, dance, act, and dimple": Temple Black, *Child Star*, p. 106.

117   "work entails no effort": "Cinema: Peewee's Progress."

117   "She just has a natural tendency": Scheuer, "Being Mama's Little Elfy."

118   "simply part of her play life": Edwards, *Shirley Temple*, p. 63.

118   "a knack for projecting myself": Temple Black, *Child Star*, p. 106.

118   "something rude and rowdy": Ibid., p. 107. The critic is Gilbert Seldes.

118   "This child frightens me": Basinger, *Shirley Temple*, p. 34.

119   "agitated and talkative": Temple Black, *Child Star*, p. 55.

119   "She gets spoiled.": Ibid.

119   "a series of conferences": Nelson B. Bell, "Little Shirley Temple Beneficiary of Contract Unique Among Movie Documents," *Washington Post*, August 9, 1934.

119   "system of relaxation": Shaffer, "The Private Life of Shirley Temple."

120   "Her routine of living": Ibid.

120   "rough-and-tumble neighborhood play": Eunice Fuller Barnard, "What Price Glory for Screen Starlets?," *New York Times*, October 11, 1936.

121   "Look, I earn all the money": Kasson, *The Little Girl Who Fought the Great Depression*, p. 228.

121   "as a human entity": Temple Black, *Child Star*, pp. 177–78.

121   "to cope with the gaping hole": Ibid., p. 178.

121   "a blood-and-thunder mentor": Ibid., p. 165.

122 "raise the gooseflesh": Ibid., pp. 90–91.

122 "I am a race man!": Kasson, *The Little Girl Who Fought the Great Depression*, p. 111. Kasson quotes from Earl J. Morris, "Morris Interviews 'Bojangles'; Learns He Is Real Race Man," *Pittsburgh Courier*, July 31, 1937.

123 "windup toy": Temple Black, *Child Star*, p. 58.

123 "is an utterly unnatural skill": Ibid., p. 130.

123 "to elevate my ability": Ibid., p. 190.

123 Robinson made the stair dance: Jim Haskins and N. R. Mitgang, *Mr. Bojangles: The Biography of Bill Robinson* (1988, reprinted Linus Multimedia, 2013), p. 225.

123 the first interracial couple: Temple Black, *Child Star*, p. 98. See also Donald Bogle, *Toms, Coons, Mulattoes, Mammies, and Bucks: An Interpretive History of Blacks in American Films* (New York: Bloomsbury, 2016), p. 41; Brian Seibert, *What the Eye Hears: A History of Tap Dancing* (New York: Farrar, Straus & Giroux, 2015), pp. 255–56.

123 He deftly choreographed around the problem: Joan Acocella, "Not a Pink Toy," newyorker.com, March 18, 2014.

123 "imperturbable and kind": Temple Black, *Child Star*, p. 92.

123 Robinson knew how it felt: Robinson sometimes played the role of "natural" for white journalists. "I don't know how I do it," he said to S. J. Woolf of *The New York Times*. "I just dance, I hear the music and something comes into my head which I just send down to my feet. And that's all there is to it." Quoted in Kasson, *The Little Girl Who Fought the Great Depression*, p. 109. See also Karen Orr Vered, "White and Black in Black and White: Management of Race and Sexuality in the Coupling of Child-Star Shirley Temple and Bill Robinson," *The Velvet Light Trap* 39 (Spring 1997): 52.

124 "a final moment of elation": Temple Black, *Child Star*, p. 92.

124 the only real grown-up: Bogle, *Toms, Coons, Mulattoes, Mammies, and Bucks*, pp. 40–42.

124 "and there is a definite expansion": Edwards, *Shirley Temple*, p. 92.

124 "life with other girls and boys": Eliza Schallert, "Shirley Out of Pictures," *Los Angeles Times*, May 12, 1940.

125 "honoring family unity over material cupidity": Temple Black, *Child Star*, p. 487.

125 "There's no use in going through life": Kasson, *The Little Girl Who Fought the Great Depression*, p. 96. He cites S. J. Woolf, "Bill Robinson, 60, Taps Out the Joy of Living," *New York Times*, May 22, 1938.

126 "Our White Folks": George S. Schuyler, "Our White Folks," *American Mercury* 12, no. 48 (December 1927): 388–89.

126 "spiritually depleted": Jeffrey B. Ferguson, *The Sage of Sugar Hill: George S. Schuyler and the Harlem Renaissance* (New Haven, Conn.: Yale University Press, 2005), p. 145.

126 "He needs to be cherished": Ibid.

126 "Do you know, Josephine": Ibid., p. 148.

126 "dropped completely out of sight": Talalay, *Composition in Black and White*, p. 42.

126 Josephine touted "extra vitality": "Child Pianist Gets 'Extra Vitality' from Raw Foods, Mother Says," *Courier-Journal* (Louisville, Ky.), May 12, 1941.

127 "a splendid example of courage": Anonymous, "The Fall of a Fair Confederate," *Modern Quarterly* (Winter 1930–31): 528–33.

127 "the peace of humility": Ibid., p. 536.

127 "go to extremes": G. Schuyler, "Our White Folks," p. 391.

127 "too much mother love": On John Broadus Watson, see Ann Hulbert, *Raising America: Experts, Parents, and a Century of Advice About Children* (New York: Alfred A. Knopf, 2003), chap. 5.

127 The newspaper sent Joseph W. Alsop: Joseph W. Alsop, Jr., "Harlem's Youngest Philosopher Parades Talent on 3d Birthday," *New York Herald Tribune*, August 3, 1934. Quotations in the next two paragraphs come from this article.

129 "have learned how to enjoy themselves": G. Schulyer, "Our White Folks," p. 391.

129 "Jo,". . . "Daddy," "God damn": Talalay, *Composition in Black and White*, p. 13.

129 "exceptional sense of humor": Ibid., p. 14.

130 "go crooked to bed": Ibid., p. 47.

130 "Everywhere your Daddy goes": Josephine Schuyler, Scrapbook, August 12, 1934, ibid., p. 50.

130 "You are stubborn and self-willed": J. Schuyler, Scrapbook, November 2, 1934, ibid., p. 57.

130 "Beat me and then love me": Ferguson, *The Sage of Sugar Hill*, p. 145. Ferguson notes that there is no sign that George complied.

131 "Your respect for and confidence in": Ibid., p. 150.

131 "You and Philippa are growing together": George Schuyler to Philippa Schuyler, October 20, 1935, in Talalay, *Composition in Black and White*, pp. 74–75.

131 "almost killed him": Josephine Schuyler, diary entry for July 2, 1934, in Talalay, *Composition in Black and White*, p. 58.

131 "she excels chiefly in her capacity": Columbia University Child Development Institute report, June 15, 1934, in Schuyler Family

Papers (hereafter SFP), Box 1, Schomburg Center for Research in Black Culture, Manuscripts, Archives, and Rare Books Division, New York Public Library.

132 **Scores of her songs:** No recordings exist, but John McLaughlin Williams revisited scores of some music she wrote between the ages of seven and nine. See "A Philippa Schuyler Moment," August 2, 2011, http://www.overgrownpath.com/2011/08/philippa-schuyler-moment.html.

132 **"make a better rule about whipping me":** J. Schuyler, Scrapbook, January 1, 1936, in Talalay, *Composition in Black and White,* p. 57.

132 **"You nearly scared me to death":** J. Schuyler, Scrapbook, 1938, in SFP, Box 46.

133 **"Jody, I want to do this":** Ibid.

133 **"You can do *anything* if you try":** George Schuyler to Philippa Schuyler, 1938, in SFP, Box 22, Folder 3.

133 **"Love was the thing that freed me":** Temple Black, *Child Star,* p. 63.

134 **"I realize, darling":** J. Schuyler, Scrapbook, November 1936, in Talalay, *Composition in Black and White,* p. 53.

135 **"If I just wanted to play games":** Scrapbook, 1938, in Talalay, *Composition in Black and White,* p. 85.

135 **Assessing her "social relationships":** School report, May 1938, on Philippa Schuyler, Scrapbook, 1938, in SFP, Box 46.

136 **"just the most delicious thing":** Talalay, *Composition in Black and White,* p. 89.

137 **"If there's any pushing done":** Joseph Mitchell, "Evening with a Gifted Child," *McSorley's Wonderful Saloon* (New York: Pantheon, 2001), p. 117.

137 **"vicious barriers of prejudice":** Philippa Schuyler, "My Black and White World," *Sepia,* June 1962, p. 13, clippings, in SFP, Box 69.

137 **"of the weighty importance":** Philippa Duke Schuyler, *Adventures in Black and White* (New York: Robert Speller & Sons, 1960), p. ix.

137 **"truly poetic, the expression of genuine feeling":** "Ganz Plays Works by Girl, 13, Boy, 14," *New York Times,* April 8, 1945, in Talalay, *Composition in Black and White,* p. 102.

138 **"the uncertainties, confusion, anger":** Schuyler, *Adventures in Black and White,* p. ix.

138 **"I have to work now":** "Teen-age Prodigy," *Picture News,* Sunday Magazine section of *PM,* July 21, 1946, Scrapbooks, 1946–1949, in SPF, Box 49.

138 **"expertly written":** "Philippa Schuyler in Stadium Debut," *New York Times,* July 14, 1946.

138 "She plays music, not Philippa Schuyler": Virgil Thomson, "University Festival," *New York Herald Tribune*, May 4, 1947. See also Talalay, *Composition in Black and White*, p. 108.

138 "Do you know how many blacks": Talalay, *Composition in Black and White*, p. 84.

139 "She sits all day at the piano": Josephine Schuyler to George Schuyler, March 27, 1948, ibid., pp. 110–11.

139 "Ten hours a day": George Schuyler to Josephine Schuyler, July 25, 1949, ibid., p. 116.

139 "breaking under the strain": P. Schuyler, "My Black and White World," p. 13.

139 "STAYING. AM COMMITTED": Philippa Schuyler to Josephine Schuyler, September 4, 1952, in Talalay, *Composition in Black and White*, p. 124.

140 "Do you realize what you are expecting": Philippa Schuyler to Josephine Schuyler, July 1960, ibid., p. 204.

140 "the turmoils, threats, hazards": Schuyler, *Adventures in Black and White*, pp. 299–300. Further quotations in this paragraph and the next are from the same source.

142 "We have tried to make you important": Josephine Schuyler to Philippa Schuyler, n.d., SFP, Box 22, Folder 3.

PART III
REBELS WITH CAUSES

Chapter 5. Bobby Fischer's Battles

Where not otherwise indicated, biographical details are drawn from Frank Brady, *Endgame: Bobby Fischer's Remarkable Rise and Fall—from America's Brightest Prodigy to the Edge of Madness* (New York: Crown, 2011).

145 "Wanna have a game?": Arnold Denker and Larry Parr, *The Bobby Fischer I Knew and Other Stories* (San Francisco: Hypermodern Press, 1995), p. 102.

145 "a football country, a baseball country": Rene Chun, "Bobby Fischer's Pathetic Endgame," *Atlantic*, December 2002, p. 93.

146 *I've Got a Secret:* Brady, *Endgame*, p. 89.

146 the *Quiz Kids* on TV: *Quiz Kids* debuted on television in 1949 and aired for four years. A short-lived effort to revive it in 1956 featured William James Sidis's cousin Clifton Fadiman as the moderator. See

the introduction to Ruth Duskin Feldman, *Whatever Happened to the Quiz Kids?: Perils and Profits of Growing Up Gifted* (Chicago: Chicago Review Press, 1982).

147 **An early champion of the SAT:** Nicholas Lemann, *The Big Test: The Secret History of the American Meritocracy* (New York: Farrar, Straus & Giroux, 1999), pp. 39–41.

147 **What if this fiercely competitive young maverick:** Harold C. Schonburg, "Russians Scored by Bobby Fischer," *New York Times,* August 18, 1962.

148 **dismissed school as a place for "weakies":** Ralph Ginzburg, "Portrait of a Genius as a Young Chess Master," *Harper's,* January 1962, p. 51.

149 **"Stilted (paranoid) personality":** Regina Fischer's FBI file, made available on August 11, 2010, in response to a FOIA request. This entry is dated June 22, 1943.

149 **She followed him to the Soviet Union:** Daniel Johnson, *White King and Red Queen: How the Cold War Was Fought on the Chessboard* (Boston: Houghton Mifflin, 2008), p. 118.

150 **the evidence points strongly to Nemenyi:** The most forceful version of the case for Nemenyi being Fischer's father is made in Peter Nicholas and Clea Benson, "Life Is Not a Board Game," *Philadelphia Inquirer,* February 8, 2003. See also Peter Nicholas, "Chasing the King of Chess," *Los Angeles Times,* September 21, 2009.

150 **"considered the subject to be mentally upset":** Nemenyi consulted the Family Service Association, December 1946, and then again, n.d., R. Fischer FBI file.

150 **in a trailer "out west":** Brady, *Endgame,* p. 9.

150 **warm home support for playful exploration:** Benjamin S. Bloom, ed., *Developing Talent in Young People* (New York: Ballantine Books, 1985), p. 512.

150 **"My mother has an anti-talent":** Brady, *Endgame,* p. 11.

150 **"MOMMY I WANT TO COME HOME":** Ibid., p. 15.

151 **in defense of a "colored family":** R. Fischer FBI file.

151 **"antagonistic" and "argumentative":** All quotations in this paragraph are from R. Fischer FBI file.

152 **more positional variations:** Garry Kasparov, in *Bobby Fischer Against the World* (2011), directed by Liz Garbus, HBO.

152 **"Thought that leads nowhere":** Stefan Zweig, *The Royal Game and Other Stories,* trans. Jill Sutcliffe (New York: E. P. Dutton, 1983), p. 8.

152 **"my little chess miracle":** Brady, *Endgame,* p. 16.

152 "He crushed me": Ibid, p. 18.
152 the notion of a "crystallizing experience": Howard Gardner, *Creating Minds: An Anatomy of Creativity Seen Through the Lives of Freud, Einstein, Picasso, Stravinsky, Eliot, Graham, and Gandhi* (New York: Basic Books, 1993), p. 31, citing David Henry Feldman.
153 "shadowy, unhappy": H. G. Wells, "Concerning Chess," in *Certain Personal Matters* (London: Lawrence & Bullen, 1898), p. 213.
153 "I may get back after 3": Brady, *Endgame*, p. 26.
153 Nemenyi stopped by on trips: Nicholas, "Chasing the King of Chess."
154 he didn't reveal his identity: David Edmonds and John Eidinow, *Bobby Fischer Goes to War: How a Lone American Star Defeated the Soviet Chess Machine* (New York; HarperPerennial, 2005), p. 321. The authors say Bobby was probably never told. According to Nicholas, "Chasing the King of Chess," he learned who his real father was after Nemenyi's death.
154 It's polite to break your roll: Nicholas, "Chasing the King of Chess."
154 "get up and walk around": Brady, *Endgame*, p. 49.
154 "He *had* to come out ahead": Harold C. Schonburg, "Fourteen-Year-Old 'Mozart of Chess,'" *New York Times*, February 23, 1958.
154 a "special list": R. Fischer FBI file.
155 Teachers recalled his pockets bulging: Schonburg, "Fourteen-Year-Old 'Mozart of Chess.'"
155 a postwar talent development formula: Bloom, *Developing Talent in Young People*, pp. 512–23.
155 "For four years I tried everything": Johnson, *White King and Red Queen*, p. 120.
156 struggling to put decent meals on the table: Nicholas and Benson, "Life Is Not a Board Game."
156 "I don't know. I just go for it": Brady, *Endgame*, p. 29.
156 "When I was eleven, I just got good": Frank Brady, *Portrait of a Prodigy: The Life and Times of Bobby Fischer* (Philadelphia: David McKay, 1965), p. 8.
157 "They are out to win": Samuel Reshevsky, "Chess Is Another Soviet Gambit," *New York Times*, June 13, 1954, in Brady, *Endgame*, p. 31.
157 "indisputable proof of the superiority": Edmonds and Eidinow, *Bobby Fischer Goes to War*, p. 33.
157 the number of registered chess players: Johnson, *White King and Red Queen*, p. 74.
157 "I dreamed about caressing her": Edmonds and Eidinow, *Bobby Fischer Goes to War*, pp. 39–41.

158 "fighting spirit": Garry Kasparov, "The Bobby Fischer Defense," *New York Review of Books*, March 10, 2011.

158 "Mr. Nigro, when is the food coming?": Brady, *Endgame*, p. 36.

160 playing blindfold chess: John W. Collins, *My Seven Chess Prodigies* (New York: Simon & Schuster, 1974), pp. 38–39.

161 "ability to look": Kasparov, "The Bobby Fischer Defense."

161 surpassed Morphy's legendary win: A month before his thirteenth birthday, Paul Morphy played against the Hungarian master János Jakab Löwenthal, who had recently won a match against Charles Stanley, considered the U.S. champion. See "János Jakab Löwenthal," *Paul Morphy*, n.d., http://www.edochess.ca/batgirl/Lowenthal .html.

161 "Mozart of Chess": Schonburg, "Fourteen-Year-Old 'Mozart of Chess.'"

161 "They shoulda made me a Grand Master": "Master Bobby," *Time*, March 28, 1958.

161 worry about his obsessiveness: Regina contacted Jewish Family Services in 1957 with concerns about her son and "described him as temperamental, unable to get along with others, without friends his age and without interest other than chess. She requested the assistance of the Service but again refused guidance, insisting she wanted to work things out her own way." R. Fischer FBI file.

162 "lives in terror of him": Edmonds and Eidinow, *Bobby Fischer Goes to War*, p. 318.

162 "perhaps the most accurate": Ibid., p. 77.

163 division of chess greats: Reuben Fine, *The Psychology of the Chess Player* (New York: Ishi Press, 2009), pp. 66–67. First published as "Psychoanalytic Observations on Chess and Chess Masters," *Psychoanalysis* 4, no. 3 (1956): 7–77.

163 "Lucky," he seethed: Reuben Fine, *Bobby Fischer's Conquest of the World's Chess Championship: The Psychology and Tactics of the Title Match* (New York: David McKay, 1973), p. 24.

163 "professional protester": Brady, *Endgame*, p. 88.

164 A fellow participant: Roy Hoppe and Eric Hicks, "Fischer's Dominance of Scholastic Chess," n.d., http://bobbyfischer.net/bobby36 .html.

165 "Yes, sometimes I did cry": Gay Talese, "Another Child Prodigy Stirs Chess World," *New York Times*, June 23, 1957.

165 the Soviets' "determined effort": Fine, *The Psychology of the Chess Player*, pp. 63–64.

165 "ahead of any plans": Brady, *Profile of a Prodigy*, p. 7.

165 "Some of what he did": Nicholas and Benson, "Life Is Not a Board Game."

166 "not one word from the Government": Schonburg, "Fourteen-Year-Old 'Mozart of Chess.'"

166 Government money hadn't been available: Nigel Cliff, *Moscow Nights: The Van Cliburn Story—How One Man and His Piano Transformed the Cold War* (New York: HarperCollins, 2016), p. 108.

167 "a boy, not a young man": Ibid., p. 152.

167 "play against the best": "Bobby Fischer a Hit in Soviet Chess, Though He Made First Move Too Fast," *New York Times*, June 29, 1958.

167 "We have to throw him out": Ibid.

167 Morphy's "genial disposition": "The Achilles of American Chess," *Chess Monthly* 1, no. 12 (December 1857): 384.

167 "I'm fed up with these Russian pigs": Johnson, *White King and Red Queen*, p. 121.

167 "I don't like Russian hospitality": Bobby Fischer to Jack Collins, July 1958, in Brady, *Endgame*, p. 94.

168 "laconic as the hero": Paul Underwood, "Yugoslavs Lionize Fischer, U.S. Chess Prodigy," *New York Times*, September 11, 1958.

168 "That's very Continental": Emma Harrison, "Bobby Fischer, Chess Hero, Back to Realities of Brooklyn Home," *New York Times*, September 16, 1958.

168 To Bobby's fury, she picketed: Brady, *Profile of a Prodigy*, p. 36. See also "Chess Protest Is Over," *New York Times*, October 12, 1960.

168 "It sounds terrible to leave a 16-year-old": Ben Quinn and Alan Hamilton, "Bobby Fischer, Chess Genius, Heartless Son," *Times* (London), January 28, 2008.

168 "Chess and me": Andrew Anthony, "Bobby Fischer: From Prodigy to Pariah," *Guardian*, May 14, 2011.

169 "began to weep quietly": Brady, *Endgame*, p. 129.

169 the image of an "uncouth kid": Ginzburg, "Portrait of a Genius as a Young Chess Master," p. 53.

169 "unintellectual, lopsidedly developed": Johnson, *White King and Red Queen*, p. 154.

169 "colossal egotism": See Ginzburg, "Portrait of a Genius as a Young Chess Master," for the quotations in this and the next paragraph.

170 he accused the Soviets: "There really was a conspiracy against him, although it was not quite as extensive as he supposed," Johnson writes. "What is not clear is whether Fischer could have won the tournament without the combine." Johnson, *White King and Red Queen*, pp. 124–26.

"The Russians do not need to cheat or fix anything; the odds will do it for them," concludes Brady, *Profile of a Prodigy*, p. 72. "Chess watchers seem to agree that it was likely the Soviets had colluded, on *some* level, at Curacao," according to Brady, *Endgame*, p. 148.

170 **"Finally the U.S.A. produces"**: Brady, *Profile of a Prodigy*, p. 99.

171 **"He is still very young"**: Ibid., p. 100.

171 **"an awful lot of prestige"**: Brady, *Endgame*, pp. 183–84.

171 **"the free world against"**: Johnson, *White King and Red Queen*, p. 180.

171 **a master of mind games**: Fischer claimed his delays and ultimatums weren't that. "I don't believe in psychology. I believe in good moves," he said. Edmonds and Eidinow, *Bobby Fischer Goes to War*, p. 136. Perhaps they were ploys designed to goad himself, not to put Spassky on edge, but they had that effect.

171 **not that the match was a policy priority**: Louis Menand, "Game Theory: Spassky vs. Fischer Revisited," *New Yorker*, March 1, 2004.

171 **Spassky, to his regime's displeasure**: Edmonds and Eidinow, *Bobby Fischer Goes to War*, p. 290.

172 **"taken on his own"**: Ibid., p. 288. For Bobby's demands, see pp. 237–38.

172 **"a propagandist for the free world"**: Ibid., p. 270.

172 **But Bobby proved immediately effective**: Ann Hulbert, "Chess Goes to School: How, and Why, the Game Caught on Among Young Americans," *Slate*, May 2, 2007.

172 **"the object is to crush"**: Fred Waitzkin, *Searching for Bobby Fischer: The Father of a Prodigy Observes the World of Chess* (New York: Penguin, 1993), p. 15.

172 **"a gift for democratizing"**: Ibid., pp. 12–13.

172 **In the USSR, Spassky's loss elicited**: Edmonds and Eidinow, *Bobby Fischer Goes to War*, p. 291.

173 **"Nobody is going to make a nickel"**: Brady, *Endgame*, pp. 209–10.

173 **He demanded rule changes**: Fischer proposed that the first player who won ten games be named the victor of the match. There would be no limit to the total number of games, and draws would not count. The reigning champion would keep his title if the score reached 9–9. See Brady, *Endgame*, pp. 217–18.

173 **a streamlined, hierarchical enterprise**: To be sure, the Soviet system wasn't as well oiled in reality as it was in theory: Spassky was surrounded by hapless advisers in Reykjavík.

174 *A Nation at Risk:* The report was issued in April 1983 by the National Commission on Excellence in Education, formed by Secretary of Education Terrel H. Bell.

174 "chess parents" nursed proto-prodigy dreams: Waitzkin, *Searching for Bobby Fischer*, p. 161.

174 studies correlating chess programs: See, for example, "Benefits," Gardener Chess, n.d., https://gardinerchess.com.au/benefits/.

174 the neural plasticity that also makes: Tom Vanderbilt, "Learning Chess at 40," *Nautilus*, May 5, 2016.

174 "effortful training": See, for example, K. Anders Ericsson, Roy W. Roring, and Kiruthiga Nandagopal, "Giftedness and Evidence for Reproducibly Superior Performance: An Account Based on the Expert Performance Framework," *High Ability Studies* 18, no. 1 (June 2007): 41; see also K. Anders Ericsson and Neil Chamess, "Expert Performance: Its Structure and Acquisition," *American Psychologist* 49, no. 8 (August 1994): 738. "In summary," they write, "deliberate practice is an effortful activity motivated by the goal of improving performance."

175 "a strong memory, concentration, imagination": Ginzburg, "Portrait of a Genius as a Young Chess Master," p. 50.

175 tested with random positions: Philip E. Ross, "The Expert Mind," *Scientific American*, July 24, 2006.

175 don't transfer seamlessly: Fernand Gobet and Guillermo Campbell, "Educational Benefits of Chess: A Critical Review," in Tim Redman, ed., *Chess and Education: Selected Essays From the Koltanowski Conference* (Dallas: Chess Program at the University of Texas at Dallas, 2006).

175 "the greatest natural player": Schonburg, "Russians Scored by Bobby Fischer."

175 yet another corroboration: Brooke N. Macnamara, David Z. Hambrick, and Frederick L. Oswald, "Deliberate Practice and Performance in Music, Games, Sports, Education, and Professions: A Meta-Analysis," *Psychological Science* 25, no. 8 (2014).

175 "The ability to put in those hours": Kasparov, "The Bobby Fischer Defense."

176 "Remember," her letter went on: Regina Fischer to Bobby Fischer, June 26, 1974, in Brady, *Endgame*, p. 215.

Chapter 6. The Programmers

177 the darkened office: Walter Isaacson, "In Search of the Real Bill Gates," *Time*, January 13, 1997.

177 secretly scheming with his good friend: Walter Isaacson, *Steve Jobs* (New York: Simon & Schuster, 2015), pp. 27–30.

177 "fell in love": Ibid., p. 17.

177 The Lakeside Mothers Club: Walter Isaacson, *The Innovators: How a Group of Hackers, Geniuses, and Geeks Created the Digital Revolution* (New York: Simon & Schuster, 2015), p. 322.

178 a *Baltimore Sun* article: Martha Jablow, "Hopkins Students Who Skipped High School," *Baltimore Sun,* June 25, 1972.

178 "I knew more than he did": James Wallace and Jim Erickson, *Hard Drive: Bill Gates and the Making of the Microsoft Empire* (New York: HarperBusiness, 1993), p. 21.

179 "The state of mind demanded": Michael Lewis, *Next: The Future Just Happened* (New York: W. W. Norton, 2002), p. 235.

179 Apple's "think different" ad campaign: Isaacson, *Steve Jobs,* p. 329.

179 "personal computer movement": Isaacson, *The Innovators,* pp. 300–303.

179 "Like infants discovering the world": Seymour Papert, *The Children's Machine: Rethinking School in the Age of the Computer* (New York: Basic Books, 1993), p. 33.

179 "the youthful fervor": Stewart Brand, "Spacewar: Fanatic Life and Symbolic Death Among the Computer Bums," *Rolling Stone,* December 7, 1972.

180 "usable in the woods": Isaacson, *The Innovators,* p. 289.

180 "A realm of intimate, personal power": Isaacson, *Steve Jobs,* p. 58.

180 "bundles of aptitudes and ineptitudes": Seymour Papert, *Mindstorms: Children, Computers, and Powerful Ideas* (New York: Basic Books, 1980), p. 8.

180 For radical "Yearners": Papert, *The Children's Machine,* pp. 2, 13.

180 "hackers" and "planners": See Brand, "Spacewar," for the "hackers" versus "planners" idea.

180 "Remember this was the 70s": Carole Cadwalladr, "Stewart Brand's Whole Earth Catalog, The Book That Changed the World," *Guardian,* May 4, 2013. See also John Markoff, *What the Dormouse Said: How the Sixties Counterculture Shaped the Personal Computer Industry* (New York: Viking, 2005), p. xii.

180 a fellowship at Stanford: Howard Wainer and Dan Robinson, "Profiles in Research: Julian Cecil Stanley," *Journal of Educational and Behavioral Statistics* 31, no. 2 (Summer 2006): 232.

180 had chaired the College Board's Committee of Examiners: Julian C. Stanley, "A Quiet Revolution: Finding Boys and Girls Who Reason Exceptionally Well Mathematically and/or Verbally and Helping Them Get the Supplemental Educational Opportunities They Need," *High Ability Studies* 16, no. 1 (June 2005): 8.

181   "'drybones methodologist'": Wainer and Robinson, "Profiles in Research," p. 232.

181   "Sick and tired" of the arid formulas: Camilla Persson Benbow and David Lubinski, "Julian C. Stanley Jr. (1918–2005)," *American Psychologist* 61, no. 3 (April 2006): 251.

181   "quiet revolution": Stanley, "A Quiet Revolution."

181   "plenty of time for screwing around": Brand, "Spacewar."

181   better known by now as "nerd camp": Bukhard Bilger, "Nerd Camp," *New Yorker,* July 26, 2004, p. 65.

182   "It seemed to many persons then": Stanley, "A Quiet Revolution," p. 8.

182   For Joe, who loved machines: Joseph Bates, interview by author, June 19, 2016.

182   "calm and compliant kid": Ibid. For other details, see Jablow, "Hopkins Students Who Skipped High School."

183   "One swallow does not make a spring": Julian C. Stanley, "Reflections from Julian Stanley: Supplementing the Education of Children with Exceptional Mathematical or Verbal Reasoning Ability," presented as the Esther Katz Rosen (invited) Lecture at the annual meeting of the American Psychological Association, Chicago, August 24, 2002.

183   "very, very aggressive": "Reminiscences of Julian Stanley," June 18, 1984, p. 32, Spencer Foundation Project, Columbia Center for Oral History Archives, Rare Book and Manuscript Library, Columbia University.

183   a son whose obvious "maladjustment": Evan Jenkins, "Express Route to Learning Fashioned for the Precocious," *New York Times,* February 28, 1973.

183   Jonathan's 3.75 grade-point average: Jablow, "Hopkins Students Who Skipped High School."

183   "My life and career thereafter": Stanley, "A Quiet Revolution," p. 8.

184   "the scientific method": "Reminiscences of Julian Stanley," p. 75.

184   "the shortest and probably quickest": Ibid., p. 6.

184   "do something, I hardly knew what": Stanley, "Reflections from Julian Stanley."

184   "As far as external controls": "Reminiscences of Julian Stanley," pp. 7, 23.

184   The Marland Report of 1972: Steven I. Pfeiffer, ed., *Handbook of Giftedness in Children: Psycho-Educational Theory, Research, and Best Practices* (New York: Springer, 2008), p. 390.

184   Congress appropriated a budget: Congress appropriated $290,000.

See James R. Delisle, "A Millennial Hourglass," *Gifted Child Today* 22, no. 6 (November–December 1999).

185   **"We decided we didn't find"**: "A Nation Deceived: How Schools Hold Back America's Brightest Students," *Templeton National Report on Acceleration*, vol. 1 (Iowa City: University of Iowa, 2004), p. 26.

185   **which had become "very weak"**: "Reminiscences of Julian Stanley," p. 36.

185   **"the assurance that we were not going to find"**: Ibid., p. 16.

185   **"Perhaps, if given the same opportunity"**: J. C. Stanley, "Psychology in Action: Test Better Finder of Great Math Talent Than Teachers Are," *American Psychologist*, April 1976, p. 314.

185   **Ten percent of the male participants**: Julian C. Stanley, "Uses of Tests to Discover Talent," in Daniel P. Keating, ed., *Intellectual Talent Research and Development: Proceedings of the Sixth Annual Hyman Blumberg Symposium on Research in Early Childhood Education* (Baltimore: Johns Hopkins University Press, 1976), pp. 10–11.

185   **likely to have attentive parents**: Stanley, "A Quiet Revolution," p. 11.

185   **younger female colleagues**: Linda Brody and Lynn H. Fox, "An Accelerative Intervention Program for Mathematically Gifted Girls," in Lynn H. Fox, Linda Brody, and Dianne Tobin, eds., *Women and the Mathematical Mystique* (Baltimore: Johns Hopkins University Press, 1980), pp. 173–75.

186   **"Fortunately," he remarked**: "Reminiscences of Julian Stanley," p. 32. By 1987, 27,000 students were reporting SAT scores in the Hopkins talent search. Julian C. Stanley, "Some Characteristics of SMPY's '700–800 on SAT-M Before Age 13 Group': Youths Who Reason *Extremely* Well Mathematically," *Gifted Child Quarterly* 32, no. 1 (Winter 1988): 205.

186   **"Our intent is to supplement"**: Stanley, "A Quiet Revolution," p. 10.

186   **"our 'prodigies,'" as Stanley called them**: Ibid.

186   **"little creeps"**: Gina Bari Kolata, "Math and Sex: Are Girls Born with Less Ability?," *Science* 210 (December 12, 1980): 1235.

186   **"smorgasbord of accelerative opportunities"**: Julian C. Stanley, "The Case for Extreme Educational Acceleration of Intellectually Brilliant Youths," *Gifted Child Quarterly* 20, no. 1 (1976): 73.

186   **After 18 hours devoted**: Stanley, "Uses of Tests to Discover Talent," p. 15.

186   **"But we decided we didn't want"**: "Reminiscences of Julian Stanley," p. 39.

186 **Mr. Acceleration:** Benbow and Lubinski, "Julian C. Stanley Jr.," p. 252.

186 **it was a "clumsy phrase":** Jablow, "Hopkins Students Who Skipped High School."

186 **"tragic waste of a rare national resource":** Ron Brandt, "On Mathematically Talented Youth: A Conversation with Julian Stanley," *Educational Leadership,* November 1981, p. 101.

187 **"High test scores at an early age":** Stanley, "Uses of Tests to Discover Talent," pp. 5–6.

187 **"For example, skills such as idea generation":** Peter V. McGinn, "Verbally Gifted Youth: Selection and Description," in Keating, *Intellectual Talent Research and Development,* pp. 179–80.

187 **"vacuous talk about creativity":** "Reminiscences of Julian Stanley," pp. 36, 47–49.

187 **his "mathematical wizards":** "Education: Smorgasbord for an IQ of 150," *Time,* June 6, 1977.

187 **More teens were in the pipeline:** Stanley, "Uses of Tests to Discover Talent," p. 10.

188 **"Our goal," he declared elsewhere:** Brandt, "On Mathematically Talented Youth," p. 105.

188 **"most productive years":** "Education: Smorgasbord for an IQ of 150."

188 **"a precious human-capital resource":** Harrison J. Kell, David Lubinski, and Camilla P. Benbow, "Who Rises to the Top? Early Indicators," *Psychological Science* 24, no. 5 (2013): 648.

188 **"We're not a talent *development* group":** "Reminiscences of Julian Stanley," p. 108.

188 **book of *Guinness World Records:* ** Ibid., pp. 90–91.

188 **"Scientists are stable introverts":** "Education: Smorgasbord for an IQ of 150."

188 **"discomfited socially":** Wainer and Robinson, "Profiles in Research," p. 233.

188 **"I try to appear as normal as possible":** "Education: Smorgasbord for an IQ of 150."

189 **"'maladjustment' disappeared completely":** Jenkins, "Express Route to Learning Fashioned for the Precocious."

189 **"Given that you have the raw ability":** Jablow, "Hopkins Students Who Skipped High School."

189 **"they were willing to defer":** Isaacson, *Steve Jobs,* p. 11.

190 **The therapist's verdict after a year:** Isaacson, *The Innovators,* p. 315.

190 **"not socially well-adjusted":** Jonathan Edwards, interview by author, September 22, 2010.

190 "drank the Kool-Aid": Ibid.

191 "I know I could do very well": Jablow, "Hopkins Students Who Skipped High School."

191 "if I hadn't gone to college": Edwards interview.

191 "You really have to be great": Jablow, "Hopkins Students Who Skipped High School."

191 "let loose in wonderland": Edwards interview.

192 "People imagine that programming": Ellen Ullman, "Out of Time: Reflections on the Programming Life," in James Brook and Iain Boal, eds., *Resisting the Virtual Life: The Culture and Politics of Information* (San Francisco: City Lights Books, 1995), p. 131.

192 "hard core": Wallace and Erickson, *Hard Drive*, p. 30.

192 "day and night": Ibid., p. 22.

192 "tried to be normal": Ibid., p. 35.

192 "monetary benefits": Ibid., p. 43.

192 relieved not to have to deal: Bates interview.

193 "It was just obvious": Melissa Hendricks, "Yesterday's Whiz Kids: Where Are They Today?," *Johns Hopkins University Magazine*, June 1997.

193 the Go and chess games: Wallace and Erickson, *Hard Drive*, p. 36.

193 collaborating with assorted graduate students: Edwards interview.

193 Joe hadn't in fact yet dared to date: Bates interview.

193 "An act of taking dictation": Ullman, "Out of Time," p. 132.

194 "romantic view": Edwards interview. Quotations in the following paragraphs are also from this interview.

196 "the fusion of flower power and processor power": Isaacson, *Steve Jobs*, p. 57.

196 "The kids who went to Stanford": Ibid., p. 33.

196 the mantra on the back cover: Ibid., p. 59.

196 "making some big change": Edwards interview.

197 Joe decided to carry on: Bates interview.

197 As Stanley's Study of Mathematically Precocious Youth: Julian C. Stanley, "Radical Acceleration: Recent Educational Innovation at JHU," *Gifted Child Quarterly* 22, no. 1 (Spring 1978): 62–67.

197 "An alien, a Martian plopped down": Edwards interview.

198 *Cybernetics* claimed a spot: Isaacson, *The Innovators*, p. 272.

198 working on mainframes at nearby Honeywell: Wallace and Erickson, *Hard Drive*, p. 59.

198 "prodded me to grow up": Edwards interview.

198 "mathematical, Spartan feel": Patti Hartigan, "Young and Brilliant, Blessed and Cursed," *Boston Globe Magazine*, March 6, 2005.

198 **"big, philosophical decisions"**: Hendricks, "Yesterday's Whiz Kids."
198 **"the room for the wild stuff"**: Edwards interview.
198 **"decided that computers were"**: Hendricks, "Yesterday's Whiz Kids."
199 **paving the way for automating:** Teletype machines were replaced by computer networks, punch cards made way for computer screens, and an online database turned nightly accounting into a relic of the past. These innovations paved the way for many automating practices in business in the 1980s. Jonathan Edwards to author, December 8, 2011.
199 **"that if I made one mistake"**: Hartigan, "Young and Brilliant, Blessed and Cursed."
199 **"gave my kind a way to live"**: Edwards interview.
199 **"By 1979 we of SMPY were nearly exhausted"**: Stanley, "A Quiet Revolution," p. 11.
199 **"It usually takes a viable idea"**: "Reminiscences of Julian Stanley," p. 71.
199 **"propitious *zeitgeist*"**: Stanley, "A Quiet Revolution," p. 9.
199 **Meritocratic pressure had been on the rise:** Jillian Kinzie et al., "Fifty Years of College Choice: Social, Political and Institutional Influences on the Decision-making Process," *Lumina Foundation for Education, New Agenda Series* 5, no. 3 (September 2004): 22–30.
200 **"the typical French camp"**: "Reminiscences of Julian Stanley," p. 44.
200 **"encourage participants to be"**: Julian C. Stanley, "An Academic Model for Educating the Mathematically Talented," *Gifted Child Quarterly* 35, no. 1 (Winter 1991): 38.
200 **"It was a wonder beyond any experience"**: Matthew Belmonte, "On Leaving CTY," 1998, http://www.mattababy.org/CTY/People/leaving_cty.html.
200 **"hot topic"**: "Reminiscences of Julian Stanley," p. 57.
200 **"personal project, if not a passion"**: Benbow and Lubinski, "Julian C. Stanley Jr.," p. 252.
200 **"700–800 on SAT-M Before Age 13 Group"**: Stanley, "Some Characteristics of SMPY's '700–800 on SAT-M," pp. 205–6. In 1991, SMPY was renamed the Study of Exceptional Talent.
200 **By 1983, he and a collaborator:** Camilla Persson Benbow and Julian C. Stanley, "Sex Differences in Mathematical Reasoning Ability: More Facts," *Science* 222 (December 2, 1983): 1030.
200 **That a gap existed:** Among students who scored 600 or higher in the Johns Hopkins regional search, boys outnumbered girls by a ratio of 4.1 to 1; at 500 and above, it was 2.1 to 1; at 700 and above, it was 13 to 1. Ibid.

201 "need to be investigated by other people": "Reminiscences of Julian Stanley," p. 70.

201 "because of the hormones": David A. Vise and Mark Malseed, *The Google Story* (New York: Delacorte Press, 2005), p. 18.

201 a rendition of "American Pie": Meghan O'Rourke, "My Summers at Nerd Camp," *Slate*, July 20, 2006. See also Bilger, "Nerd Camp."

202 "Those Asian American Whiz Kids": David Brand et al., "The New Whiz Kids: Why Asian Americans are Doing So Well, and What It Costs Them," *Time*, August 31, 1987.

202 that attitude especially inspired her: "Bionic Woman," *NOVA Science-NOW*, July 1, 2008.

202 "wealth of facilitative options": Stanley, "Reflections from Julian Stanley." See also Linda E. Brody, "The Study of Exceptional Talent," *High Ability Studies* 16, no. 1 (June 2005): 88.

202 "tennis factory" model: Barry McDermott, "He'll Make Your Child a Champ," *Sports Illustrated*, June 9, 1980.

203 unnecessarily "flamboyant": Hendricks, "Yesterday's Whiz Kids."

203 "think that I'm actually cute": Yoky Matsuoka, interview by author, November 15, 2010.

204 daughters of Asian-born-and-educated parents: Linda Boliek Barnett and William G. Durden, "Education Patterns of Academically Talented Youth," *Gifted Child Quarterly* 37, no. 4 (Fall 1993): 163.

204 "more nerdy interests than most": Ken Auletta, *Googled: The End of the World as We Know It* (New York: Penguin, 2010), p. 30.

205 "Oh, I'm one of those men": Matsuoka interview, November 15, 2010.

205 "embrace her inner geek": "Bionic Woman," *NOVA ScienceNOW*.

205 "if he was taking any advanced courses": Auletta, *Googled*, p. 31.

205 "I tried so many different things": Vise and Malseed, *The Google Story*, p. 29.

206 stereotype threat: See Claude M. Steele and Joshua Aronson, "Stereotype Threat and the Intellectual Test Performance of African Americans," *Journal of Personality and Social Psychology* 69, no. 5 (1995): 797–811.

206 the pathbreaking roboticist Rodney Brooks: Joseph Guinto, "Machine Man: Rodney Brooks," *Boston Magazine*, November 2014.

206 a brain-linked artificial hand: In the early 1960s, recovering from hip surgery, Norbert Wiener had generated ideas about a brain-operated artificial limb, which inspired work on the "Boston arm." "Boston Elbow ('Arm') Prototypes, Robert Mann, 1966–1973," MIT Museum, n.d., http://museum.mit.edu/150/10.

206 Still, she thought her path: Yoky Matsuoka, interviews by author,

November 15 and 16, 2010. See also Amy Hodson Thompson, "Cogito Conversation: Yoky Matsuoka," Cogito.org, September 28, 2009, accessed in 2009.

207 **math is only for geniuses:** Jordan Ellenberg, a student tracked by Stanley's SMPY, made this point in "The Wrong Way to Treat Child Geniuses," *Wall Street Journal,* May 30, 2014.

207 **verdicts on their potential:** See Carol S. Dweck, *Mindset: The New Psychology of Success* (New York: Ballantine Books, 2008), pp. 78–79, on women's tendency to trust other people's opinions too much.

207 **she shared thoughts in a 2009 interview:** Thompson, "Cogito Conversation: Yoky Matsuoka."

207 **a tripling over the course of two decades:** Stephen J. Ceci and Wendy M. Williams, *The Mathematics of Sex: How Biology and Society Conspire to Limit Talented Women and Girls* (New York: Oxford University Press, 2009), p. 155. The 13:1 ratio of boys to girls in the above 700M group in 1983 had become a 3.2:1 ratio in 2005. In other words, girls' representation in that cohort had more than tripled, rising from 7 percent to almost 24 percent. The near parity of boys' and girls' scores in other countries made further increases among girls in the United States seem likely. See Janet S. Hyde and Janet E. Mertz, "Gender, Culture, and Mathematics Performance," *PNAS* 106, no. 22 (June 2, 2009).

207 **"I am very interested in changing":** Thompson, "Cogito Conversation: Yoky Matsuoka."

208 **"all heart" to his "all brains":** Hartigan, "Young and Brilliant, Blessed and Cursed."

208 **"many years of toil and tears":** Jonathan Edwards, "I Scare Myself," *Alarming Development* (blog), February 8, 2016, http://alarming development.org/?p=1049.

208 **stock worth $49.1 million:** Hartigan, "Young and Brilliant, Blessed and Cursed."

208 **"intellectual legacy":** Edwards interview.

208 **"vision of bringing programming":** "YOW! 2015 Speakers: Jonathan Edwards," http://bit.ly/2nUHf5x.

208 **Communications Design Group:** It has since become the Human Advancement Research Company.

208 **"Our nerd culture embraces":** Jonathan Edwards, "ch-ch-changes," *Alarming Development* (blog), January 31, 2016, http://alarming development.org/?p=952.

209 **"brilliant, compulsive achievers":** Edwards interview.

209 **the downward creep:** Bilger, "Nerd Camp."

209 **"moaning about transfer credit"**: Belmonte, "On Leaving CTY."
209 **Younger alumni on the site:** Matthew Belmonte's essay, widely circulated on the Internet, prompted lots of responses, posted on "The Real CTY." See http://web.archive.org/web/20040113223443 /http://www.eviliza.org/cty/news/essays.html.
210 **"how life works, [how] to be balanced"**: Edwards interview.
210 **"absorb as normal"**: Bates interview.
210 **"an obnoxious human being"**: Isaacson, *The Innovators,* p. 329.
210 **he considered many of them "dumb shits"**: Isaacson, *Steve Jobs,* p. 43.
210 **"the cult of the boy engineer"**: Ullman, "Out of Time," p. 140.
210 **"the culture of programming unfairly excludes"**: Jonathan Edwards, "Developer Inequality and the Technical Debt Crisis," *Alarming Development* (blog), July 7, 2014, http://alarmingdevelopment .org/?p=865.
211 **"a Mad Computer Scientist"**: Jonathan Edwards, email to author, December 11, 2011.

PART IV

MIRACLES AND STRIVERS

Chapter 7. The Mystery of Savant Syndrome

Where not otherwise indicated, biographical details about Jacob Barnett are drawn from Kristine Barnett, *The Spark: A Story of Nurturing, Genius, and Autism* (New York: Random House, 2014).

215 **Reclusive William James Sidis:** In Michael Fitzgerald and Ioan James, *Mind of the Mathematician* (Baltimore: Johns Hopkins University Press, 2007), pp. 35–39, the authors argue that it is "highly likely" that not just William James Sidis, but Norbert Wiener and their fathers as well, "suffered from Asperger syndrome." Yeats and Wittgenstein are discussed in Michael Fitzgerald, *Autism and Creativity: Is There a Link Between Autism in Men and Exceptional Ability?* (New York: Routledge, 2004). See also "Famous People with Asperger Syndrome or Similar Autistic Traits," http://www.asperger -syndrome.me.uk/people.htm, and "Famous People with Aspergers Syndrome," https://www.disabled-world.com/artman/publish/article _2086.shtml.
215 **Jonathan Edwards raised this possibility:** Jonathan Edwards, interview by author, September 22, 2010.

215 **in 2013, the Asperger's label:** As of 2013, with the publication of the *DSM-V,* Asperger's was eliminated as a separate category of the spectrum disorder and is now synonymous with high-functioning autism.

215 **"a signature disorder of the high-tech information age":** Hanna Rosin, "Letting Go of Asperger's," *Atlantic,* March 2014, p. 40.

215 **Viennese pediatrician Hans Asperger:** Hans Asperger, "Autistic Psychopathy in Childhood," in Uta Frith, ed., *Autism and Asperger Syndrome* (Cambridge, U.K: Cambridge University Press, 1991), pp. 37–92.

215 **"for success in science and art":** Hans Asperger, "Problems of Infantile Autism," *Communication: Journal of the National Autistic Society* 13 (1979): 45–52.

216 **was surprised by how often:** Darold A. Treffert, interview by author, March 1, 2011.

216 **"without lessons or training":** Darold A. Treffert, *Islands of Genius: The Bountiful Mind of the Autistic, Acquired, and Sudden Savant* (Philadelphia: Jessica Kingsley, 2010), p. 12.

216 **disproportionately associated with autism:** Darold A. Treffert, "The Savant Syndrome: An Extraordinary Condition; A Synopsis: Past, Present, Future," *Philosophical Transactions of the Royal Society B: Biological Sciences* 364 (2009): 1351–57.

216 **Treffert had a new prefix:** Treffert, *Islands of Genius,* pp. 24–25.

217 **"Mozart of jazz":** Ibid., p. xiiv. See also Daniel Tammet, *Embracing the Wild Sky: A Tour Across the Horizons of the Mind* (New York: Free Press, 2009), pp. 25, 254.

217 **roughly one in ten people:** Treffert, "The Savant Syndrome."

217 **didn't officially belong:** Treffert sounded baffled by Jay: "Then there is Jay. Jay is not a savant." Treffert, *Islands of Genius,* p. 55.

217 **whose mother had found her way:** Darold A. Treffert, "The Spark: A Mother's Story of Nurturing Genius," Wisconsin Medical Society blog, June 25, 2013, https://www.wisconsinmedicalsociety.org/professional/savant-syndrome/archive/2013-archive/.

218 **She called Treffert:** Barnett, *The Spark,* pp. 130–33.

218 **dreaded that ever happening again:** Ibid., p. 137.

219 **christened a "miracle worker":** See Josh Jones, "Mark Twain & Helen Keller's Special Friendship," Open Culture, May 13, 2015, http://www.openculture.com/2015/05/mark-twain-helen-kellers-special-friendship.html.

219 **Keller's "soul-sense":** Helen Keller, *The Story of My Life: The Restored Classic,* ed. Roger Shattuck and Dorothy Hermann (New York:

W. W. Norton, 2003), pp. 92, 100. See also Shattuck's commentary on p. 450.

219 **"mind blindness," the inability to extrapolate:** John Donovan and Caren Zucker, *In a Different Key: The Story of Autism* (New York: Crown, 2016), pp. 300–304. See also Simon Baron-Cohen, *Mindblindness: An Essay on Autism and Theory of Mind* (Cambridge, Mass.: MIT Press, 1995).

219 **"So a problem child?":** "Prodigy, 12, Compared to Mozart," *60 Minutes,* CBS News, November 24, 2004.

220 **"She has one advantage":** Anne Sullivan wrote in one of her reports, "I believe every child has hidden away somewhere in his being noble capacities which may be quickened and developed if we go about it in the right way; but we shall never properly develop the higher natures of our little ones while we continue to fill their minds with the so-called rudiments." Keller, *The Story of My Life,* pp. 198, 212.

220 **"This child told me, he said":** "Prodigy, 12, Compared to Mozart," *60 Minutes.*

221 **"He's so busy learning things":** Diane Savage, interview by author, May 24, 2014.

221 **"Your son," Diane was stunned to hear:** Steve Silberman, "The Key to Genius," *Wired,* December 2003.

222 **Matt wasn't following the plots:** Matt Savage, interview by author, May 10, 2014.

222 **the "full-blown autism" category:** Barnett, *The Spark,* pp. 28, 32.

222 **"We research the hell out of everything":** Larry Savage and Diane Savage, interview by author, April 10, 2015.

223 **Auditory Integration Training:** Rosalie Seymour, "A Brief History of Auditory Integration Training," n.d., http://aitinstitute.org/ait_history.htm.

223 **"ulterior motive":** L. Savage and D. Savage interview.

223 **"My mind is made of math problems":** Silberman, "The Key to Genius."

223 **by now more systematized:** Barry M. Prizant with Tom Fields-Meyer, *Uniquely Human: A Different Way of Seeing Autism* (New York: Simon & Schuster, 2015), p. 3.

223 **"The calendar on the kitchen wall":** Barnett, *The Spark,* p. 33.

224 **pestering (her word):** Ibid., p. 45.

224 **"his focus was ferocious":** Ibid., p. 46.

224 **"terrible, tangled mess":** Ibid., p. 47.

224 **"night-night":** Ibid., p. 42.

225   "Did you get in your hours?": Ibid., p. 51.

225   "I always believed": Sanjay Gupta, "Genius: Quest for Extreme Brain Power," CNN, October 10, 2006.

225   "I knew my child better": Barnett, *The Spark,* p. 58.

226   he grasped its structure and harmonies: Samuel Zyman, interview by author, February 14, 2011.

227   pretty sure he had skipped around: M. Savage interview, May 10, 2014.

227   here was a "special situation": D. Savage interview.

227   noting several tracks in the nine-minute range: M. Savage interview, May 10, 2014.

227   "to admit sheepishly": L. Savage and D. Savage interview.

228   "I came to see my maternal intuition": Barnett, *The Spark,* p. 102.

228   "the over-the-top 'muchness'": Ibid., p. 75.

229   "port of last resort": Ibid., p. 66.

229   "a highly unorthodox kindergarten": Ibid., p. 67.

229   "match up with some so-called normal template": Ibid., p. 58.

229   "the room went silent": Ibid., p. 86.

229   "the awe and veneration": Ibid., p. 90.

229   "hadn't been missing after all": Ibid., p. 94.

229   detail-oriented curiosity: See, for example, Francesca Happé and Pedro Vital, "What Aspects of Autism Predispose to Talent?," *Philosophical Transactions of the Royal Society B: Biological Sciences* 364, no. 1522 (2009): 1369–75.

229   "Rage to master": Ellen Winner, *Gifted Children: Myths and Realities* (New York: Basic Books, 1996), pp. 3–4.

230   "Nobody was telling Jake": Barnett, *The Spark,* p. 95.

230   "rubs me the wrong way": Keller, *The Story of My Life,* p. 179.

230   "What would you do": Samuel Zyman, "New Music from a Very New Composer," *Juilliard Journal* 18, no. 8 (May 2003).

230   started cello lessons at three: "Jay Greenberg, Composer," IMG Artists, http://imgartists.com/artist/jay_greenberg; in Jay's own later notes on several pieces, he says he started at four.

230   all about theory and composition: Jay Greenberg, email to author, February 24, 2011. Greenberg said he started studying in 1998 with Antony John, whom he called a "key figure."

231   "the likes of Mozart, and Mendelssohn": "Prodigy, 12, Compared to Mozart," *60 Minutes.*

231   "It's hard to convey": Zyman compared the feat to stories of Mozart at work on the overture to *The Marriage of Figaro* the evening before

its debut performance, writing out individual parts because there was no time to produce a full score. Zyman interview.

231 "It's as if the unconscious mind": "Prodigy, 12, Compared to Mozart," *60 Minutes.*

232 "I was an unwelcome arrival": Jay Greenberg, email to author.

232 "being surrounded by other super musically gifted kids": Zyman interview.

232 "We had real problems at the beginning": Samuel Adler, interview by author, February 16, 2011.

232 a plaque noting that Mozart: Frank J. Oteri, "Samuel Adler: Knowing What You're Doing," a conversation at the German Consulate to the United Nations, March 12, 2015, http://www.newmusicbox.org /articles/samuel-adler-knowing-what-youre-doing/.

232 "everything I said": This and other quotations from Adler in this section are from Adler interview.

233 Not that the way ahead: Joan Acocella, "I Can't Go On!," *New Yorker,* August 3, 2015. She comments on the price of rigorous musical education in preparation for a solo career: "At least by adolescence, a person aiming at a soloist career in classical music is practicing about five hours a day. This means that he is alone for at least a third of his waking hours and therefore, unlike his peers, is not engaged in what psychologists call 'ego development.' He is not finding out what other people are like; he is not learning how to handle doubt, fear, envy, delay, failure—indeed, success."

233 "spurt of productivity and growth": Jay Greenberg, "Composer Note: Sonata for Cello and Piano" (2004), http://www.musicsalesclassical .com/composer/work/37027.

233 "Genius is an abnormality": Andrew Solomon, "Would You Wish This on Your Child?," *New York Times Magazine,* November 4, 2012.

233 "Matt comes with software installed": Quoted in *Beautiful Minds: A Voyage into the Brain* (2006), directed by Petra Höfer and Freddie Röckenhaus.

235 "some . . . that are very far ahead": Eyran Katsenelenbogen, interview by author, November 6, 2014.

235 "I used to play a lot" . . . "Bouncy": M. Savage interview, May 10, 2014.

235 "wouldn't make eye contact": John Funkhouser, interview by author, October 30, 2014.

236 "I just understood jazz theory": M. Savage interview, May 10, 2014.

236 "Everything visual comes to me": Ibid.

237 "They really clicked": Funkhouser interview.

237 conveying "life lessons": M. Savage interview, May 10, 2014.

237 Banacos didn't just work with Matt: See Lefteris Korids, "Top Speed and in All Keys: Charlie Banacos's Pedagogy of Jazz Improvisation," D.Mus.A. thesis, New England Conservatory of Music, 2012.

237 "We definitely did extreme things for our kids": L. Savage and D. Savage interview.

238 looking back, called them "clichéd": Matt Savage, interview by author, November 3, 2014.

238 "he evolved very quickly": Funkhouser interview.

238 "between softly gliding passages": Christopher Porterfield, "Debut of an Odd Couple," *Time*, November 17, 2003.

238 "a musical term meaning": Matt Savage Trio, *Cutting Loose* (2004), Savage Records, http://savagerecords.com/wordpressnew/music/cutting-loose/.

238 "What I love about jazz": Chris Elliott, "Savage Genius," *Seacoast Online*, September 28, 2006, http://archive.seacoastonline.com/news/09282006/health-f-s28-matt-savage22.html.

238 "huge strides emotionally": Porterfield, "Debut of an Odd Couple."

238 "a turbocharged working memory": Barnett, *The Spark*, p. 237.

239 "As long as Jake could get": Ibid., p. 137.

239 "If I had stopped and let myself bask": Ibid., p. 238.

239 "from a private school in Manhattan": Ibid., p. 230.

239 "trying to 'fix'": Ibid., p. 165.

239 "play and ordinary childhood experiences": Ibid., p. 160.

240 their son was "profoundly gifted": Ibid., pp. 229–30.

241 "creative fugue state": Ibid., p. 204.

241 on the road to a Nobel Prize: Ibid., p. 210.

241 "several of the toughest problems": Michelle Castillo, "12-Year-Old Genius Expands Einstein's Theory of Relativity, Thinks He Can Prove It Wrong," *Time*, March 26, 2011.

241 often called "Mama Jane": Barnett, *The Spark*, p. 215.

242 "The biggest change": Ibid., p. 221.

242 quietly humming musical phrases: Ian VanderMeulen, "Sounds Like Teen Spirit," *Symphony*, March–April 2009, p. 40.

242 in the hands of ICM Artists: Charles Letourneau, interview by author, February 7, 2011. Letourneau was Jay's ICM agent.

242 "hazardous transition to maturity": Alex Ross, "Jay Greenberg," *The Rest Is Noise* (blog), therestisnoise.com, November 30, 2004, http://www.therestisnoise.com/2004/11/jay_greenberg.html.

242 **"the disappointing realization"**: Alex Ross, "Ignore the Conductor," *New Yorker,* May 17, 2004.

242 **"a validation"**: Matthew Gurewitsch, "Early Works of a New Composer (Very Early, in Fact)," *New York Times,* August 13, 2006.

243 **the "divine inspiration" aura**: VanderMeulen, "Sounds Like Teen Spirit," p. 41.

243 **"at the age of 12"**: Porter Anderson, "Driven to Music: A Prodigy at Age 15," CNN, November 14, 2007.

243 **"I really don't spend much time"**: Ibid.

243 **"I don't know"**: Martin Steinberg, "Premiere of Teen Composer's Concerto," Associated Press, October 30, 2007.

243 **"for about 10 years"**: Anderson, "Driven to Music."

243 **writing, tae kwan do, and photography**: Gurewitsch, "Early Works of a New Composer."

243 **"to reach the point where"**: VanderMeulen, "Sounds Like Teen Spirit," p. 43.

244 **"emo-listening, hip-hop-dancing"**: Ross, "Ignore the Conductor."

244 **"Thus, no longer can I remain"**: Jay Greenberg, "Salutations," Facebook, February 27, 2010, https://www.facebook.com/notes/jay -greenberg/salutations/358020974594.

244 **"cutting or the bleeding edge of music"**: Jay Greenberg, "Pardon Me, Which Way Is the Avant-Garde?," Facebook, March 12, 2010, https://www.facebook.com/notes/jay-greenberg/pardon-me-which -way-is-the-avant-garde/387931749594.

244 **"So, although I'm aware very few"**: Jay Greenberg, "The Value of Recordings," Facebook, March 18, 2010, https://www.facebook.com /notes/jay-greenberg/the-value-of-recordings/402869739594.

244 **"inner scientist"**: Jay Greenberg, "Why Study Music, Anyway?," Facebook, March 5, 2010, https://www.facebook.com/notes/jay -greenberg/why-study-music-anyway/370966914594.

244 **"conducting in my head"**: Jay Greenberg, email to author.

245 **"to go to Radcliffe"**: Helen Keller to Mrs. Samuel Richard Fuller, October 20, 1899, in Keller, *The Story of My Life,* p. 368.

245 **Berklee College of Music**: M. Savage interview, May 10, 2014; D. Savage interview; D. Savage and L. Savage interview.

245 **"almost a gimmick"**: Joseph P. Kahn, "Playing the Changes," *Boston Globe,* February 9, 2010.

246 **"That's a tune all about"**: Matt Savage, performance at Dizzy's Club Coca-Cola, February 21, 2011, author's notes.

246 *Big Apple Suite:* Ibid. See description of *Big Apple Suite* in Corinna Da

Fonseca-Wollheim, "The Musical Maturing of Matt Savage," *Wall Street Journal,* October 29, 2008.

246 **"straight-ahead jazz"**: M. Savage interview, May 10, 2014.

246 **"It's a journey from chaos to order"**: Matt Savage, comments at master's recital at Manhattan School of Music, April 10, 2015.

247 **"It's all about attention span"**: M. Savage interview, November 3, 2014.

247 **"He's been developing"**: L. Savage and D. Savage interview.

247 **a TEDxTeen talk**: Jacob Barnett, "Forget What You Know," TEDxTeen, April 9, 2012, https://www.youtube.com/watch?v=Uq-FOOQ 1TpE.

248 **the most successful TED talk**: Nathan Heller, "Listen and Learn," *New Yorker,* July 9, 2012.

248 **"the wonderland of Mind"**: Keller, *The Story of My Life,* pp. 81–82.

248 **"became the youngest person ever"**: Barnett, *The Spark,* p. 252.

249 **"It's the outliers, the oddballs"**: Paul Wells, "Jacob Barnett, Boy Genius," *Maclean's,* September 9, 2013.

249 **"My main job with Jacob"**: Ibid.

Chapter 8. Tiger Parents, Super Children

Where not otherwise indicated, biographical details about Lang Lang are drawn from Lang Lang with David Ritz, *Journey of a Thousand Miles: My Story* (New York: Spiegel & Grau, 2008), and Lang Lang with Michael French, *Lang Lang: Playing with Flying Keys* (New York: Delacorte Press, 2008).

251 **"my hallmark"**: Lang, *Playing with Flying Keys,* p. 55.

251 **"It's one of those magical places"**: Steve Smith, "Pianists of the Age to Put on a Show," *New York Times,* October 28, 2009.

252 **"You should play Game Boy less"**: Ann Hulbert, "The Prodigy Puzzle," *New York Times Magazine,* November 20, 2005. The Davidson Institute fellows' reception was held at the Library of Congress on September 28, 2005.

252 **remarkable surge in classical music**: Joseph Kahn and Daniel J. Wakin, "Classical Music Looks Toward China with Hope," *New York Times,* April 3, 2007.

252 **"If one word applies to Lang Lang"**: "Biography," n.d., http://lang lang.com/en/me.

252 **"never left my consciousness"**: Lang, *Journey of a Thousand Miles,* p. 48.

253 **"the robot stereotype"**: Mike Paarlberg, "Lang Lang with the National Symphony Orchestra at the Kennedy Center, Reviewed," *Washington City Paper,* October 30, 2015.

253 **"The Lang Lang Effect"**: "Biography."

253 **a high-prestige extracurricular pursuit**: Alex Ross, "Symphony of Millions," *New Yorker,* July 7, 2008.

253 **no choice but to comply**: Michael Ahn Paarlberg, "Can Asians Save Classical Music?," *Slate,* February 2, 2012.

253 **"Mozart Effect"**: Claudia Hammond, "Does Listening to Mozart Really Boost Your Brainpower?," BBC, January 8, 2013.

254 **pianists, chess players, athletes**: K. Anders Ericsson, Kiruthiga Nandagopal, and Roy W. Roring, "Giftedness Viewed from the Expert-Performance Perspective," *Journal for the Education of the Gifted* 28, no. 3/4 (2005): 294–95. See also Paul Voosen, "Bringing Up Genius: Is Every Healthy Child a Potential Prodigy?," *Chronicle Review,* November 8, 2015.

254 **"10,000 hour rule"**: Malcolm Gladwell, *Outliers: The Story of Success* (New York: Little, Brown, 2008), p. 38.

254 **"The scientific formulation"**: Voosen, "Bringing Up Genius."

254 **"magic number of greatness"**: Gladwell, *Outliers,* p. 41.

254 **"Dear Children of the World"**: Lang, *Playing with Flying Keys,* p. xv.

254 **the term *grit***: Angela L. Duckworth, Christopher Peterson, Michael D. Matthews, and Dennis R. Kelly, "Grit: Perseverance and Passion for Long-Term Goals," *Journal of Personality and Social Psychology* 92, no. 6 (2007): 1087–101.

255 **In a tell-all account**: Amy Chua, *Battle Hymn of the Tiger Mother* (New York: Penguin Press, 2011).

255 **talent is like sex in marriage**: Andrew Solomon, *Far from the Tree: Parents, Children, and the Search for Identity* (New York: Scribner, 2012), pp. 450–51.

255 **"To me, the most shocking"**: Angela Duckworth, "Grit: The Power of Passion and Perseverance," TED talk, April 2013, https://www.ted.com/talks/angela_lee_duckworth_grit_the_power_of_passion_and_perseverance/transcript?language=en.

256 **"You know, you're no genius!"**: Angela Duckworth, *Grit: The Power of Passion and Perseverance* (New York: Scribner, 2016), p. xiii.

256 **"Never, never disgrace me"**: Chua, *Battle Hymn of the Tiger Mother,* p. 17.

256 **lots of other Americans, too**: In *Grit,* Duckworth notes that, according to national surveys, Americans are about twice as likely to say that effort is more important to success than talent is. But the research of

a psychologist named Chia-Jung Tsay suggests that when attitudes are probed less directly, a bias toward "naturals," or talent, emerges. Duckworth, *Grit*, pp. 23–25.

256 **"You may face a competitor"**: Lang, *Journey of a Thousand Miles*, p. 33.

256 **"little emperors"**: Quanyu Huang, *The Hybrid Tiger: Secrets of the Extraordinary Success of Asian-American Kids* (New York: Prometheus Books, 2014), pp. 30, 134.

256 **The race was on to dedicate**: Huang defines *guan* as an "incredibly important concept of Chinese parenting culture ... [which] means to manage and, when necessary, to control or restrain your child—but it also means to care for and about them, to be involved and invested in their lives, and to offer protection and guidance for them." Ibid., pp. 140–41. Yo-Yo Ma says, "One of the duties of an Oriental child is unquestioning obedience to the parents; this is supposed to continue throughout one's life. It goes beyond obedience; the parents identify completely with the child." David Blum, "A Process Larger Than Oneself," *New Yorker*, May 1, 1989, p. 50.

257 **anything but relaxing**: Lang, *Journey of a Thousand Miles*, p. 24.

257 **"a sensitive child"**: Ibid., p. 1.

258 **"the importance of balance"**: Wang Liping and Li Wen, "Zhu Yafen: The Elegance of Piano Education," *China Today*, December 9, 2014, http://www.chinatoday.com.cn/english/culture/2014-12/09/content _657660.htm.

258 **"winning, winning, winning"**: Lang, *Journey of a Thousand Miles*, p. 27.

258 **"unchallenged power"**: Ibid., p. 168.

258 **"It's not fair!"**: Ibid., p. 46.

258 **"Achievement motivation"**: Adam Grant, *Originals: How Non-Conformists Move the World* (New York: Viking, 2016), p. 10.

259 **"When I played the piano"**: Lang, *Journey of a Thousand Miles*, p. 60.

259 **"a lost cause"**: Ibid., p. 72.

259 **"Die now rather than live in shame!"**: Ibid., pp. 75–76.

260 **"rage to master"**: Ellen Winner, *Gifted Children: Myths and Realities* (New York: Basic Books, 1996), pp. 3–4.

260 **Mihaly Csikszentmihalyi, a leading figure**: Mihaly Csikszentmihalyi et al., *Talented Teenagers: The Roots of Success and Failure* (Cambridge, U.K.: Cambridge University Press, 1993), p. 215.

260 **"make some kind of a raid"**: Howard Gardner, "The Creators' Patterns," in Margaret A. Boden, ed., *Dimensions of Creativity* (Cambridge, Mass.: MIT Press, 1996), p. 156.

260 **"I was ten years old"**: Lang, *Playing with Flying Keys*, p. 64.

260 "stuck in hell": Lang, *Journey of a Thousand Miles,* p. 79.

261 "was in my blood": Ibid., p. 32.

261 "a golden boy who danced": Ibid., p. 38.

262 "I understood at a very early age": Lang, *Playing with Flying Keys,* p. 17.

262 "turn a child's play": Ibid., p. 18.

263 "even if my hands grew tired": Ibid.

263 "autotelic experience": Csikszentmihalyi et al., *Talented Teenagers,* pp. 15–16. See also Mihaly Csikszentmihalyi, *Flow: The Psychology of Optimal Experience* (New York: HarperPerennial, 2008), p. 47, and chapter 7, "Work as Flow"; Daniel H. Pink, *Drive: The Surprising Truth About What Motivates Us* (New York: Riverhead, 2009), p. 113.

263 "usually occur when a person's body or mind": Csikszentmihalyi, *Flow,* p. 3.

264 "my father and I shared": Lang, *Journey of a Thousand Miles,* p. 91.

264 "chasing the music": Ibid.

264 a "midlife crisis": Jeanne Bamberger, "Growing-Up Prodigies: The Midlife Crisis," in Gary E. McPherson, ed., *Musical Prodigies: Interpretations from Psychology, Education, Musicology, and Ethnomusicology* (Oxford: Oxford University Press, 2016).

265 "the path to success in China": Lang, *Playing with Flying Keys,* p. 153.

265 "feverish state": Lang, *Journey of a Thousand Miles,* p. 118.

265 "to practice ten hours a day": Ibid., p. 230.

265 "He wasn't trying to capture": Ibid., p. 125.

265 "I was meshuga": Blum, "A Process Larger Than Oneself," pp. 52, 61.

266 "practice-crazed" young pianist: Lang, *Journey of a Thousand Miles,* p. 177.

266 "it can't be about the prize": Ibid., p. 171.

266 "Simply concentrate on the music": Ibid., p. 230.

266 "think culturally": Lang Lang, interview by author, October 24, 2011.

266 "If I were not preparing for some contest": Lang, *Journey of a Thousand Miles,* p. 171.

266 "Was I ever really a normal teenager?": Ibid., p. 230.

267 "You don't have to sacrifice everything": Solomon, *Far from the Tree,* p. 449.

267 "Lang Lang's avuncular gentleness": Ibid., p. 453.

267 "play it forward": Lang Lang International Music Foundation Young Scholars Program, http://langlangfoundation.org/our-pro grams/young-scholars-program/. Ariela Rossberg, interview by author, October 28, 2015.

268 **"eating bitterness"**: Nicholas Kristof, "China Rises, and Checkmates," *New York Times,* January 8, 2011.

268 **"All you have to do is practice"**: *My Life as a Child* (2007), TLC. In this six-part TLC documentary, Marc was equipped with a camera; he appears in episode 1, "Hopes and Hurdles." For a description of the series, see Felicia R. Lee, "Children Tell Their Own Stories in New Series," *New York Times,* February 26, 2007.

268 **"As much time as an average kid"**: *My Life as a Child.*

268 **"My technique is much better"**: Bill Whitaker, "Ten-Year-Old Prodigy Plays Carnegie Hall," *CBS Evening News,* November 21, 2009.

269 **"When I was three, I asked"**: Bill Whitaker, "Concert Piano's Littlest Star," *CBS Evening News,* October 9, 2008.

269 **a teacher can pick up on**: Gary Graffman, interview by author, October 31, 2015.

270 **"I don't know where he begins"**: Nora Zamichow, "Pint-Size, but Grand on Piano," *Los Angeles Times,* June 22, 2005.

270 **a National Geographic documentary**: *My Brilliant Brain,* http://nat geotv.com/asia/my-brilliant-brain/about.

270 **"encourage children to work"**: Duckworth et al., "Grit," p. 1110.

271 **grit, the key to putting in hours**: Duckworth, "Grit: The Power of Passion and Perseverance," TED talk.

271 **"the diligent, disciplined"**: Chua, *Battle Hymn of the Tiger Mother,* p. 8.

271 **"soft, entitled"**: Ibid., p. 22.

271 **"weird Asian automatons"**: Ibid., p. 8.

271 **proudly contrasted fervent dedication**: Solomon, *Far from the Tree,* p. 453.

272 *Los Angeles Times* **story about him**: Zamichow, "Pint-Size, but Grand on Piano."

272 **"My mom is my manager"**: *My Life as a Child.*

272 **"his protector"**: Chloe Hui, "Riding Out a Tornado," preliminary book proposal, sent to author February 29, 2012.

273 **the risks of the prodigy circuit**: Marie Winn, "The Pleasures and Perils of Being a Child Prodigy," *New York Times Magazine,* December 23, 1979. She writes of a "benevolent conspiracy" among "powerful figures in the music world" to discourage precocious performance and the prodigy treatment.

273 **occasions to discuss passion**: Hulbert, "The Prodigy Puzzle."

273 **"growth mindset"**: Carol S. Dweck, *Mindset: The New Psychology of Success* (New York: Random House, 2006).

273 **"I want to achieve incredible things"**: Whitaker, "Concert Piano's Littlest Star."

273 "can't give up too easily": Meera Vijayan, "A Piano Star Is Born," *Star Online*, November 25, 2007, http://www.thestar.com.my/lifestyle /entertainment/tv/news/2007/11/25/a-piano-star-is-born/.

274 "not-so-fun-in-the-moment exertion": Duckworth, *Grit*, p. 130.

274 can stunt progress: Toby Perlman, creator of the Perlman Music Program, says that performing too early cramps growth. She is quoted in Lois B. Morris and Robert Lipsyte, "A Musical Dream Come True; Thou Shalt Learn to Play Without Being Tortured," *New York Times*, July 25, 2002. In David Blum's *New Yorker* profile of him, Yo-Yo Ma says, "One good thing is that as a child I didn't perform much. It's risky to create careers for 'geniuses' at age nine. The tendency is to make do with your technical limitations in order to get through your performances. The weaknesses then easily become ingrained." Blum, "A Process Larger Than Oneself," p. 51.

274 "The thing is," Marc said: Marc Yu, *The Thing Is, You Have to Love Music*, IdeaFestival TV, May 11, 2010, https://www.youtube.com /watch?v=pQpC2OeNP3k&feature=related.

274 "I think with an ordinary mom": *My Life as a Child*.

275 a new teacher: Solomon, *Far from the Tree*, p. 452.

275 "It was so much abuse": Chloe Hui, interview by author, July 5, 2011.

275 "Marc will be telling people": Solomon, *Far from the Tree*, p. 452.

276 "I don't want to hear the word *pushy*": Ibid., p. 453.

276 "He was showing a lot": Chloe Hui, interview by author, August 16, 2011.

276 "the toughest time of our lives": C. Hui interview, July 5, 2011.

276 "its distinctive inquiry-based": "Mission and Philosophy," Nueva, n.d., http://www.nuevaschool.org/about/mission-and-philosophy.

276 "reflection [as] an essential practice": "Reflection: An Essential Practice for Learning," January 29, 2016, Nueva, http://www.nuevaschool .org/news/nueva-now/1418-reflection-an-essential-practice-for -learning.

277 "so exciting!": Marc Yu, interview by author, August 16, 2011.

277 "Shut up, Mom!": Chloe Hui, interview by author, March 2, 2012.

277 "an inherently closet practice": Chua, *Battle Hymn of the Tiger Mother*, p. 172.

277 She was "huggy": Amy Chua, interview by author, May 31, 2011.

277 "you're diseased": Chua, *Battle Hymn of the Tiger Mother*, p. 173.

278 "I HATE YOU": Ibid., p. 205.

278 "I don't want you controlling": Ibid., p. 221.

278 "We cried over each other's shoulders": Chloe Hui, email to author, July 22, 2011.

278 "all the yelling, screaming": C. Hui interview, August 16, 2011.

278 "When I was younger": M. Yu interview.

278 spurred on less by Chinese-style duress: Chua, *Battle Hymn of the Tiger Mother*, p. 226.

279 "I am and will always be grateful": M. Yu interview.

279 "To play professionally": C. Hui interview, July 5, 2011.

279 "Isn't it too risky": C. Hui interview, August 16, 2011.

279 "compromised my own values": Hui, "Riding Out a Tornado."

279 "That's going to be hard": Chua, *Battle Hymn of the Tiger Mother*, p. 226.

279 "had a prodigy dropped": Hui, "Riding Out a Tornado."

280 "I feel deprived": M. Yu interview.

Epilogue

281 "each child is a complex": Julian C. Stanley and Camilla P. Benbow, "Youths Who Reason Exceptionally Well Mathematically," in Robert J. Sternberg and Janet E. Davidson, eds., *Conceptions of Giftedness* (Cambridge, U.K.: Cambridge University Press, 1986), p. 370.

282 The tiger mother's guiding tenets: Ann Hulbert, "Hear the Tiger Mother Roar," *Slate*, January 11, 2011.

283 the notion that a "midlife crisis": Jeanne Bamberger, "Growing-Up Prodigies: The Midlife Crisis," in Gary E. McPherson, ed., *Musical Prodigies: Interpretations from Psychology, Education, Musicology, and Ethnomusicology* (Oxford: Oxford University Press, 2016).

284 "life with other girls and boys": Shirley Temple Black, *Child Star: An Autobiography* (London: Headline, 1989), p. 313.

285 "So much has happened that is so intense": Chloe Hui and Marc Yu, interviews by author, May 2, 2016. All other quotes from Chloe and Marc in the Epilogue are from these interviews.

289 a wider world that helps: Mihaly Csikszentmihalyi, *Creativity: Flow and the Psychology of Discovery and Invention* (New York: HarperCollins, 1996), p. 185. He emphasizes that creativity thrives on inner-focused drive and on curiosity and openness to external stimuli.

290 "a tragic misunderstanding": Andrew Solomon, *Far from the Tree: Parents, Children, and the Search for Identity* (New York: Scribner, 2012), p. 441.

290 "chance to develop a reasonably thick skin": Norbert Wiener, "Analysis of the Child Prodigy," *New York Times Magazine*, June 2, 1957, p. 34.

Index

Page numbers in *italics* refer to illustrations.

ILLUSTRATION CREDITS

13 Courtesy MIT Museum

18 Public domain

43 Henry Cowell c. 1902. The Henry Cowell Collection, Music Division, The New York Public Library for the Performing Arts. Courtesy of the David and Sylvia Teitelbaum Fund, Inc.

74 Wikimedia Commons

93 Barbara Follett c. 1924. Barbara Newhall Follett Papers, Rare Book & Manuscript Library, Columbia University in the City of New York. Courtesy of Stefan Cooke

117 Bettmann/Bettmann Collection/Getty Images

135 Photographs and Prints Division, Schomburg Center for Research in Black Culture, The New York Public Library, Astor, Lenox and Tilden Foundations

155 Copyright 2017 The Marshall Chess Foundation

159 Copyright 2017 The Marshall Chess Foundation

183 Photograph by William L. Klender. Permission from the Baltimore Sun Media Group.

194 Photograph by William L. Klender. Permission from the Baltimore Sun Media Group.

203 From *Florida Today,* October 25 © 1987 Gannett-Community Publishing. All rights reserved. Used by permission and protected by the Copyright Laws of the United States. The printing, copying, redistribution, or retransmission of this Content without express written permission is prohibited.

226 Courtesy of Diane Savage

231 Bill Phelps © Sony Music Entertainment/Courtesy of Sony Classical

240 Photograph by Jessica Darmanin. Originally published in Maclean's™ magazine on September 9, 2013. Used with permission of Rogers Media Inc. All rights reserved.

257 Courtesy of Lang Lang

270 Courtesy of Chloe Hui

PERMISSIONS ACKNOWLEDGMENTS

Grateful acknowledgment is made to the following for permission to reprint the following previously published material:

The MIT Press: Excerpt from *Ex-Prodigy: My Childhood and Youth* by Norbert Wiener, published by The MIT Press. Reprinted by permission of The MIT Press.

Oxford University Press: Excerpts from *Composition in Black and White: The Life of Philippa Schuyler* by Kathryn Talalay, copyright © 1995 by Kathryn Talalay. Reprinted by permission of Oxford University Press, USA.